The Blackwell Companion to Major Contemporary Social Theorists

BLACKWELL COMPANIONS TO SOCIOLOGY

The *Blackwell Companions to Sociology* provide introductions to emerging topics and theoretical orientations in sociology as well as presenting the scope and quality of the discipline as it is currently configured. Essays in the Companions tackle broad themes or central puzzles within the field and are authored by key scholars who have spent considerable time in research and reflection on the questions and controversies that have activated interest in their area. This authoritative series will interest those studying sociology at advanced undergraduate or graduate level as well as scholars in the social sciences and informed readers in applied disciplines.

1 *The Blackwell Companion to Social Theory*, Second Edition
Edited by Bryan S. Turner

2 *The Blackwell Companion to Major Social Theorists*
Edited by George Ritzer

3 *The Blackwell Companion to Political Sociology*
Edited by Kate Nash and Alan Scott

4 *The Blackwell Companion to Medical Sociology*
Edited by William C. Cockerham

5 *The Blackwell Companion to Sociology*
Edited by Judith R. Blau

6 *The Blackwell Companion to Major Classical Social Theorists*
Edited by George Ritzer

7 *The Blackwell Companion to Major Contemporary Social Theorists*
Edited by George Ritzer

8 *The Blackwell Companion to Criminology*
Edited by Colin Sumner

9 *The Blackwell Companion to Sociology of Families*
Edited by Jacqueline Scott, Judith Treas, and Martin Richards

Forthcoming

The Blackwell Companion to Social Movements
Edited by David Snow, Sarah Soule, and Hanspeter Kriesi

The Blackwell Companion to Social Inequalities
Edited by Mary Romero and Eric Margolis

The Blackwell Companion to the Sociology of Culture
Edited by Mark Jacobs and Nancy Hanrahan

The Blackwell Companion to Major Contemporary Social Theorists

Edited by

George Ritzer

350 Main Street, Malden, MA 02148-5018, USA
108 Cowley Road, Oxford OX4 1JF, UK
550 Swanston Street, Carlton South, Melbourne, Victoria 3053, Australia
Kurfürstendamm 57, 10707 Berlin, Germany

First published 2003 by Blackwell Publishing Ltd

This edition and *The Blackwell Companion to Major Classical Social Theorists* originally published together as *The Blackwell Companion to Major Social Theorists* in 2000 by Blackwell Publishing Ltd

Library of Congress Cataloging-in-Publication Data

ISBN 1-4051-0595-X (paperback)

A catalogue record for this title is available from the British Library.

Set in 10.5 on 12 pt Sabon
by Kolam Information Services Pvt Ltd, Pondicherry, India
Printed and bound in the United Kingdom
by MPG Books Ltd, Bodmin, Cornwall

For further information on
Blackwell Publishing, visit our website:
http://www.blackwellpublishing.com

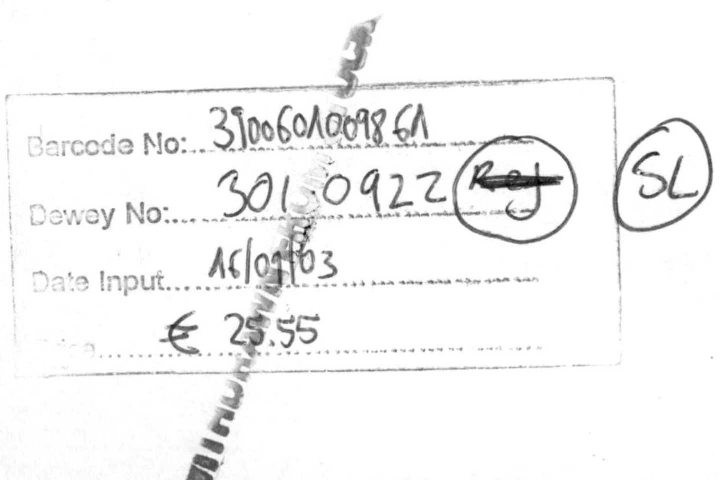

Contents

Preface

The publication of this two-volume paperback edition is a welcome event. While many social scientists and libraries added the original hardback, single-volume edition of *The Blackwell Companion to Major Social Theorists* to their collections, its price put it beyond the reach of all but the most well-heeled students. Thus instructors were unable, by and large, to assign it to their classes. The publication of these two volumes in paperback solves that problem by making the books much more affordable. Furthermore, dividing the original volume more-or-less in half allows those who teach classical theory to assign volume I, *The Blackwell Companion to Major Classical Social Theorists*, and those who teach contemporary theory to use volume II, *The Blackwell Companion to Major Contemporary Social Theorists*. In addition, for those who teach general courses in theory, both volumes can be assigned. The books can be used as basic texts, or as supplements to more conventional textbooks in social and sociological theory. Since the essays are original contributions authored by experts on particular theorists, the two volumes should also be useful to scholars looking for up-to-date and authoritative overviews of the work of the major social theorists.

Some minor changes have been made to the text, but in the main the essays are the same as those that appeared in the original hardback edition. One major change is that the original introductory essay has been used as the basis for new introductory essays, each directed at the unique concerns of the volume in which it appears. Thus the volume of the classics opens with an essay by Douglas Goodman entitled, "Narratives, *Geistesgeschichtes*, and the History of Social Theory." Goodman's essay outlines five narrative approaches to the history of sociology, making the case for critical and effective histories of social theory that place classical theoretical perspectives in dialogue with present-day theoretical orientations and challenge the ideal of theoretical progress. The volume on contemporary theory begins with an essay by Todd Stillman, "Metatheorizing Contemporary Social Theorists." Stillman catalogues the forces that contribute to intellectual breakthroughs and develops a systematic approach to the intellectual and social factors that have influenced contemporary social theorists.

Overall, these volumes present essays by leading contemporary social theorists on their classical predecessors and contemporary peers. Having written chapters or essays on many of the people covered here, I have a great appreciation for these essays. In fact, I learned a great deal from each of them and I believe that most, if not all, readers will find these essays edifying.

Beyond the contributors, there are a number of other people to thank. I begin with Susan Rabinowitz, who proposed that I undertake this project and was of great help throughout its creation and development. Ken Provencher at Blackwell helped to put the paperback volumes into print. I could not have done these books without the help of Douglas Goodman, who not only wrote the introductory essay to the classical volume but read and commented on all of the essays and helped with the innumerable details involved in bringing this project to fruition. I also need to thank Todd Stillman, who authored the introduction to the contemporary volume and kept track of the revisions. My undergraduate research assistants Zinnia Cho and Jan Geesin also provided valuable research assistance.

Contributors

Christopher G. A. Bryant is Professor of Sociology, and Dean of the Faculty of Arts, Media and Social Sciences, at the University of Salford. He is the author of *Sociology in Action* (1976), *Positivism in Social Theory and Research* (1985), and *Practical Sociology: Postempiricism and the Reconstruction of Theory and Application* (1995) and co-editor of five other books, including two with David Jary: *Giddens' Theory of Structuration* (1991) and *Anthony Giddens: Critical Assessments* (four volumes, 1997). In addition to social theory, he has research interests in: the post-communist transformation of Eastern Europe; George Soros and the Central European University; and the nations of Britain.

Craig Calhoun is President of the Social Science Research Council and Professor of Sociology and History at New York University. Among his books are *Nationalism* (1997), *Critical Social Theory: Culture, History, and the Challenge of Difference* (1995), and *Neither Gods nor Emperors: Students and the Struggle for Democracy in China* (1994). He was the editor of the ASA journal *Sociological Theory* from 1994 to 1999, and is the editor-in-chief of the *Oxford Dictionary of the Social Sciences*.

Patricia T. Clough is Professor of Sociology, Women's Studies and Intercultural Studies at Queens College and The Graduate Center of CUNY. She is author of *The End(s) of Ethnography: from Realism to Social Criticism* (second edition 1998), *Feminist Thought: Desire, Power and Discourse* (1994), and *Autoaffection: Unconscious Thought in the Age of Teletechnology* (in the press). Clough is interested in the transformation of sociality, subjectivity, and political economy in relationship to changes in technology. She is presently working on a book on psychoanalysis, mass media, and trauma.

Karen S. Cook is the Ray Lyman Wilbur Professor of Sociology at Stanford University. She is currently conducting research on social exchange, social networks, trust, and physician referral networks. Her recent publications include work on social psychology, social exchange, distributive justice (with K. Hegtvedt), and trust in the USA and Japan (with T. Yamagishi and M. Watabe, *American Journal of Sociology*, July 1998).

Gary Alan Fine is Professor of Sociology at Northwestern University. He received a PhD in social psychology from Harvard University in 1976. He is most recently the author of *Morel Tales: the Culture of Mushrooming* (1998) and *Kitchens: the Culture of Restaurant Work* (1996). His current research is an examination of the creation of a market for self-taught art.

David Jary is Professor of Sociology and Dean of the Graduate School at Staffordshire University, UK. Previously, he was Senior Lecturer in Sociology at the University of Salford, UK. His writings include *The Middle Class in Politics* (with J. Garrard et al.), *Sport, Leisure and Social Relations* (with J. Horne and A Tomlinson), *The New Higher Education* (with M. Parker), *Giddens's Theory of Structuration* (with C. Bryant) and recently *Anthony Giddens: Critical Assessments* (four volumes, with C. Bryant).

Douglas Kellner is George Kneller Chair in the Philosophy of Education at UCLA and is author of many books on social theory, politics, history, and culture, including *Herbert Marcuse and the Crisis of Marxism, Critical Theory, Marxism, and Modernity, Jean Baudrillard: from Marxism to Postmodernism and Beyond, Postmodern Theory: Critical Interrogations* (with Steven Best), *Television and the Crisis of Democracy, The Persian Gulf TV War, Media Culture*, and *The Postmodern Turn* (with Steven Best).

Richard Kilminster is Senior Lecturer in Sociology at the University of Leeds, where he also gained his PhD under Zygmunt Bauman in 1976, having previously studied sociology at the Universities of Essex and Leicester. In the 1980s he worked with Norbert Elias at the University of Bielefeld and in Amsterdam, and edited his last major work, *The Symbol Theory* (1991). He is author of *Praxis and Method* (1979) and *The Sociological Revolution: from the Enlightenment to the Global Age* (1998), and editor (with Ian Varcoe) of *Culture, Modernity and Revolution: Essays in Honour of Zygmunt Bauman* (1995). His research interests are in the fields of sociological theory, the sociology of knowledge, and psychoanalysis. He is currently researching social identity.

Siegwart Lindenberg holds a chair of theoretical sociology at the University of Groningen, the Netherlands, and is co-director of the Interuniversity Center for Social Science Theory and Methodology (ICS). He received his PhD from Harvard University in 1971 and is a member of the Royal Netherlands Academy of Arts and Sciences. His research interests focus mainly on developing a sociological approach to rational choice and applying it to questions of contracting, solidarity in groups and organizations, and quality of life. Some recent publications are: "Contractual Relations and Weak Solidarity: the Behavioral Basis of Restraints on Gain-maximization," *Journal of Institutional and Theoretical Economics* (1988); "An Extended Theory of Institutions and Contractual Discipline," *Journal of Institutional and Theoretical Economics* (1992); "Framing, Empirical Evidence, and Applications," in *Jahrbuch für Neue Politische Öekonomie, volume 12* (1993); "Alternatives, Frames, and Relative Prices: a Broader View of Rational Choice," *Acta Sociologica* (with B. Frey, 1993); "Grounding Groups in Theory: Functional, Cognitive, and Structural Interdependencies," in *Advances in Group Processes volume 14* (1997); "Solidarity: Its Microfoundations and Macro/dependence," in *The Problem of Solidarity: Theories and Models* (1998).

Philip Manning is Associate Professor of Sociology at Cleveland State University. Recent publications include "The Deinstitionalization and Deinstitutionalization of the Mentally Ill: Lessons from Goffman," in *Counseling and Therapeutic State* (1999) and "Ethnographic Coats and Tents," in *Goffman and Social Organization: Studies in a Sociological Legacy* (1999). He is presently working on a study of Freud's impact on American sociology.

Stephen Mennell has been Professor of Sociology and Head of Department at University College Dublin (National University of Ireland, Dublin) since 1993. He read economics at the University of Cambridge and spent the year 1966–7 as a Frank Knox Memorial Fellow in the Department of Social Relations at Harvard University. Between 1967 and 1990 he taught in the Department of Sociology at the University of Exeter, England, and was awarded the degree of Doctor in de Sociale Wetenschappen by the University of Amsterdam in 1985. From 1990 to 1993 he was Professor of Sociology and Head of the Department of Anthropology and Sociology at Monash University, Melbourne, Australia. His book *All Manners of Food* was awarded the Grand prix international de littérature gastronomique and the Prix Marco Polo. He is a Trustee of the Norbert Elias Foundation, Amsterdam. He has written and edited a number of other books

William Outhwaite, born in 1949, studied at Oxford and Sussex Universities and is Professor of Sociology in the School of European Studies at Sussex, where he has taught since 1973. His research interests include the philosophy of social science (espeically realism), social theory (especially critical theory and contemporary European social theory), political sociology, and the sociology of knowledge. He is the author of *Understanding Social Life: the Method Called Verstehen* (1975; 2nd edn 1986), *Concept Formation in Social Science* (1983), *New Philosophies of Social Science: Realism, Hermeneutics and Critical Theory* (1987), and *Habermas: A Critical Introduction* (1994). He edited *The Habermas Reader* (1996), *The Blackwell Dictionary of Twentieth-Century Social Thought* (1993, with Tom Bottomore), and *The Sociology of Politics* (with Luke Martell,

1998). He is currently working on books on social theory and post-communism, contemporary Europe and Germany. He has been a deputy editor of *Sociology*, editor of *Current Sociology*, and chair of the International Sociological Association's Publications Committee, and is now an associate editor of the *European Journal of Social Theory*.

Anne Warfield Rawls is an Associate Professor of Sociology at Wayne State University. Her interests are in the areas of social theory and interaction. In that regard she has published papers that attempt to connect various writings on interaction with issues developed by classical social theorists. This synthesis has in turn been applied to the analysis of "race" and intercultural communication. Publications include "The Interaction Order *Sui Generis*: Goffman's Contribution to Social Theory," "Durkheim's Epistemology: the Neglected Argument," and "'Race' as an Interaction Order Phenomenon: W. E. B. Du Bois' Double Consciousness Thesis Revisited." She is currently completing books on Durkheim's epistemology and on interaction between "races" in the United States. For the past ten years Professor Rawls has worked closely with Harold Garfinkel, preparing several edited volumes of his collected works for publication.

George Ritzer is Professor of Sociology at the University of Maryland, where he has been a Distinguished Scholar-Teacher and won a Teaching Excellence Award. He has chaired the American Sociological Associations's sections on Theoretical Sociology and Organizations and Occupations. George Ritzer has held a Fulbright-Hays Fellowship, has been a Fellow at the Netherlands Institute for Advanced Study and the Swedish Collegium for Advanced Study in the Social Sciences, and has held the UNESCO Chair in Social Theory at the Russian Academy of Sciences. His major areas of interest are sociological theory and metatheory, as well as the application of theory to the sociology of consumption. In the former, his major publications are *Sociology: a Multiple Paradigm Science* (1975/1980), *Toward an Integrated Sociological Paradigm* (1981) and *Metatheorizing in Sociology* (1991). In the latter, he has written *The McDonaldization of Society* (1993, 1996), *Expressing America: a Critique of the Global Credit Card Society* (1995), *The McDonaldization Thesis: Explorations and Extensions* (1998) and *Enchanting a Disenchanted World: Revolutionizing the Means of Consumption* (1999). His work has been translated into many languages: *The McDonaldization of Society* alone has been, or is being, translated into more than a dozen languages. He is currently co-editing the *Handbook of Social Theory* with Barry Smart.

Barry Smart is Professor of Sociology in the School of Social and Historical Studies. He is the author of a number of books, including *Michel Foucault*, *Modern Conditions*, *Postmodern Controversies*, and *Postmodernity*. Recent publications include *Facing Modernity* and *Resisting McDonaldization*. He is also the co-editor (with George Ritzer) of *The Handbook of Social Theory* (2001).

Todd Stillman is a PhD candidate at the University of Maryland at College Park. His research interests include classical and contemporary sociological theory, the sociology of consumption, and nationalist movements.

Piotr Sztompka is a Professor of Theoretical Sociology at the Jagiellonian University in Krakow, Poland. He has taught at several American and European universities, most often at Columbia and UCLA. He has been a fellow at the Institutes for Advanced Study at Uppsala, Berlin, Vienna, and Stanford. He was a recipient of the New Europe Prize 1995, is a Member of Academia Europaea (London), the American Academy of Arts and Sciences (Cambridge, MA) and the Polish Academy of Sciences, and Vice-President of the International Sociological Association. His twelve books published in English include *System and Function* (1974), *Sociological Dilemmas* (1979), *Robert Merton: an Intellectual Profile* (1986), *Society in Action* (1991), *The Sociology of Social Change* (1993), and *Trust: a Sociological Theory* (1999). He has also edited a number of volumes, including *Robert Merton on Social Structure and Science* (1996). He is currently working on a book on cultural trauma in post-communist societies.

Jonathan H. Turner is Distinguished Professor of Sociology at the University of California at Riverside. He is the author of twenty-four books and many articles on sociological theory, ethnic relations, institutional systems, stratification dynamics, and evolutionary processes. His most recent research has been on the biology and sociology of human emotions.

Malcolm Waters is Professor of Sociology and Dean of Arts at the University of Tasmania, Australia. He is the author or co-author of *Postmodernization*, *Modern Sociological Theory*, *The Death of Class*, *Globalization*, and *Daniel Bell*. Waters is a Fellow of the Academy of the Social Sciences in Australia.

Joseph M. Whitmeyer is Associate Professor of Sociology at the University of North Carolina at Charlotte. He is interested in developing actor models and using them deductively to analyze social phenomena such as associational networks, reputation systems, social power, and nationalism. A recent article in *Rationality and Society* presents an experimental test of how negatively connected exchange networks produce power inequality.

Introduction: Metatheorizing Contemporary Social Theorists

Todd Stillman

The lives of contemporary social theorists can illuminate the foundations of contemporary social theory. Theories are tools for looking at the social world. Yet theorists who are not themselves immune to the influences of the social world conceive them. Because these tools are shaped by personal experiences, theoretical work bears the imprint of the social context in which it is produced. It follows that readers and researchers should use a theorist's work critically and reflexively; to understand the strengths and limitations of the theory, they must be sensitive to the context in which it is produced. Anthony Giddens says as much in reference to classical social theory: "[There are] deficiencies deriving from the context of their formation."[1] This holds true for contemporary theory as well.

Taking their cue from the sociologies of knowledge and science, the authors of these essays place the work of thirteen thinkers in the context of these thinker's lives and times. Factors such as sociohistorical developments, social networks and mentorship, and the idiosyncrasies of biography, combine with intellectual influences that range from nineteenth-century German philosophy to French existentialism to Freudian psychoanalysis. The chapters also chart the development of the theorists' thought over the course of their careers as they refine their ideas and extend their analyses to new theoretical problems. Authored by a practicing sociologist, each of these essays is an exercise in reflexive thinking; they turn the tools of the discipline on to major figures in the discipline.

The purpose of this introduction is to outline a systematic account of the major kinds of influences on these theorists and their work. It will draw on the ideas of metatheory, the systematic study of theory, to suggest that there are four general sources of influence on theory formation.[2] Influences are not wholly constitutive of a body of work, but they do provide clues to the social and intellectual resources that a theorist drew on. Much of what is distinctive in the work of social theorists can be understood as attempts to assimilate their social and intellectual influences into a theoretical framework.

METATHEORETICAL ANALYSIS

Most theorizing takes an aspect of the social world as the object of analysis. It should go without saying that most social theory is developed in the context of an empirical case or comparatively across cases. The value of a theory, nonetheless, is found in whether it transcends the specificity of its cases. For example, Pierre Bourdieu developed his theory of cultural capital in the context of his work on the French educational system. Although conceived in the French context, Bourdieu's has been an influential theory of social reproduction, a useful analytic in a variety of empirical contexts. Most good theorizing follows this pattern.

Metatheorizing, by contrast, is a step removed from empirical research. Rather than take the social world as the object of analysis, it takes theories themselves as its object in an effort to understand their individual strengths and limitations as well as to develop overarching perspectives on sets of theories. A metatheoretical analysis of the theory of cultural capital might weigh which elements of the theory are nationally specific or consider how Bourdieu's own experiences with the French system influenced his views. Either one of these would help a reader to assess Bourdieu's contribution not merely to the study of French academe but also to the corpus of general theory on which sociologists draw. Thus the value of metatheorizing is that it examines the intellectual commitments of a theory with an eye toward critical assessment.

Metatheorizing is employed for a variety of ends. Although it is not always labeled as such, most theorists use metatheoretical analysis to clarify a central problem in extant theory as a prelude to proposing a theoretical perspective to deal with this problem. A good example of this sort of metatheorizing is Giddens's *Central Problems in Social Theory*, which develops a critical reading of structuralism into the influential theory of structuration. A second type of metatheory develops an overarching perspective on a set of theories. One prevalent variety sets out to synthesize a set of ideas by ratcheting up the level of abstraction. A good example of this type of metatheorizing is the first volume of Jeffrey Alexander's *Theoretical Logic in Sociology* (1982), which develops an overarching perspective on classical sociology.[3] Metatheorizing can also be undertaken as an end in itself. An intellectual biography of an influential theorist, for example, can develop a rich reading of the theorist's work. The authors of the essays in this volume have produced this sort of metatheory. They have synthesized the work of an important figure and placed it in an intellectual and social context that clarifies the origins and influence of the theory. No matter what the ends, metatheorizing is a useful term to capture what people do when they think about theory.

This introductory essay is primarily concerned with metatheorizing as a tool for better understanding social theory. Our basic proposition is that an

Intellectual

	Internal	External
Intellectual	Cognitive paradigms Schools of thought Changes in paradigms, schools of thought Metatheoretical tools Theories	Use of concepts borrowed from: Philosophy Economics Linguistics, etc. Impact of disciplines outside sociology
Social	Communal paradigms Invisible colleges Schools Networks Individual backgrounds	Impact of society Impact of social institutions Historical roots

Social

understanding of the context in which theories are formed is useful for assessing the strengths and limitations of a theory. To this end, the analytic presented in the figure will be useful to codify types of influences on the development of a social theory.[4]

Theorists are influenced by both intellectual and social factors. These can be further subdivided into factors internal to the discipline and factors external to the discipline. Internal intellectual factors include the influence of schools and traditions of thought on a theorist. External intellectual factors include ideas borrowed from other disciplines. Internal social factors include the influence of social networks and mentorship on a theorist's work. External social factors include the impact of historical change on the structures and institutions of the society being theorized.

Although these categories are logically exhaustive, they are not mutually exclusive; some factors fit into more than one quadrant. It is therefore instructive to consider how each factor relates to the others. A class of relationships of interest to metatheorists is cases of external social factors having an effect on internal social ones. External social factors such the disintegration of the Soviet Union clearly had an effect on internal social factors such as the number of seminars and conferences dedicated to the post-communist transition. Another mechanism relates internal intellectual and internal social factors insofar as traditions of thought exert influence through social networks and mentorship. Exploring such relationships can offer a window into the workings of subdisciplines. Cast more broadly, this analytic is a serviceable way to conceptualize the variety of factors that contribute to a theorist's social location and intellectual makeup.

Contemporary social theory is a product of this complex of influences on the work of social theorists. Fundamental changes to social institutions (e.g., the rise of compulsory education), advances in other disciplines (such as cognitive psychology and linguistics), the institutional power of major programs and "hot" new programs, the continuing influence of the sociological classics, along with other factors too numerous to list, form the backdrop in which new social theory is formed. The remainder of this essay turns to specific examples of such influences drawn from the experiences of the thinkers covered in this volume.

Internal Intellectual Influences

The norm in more recent years is for theorists to be most powerfully influenced by ideas internal to sociology, but to have a smattering of external inputs as well. Perhaps of greatest importance is the fact that many of the thinkers discussed in this book are famous for playing a major role in the creation of a perspective that has shaped social thinking. They themselves have become major internal intellectual influences on the thinkers and researchers who have been inspired by their ideas.

Among the thinkers in this volume the classical theorists Karl Marx, Émile Durkheim, and Max Weber are, doubtless, the most important internal intellectual influences on contemporary social theorizing. The so-called "holy trinity" set out the major problems for social theory that continue to occupy contemporary thinkers. Marx provided a rationale for integrating social theory, empirical historical inquiry, and normative critique. Durkheim gave sociology the social fact, as a justification for studying society and as a powerful analytical tool. Weber's ideas are founding principles in the sociology of religion, organizations, development, and politics, among many other fields.

Naturally, contemporary theorists have drawn unequally on the classics. They have their own orientation toward classical theory, which is rooted in a vision of what the practice of theory is and how the classical tradition informs this practice. A salient distinction can be drawn between two kinds of thinkers. Scientific thinkers like Merton rummage the classics in search of testable hypotheses. Critical thinkers like Habermas engage the classics as an interpretive exercise, developing new lines of interpretation to inform their own grand theoretical syntheses.

Robert Merton's position on the relation of contemporary theory to particular classics is well known, and controversial. He said that, "the writings of classical authors in every field of learning can be read with profit time and again, additional ideas and intimations coming freshly into view with each rereading."[5] But, as Sztompka argues in this volume, Merton also felt that the classics should only be read selectively with an eye toward critically appropriating what is relevant to current social issues and social scientific debates, while rejecting or modifying the rest. The classics best serve as a living tradition, subject to constant reinterpretation, rather than as a vast set of constraints on appropriate subjects, research methods, and theoretical orientations. As a policy, Merton always used the classics in the service of a theoretical or empirical analysis.

The mark of Durkheim on Merton's work demonstrates his ideas about the value of the classics. This influence is evident in Merton's scientific orientation, his embrace of structural functionalism, and his choice of research topics. In his influential essay on middle-range theorizing, he cites Durkheim's *Suicide* as *the* exemplar for middle-range theory because of the study's contextual, deductive approach to theory development. In his analysis of anomie and deviance, Merton draws on this landmark study of suicide but his rigorous analytic goes far beyond it in pursuit of the structural sources of deviance in a stratified society.[6] Merton's use of Durkheim to further his own theoretical projects is consistent with his vision of the role of the classics for scientific sociological inquiry.

Jürgen Habermas writes in the grand tradition of sociological theory that Merton vigorously opposed. Habermas takes social theory to be a critical rather than a scientific enterprise, that is, the aim of theory is to write a pathology report of modern society in order to find a cure for its ills. He was trained in the Weberian Marxist tradition of the Frankfurt School, and his voluminous exegesis on Marx, Weber, Durkheim, Mead, and many others, forms the basis of his theory of communicative action. Early in his career, Habermas developed a neo-Marxian theory of the historical development of late capitalism that develops a theory of the role of the interventionist state in displacing economic crises into the political and cultural spheres.

Habermas's concern for the rationalization of society is derived from Weber, but his theory of communicative action splits rationalization into two complementary processes: the rationalization of the market and bureaucratic spheres (the system) and the rationalization of the sphere of everyday life. The latter was formerly the territory of culturally grounded understanding and mutual accommodations but in modern society was threatened by the increasing reach of bureaucratic rationality. By attributing an autonomous logic to different social spheres, Habermas backs away from the totalizing claims of Weber's rationalization thesis. But he also describes a dynamic that seems better to match our experience of rationalization. In this sense, Habermas's relation to the classics can be seen as an attempt to update or revise their best parts to suit our contemporary understandings and needs. Habermas's use of the classics is at odds with Merton's scientific ambitions but nevertheless suggests how readings of the classics can give rise to new grand theoretical projects. Both are illustrative of how the classics provide a foundation for contemporary social theory.

External Intellectual Influences

While the sociological classics have the most pronounced influence on all manner of social theorizing, contemporary social theory is notable for drawing on extra-disciplinary resources to make up for some of the shortfalls and lapses of the classical tradition. Habermas's theory of communicative action, as described above, draws not only on the classics but takes significant inspiration from pragmatist philosophy when developing its ideas about discourse ethics and moral norms. External intellectual influences have become priceless sources of theoretical innovations for contemporary social theorizing by supplying fresh ideas and data to be integrated with the dominant traditions.

Such a strategy makes creative use of paradigms developed elsewhere to make interventions in key theoretical problems. Both Richard Emerson and Michel

Foucault draw on extra-disciplinary resources to address how best to study and conceptualize power. Power had been a macro-sociological issue, a means that states and other powerful actors used to exert influence, but there was little work being done on the mechanism of influence. Both Foucault and Emerson turned toward micro-theories to address this important issue. For Emerson, behaviorism was an empirically satisfactory resource to investigate the workings of power in social exchange and social networks. For Foucault, interested in what he termed the "micro-physics" of power, structuralism provided a framework for understanding how expert discourses on pressing social issues like sexuality and criminality could shape actors and actions. Both interventions are notable for setting new research agendas based on their readings of extra-disciplinary materials.

Richard Emerson's exchange theory draws part of its inspiration from B. F. Skinner's empirical research into human behavior. Emerson's commitment to behaviorism meant that he could ignore the subjective meaning of individual action while carrying out empirical studies of observable behavior. In his landmark 1972 article, Emerson wrote, "In this chapter we will not presume to know the needs and motivations of men. We will see how far we can go on this skimpy basis."[7] While many social scientists, notably the symbolic interactionists, were at the time (and are still today) committed to the investigation of meaningful behavior, Emerson's power-dependency theory puts the issue of subjective meaning in brackets, in favor of a deductive, experimentally tested power-dependency model of exchange relations. The influence of Skinnerian behaviorism allowed Emerson to put his own ideas about power relations on a scientific footing.

The influence of structuralist linguistics on social theory is another case in point. Michel Foucault's distinctive approach to the knowledge/power nexus owes something to structuralist ideas anticipated by Durkheim and Mauss but given their full expression by linguists such as Ferdinand Saussure and Roman Jakobson. These linguists adhered to a deterministic view of the relation between linguistic systems and everyday speech. Taken up by anthropologists and semioticians and applied to the study of mythic, and modern, culture, structuralism was in fashion in France during Foucault's formative years. The degree of influence that structuralism had on Foucault is debatable, but it is clear that his ideas about the power of discourse to shape actors and their actions bears the mark of structuralism's emphasis on the determining power of language. For all that is innovative, idiosyncratic, and personal in Foucault's approach, his perspective would not have been articulated in quite the same manner if structuralism was not an intellectual influence – and a foil – of his project.

Internal Social Influences

Internal social influences include factors like the stamp of social networks and individual backgrounds on a thinker's ideas. A wide range of biographical factors all leave their mark. Social experiences such as migration, travel, work, and education can all impinge on a theorist's thought. Race, class, and gender also are also influential. Finally, networks, schools, invisible colleges and intellectual communities have an effect on career and reception. All these types of social experiences can lead theorists to new insights and directions.

An example of work and college experiences leaving their mark on a theorist is found in the early career of Garfinkel, a student of Parsons and Schutz. Some of his inspiration came, surprisingly, from an accident of biography. An important concept for ethnomethodologists, traceable to his *Studies in Ethnomethodology*, is, "accountability."[8] Accountability refers to the *post hoc* justifications that actors give for their actions to the people or organizations to which they are held accountable. These justifications fail to paint a complete picture of any situation but rather are couched in terms that make a course of action comprehensible under the framework of rules and regulations in which actors operate. Garfinkel's ideas about accountability were inspired by his college experiences at the University of Newark. While in Newark, Garfinkel took a business course on double entry bookkeeping and cost accounting. Garfinkel's interrogation of this material led him to ask how accountants justify their decisions to put items in particular columns in their books, understanding that they would be accountable to their superiors and other agencies. Accountants, he understood, were clear about the fact that their indicators did not represent an underlying order but rather were a form of theorizing that developed conceptual order out of the empirical manifold of business practices. Garfinkel's insights into the relations among an organization, an accountant, and the books, found their way into his thinking about ethnomethods, particularly his argument in "Good Reasons for Bad Clinical Records," about the way in which clinicians render patient files accountable. The same sort of idea also served as an inspiration for his critique of Talcott Parsons's formal analytical theorizing, in "Parsons's Plenum."

Bourdieu's sense of how social inequality was reproduced through social institutions was deeply affected by his schooling in France. The son of a postmaster, Bourdieu entered the elite École Normale Superieure in 1951 (as a classmate of Jacques Derrida and Michel Foucault), where he was taught to think of himself as a member of the "state nobility." Although Bourdieu excelled at the school, he also conceived of himself as an outsider and found himself deeply disappointed with what he saw as the corrupt power of the institutional elite. These feelings were reinforced through the early part of his academic career, when he found himself in a marginal position in French academic life.

Bourdieu's commentary on the French educational system is marked by his having experienced the star system from the inside. Within the university system, he argued, power rather than simply merit shaped the distribution of opportunities. He said that the education system tended to promise more than it delivered. While intellectuals present themselves as working for the common good, they in fact reproduce social inequalities. They inspire devotion from those who want richer, freer lives but they disappoint them with the limits they impose. Bourdieu felt that by exposing the deep truth of the situation he could delegitimate the power of the old guard and challenge the myths in French education. This impulse to undermine the myths of modern institutions is one of the animating features of his entire corpus.

Also important is the theorist's ties to networks, schools, invisible colleges, and communities of thinkers. While attending the graduate school at the University of Chicago, Erving Goffman was the beneficiary of a rich legacy of American sociological thought. His teachers included such luminaries as Everett Hughes, Herbert Blumer, and Edward Shils. According to Fine and Manning, the institutional peculiarities of Chicago at the time – only seven faculty members and scores of graduate students – meant that the graduate students relied on each other to formulate their problems and advance their educations. They formed close friendships through their co-location in Hyde Park. At Chicago, Goffman had the good fortune of an extended intensive exchange of ideas with a succession of influential figures including Joseph Gusfield, Howard Becker, and Ralph Turner. As a group, they became skeptical of the dominant structural-functionalist perspective of the day and turned instead to rich, empirical sociological studies in the interactionist perspective. These scholars all developed a concern about totalitarian control, an interest in dramatic change, and in the bases of community and conformity. Their work set a sociological agenda for research into collective behavior, race and ethnicity, deviance, and work and occupations.

In sum, internal intellectual influences – personal experiences and other accidents of biography – place thinkers in situations that subsequently color their selection of topics, their manner of thinking, or their relation to mainstream social thought. By attending to such influences, it becomes clear that social theory is not the objective, scientific endeavor that some would have. Rather, the individual circumstances of social theorists characteristically become important resources for their theorizing.

External Social Influences

External social influences – such as long-running trends like industrialization or watershed events like World War I – can have a constitutive influence on a theorist. Economic depressions and wars have affected most of them. So have the national contexts in which they work. On the one hand, such events define the salient issues of the day and, in doing so, constitute the most pressing topics for social theory to address. Wars, revolutions, episodes of contentious politics, technological innovations, and changing modes of production are external social developments that have attracted the attention of social theorists. On the other hand, such events can affect the trajectory of a theorist's career and the reception of their ideas. A case in point would be the effects of the relocation of the Frankfurt School to the USA after the Nazis came into power and the effect that both Nazism and exposure to American popular culture had on the work of Marcuse, Horkheimer, Adorno, and Lowenthal.

Once a social problem has drawn the attention of the public, social thinkers who wish to influence policy decisions and substantive debates orient their research to bear on these salient questions. James Coleman's career-long concern for influencing public debate is evident from the beginning of his career. *The Adolescent Society* is a fine example of how a contemporary social problem can influence a thinker's agenda.[9] Policymakers understood that education is profoundly important insofar as it has the ability to reinforce or ameliorate inequalities of opportunity in an industrial society. This understanding translates into a value system that emphasizes knowledge and skills. Yet a rift has opened between these values and the values of adolescents who prefer sports or socializing to academic achievement. Coleman asked why high school students fail to assimilate academic values. His theory of the leading crowd seeks to explain the low standing of academic achievement in the adolescent's value system. Coleman's ideas about education had a notable impact on the debates over education.

Daniel Bell's writings on the contemporary scene were notable because they conceptualized important changes in the economic and social landscape in ways that highlighted the inadequacy of extant social theory. In other words, Bell described an emerging type of society that had yet to be theorized. (The impact of Baudrillard's writings on the emergence of a postmodern society is similar in this regard.) Bell's social theorizing is animated by the idea that modernity is disintegrating into a post-industrial society. Perusing the social landscape, Bell sees that the contemporary scene is no longer centered on the manufacturing of tangible goods. The post-industrial society is one in which information technology and a service economy rise alongside the machine technology of industrial society. Within this society, the relative importance of the professional and technical class increases *vis-à-vis* other occupational classes. In this society, codified theoretical knowledge becomes the basis for social planning and social control. Such observations may seem commonplace today but, in the 1960s and 1970s, were prescient. Bell's theoretical ideas are elaborated from his observation of the contemporary scene, especially changing economic roles and technological innovation. Such developments are consistently a source of theoretical inspiration because they suggest that existing categories of analysis are inadequate and in need of rethinking.

Coleman and Bell can be seen as taking very different approaches to theorizing insofar as Coleman attempts to focus in on the detailed workings of particular social problem while Bell uses broad brushstrokes to characterize whole segments of social life. Yet the fundamental similarity of their approaches is that they are each reacting to the changing contemporary scene. Such an impulse is among the most common sources of new social theory.

METATHEORY AS A REFLEXIVE ACTIVITY

More than thirty years have passed since Alvin Gouldner made his plea for reflexive sociology in *The Coming Crisis of Western Sociology.*[10] Gouldner believed a "sociology of sociology" was needed to move beyond the "methodological dualism" of practitioners who assume they view the social world from a special objective vantage. A deepened understanding of the sociologist's position in the world, gained by turning the sociologies of knowledge, science, and occupations on the worlds of sociologists themselves, would create a new awareness of how sociologists' roles and their personal praxis affect their work. In turn, this awareness might free sociologists from the strictures of their theoretical and methodological biases to produce valid and reliable information about the social world.

Although Gouldner's attack on scientific sociology became famous, reflexive thinking about theory did not begin with *The Coming Crisis of Western Sociology*. Randall Collins claims that as a general phenomenon reflexivity "comes increasingly to the fore as the intergenerational sequence lengthens."[11] In a wide-ranging survey of several thousand years of philosophical thought, Collins finds reflexive thinking among such traditions as the Greek Sophists, nineteenth-century German thought, and the logical formalists. This suggests that reflexivity is a natural feature of intellectual communities. One way to interpret the dearth of reflexive thinking in mid-twentieth-century sociology is as the proverbial exception to the rule. In a quest for cumulative knowledge of society, reflexivity was for a time arrested. This is not to say that science is incapable of reflexively assessing its theories, methods, and practices – as all good science should – but rather that "normal science" is characterized by a community's general acceptance of foundational assumptions. Reflexive thinking is, and probably always has been, a key component of a vigorous intellectual community because critical assessment spurs innovation.

This volume is a testament to the value of reflexive thinking about key figures using the tools of our discipline. Each of these chapters provides insights into the structure of a major thinker's thought and the forces that contributed to the development of his or her ideas. Only when these forces are taken into account, can the context-specific elements of a body of work be appreciated. It is up to the readers of this volume to make the most of this contextual approach to social theory and to decide which elements of a theory remain useful when they are taken from the context of their formation and applied to emerging areas of interest.

Metatheory is a systematic tool for theorizing reflexively. The tools of metatheory are useful because they codify the many ways in which theory can be appraised and investigated as an object of analysis. By turning the tools of the discipline on its major thinkers, this volume reveals some of the important sources of contemporary social theory, be they accidents of biography or world-historical transformations. By revealing these sources, this volume will be a valuable tool for students of social theory to better appraise the works they study.

How much of contemporary social theory can be attributed to the circumstance under which it was creation? Quite a bit – as this volume shows. Metatheory is our best available tool for making this point and for continuing to think reflexively about our discipline.

Notes

1 A. Giddens (1979) *Central Problems in Social Theory: Action, Structure, and Contradiction in Social Analysis*. London: Macmillan, p. 1.
2 G. Ritzer (1991) *Metatheorizing in Sociology*. Lexington, MA: Lexington Books.

3 J. Alexander (1982) *Theoretical Logic in Sociology*, vol. 1: *Positivism, Presuppositions, and Current Controversies*. Berkeley: University of California Press.
4 This figure appears in Ritzer 1991, p. 18.
5 R. K. Merton (1968) *Social Theory and Social Structure*. New York: Free Press, p. 65.
6 É. Durkheim (1897/1951) *Suicide*. New York: Free Press.
7 R. Emerson (1972) Exchange Theory, Part 1: A Psychological Basis for Social Exchange. In J. Berger, M. Zelditch, Jr., and B. Anderson (eds) *Sociological Theories in Progress*, vol. 2. Boston: Houghton Mifflin, p. 44.
8 H. Garfinkel (1967) *Studies in Ethnomethodology*. Englewood Cliffs, NJ: Prentice Hall.
9 J. Coleman (1961) *The Adolescent Society*. Glencoe, IL: Free Press.
10 A. Gouldner (1970) *The Coming Crisis of Western Sociology*. New York: Basic Books.
11 R. Collins (1999) *The Sociology of Philosophies: a Global Theory of Intellectual Change*. Cambridge, MA: Harvard University Press, p. 787.

1

Robert K. Merton

Piotr Sztompka

The Person

Robert King Merton was born on July 4, 1910 in Philadelphia, to a family of working-class Jewish immigrants from Eastern Europe. As a journalist puts it, he started "almost at the bottom of the social structure" (Hunt, 1961, p. 39).

Obviously gifted, from the earliest days he encountered conducive opportunities for his talents to unfold. Close to his Philadelphia home he found the Andrew Carnegie Library, where as a child he spent endless hours, voraciously consuming works in literature, science, and history, and especially biographies and autobiographies (apparently looking for a "role model," as he was to call it later). Since that time he has always remained, to use his own words, "the inveterate loner working chiefly in libraries and in my study at home" (Merton, 1994, p. 16). The Academy of Music, with Leopold Stokowski at the helm, was within walking distance and a place of frequent visits. And later, in the mid-1920s, new institutions were added in the vicinity: the Central Library and the Museum of Art. Thus, outside of formal education at the South Philadelphia High School, young Merton was exposed to a rich educative environment (see Merton, 1994).

There were other opportunities though, having more to do with luck: meeting the right people at the right moments of his life. Among those there were: the librarians at Carnegie Library, who took an interest in the young book addict; George E. Simpson, young sociology instructor at Temple College, who made him a research assistant to the study of the public imagery of Blacks, and thus awoke a lifelong passion for social inquiry; Pitirim A. Sorokin, who after a brief encounter at an American Sociological Association convention encouraged Merton to apply for graduate study at Harvard, and soon after made him his research and teaching assistant, as well as a co-author of his work on social time and a chapter in his monumental *Social and Cultural Dynamics* (1937–41); Talcott Parsons, who pushed his inquisitive mind toward the European founders of sociology – Durkheim, Weber, Marx, Simmel – and taught him analytic skills and conceptual sophistication; George Sarton, who seduced him toward the history of science; and finally a wartime immigrant from Vienna, mathematician-psychologist turned sociologist Paul F. Lazarsfeld, with whom Merton established the long-lasting collaboration at Columbia University and the famous Bureau of Applied Social Research, which they co-directed for several decades.

Let us return to more formal biographical facts. In 1927 Merton entered Temple College at Philadelphia, from which he graduated in 1931. Right after, he won a fellowship for graduate study at Harvard University, and in 1936 defended his doctoral dissertation "Science, Technology and Society in Seventeenth-century England," written under the guidance of George Sarton, and published as a book two years later (Merton, 1938). Here he put forward a hypothesis, akin to Max Weber's famous claim on the link between Protestant ethic and the capitalist economy, arguing for a similar link between Protestant pietism and early experimental science. The "Merton Thesis" has been subjected to criticism, particularly from historians (see Kearney, 1973), and started continuous debates. Some of them have been recently put together in a book by I. Bernard Cohen (1990). Even before his doctoral dissertation, Merton's first influential articles came out in print: "The Unanticipated Consequences of Purposive Social Actions" in 1936 (Merton, 1996, pp. 173–82), and, in 1938, one of his crucial contributions, the article "Social Structure and Anomie" (Merton, 1996, pp. 132–52), starting a whole school in the theory of deviance and becoming a subject of continuing debate for more than half a century. From 1936 to 1939 Merton served as a tutor and instructor at Harvard, and then from 1939 until 1941 he held the positions of professor and chairman at the Department of Sociology at Tulane University in New Orleans. In 1941, choosing between job offers from Harvard and Columbia, Merton moved to Columbia University, where he remained on the faculty of the Sociology Department for 38 years, going through the positions of Assistant Professor, Associate Professor (1944), Full Professor (1947), Chairman (succeeding Paul Lazarsfeld in 1961), Giddings Professor of Sociology (1963), and University Professor (1974). After retirement, from 1979 to 1984 he remained active as a Special Service Professor. He withdrew from teaching in 1984.

Apart from the university, Merton has been much involved in wider academic life, both in the United States and internationally. Among his many official positions are the Presidencies of the American Sociological Association (1956), the Eastern Sociological Society (1968), and the Society for Social Studies of Science (1975). He has held innumerable posts on editorial boards, professional committees, and advising positions to publishing houses. Academic recognition includes membership of the National Academy of Sciences, Academia Europaea, and numerous foreign academies (the Polish Academy of Science was added to this list in 1997). He has received more than twenty honorary doctoral degrees from universities including Yale, Chicago, Harvard, Columbia, Leiden,

Jerusalem, Wales, Ghent, Oxford, and Krakow. He was a Fellow of the Guggenheim Foundation (1962), and the Center for Advanced Studies in Behavioral Science, the Resident Scholar at the Russell Sage Foundation (1979 until the present time), and MacArthur Prize Fellow (1983–8). From the American Sociological Association he received a Career of Distinguished Scholarship award, and in 1994 the President of the United States granted him the highest academic honor: the National Medal of Science.

Married twice, he has a son and two daughters from the first marriage. His son, Robert C. Merton, a professor at Harvard and an eminent specialist in the study of financial markets, won the Nobel Prize in economics in 1997.

The Social Context

Merton's life covers the major part of twentieth-century American history. Even though he has always been a man of academia, surrounded by and totally devoted to the intellectual community, he has also been touched by the turns of political and economic events. A perfect example of a self-made man, coming from the lowest echelons of class structure and advancing to the narrowest New York elite, as well as to worldwide fame, he could not but recognize the mobility, openness, and democratic virtues of American society making that feat possible. This led him quite early to embrace the liberal-democratic political creed to which he has remained faithful all his life. The experience of the Great Depression raised his sensitivity to social issues, racial discrimination, poverty, deviance, and anomie. And the drama of Stalinist terror, the Nazi ascendance to power and the Second World War, the Holocaust and the Gulag, and other atrocities, brought him to a strong condemnation of totalitarianism. He lived through the defeat of Nazism in 1945 as well as the the final collapse of communism in 1989, which provided happy corroboration of his political commitments.

He reacted to political events with the tools of his academic profession, mostly through research and writing, but was always concerned with the "potentials of relevance" of scientific ideas. He devoted systematic reflection to the role of the intellectual in public bureaucracy (1945), social responsibilities of technologists (1947), and the role of applied social science in the formation of policy (1949). The most "practical" of his own theoretical studies include work on deviance and anomie, racial discrimination, marriage patterns, political "machines," housing, propaganda and the "war-bond drive," and medical education. The most "ideological" of his articles dealt with the destruction of science in Nazi Germany and the defense of the "scientific ethos" (Merton, 1996, pp. 277–85), which for him was a kind of micro-model for the democratic polity. As a co-director of the Bureau of Applied Social Research, he managed and supervised numerous other programs directed at pressing social issues.

As was mentioned above, his most significant social environment was academia. His graduate studies and the beginnings of his professional career coincided with the renaissance of American sociology in the 1930s, with Harvard

University as its most lively center, in Robert Nisbet's metaphor "the Venice" of that time (Coser and Nisbet, 1975, p. 6). His mature career was linked to "the Florence" of American sociology (ibid.) in post-war years, Columbia University. He stayed at Columbia Sociology Department through the peak period of its eminence, in the 1950s and 1960s, to which he himself contributed in considerable measure.

From the "core" of Columbia University, the concentric circles of his "significant others," whom he reciprocally influenced as a highly recognized and esteemed partner, extended to the intellectual, cultural, and artistic community of New York, then Western and Eastern Europe, and eventually an even wider world. He became a true cosmopolitan, maintaining permanent links with international academic communities, not limited by political or ideological biases. One of the founders, in 1948, of the International Sociological Association (ISA), as early as the 1950s he went with the first group of American sociologists to the USSR, paid numerous visits to Poland, Hungary, and Czechoslovakia, visited China, and was always ready to give a generous helping hand to the young apprentices in sociology from those politically exotic parts of the world (here I am happy to record my own personal debt). It would be hard to find a better example of the true "man of the world."

THE INTELLECTUAL CONTEXT

Merton believed that science develops cumulatively and incrementally by standing "on the shoulders of giants" (Merton, 1965). Hence, the crucial importance of scientific traditions. "I have long argued," Merton says, "that the writings of classical authors in every field of learning can be read with profit time and again, additional ideas and intimations coming freshly into view with each re-reading" (Merton, 1965, p. 45). This is particularly relevant for the adept of a young science like sociology: "the sociologist qua sociologist rather than as historian of sociology, has ample reason to study the works of a Weber, Durkheim, and Simmel and, for that matter, to turn back on occasion to the works of a Hobbes, Rousseau, Condorcet or Saint-Simon" (Merton, 1968, p. 35). But sociology limited to the intepretation of the masters would be sterile. In an attempt to avoid both narrow dogmatism and uncritical novelty, Merton's policy of relating to the masters seems to imply three directives. First is a selective approach; that is, the constant effort to derive from the masters of the past the core of their ideas and to sift it from inevitable marginal contributions, blind alleys, or outright mistakes. Second is reading the masters anew; that is, entering into a sort of critical dialogue with them, reworking their ideas in the light of new perspectives and approaches, later discoveries and experiences, newly acquired data. Third is the injunction to critically enrich, partly supplant, or reject past ideas, if found incomplete, deficient or obsolete: "the founding fathers are honored, not by zealous repetition of their early findings, but by extensions, modifications and, often enough, by rejection of some of their ideas and findings" (Merton, 1968, p. 587).

Merton is quite faithful to this professed policy. Various commentators have noted that he was among the first in his generation of American sociologists to turn their attention to the heritage of European sociology, to have mastered it in depth and to have "assimilated European thought patterns more thoroughly than most of his predecessors" (Coser and Nisbet, 1975, p. 4). But his attitude toward "founding fathers" has never been exegetic or dogmatic. Rather, it has been self-consciously critical, with an emphasis on possible continuities.

Who are those giants "on the shoulders" of which Merton self-consciously places himself? To begin with, there is his pre-eminent indebtedness to Émile Durkheim. In the list of his recognized idols he unfailingly places Durkheim in the forefront, and indicatively Durkheim is quoted more often than any other author in Merton's major volume, *Social Theory and Social Structure* (1968). There is a striking similarity in the dominant orientation of their sociologies: their common attempt to have sociology develop into a reasonably rigorous, "hard" science of a specifically social subject matter, with explanations in terms of identified social factors. Merton's sociology is also in continuity with Durkheim's in terms of common theoretical approach: functional and structural analysis. Finally, there are obvious substantive continuities: from Durkheim's study of suicide, and particularly "anomic suicide," to Merton's analyses of anomie and deviance; and from Durkheim's sociological research on religion, focusing on religious communities, to Merton's sociological analysis of science, undertaking detailed analysis of the structure and functioning of the communities of scholars.

Next in line of Merton's intellectual ancestors comes Karl Marx. In his approach to Marx, Merton rejects dogmatism: "I have long since abandoned the struggle to determine what 'Marxism' is or is not. Instead, I have taken all that I find good in Marxian thought – and that is a considerable amount – and neglected conceptions which do not seem to me to meet tests of validity" (Merton, 1982b, p. 917). Such an approach allows him to follow some Marxian ideas, while remaining far removed from Marxism in the political or ideological sense. Many common methodological and substantive ideas would include the emphasis on sociological, and particularly structural, factors in the explanation of human phenomena; or the focus on contradictions, conflicts, and circularity of social processes. Then, the idea of the existential determination of knowledge, turned into the idea of the social-structural determination of science, has uncontestable Marxian roots.

Third in line of ancestry comes Georg Simmel. There is some commonality in their general approach to sociology: an emphasis on relationships and structures, the "form" or "geometry" of social reality. But Merton's indebtedness to Simmel becomes all the more apparent in the context of conceptual analyses. He reaches some quite similar substantive results. For example, Merton starts from Simmel's hunches in his analysis of patterned interactions, social visibility, and observability (Jaworski, 1990), in-group integration and inter-group conflicts, the completeness, openness, and closedness of groups, reference groups, and several others.

Max Weber has had less influence on Merton's work. To be sure, Merton explicitly identifies Weber as one of his "masters-at-a-distance," but except for the doctoral dissertation on the Puritan ethic and the origins of modern science, and the discussion of bureaucratic structure, it is hard to discover Weberian themes in Merton's work. On the rare occasions when Merton enters the world of Weber's sociology, he mostly accepts Weber's results as given. This is the case with the theory of action, the idea of "value-free" sociology, or the ideal type of bureaucratic organization.

So much for the classics of an earlier time. Among the later twentieth-century masters, some of whom were Merton's contemporaries or even immediate teachers, four names should be mentioned. An important influence on Merton's ideas, particularly in the field of sociology of science, was exerted by George Sarton, at the time of Merton's graduate studies undoubtedly "the acknowledged world dean among historians of science" (Merton, 1985, p. 477). The influence of Sarton can be found at the level of general interests: in science, its development, the operation of scientific communities, and specific techniques for studying historical sources. Apart from that, at the centennial of Sarton's birth, held at the University of Ghent, Merton acknowledged numerous tangible and intangible "gifts" that he received from his mentor; including the conducive micro-environment for the work on his doctoral dissertation, opening the pages of the newly established journal *Isis* for Merton's first publications, and publishing Merton's doctoral thesis in another of Sarton's periodicals, *Osiris* (1938).

Then come the two most influential teachers, under whom, and later with whom, Merton learned and worked: Pitirim Sorokin and Talcott Parsons. It was not entirely a direct and solely positive influence. Merton was apparently not an easy pupil. Admiring his teachers, he did not hesitate to criticize them and to build his own intellectual system partly in opposition to theirs. The case of Sorokin is particularly telling. Having the young Merton collaborate with him on one important chapter of his treatise *Social and Cultural Dynamics* (1937–41) and on an article on "Social Time" (1937), and some thirty years later publicly praising *On the Shoulders of Giants* (1965) as a masterpiece, Sorokin also went so far as to label Merton's paradigm of functional analysis as "a modern variation on Alexandrian or medieval scholasticism in its decaying period. It is heuristically sterile, empirically useless, and a logically cumbersome table of contents" (Sorokin, 1966, pp. 451–2). The same skepticism was expressed toward Merton's theory of reference group: "A multitude of Merton's propositions, especially in his theory of the reference groups, represent a codification of trivialities dressed up as scientific generalizations" (ibid., p. 452). The ambivalence of Sorokin's attitude is beautifully rendered by the personal inscription in one of his books: "To my darned enemy and dearest friend – Robert – from Pitirim."

Another of Merton's teachers is Talcott Parsons. Speaking for his entire generation of Harvard sociologists, Merton remarks: "Talcott was both cause and occasion for our taking sociological theory seriously" (Merton, 1980, p. 70). His influence on steering Merton's interest toward theoretical considerations was certainly immense. But for almost forty years, since a meeting of the ASA in the

1940s, which witnessed their first major, public clash, Parsons's abstract manner of theorizing was a subject of Merton's persistent challenge, leading him to propose in 1945 the notion of a "middle-range theory" (Merton, 1996, pp. 41–50). Similarly, the static and ahistoric "structural functionalism" proposed by Parsons was a subject of Merton's strong critique, contributing to the birth of his own dynamic "functional analysis" in 1949 (ibid., pp. 65–86). But their theoretical debate always stayed within the borders of exemplary civility. As Merton recollects, "I remember the grace with which, some thirty years ago, he responded in a forum of this same Association to my mild mannered but determined criticism of certain aspects of his theoretical orientation" (Merton, 1980, p. 70). Years later Parsons came to acknowledge Merton's "major contribution to the understanding and clarification of the theoretical methodology of what he, I think quite appropriately, called 'functional analysis'" (Parsons, 1975, p. 67), and then saluted him "for his highly creative role in developing the foundations of this challenging intellectual situation" (ibid., p. 80).

Finally, one must recognize Merton's decades-long "improbable collaboration" (Merton, 1994, p. 15) with Paul Lazarsfeld, producing fruit in several co-authored works, as well as in numerous research projects. It is a rare case of basically different styles of research and theorizing supplementing and enriching each other: Merton's focus on discursive, conceptual clarifications and elaborations, and Lazarsfeld's emphasis on turning concepts into operationalized, testable variables. A good example of the collaboration, their common study of friendship formation (Merton, 1954), came as close to real complementarity as could be expected in the case of two strong, independent individualities, with divergent backgrounds, thought patterns and scholarly goals.

THE WORK

Merton has been a very prolific writer. In his bibliography we find over a dozen books, another dozen edited, or coedited, volumes, and 180 major articles. These numbers continue to grow, as Merton retains his creative powers, and continuously adds new items to his impressive academic output.

There are some characteristic formal traits of his printed work. Most of his formidable output is in the form of extended essays, long articles, introductions, reviews, discussions: sometimes getting so long as to turn imperceptibly into a book, such as the "Shandean postscript" of 290 pages, his favorite *On the Shoulders of Giants* (Merton, 1965), or the "Episodic Memoir" of 150 pages, tracing the development of the sociology of science (Merton, 1979); but most often gathered up in collections, among which *Social Theory and Social Structure* (in its three major editions of 1949, 1957, and 1968), *The Sociology of Science* (1973), *Sociological Ambivalence* (1976), *Social Research and the Practicing Professions* (1982a) and *On Social Structure and Science* (1996) are most significant. Of true "books," in the sense so dear to the humanists and so alien to the natural scientists, he has written only one and only when he had to for formal reasons: his doctoral dissertation.

The thematic range of his interests is very wide: from drug addicts to professionals, from anomie to social time, from friendship formation to role conflicts, from functional analysis to scientific ethos, from medical education to multiple discoveries, from bureaucratic structure to the origins of medieval aphorisms. He seems to pick up various topics, here and there, and then pursue them methodically, meticulously, in depth, sometimes for many years. One of his strongest contributions is insightful concepts. As he identifies new aspects of social life which he finds sociologically significant, he coins neologisms to designate them. A number of these have entered the vocabularies of not only social science but the vernacular of everyday life. Some have already become cases of the process in the history of thought which Merton has identified as "obliteration by incorporation (OBI)," in which "the sources of an idea, finding or concept become obliterated by incorporation in canonical knowledge, so that only a few are still aware of their parentage" (Merton, 1968, pp. 27–8). Merton has also highlighted earlier concepts and terms which had gone largely unregarded, performing what he calls a "cognitive conduit." The list of concepts coined by Merton which entered the canon of contemporary sociology contains manifest and latent functions, dysfunctions, self-fulfilling prophecy, homophily and heterophily, status-sets and role-sets, opportunity structures, anticipatory socialization, reference group behavior, middle-range theories, sociological ambivalence, and others. The supplements to *Oxford English Dictionary* (volumes 1–3) credit ten neologisms to Merton. His theoretical and methodological orientations of functional analysis and structural analysis are widely applied, often without recognition of the authorship. This sort of acceptance is perhaps the strongest proof of Merton's impact on contemporary sociology.

In chronological order one may distinguish a number of phases in his lifelong work (Crothers, 1987, pp. 34–40; Clark, 1990, p. 15). In the 1930s, during his Harvard years, Merton was involved in empirical projects on the homeless of Boston, and prepared his doctoral dissertation on the link between Protestant pietism and the origins of science, to be published in 1938. He also worked on major theoretical articles: "Civilization and Culture" (1936), "The Unanticipated Consequences of Purposive Social Actions" (1936), and "Social Structure and Anomie" (1938). His early interest in European sociology is documented by two review articles: "Recent French Sociology" (1934) and "Durkheim's Division of Labor in Society" (1934). He was to become one of the most cosmopolitan of American sociologists, acquiring a deep knowledge of the European heritage, and long after retirement insisted on his yearly routine of a summer tour of European capitals, savoring their cultural riches and rekindling his vast personal and professional networks of collaborators and friends.

In the 1940s he took part in a number of empirical projects carried out in the Bureau of Applied Social Research, including the study of a radio campaign known as the "war-bond drive," summarized in 1946 in the volume *Mass Persuasion*. Another of his contributions was the reinterpretation of the findings of wartime studies carried out by Samuel Stouffer and his team on the "American soldier," which resulted in an article (with A. Kitt Rossi) on reference groups, published for the first time in 1950 (Merton, 1968, pp. 279–334). The concept of reference group was purged of its early psychological bias, and rephrased in sociological, structural terms. The distinction of normative and comparative reference groups, as well as various subtle permutations of "reference group behavior," have inspired a number of later scholars (Merton, 1968, pp. 335–440). At the same time Merton worked on several methodological and theoretical topics. In 1948 his seminal article "Self-fulfilling prophecy" came out (Merton, 1996, pp. 183–204), and in 1949 his major volume *Social Theory and Social Structure*, including articles on "middle-range strategy" and "manifest and latent functions," where the research program of linking empirical research and theoretical reflection, within the framework of so-called functional analysis, was put forward for the first time. It was particularly the idea of middle-range theorizing which, despite some criticisms (e.g. Opp, 1970), became widely adopted by sociologists.

In the 1950s his research work was still linked to the Bureau of Applied Social Research, but he also became involved in graduate training, and his lectures and seminars became arenas of conceptual and theoretical developments, unraveled in what he calls "oral publication," only to be published in print much later. The empirical studies of medical education left two products, a methodological volume, *The Focused Interview* (with M. Fiske and P. Kendall, 1956), and a more substantive book, *The Student-Physician* (1957). There are also two theoretical papers, which joined the list of those widely followed and discussed later, and were destined to enter the canon of sociological knowledge: "The Role-set: Problems in Sociological Theory" in 1957 (Merton, 1996, pp. 113–22), where Merton painted a picture of complex and overlapping relationships among social roles and statuses; and "Social Conformity, Deviation and Opportunity-structures" (1959), where he returned after twenty years to the theory of anomie, expanding his argument in considerable measure, only to enrich it even more in 1964 in the article "Anomie, Anomia and Social Interaction: Contexts of Deviant Behavior." The deviant adaptations were shown to result not merely from the condition of anomie, but also from the structurally given, available set of legitimate and illegitimate opportunities for pursuing the chosen goals.

In the 1960s and 1970s Merton returned to his "first love" (Lazarsfeld, 1975, p. 43), namely the sociology of science, a subdiscipline which he initiated, and significantly helped to build and institutionalize. The first sign of a thematic shift came in 1957 when he delivered a presidential lecture to an ASA convention: "Priorities in Scientific Discovery: a Chapter in the Sociology of Science" (Merton, 1996, pp. 286–304). Then a series of essays addressed various problems of the sociology of science: "Singletons and Multiples in Scientific Discovery" in 1961 (Merton, 1996, pp. 305–17); "The Matthew-effect in Science: the Reward and Communication Systems of Science" in 1968, revised in 1988 (Merton, 1996, pp. 318–36); "Insiders and Outsiders: a Chapter in the Sociology of Knowledge" in 1972 (Merton, 1996, pp. 241–66); and others. In 1965, what he called his "prodigal brainchild" appeared under the title *On the Shoulders of Giants*, presenting a number of theoretical points in the sociology of science in the guise of eruditional search for the origins of the medieval metaphor. The story of his favorite subdiscipline came out in 1979 as *The Sociology of Science:*

an Episodic Memoir. But in this period he also published crucial statements in general sociological theory: the essay on "structural analysis" in 1975 (Merton, 1996, pp. 101–12), and an earlier study of "sociological ambivalence" (with E. Barber) in 1963 (Merton, 1996, pp. 123–31).

In the 1980s and 1990s Merton has continued his work in various directions. Part of that is devoted to rewriting, polishing, and editing earlier, unpublished manuscripts and preparing collected volumes of essays for print. An example is *Social Research and the Practicing Professions* (1982a). But he also contributed new, original articles of considerable importance: "Client Ambivalences in Professional Relationships" (with V. Merton and E. Barber, 1983), "Socially Expected Durations" (1984), and "The Fallacy of the Latest Word: the Case of Pietism and Science" (1984). At the same time, he started a new *genre* in his work: erudite and dense reminiscences about his collaborators and friends: George Sarton, Talcott Parsons, Florian Znaniecki, Alvin Gouldner, Louis Schneider, Franco Ferrarotti, James Coleman, and Paul Lazarsfeld.

His most recent work returns to the area of the sociology of science with particular emphasis on the fate of scientific concepts and phrases. This starts with the monumental *Social Science Quotations* (Sills and Merton, 1991), and continues with articles on "serendipity," "opportunity structure," "the Matthew Effect," and "the Thomas Theorem," ending with a study of the very term "scientist" as the example of the gendered use of language. In 1994, at the instigation of friends, he turned his reflective focus on himself, and produced the "slight remembrance of things past" titled "A Life of Learning," "orally published" as the C. H. Haskins memorial lecture at Philadelphia (Merton, 1994, reprinted in Merton, 1996, pp. 339–59).

The Theory

From the rich mosaic of Merton's substantive contributions, produced at various levels of generality, in various areas, in various periods of his long career, there emerges a coherent system of ideas. Some of them refer to sociology: its goals, orientation, and methods. Some of them refer to society: its constitution and transformations. And in the background of all that, there is a particular image of science, as a cognitive enterprise, social institution and community of scholars. In my interpretation Merton has given us a comprehensive theory of society. But this is a contentious point, and some commentators see only the multiple, fragmentary contributions of Merton to many sociological problems and complain about the "curious omission" of "a systematic theory or a system of sociology" (Bierstedt, 1981, p. 445). I have entered into extensive debate with Robert Bierstedt on this issue, which for lack of space cannot be summarized here (see Sztompka, 1990, pp. 53–64; Bierstedt, 1990, pp. 67–74).

Two of Merton's formulations come closest to his definition of what sociology is all about. The calling of a sociologist is described as "lucidly presenting claims to logically interconnected and empirically confirmed propositions about the structure of society and its changes, the behavior of man within that structure and the consequences of that behavior" (Merton, 1968, p. 70). And the goal of the whole discipline is characterized as follows: "In the large, sociology is engaged in finding out how man's behavior and fate are affected, if not minutely governed, by his place within particular kinds, and changing kinds, of social structure and culture" (Merton, 1976, p. 184). Thus, clearly the prime subject matter of sociology is conceived as the social structure, and it is to be studied in its multiple and varied aspects: genetic (how it came to be), as well as functional (how it affects behavior); static (how it operates), as well as dynamic (how it changes). The *focus on social structure* appears from the beginning as the defining trait of Merton's sociology. In my reading this is his main focus, but here I differ with some other commentators, who would classify Merton together with Parsons simply as "functionalists" (e.g. Turner, 1974).

It is true that Merton started from an approach he called "functional analysis," but he immediately distanced himself, even by introducing that name, from doctrinaire "functionalism." For him, "the central orientation of functionalism" is "the practice of interpreting data by establishing their consequences for larger structures in which they are implicated" (Merton, 1968, pp. 100–1). In his famous "paradigm for functional analysis" in 1949, he outlined a strikingly open, deeply revised version of functionalism, allowing for the conceptualization of social conflict and social change. Thus, when a quarter century later in 1975 he wrote the important paper "Structural Analysis in Sociology" (Merton, 1996, pp. 101–12), it was not a radical break with functional analysis, but rather its logical extension. Structural analysis was a natural outgrowth of functional analysis, complementing but not at all supplanting it. Merton's own position is explicit: "The orientation is that variant of functional analysis in sociology which has evolved, over the years, into a distinct mode of structural analysis" (Merton, 1976, p. 9). Functional analysis specifies the consequences of a social phenomenon for its differentiated structural context; structural analysis searches for the determinants of the phenomenon in its structural context. Obviously, both orientations refer to the different sides of the same coin; they scrutinize two vectors of the same relationship, between a social phenomenon and its structural setting. There is no opposition of Merton the functionalist to Merton the structuralist; both theoretical orientations have been consolidated into one.

Merton's idea of the social structure, already central for his "functionalist" writings, includes four defining criteria. The focus on relations linking various components of society is clear in the early characterization of social structure: "by social structure is meant that organized set of social relationships in which members of the society or group are variously implicated" (Merton, 1968, p. 216). The emphasis on the patterned, regular, repetitive character of relations is one of the central themes pervading Merton's work, as is the term "patterned," a qualifier he is particularly fond of. As Paul Lazarsfeld noted: "Throughout his writings, this is probably the technical term he uses most often" (Lazarsfeld, 1975, p. 57). The third constitutive criterion of social structure – the idea of a deep, hidden, underlying level (corresponding to the concept of latent functions in functional analysis) – is the only aspect of Merton's approach directly influenced by the "logical-linguistic structuralism" of Claude Lévi-Strauss or Noam

Chomsky. As he puts it: "It is analytically useful to distinguish between manifest and latent levels of social structure" (Merton, 1976, p. 126).

But perhaps most important for Merton's notion of social structure is the fourth criterion, the idea of constraining or facilitating influences exerted by social structure on more concrete, and more directly accessible, social phenomena and events (behaviors, beliefs, attitudes, motivations, etc.). The concept of "structural context," and especially "structural constraint," as limiting the effective field of action, appeared in the early "paradigm for functional analysis," and was developed later: "Behavior is a result not merely of personal qualities, but of these in interaction with the patterned situations in which the individual behaves. It is these social contexts which greatly affect the extent to which the capacities of individuals are actually realized" (Merton, 1982a, p. 174). But the structural context was not conceived only in negative terms, as a limiting constraint, but also as a positive influence, facilitating, encouraging, stimulating certain choices by actors or agents: "the social structure strains the cultural values, making action in accord with them readily possible for those occupying certain statuses within the society and difficult or impossible for others.... The social structure acts as a barrier or as an open door to the acting out of cultural mandates" (Merton, 1968, pp. 216–17).

The best example of Merton's structural analysis is his famous theory of anomie. Understood as a structural condition of dissociation between uniform cultural demands of success and the differentiated opportunities for success, anomie is shown to generate various forms of deviant conduct: 'innovation', 'ritualism', 'retreatism' or 'rebellion', depending on the wider structural context within which it appears (Merton, 1938).

Starting from the general framework provided by his functionalist and structuralist orientation, Merton develops a more detailed image of the social structure. There are two traits which endow it with a distinct, unmistakably Mertonian flavor. First, social structure is seen as complex and multidimensional. It covers a plurality of components, elements, and items shaped into various kinds of networks or interlinkages. There are statuses, roles, role-sets, status-sets, norms, values, institutions, collectivities, groups, organizations, interests, etc., and they are depicted as cohering on numerous levels. A related, second property of Merton's idea of social structure is the emphasis on asymmetrical relationships: conflicts, contradictions, dysfunctions, strains, tensions, ambivalence. As Merton emphasizes: "It is fundamental, not incidental to the paradigm of structural analysis that social structures generate social conflict by being differentiated in historically differing extent and kind, into interlocking arrays of social statuses, strata, organizations, and communities that have their own and therefore potentially conflicting as well as common interests and values" (Merton, 1976, pp. 124–5). Merton's core idea is to consider human individuals (and their actions) as structurally located, anchored in the network of social relationships.

Attempting to cope with the immense variety of structural components, Merton proposes the distinction between the social structure in the narrow sense and the cultural structure: "the salient environment of individuals can be usefully thought of as involving the cultural structure, on the one hand, and the social structure, on the other" (Merton, 1968, p. 216). Cultural structure comes to be characterized exclusively in normative terms: as a network of norms, values, roles and institutions. Similarly, the idea of social structure in the narrow sense is gradually enriched with the help of the notion of "opportunity-structure," inspired by the idea of "life-chances," and "vested interests," taken probably from Max Weber and Karl Marx. It is understood as a hierarchically differentiated access to resources, facilities, and valuables (wealth, power, prestige, education, etc.).

The components of social structure at both levels – of social structure proper and of cultural structure – are variously interrelated, both within each level, and across distinct levels. It is, in fact, only the study of those interrelations that reveals the complex quality of the social structure as a relational network. The most important feature of Merton's analysis, which sets him apart from traditional functionalists and other proponents of social equilibrium, consensus, and harmony, is his treatment of integration as problematic and contingent, not as given. The differing degrees of integration span the spectrum, from complete consensus to complete dissensus, with these extreme poles being only analytic possibilities, rarely occurring in empirical reality. And it is striking that, perhaps to counterbalance the bias of "normative functionalism," Merton focuses his analysis on situations closer to the pole of dissensus: various kinds of strains, tensions, contradictions and conflicts in the social structure. He treats them as normal, typical, permanent, and not as pathological disturbances or deviations. Against the predominant stereotype of Merton the functionalist, I believe that his is a conflictual image of society *par excellence*, as distant as can be from the image of a harmonious utopia. Look at some of his central theoretical categories: dysfunction, role-conflict, sociological ambivalence, anomie. All of them refer to the "ugly face" of society, as Ralf Dahrendorf would put it (Dahrendorf, 1968, pp. 129–50).

The image of society underlying Merton's social theory is dynamic, incorporating structurally produced change in and of social structures: "social structures generate both changes within the structure and changes of the structure and . . . these types of change come about through cumulatively patterned choices in behavior and the amplification of dysfunctional consequences resulting from certain kinds of strains, conflicts, and contradictions in the differentiated social structure" (Merton, 1976, p. 125). As the Loomises noted long ago, Merton is "irrevocably committed to a study of the dynamics of social change no less than to stabilities of social structures" (Loomis and Loomis, 1961, p. 315).

There are two types of structural change which fall within the purview of Merton's dynamics. The first type involves the regular "functioning" or everyday "operation" of society. Such changes consist in ongoing adaptive processes which reproduce specified states of a social structure, or at least keep them within the limits which give that structure its identity. The second type of changes involves the "transformation" of society. This consists of the morphogenetic processes that disrupt the existing structure and create a basically new one in its place. The first type of change brings about the reproduction of an old social order; the second type of change brings about the production of a new social order.

The illustrations of Merton's study of adaptive processes are relatively well known. His analyses of the articulation of roles in the role-set and of the social mechanisms of adaptation in status-sets are particularly telling (Merton, 1968, pp. 425, 434). They attempt to face "the general problem of identifying the social mechanisms which serve to articulate the expectations of those in the role-set so that the occupant of a status is confronted with less conflict than would obtain if these mechanisms were not at work" (Merton, 1968, p. 425).

But adaptive processes cover only a part of social dynamics. Changes in social structure reducing inefficiency, conflict, strains, and tensions from what they would otherwise be must be distinguished from the changes of social structure which transform it significantly to produce new structural arrangements. It is rarely recognized that Merton's theory also contributes to this area of social dynamics. In Merton's theoretical orientation, the general scheme of structure-building process can be condensed as follows: under conditions still little understood, structural conflict brings about transformations of social structure up to a point when a new structure emerges and the structural conflict is reproduced in a new form. The basic logic underlying the process is that of amplification rather than compensation or, to put it differently, positive rather than negative feedback.

Merton singles out two general mechanisms of structure-building. The first may be described as the mechanism of accumulated dysfunctions; the second as the mechanism of accumulated innovations. The accumulation of dysfunctions occurs when certain structural elements are dysfunctional for a social system as a whole, or some of its core segments. For example, the unrestrained pattern of egoistic hedonism, if sufficiently widespread, may lead to the disruption of the social system. The larger the number of such dysfunctional elements, and the more dysfunctional each of them, the more likely is the system to break down. Another case appears when some elements are basically functional for a social system, but have some additional, dysfunctional side-effects. For example, the competitive success orientation or "achievement syndrome" may be beneficial for the economy, but at the same time may lead to the neglect of family life and consequent breakdown of family structure. The question now becomes that of the relative weight of the accumulated dysfunctional side-effects, which, passing over a hypothetical threshold, outbalance functional outcomes and lead to institutional breakdown and "basic social change" in the form of replacement of structure. A different and, in Merton's conception, basic and empirically frequent case obtains when certain structures are functional for certain groups or strata in the society and dysfunctional for others. Examples are progressive taxation, social security, apartheid, affirmative action. The net outcome – toward stability or toward change – is then determined by the comparative (relative) power of the diverse groups or strata beneficially or adversely affected by those patterned social arrangements. As groups or strata dysfunctionally affected attain sufficient power, they are likely to introduce structural changes. The final type occurs when some structural elements are functional for certain subsystems and dysfunctional for others. For example, traditional mores or *Gemeinschaft* forms of collectivities, certainly beneficial for the integration of society may often stand in the way of economic modernization, thus becoming dysfunctional for the economic subsystem. The pressure for change here depends on the complex set of historical circumstances determining the relative functional significance of the subsystems dysfunctionally affected. If the dysfunctions touch the subsystems of strategic, core significance – in a modern society the economic institutions, political regime, etc. – structural change is likely.

The alternative mechanism of structure-building is the accumulation of innovations. Here Merton focuses on one selected case: the crescive change of normative structures, particularly through the "institutionalized evasions of institutional rules." Structure-building *via* norm evasion starts from incidents of aberrant behavior by individuals who find the norms too demanding for them, even though generally legitimate. For example, the thief who does not question the legitimacy of the fifth commandment will be outraged if something is stolen from him, and not particularly surprised if caught and sentenced. Some part of evasions from norms remains fully private, invisible, undetected. But when evasions become more widespread, undertaken by a plurality of individuals, repeated on various occasions, the public awareness is apt to be awakened. When villains get identified, the examples of particularly skillful evaders may become the subject of public lore, often tainted with envy. The occurrence of common incentives to evasion among the large collectivities of individuals – coupled with the widespread belief that "everybody does it" and the tendency to imitate successful evaders – accounts for the patterning of evasions: their regular and repeatable character. Tax evasions, cheating on exams, avoidance of customs duties and currency controls, petty theft in business firms, etc., provide familiar examples. But note that, even though rarely sanctioned, the norms are here still accorded some legitimacy. The most crucial phase comes when, as Merton puts it, "A mounting frequency of deviant but 'successful' behavior tends to lessen and, as an extreme potentiality, to eliminate the legitimacy of the institutional norms for others in the system" (Merton, 1968, p. 234). It is only now that his early concept of "institutionalized evasions" fully applies. Institutionalization in this sense is more than the mere patterning, since it involves not only repetition or regularity of behavior but the granting of a degree of legitimacy, widespread acceptance, or even positive sanctioning of evasive behavior.

This leads to the final phase of a structure-building: attaining by evasions the status of sanctioned norms, fully legitimized and embedded in a new normative structure. A cycle of structure-building ends, and of course a next one is opened, as new norms inevitably begin to be evaded, at least by some members of society, and the process of normative change starts to operate again.

A particular implementation of structural orientation is to be found in Merton's sociology of science, the field that comprises the empirical sociology of scientific communities as producing, selecting, and distributing scientific knowledge. Apart from mapping the whole field of this new sociological subdiscipline, Merton has contributed influential ideas to its three focal topics: the scientific ethos, the scientific community, and the origins of modern science.

The analysis of scientific ethos was introduced in the context of penetrating critique of the fate of science under the totalitarian, Nazi regime in Germany. Merton shows that the context functionally indispensable for the proper operation of the system of science is the liberal-democratic order. He believes that the future of science is allied with the spread of the democratic attitude and institutions. The scientific ethos appears as a micro-model of the democratic ethos. It is defined as follows: "The ethos of science is that affectively toned complex of values and norms which is held to be binding on scientists" (Merton, 1968, p. 595). The paramount values are: objectivity, the commitment to the pursuit of knowledge as adequate and as complete as possible; and originality, the commitment to the pursuit of new knowledge. Norms, or "institutional imperatives," define the acceptable or preferred means for realizing those values. There are four of them. "Universalism" requires science to be impersonal. "Communism" requires that scientific knowledge be treated not as private property of its creator, but rather as a common good, to be freely communicated and distributed. "Disinterestedness" demands the subordination of extrinsic interests to the intrinsic satisfaction of finding the truth. "Organized scepticism" requires the scientist to doubt, and then to check whether the doubt is well founded. This is carried out through public criticism by scientists of claimed contributions to scientific knowledge (Merton, 1996, pp. 267–76).

Merton is well aware that this idealized picture of the scientific ethos is rarely found in reality. The most interesting reason for deviance is found in the internal ambivalences and anomie inherent in the ethos itself. Anomic conduct in science derives primarily from the great values placed upon originality, and uniformly so for all working scientists, whereas the opportunities and possibilities of achieving original results are most variable, owing to personal constraints (talents, abilities, competences), as well as to structural constraints (limited resources, underdeveloped scientific culture, unavailable experimental technologies etc.). "In this situation of stress, all manner of adaptive behaviors are called into play, some of these being far beyond the mores of science" (Merton, 1973, p. 323). Examples include outright fraud, the fabrication of data, the denouncing of rivals, aggressive self-assertion, and plagiary.

The other aspect of science that Merton vigorously investigates is the scientific community, a specific type of social organization made up of scientists in their role behavior and mutual, interactive relationships. There are several subsystems that are singled out within the scientific community. The first is the "system of institutionalized vigilance": the examination, appraisal, criticism, and verification of scientific results by academic peers. The second is the "communication system of science": the complex mechanism of scientific publication, making the results visible. Here Merton introduces the biblical metaphor and the concept of the "Matthew Effect," observing that the works published by recognized scholars have much better chances of visibility in the scientific community than equally significant or original contributions by scholars of less renown. Another concept of "obliteration by incorporation" signifies the situation in which both the original source and the literal formulation of an idea are forgotten, owing to its long and widespread use. The notion of "cognitive conduits" refers to the spreading and inheriting of ideas over time. Another subsystem of the scientific community is the evaluation and reward system of science, the complex mechanisms of scientific recognition and reward-allocation, again biased in favor of already recognized scholars. All these processes lead to the emergence of the stratification system of science, the patterned differentiation of scholars according to identifiable criteria. Finally, there is the informal influence system of science: the network of personal ties, acquaintanceships, friendships, and loyalties that cut across other systems and significantly modify their operation. Merton pays ever-growing attention to this elusive domain giving new prominence to the seventeenth-century concept of the "invisible college" (used earlier by D. de Solla Price), as well as the twentieth-century idea of the "thought collective" (introduced by Ludwig Fleck).

The third focus of Merton's concern with science, in fact the earliest in his own research biography, is the historical origins of science and its subsequent development. In his doctoral dissertation (Merton, 1938) he put forward the widely discussed "Merton's Thesis," in some ways parallel to the earlier "Weber's Thesis" concerning the origins of capitalism. Studying the origins of empirical science in seventeenth-century England, Merton observed a linkage between religious commitments and a sustained interest in science. He noted that English scientists in that period were disproportionately ascetic Protestants or Puritans. The values and attitudes characteristic of Puritanism were seen to have had the effect of stimulating scientific research by inviting the empirical and rational quest for identifying the God-given order in the world and for practical applications; just as they legitimized scientific research through religious justification. Once having obtained institutional legitimacy, science largely severed its link with religion, finally to become a counterforce, curbing the influence of religion. But as the first push, religion was seen as crucially important.

Impact

There are various measures that can be applied to evaluate a scholar's impact on his or her discipline. One is the existence of a "school," the wide network of pupils, collaborators, and followers creatively working out the bits and pieces of the master's heritage, as well as the amount of critical evaluation that his work merits. Another is the extent of reception that the work receives, which can be estimated by looking at the number of editions and translations, the time staying in print, and the citation indexes. The third, a bit paradoxical, is the degree to which the concepts and ideas undergo what Merton himself called "obliteration by incorporation," i.e. melt into the accepted, textbook canon of sociology, no longer linked to their originator.

On all three counts Merton ranks very high. As an academic teacher he had the good luck to encounter "successive cohorts of brilliant students" (Merton, 1994, p. 17). It is perhaps not an accident that so many of Merton's students at Columbia found their way into the pages of sociological textbooks: Rose and Lewis Coser, James Coleman, Robert Bierstedt, Peter Blau, Seymour M. Lipset,

Irving L. Horowitz, Alvin Gouldner, Philip Selznick, Louis Schneider, Robin Williams, Alice and Peter Rossi, Jonathan and Steven Cole, Juan Linz, Franco Ferrarotti, Hans L. Zetterberg, Ralf Dahrendorf, and many others. Now, after so many years Merton may be proud "writing papers designed specifically for those honorific volumes known as *Festschriften*. Not, as might be supposed, *Festschriften* in honor of teachers or aged peers but in honor of onetime students" (Merton, 1994, p. 17). The network of close collaborators would embrace other towering figures of twentieth-century sociology: Talcott Parsons, Paul Lazarsfeld, Robert Lynd, C. Wright Mills, Shmuel Eisenstadt. He served innumerable others, freely accepting their manuscripts for reviewing and editing. The number of published books that went through his meticulous editorial grinding exceeds two hundred. There are also hundreds of sociologists worldwide with whom he exchanged correspondence, thoroughly discussing their ideas. The bibliography of writings about Robert Merton amounts to more than four hundred items, including several monographs and collective books.

Most of his own books have gone through a series of printings and multiple foreign editions, with *Social Theory and Social Structure* appearing in almost twenty languages. Some articles are frequently republished in sociological "readers." Most of them are still in print, sometimes half a century after original publication. And the citation indexes are truly impressive. For a period from 1969 to 1989 his Social Science Citation Index count totals 6800, and his Science Citation Index count, 1350 (Clark, 1990, p. 23). This by far exceeds the number of citations to any other living sociologist. Particularly striking is the great number of citations to works published as long as forty or fifty years ago, like *Social Theory and Social Structure* of 1949, or the two famous articles on "unanticipated consequences of social actions" of 1936, and "anomie and social structure" of 1938. Citation data show that the latter "has probably been more frequently cited and reprinted than any paper in sociology" (Cole, 1975, p. 175).

Apart from general sociological theory there are some subdisciplines of sociology whose development was strongly influenced by Merton's contributions. One could mention the sociology of science and the sociology of deviance, where strong Mertonian "schools" are still operating.

ASSESSMENT

Robert K. Merton certainly belongs to the most influential sociological theorists of the twentieth century. Two kinds of contributions make him a "modern sociological classic": his exemplary style of doing sociology and his substantive contribution to sociological theory.

The most concise characterization of Merton's style of thought may be put in three words: balance, system, and discipline. He has a strong aversion to extremes. The most famous illustration of this is his strategy of "middle-range theory," based on the rejection of both narrow empiricism and abstract, scholastic theorizing. The systematic quality of his work is emphasized by the repeated use of what he calls "paradigms," introduced long before, and in meaning different from, Kuhn's, namely as heuristic schemes destined to introduce a measure of order and lucidity into qualitative and discursive sociological analysis, by codifying the results of prior inquiry and specifying the directions of further research. The most famous are his paradigms for functional analysis, for structural analysis, for deviant social behavior, and for the sociology of knowledge. The disciplined quality of Merton's work is self-consciously expressed by his concepts of "disciplined inquiry" and "disciplined eclecticism." The first means "systematic and serious, that is to say, the intellectually responsible and austere pursuit of what is first entertained as an interesting idea" (Merton, 1968, p. xiv). Merton's persistence in tracing the implications and ramifications of his central insights is legendary. Decade after decade he returns to the same themes, each time developing them conceptually and enriching them with new empirical evidence. For example, his major reworkings of the theme of "anomie" came out in 1938, 1949, 1955, 1959, 1964, and 1997. The idea of "disciplined eclecticism" encourages openness and antidogmatism: the critical and systematic adaptation of a plurality of theoretical orientations and theories in solving sociological problems. Thus Merton presents a truly classical model of how sociology should be done, perhaps a needed reminder in the time of a certain methodological anarchy. But of course his contribution is not limited to a methodological model. He applies the model himself, reaching fundamental results, including an original and fruitful image of society.

The preceding analysis of Merton's work was intended to corroborate five claims. First, I believe that despite the dispersed, piecemeal, fragmentary nature of Merton's contributions, they add up to a coherent system of thought. Of course, the system is far from complete: there are many empty spots, many lacunae, many fields of "specified ignorance" (to use his favorite term). But all the islands of enlightenment fit nicely into the overall topography. And the dark or shadowy areas provide the system with strong potentials for elaboration, suggest further problems for fruitful inquiry.

Second, I believe that despite his own research focus on the middle level of generality ("middle range theories"), Merton has unwittingly produced a general theory of society. His contributions add up to a consistent picture of the social world. Third, against the stereotypes identifying Merton as an embodiment of functionalism, I believe that his orientation is and always has been mainly structuralist. Drawing inspiration from Durkheim, he perceives all social phenomena as located in a structural context, interlinked with other phenomena within wider social wholes. Those linkages are of two sorts: causal, when a phenomenon is constrained or facilitated by structural context; and functional, when a phenomenon produces structural effects (functions). "Functional analysis" clearly appears as a specific mode of a more general structural approach pervading Merton's inquiry.

Fourth, he is a conflict theorist *par excellence*. His image of social life is saturated with contradictions, strains, tensions, ambivalence, dysfunctions, and conflicts of all sorts. There is nothing of the tranquil, harmonious, consensual, equilibrated utopia in a human drama as depicted by Merton: with its torment of uncertainty and unintended, latent consequences of any action; with its agony of ambivalence and cross-cutting pressures of norms, roles, and statuses; with its fright of normlessness, or anomie; with its risk of defeat or "self-destroying prophecies."

Fifth, his theory is dynamic in the full sense of the term. As I attempted to illustrate in detail, he not only recognizes various modalities of change, but focuses on structural changes, i.e. those which are structurally generated and structurally consequential. And he not only studies reproductive (or adaptive) processes, but devotes considerable attention to the structure-building through which new, or fundamentally modified, structures are socially constructed.

The structural theory of society – incorporating "social statics" and "social dynamics," "social anatomy" and "social physiology," consensus and conflict, stability and change, reproduction and emergence – provides a fully fledged, multidimensional paradigm for sociology. It is deeply rooted in the classical sociological tradition of the nineteenth century. In fact, Merton synthesizes and extends the classical sociological tradition. He attains balanced, intermediate positions on various traditional issues, unravels entangled premises to reach their rational core, unmuddles the muddle of sociological controversies. This allows him to introduce a further measure of order and systematization to the classical heritage. Merton's determined effort to clarify, codify, consolidate, and organize disparate pieces of sociological wisdom results in a mosaic that is rewarding aesthetically as well as intellectually. The synthesis becomes much more than a summary of earlier ideas: it results in their selective and critical reformulation and cumulation. At many points, novel concepts, insights, and ideas are added to the classical heritage.

Thus, perhaps Merton's most important service to the development of contemporary sociology is the vindication of the classical style of doing sociology and the classical heritage of theoretical ideas. He shows with new vigor that the ideas of the nineteenth-century masters are not at all exhausted or dead. In his work, paradigms of classical thought gain new vitality, as they are shown to be fruitful: both in the explanatory sense, as means of accounting for large areas of social experience and for solving the puzzles confronting men and women in their social life; and in the heuristic sense, as means of raising new questions and suggesting new puzzles for solution.

An important, and only seemingly paradoxical, function of Merton's synthesis is to indicate directions of inquiry that will eventually elaborate and overcome it. Its systematic and lucid quality enables us to perceive not only past and current knowledge but also "the various sorts of failure: intelligent errors and unintelligent ones, noetically induced and organizationally induced foci of interest and blind spots in inquiry, promising lands abandoned, and garden-paths long explored, scientific contributions ignored or neglected by contemporaries,... serendipity lost" (Merton, 1975, p. 336). Ultimately, it leads toward mapping further domains of "specified ignorance": "what is not yet known but needs to be known in order to lay the foundation for still more knowledge" (Merton, 1976, p. 112). It is precisely here that the past and the future of our discipline meet. Merton's work provides a solid bridge from the accomplishments of the classical masters to the future vistas of sociology.

Bibliography

Writings of Robert Merton

Social Time: a Methodological and Functional Analysis (with Pitirim A. Sorokin). 1937. *American Journal of Sociology*, 42, 619–29.

Science, Technology and Society in Seventeenth Century England. 1938. In G. Sarton (ed.), *OSIRIS*. Bruges, Belgium: St Catherine Press, pp. 362–632 (reprinted New York: Howard Fertig, 1970 and 1993).

Mass Persuasion. 1948. New York: Harper & Brothers.

Friendship as a Social Process: a Substantive and Methodological Analysis (with P. F. Lazarsfeld). 1954. In M. Berger, T. Abel and C. Page (eds), *Freedom and Control in Modern Society*. New York: Van Nostrand, pp. 18–66.

The Focused Interview (with M. Fiske and P. L. Kendall). 1956. New York: Free Press.

The Student-physician: Introductory Studies in the Sociology of Medical Education (with G. G. Reader and P. L. Kendall). 1957. Cambridge, MA: Harvard University Press.

Social Conformity, Deviation and Opportunity-structure. 1959. *American Sociological Review*, 24(2), 177–89.

On the Shoulders of Giants. 1965. New York: Harcourt Brace Jovanovich ("vicennial edition" 1985, Harcourt Brace Jovanovich; "post-Italianate edition" 1993, University of Chicago Press).

Social Theory and Social Structure. 1949. New York: Free Press (revised edition 1957; enlarged and revised edition 1968).

The Sociology of Science: Theoretical and Empirical Investigations (edited by N. W. Storer). 1973. Chicago: University of Chicago Press.

Thematic Analysis in Science: Notes on Holton's Concept. 1975 *Science*, 188, April 35, 335–8.

Sociological Ambivalence and Other Essays. 1976. New York: Free Press.

Sociology of Science: an Episodic Memoir. 1979. Carbondale: Southern Illinois University Press.

Remembering the Young Talcott Parsons 1980. *The American Sociologist*, 15 (May), 68–71.

Social Research and the Practicing Professions (edited by A. Rosenblatt and T. F. Gieryn). 1982a. Cambridge, MA: ABT Books.

Alvin W. Gouldner: Genesis and Growth of a Friendship. 1982b. *Theory and Society*, 11, 915–38.

George Sarton: Episodic Recollections by an Unruly Apprentice. 1985. *ISIS*, 76, 477–86.

The Macmillan Book of Social Science Quotations (edited with D. Sills). 1991. New York: Macmillan.

A Life of Learning. 1994. New York: ACLS Occasional Paper No. 25, 20 pp. (reprinted in *On Social Structure and Science*).

On Social Structure and Science (edited by P. Sztompka). 1996. Chicago: University of Chicago Press.

Further reading

Bierstedt, R. (1981) *American Sociological Theory: a Critical History*. New York: Academic Press.

Bierstedt, R. (1990) Merton's Systematic Theory. In J. Clark, C. Modgil and S. Modgil (eds), *Robert K. Merton: Consensus and Controversy*. London: Falmer Press, pp. 67–74.

Clark, J. (1990) Robert Merton as Sociologist. In J. Clark, C. Modgil and S. Modgil (eds), *Robert K. Merton: Consensus and Controversy*. London: Falmer Press, pp. 13–23.

Clark, J., Modgil C. and Modgil, S. (eds) (1990) *Robert K. Merton: Consensus and Controversy*. London: Falmer Press.

Cohen, I. B. (1990) *Puritanism and the Rise of Modern Science: the Merton Thesis*. New Brunswick, NJ: Rutgers University Press.

Cohen, I. B. (ed.) (1990) *Puritanism and the Rise of Modern Science: The Merton Thesis*. New Brunswick: Rutgers University Press

Cole, S. (1975) The Growth of Scientific Knowledge: Theories of Deviance as a Case Study. In L. A.Coser (ed.), *The Idea of Social Structure: Papers in Honor of Robert K. Merton*. New York: Harcourt Brace Jovanovich, pp. 175–220.

Coser, L. A. (ed.) (1975) *The Idea of Social Structure: Papers in Honor of Robert K. Merton*. New York: Harcourt Brace Jovanovich.

Coser, L. A. and Nisbet, R. (1975) Merton and the Contemporary Mind: an Affectionate Dialogue. In L. A. Coser (ed.), *The Idea of Social Structure: Papers in Honor of Robert K. Merton*. New York: Harcourt Brace Jovanovich, pp. 3–10.

Crothers, C. (1987) *Robert K. Merton: a Key Sociologist*. London: Tavistock.

Dahrendorf, R. (1968) *Essays in the Theory of Society*. Stanford, CA: Stanford University Press.

Gieryn, T. F. (ed.) (1980) *Science and Social Structure: a Festschrift for Robert K. Merton*. New York: New York Academy of Sciences.

Hunt, M. M. (1961) How Does It Come to Be So? Profile of Robert K. Merton. *New Yorker*, 36, pp. 39–63.

Jaworski, G. D. (1990) Robert K. Merton's Extension of Simmel's "Ubersehbar." *Sociological Theory*, 8, 99–105.

Kearney, H. F. (1973) Merton Revisited. *Science Studies*, 3, 72–8.

Lazarsfeld, P. (1975) Working with Merton. In L. A. Coser (ed.), *The Idea of Social Structure: Papers in Honor of Robert K. Merton*. New York: Harcourt Brace Jovanovich, pp. 35–66.

Loomis, C. P. and Loomis, Z. K. (1961) *Modern Social Theories: Selected American Writers*. Princeton, NJ: Van Nostrand.

Mongardini, C. and Tabboni, S. (eds) (1997) *Merton and Contemporary Sociology*. New Brunswick, NJ: Transaction Publishers.

Opp, K. D. (1970) Theories of the Middle Range as a Strategy for the Construction of a General Sociological Theory: a Critique of a Sociological Dogma. *Inquiry*, 2, 243–53.

Parsons, T. (1975) The Present Status of "Structural-Functional" Theory in Sociology. In L. A. Coser (ed.), *The Idea of Social Structure: Papers in Honor of Robert K. Merton*. New York: Harcourt Brace Jovanovich, pp. 67–83.

Sorokin, P. A. (1937–41) *Social and Cultural Dynamics*, 4 volumes. New York: American Books Co.

Sorokin, P. A. (1966) *Sociological Theories of Today*. New York: Harper & Row.

Sztompka, P. (1986) *Robert K. Merton: an Intellectual Profile*. London and New York: Macmillan and St Martin's Press.

Sztompka, P. (1990) R. K. Merton's Theoretical System: an Overview. In L. A. Coser (ed.), *Robert K. Merton: Consensus and Controversy*. London: Falmer Press, pp. 53–64.

Turner, J. H. (1974) *The Structure of Sociological Theory*. Homewood, IL: Dorsey Press.

2

Erving Goffman

Gary Alan Fine and Philip Manning

Erving Goffman has a hold on the sociological imagination. While he was perhaps not as broad or subtle a theorist as Durkheim, Simmel, Marx, or Weber, the images and slogans of this scholar have become an integral part of the discipline. The dramaturgical metaphor has become sociology's second skin. As a consequence, Erving Goffman is arguably the most influential American[1] sociologist of the twentieth century.

While this bald statement would be accepted by many, two additional features are also widely accepted. First, Goffman himself can hardly be considered a conventional social theorist. In his thirty-year academic career Goffman did not attempt to develop an overarching theory of society; nor did he raise issues that speak to transhistorical concerns of social order. While on occasion Goffman referred to other social theorists, such references were typically included in passing, and his work does not contain a systematic confrontation with other sociological theorists. Goffman's work can be characterized equally by those central sociological issues that he did not discuss (or did so only briefly), and those that he explored so brilliantly. Second, Goffman does not easily fit within a specific school of sociological thought. Although he was often linked to the symbolic interactionist perspective, he did not readily accept this label (see Goffman (1969, pp. 136–45) for his account of the limitations of this approach). Further, Goffman did not produce a close-knit school of younger scholars who saw themselves as following his agenda (Grimshaw, 1983, p. 147). Goffman embraced and transformed the ideas of certain important social theorists (Durkheim, Simmel, Blumer, and Hughes, and Schutz), and the work of others, who might be labeled his "students," was profoundly influenced by contact with Goffman (John Lofland, Gary Marx, Harvey Sacks, Eviatar Zerubavel, Carol Brooks Gardner, Emmanuel Schegloff, David Sudnow, and Charles and Marjorie Goodwin). However, it is odd, given Goffman's influence, that there are remarkably few scholars who are continuing his work. In part, this is because Goffman has a signature style, but it is also because Goffman's stylistic approach is not broadly valued in the discipline (Abbott, 1997). This paradox must be at the heart of any analysis of Erving Goffman's theoretical legacy.

GOFFMAN'S LIFE

Erving Manual Goffman was born in Mannville, Alberta, on June 11, 1922, to Ukrainian Jewish parents. His parents, Max and Ann, were among the 200,000 Ukrainians who migrated to Canada between 1897 and 1914 (Winkin, 1988, p. 16). Along with his sister, Frances, he was brought up in Dauphin, near Winnipeg, where later, in 1937, he attended St John's Technical High School. Winkin (1988) reports that, for unknown reasons, his friends called him "Pookie." Goffman showed an initial interest in chemistry, which he pursued at the University of Manitoba in 1939.

In 1943–4 he worked at the National Film Board in Ottawa, where he met Dennis Wrong, who encouraged Goffman's interest in sociology. Soon after, Goffman enrolled at the University of Toronto, where, under the guidance of C. W. M. Hart and Ray Birdwhistell, he read widely in sociology and anthropology. The writings of Durkheim, Radcliffe-Brown, Warner, Freud and Parsons were particularly important to his intellectual development (Winkin, 1988, p. 25). At Toronto, he also developed a close friendship with the anthropologist Elizabeth Bott.

In 1945 Goffman graduated from Toronto with a degree in sociology and moved to the University of Chicago for graduate work. Winkin reports that he was initially overwhelmed by the transition. This may be a euphemistic way of saying that Goffman's grades were not impressive at the beginning of his graduate career. The University of Chicago was hectic and confusing, a situation exacerbated by the many students relying on funding from the GI Bill. After several difficult years Goffman settled into the routine of graduate life, taking numerous courses, including Everett Hughes's seminar on Work and Occupations, where he first heard the expression "total institution," which became important to his later writing (Burns, 1992, p. 101). For reasons perhaps relating to his steady stream of sarcasm, Goffman earned a nickname from his fellow graduate students: "the little dagger" (Winkin, 1988, p. 28).

Data on Goffman's early years in graduate school are sparse (Winkin, 1999), and apparently he kept to himself during that period, reading voraciously. However, in 1949 Goffman completed his MA thesis, based on a survey research project concerning audience reactions to a then popular radio soap opera. Soon after, he left for the Shetland Islands. From December 1949 to May 1951 Goffman lived on the Island of Unst, where he collected ethnographic data for his doctoral dissertation. Masquerading as an American interested in agricultural techniques, he absorbed as much as he could about everyday life on this small Scottish island, partially overcoming the initial suspicions of the islanders, who thought that he might be a spy (Winkin, 1999).

After leaving the Shetland Islands, Goffman moved to Paris, where he completed a draft of his doctoral dissertation. The following year he returned to Chicago and married the 23-year-old Angelica Choate, whom he had met earlier at the university, where she was an undergraduate majoring in psychology. Their son, Tom, was born the following year.

In 1953 Goffman successfully defended his dissertation. His examiners had mixed reactions to his study: several expected a detailed case study and were dismayed to receive what was, in effect, a general theory of face-to-face interaction (Winkin, 1998). After a brief stretch as a research assistant for Edward Shils, Goffman, his wife, and young son moved to Washington, DC, where in 1955 he began observations at St Elizabeths hospital (Goffman, 1961a). For the next three years Goffman spent time at the hospital, where he was given the position of assistant to the athletic director. This marginal position gave him access to all parts of the institution.

On January 1, 1958, Goffman was invited by Herbert Blumer to teach at the University of California at Berkeley, where he was hired as a visiting assistant professor. During the next four years Goffman progressed rapidly. *The Presentation of Self* was reissued by a prominent publisher in the United States in 1959. This was followed by *Asylums* in 1961 and *Encounters* later that year. He was promoted several times and became a full professor in 1962. In addition to his academic interests, Goffman showed himself to be a shrewd stock market analyst and a keen gambler. Goffman was proud of his stock-picking abilities: later in life he boasted that even though he was one of the highest paid sociologists in the United States, he still earned a third of his income from investments and a third from royalties. By contrast, his gambling abilities remain uncertain: there are reports that he was regularly beaten at poker by colleagues at the university; losses that he accepted with grace and good humor (Marx, 1984). He was a stronger blackjack player, and made frequent visits to casinos in Nevada. Indeed, later he trained, qualified, and worked as a blackjack dealer at the Station Plaza Casino in Las Vegas, where he was promoted to pit boss (Andrea Fontana, personal correspondence). In his published work, particularly in the essay "Where the Action Is," Goffman includes tantalizing hints of an ethnography of gambling and casino life; however, he never published a separate study.

During his stay at Berkeley, his wife, Angelica, had serious mental health problems, which resulted in her suicide in 1964. A parallel may exist between Goffman's academic interests in mental illness and his own personal observations of it at home. Perhaps nowhere is this clearer than in his 1969 essay, "The Insanity of Place," which is, arguably, autobiographical.

In 1966, Goffman spent a sabbatical year at the Harvard Center for International Affairs. At Harvard he developed a friendship with Thomas Schelling, from whom he strengthened his understanding of game theoretic accounts of human behavior. He resigned his position at Berkeley on June 30, 1968 in order to accept a Benjamin Franklin Chair in Sociology and Anthropology at the University of Pennsylvania. His salary at that time was $30,000 a year, setting a new high for a sociology professor. For a variety of reasons (perhaps including salary) Goffman was alienated from his colleagues in sociology, and he spent the first couple of years at the university working out of an office in the Anthropological Museum. The move to Philadelphia did not slow down his research productivity. In 1971 he published *Relations in Public*, in which he brought together many of his ideas about the organization of everyday conduct. Simultaneously he was also working on the book he hoped to be his magnum opus, *Frame Analysis*, eventually published in 1974. Given the long gestation period, the lukewarm reception of the book by the sociological community must have been a disappointment.

In 1981 he married the linguist, Gillian Sankoff, with whom he had a daughter, Alice, in May 1982. On November 20, 1982, he died of stomach cancer, a few weeks after he had to cancel the presentation of his Presidential Address to the American Sociological Association. This paper, "The Interaction Order," was published in the *American Sociological Review* in 1983. The dry humor of the presentation is striking: Goffman added a preface to his speech from his hospital bed, knowing that he would not be able to deliver it in person. The title of the talk was also carefully chosen: this was the title that, in 1953, Goffman had used for the conclusions to his doctoral dissertation. This gesture brought a sense of closure to his intellectual ideas.

THE SOCIAL CONTEXT

As Goffman's generation is only now passing from the scene as active scholars, the full history of the period in which he was trained is still being written. Despite Goffman's links with a number of academic and research institutions, including the University of Toronto, the Sorbonne, the University of Edinburgh, the National Institutes of Health, the University of California at Berkeley, Harvard University, and the University of Pennsylvania, the one location that has been taken as having more influence on him than all others is the University of Chicago. As a result of a chance meeting, Goffman decided to attend graduate school with Everett Hughes, a fellow Canadian, at the University of Chicago.

While less has been made of Goffman's tenure at Berkeley and at Pennsylvania than is warranted, it was the social scene in Chicago's Hyde Park in the years after the Second World War that had the most lasting and profound impression. Erving Goffman was very much a product of this time and place.

Hyde Park in the late 1940s and early 1950s was a special location for the development of sociology and sociologists. The roster of graduate students from the period reads like a who's who of the creative minds of the discipline. The most extensive set of accounts detailing the intellectual and social life at the University of Chicago in this period are included in *A Second Chicago School?* (Fine, 1995), a collection of essays that depicts the profound influence of the place and period on the development of sociology in the latter half of the twentieth century.

Prior to 1935, Chicago was the dominant sociology program in the United States, and the world. However, by the late 1940s, the development of "the

General Theory of Action" under Talcott Parsons at Harvard and survey research and functional analysis under Paul Lazarsfeld and Robert Merton at Columbia made Cambridge and Morningside Heights strong contenders, perhaps more "cutting edge" than the embattled qualitative tradition at Chicago (Bulmer, 1984; Gusfield, 1995, pp. ix–x; Camic, 1996; Abbott, 1997). Still, Chicago proved to be an intellectually exciting home for many graduate students, even if the changes in the faculty, notably the move of Herbert Blumer to Berkeley, led to misgivings by the university administration (Abbott and Graziano, 1995). Further, despite the stereotypes that have often linked Chicago sociology to the interactionist project, the department was both theoretically and methodologically diverse (Bulmer, 1984; Platt, 1995).

According to Joseph Gusfield (1995, pp. xv–xvi), himself a graduate student in the period, the cohort in which Goffman came of age as a sociologist was a large one, consisting of a high proportion of Jews and veterans. Further, aside from similarities among the members of the cohort, the very size of the cohort contributed to a sense of cohesion and engagement. The Chicago department never had a large faculty. During the late 1940s, the department had fewer than ten faculty and only seven full professors, and, as these were prominent men, several were likely to be on leave at any one time. During the high point of the postwar years over 200 students were registered in either the MA or the PhD programs. Whereas only four PhDs were granted in 1946, by 1954, twenty-eight were awarded. The explosion in the number of graduate students overwhelmed the ability of the faculty to nurture them or even to provide guidance for preliminary exams and doctoral dissertations (Lopata, 1995, p. 365), and provoked irritation or even bitterness toward the structure of the program, especially by graduate students.

As a result, graduate students banded together for social and intellectual support. In 1947, students who had been active previously in union activity formed a student grievance committee that focused on the neglect of students by the faculty (Lopata, 1995, p. 366). The fact that the committee did not achieve many changes (Chicago defined itself as a research university, with teaching graduate students a secondary priority) created graduate student cohesion. In addition, the structure of the department led graduate students to formulate their problems independently from faculty members, leading to scholarly creativity early in their careers. Thus, even Goffman's early work, such as his writings on the significance of class symbols, though clearly influenced by some Chicago faculty and by other graduate students, was also uniquely his own.

However, other factors were at work. One important feature was the geographical ecology of Hyde Park, which helped to form an aggregate of graduate students into a cohesive social group. Gusfield points out that most of the cohort lived within a few blocks of each other, near the somewhat isolated campus, surrounded by a rundown urban area. The campus was a defended neighborhood, circled by a seemingly hostile outside world. Gusfield notes that the many rundown apartment houses made it possible for most graduate students to afford housing close to campus. Students found common hangouts, such as Jimmy's

Bar, the University Tavern, the Tropical Hut eatery, and a wide array of fine bookstores. Gusfield (1995, p. xv) writes:

> The closeness of places, the then-safety of the streets, and the proximity of residence helped us to form friendships and events of solidarity that have been lasting. The classroom spilled over onto the streets and, of course, into the living rooms and kitchens. My wife still remembers the night she thought I had met foul play when a search of the streets at 1:00 A.M. found me and Erving Goffman "talking shop" under a lamp post. During one or two years there was an ongoing softball game in a 57th Street schoolyard. The Social Science building had a daily interdisciplinary coffee hour. There were the frequent parties and, above all, the talk-talk-talk.

The close friendships and networks in which Goffman participated and in which he was an active participant led to sufficient personal respect that he was anointed the "one most likely to succeed."

Although it does not appear that Goffman himself was very active politically, many of his fellow graduate students were involved politically in such causes as civil rights and union activity. His seeming apathy was continually confronted and tested by the commitments of his friends and classmates.

While Goffman's intellectual contributions stand on their own merit, the presence of a powerful social network composed of other prominent sociologists who could promote his work, as well as provide occasional advice, proved beneficial for his future status. Reputation, while grounded in the work itself, is also a function of the social situation (Fine, 1996). The impact of social settings matters in our interpretation of any theorist.

Goffman's years at the University of California at Berkeley (1958–68) were intellectually productive and socially tumultuous. By the early 1960s Berkeley's Department of Sociology was one of the strongest in the United States, situated in a rapidly growing, prestigious state university. In addition to Goffman, the department included such luminaries as Seymour Martin Lipset, Kingsley Davis, Neil Smelser, Nathan Glazer, Reinhard Bendix, John Clausen, David Matza, Philip Selznick, and, of course, Herbert Blumer. As Gary Marx (1984, p. 650) notes, the department drew scholars from the traditions at Harvard, Columbia, and Chicago, and "it was probably the only major school not dominated by one or two powerful intellectual figures and a single methodological or theoretical approach." As the decade progressed, Berkeley became synonymous with student protest, and the Department of Sociology was one of the centers of protest in this chaotic period (Heirich, 1970; Marx, 1984). While Goffman was by no means part of the radical fringe of the department and rejected political involvement (commenting, as Marx (1984, p. 658) reports, "When they start shooting students from the steps of Sproul Hall I guess I'll get involved, but not until then"), his sometimes cynical, always corrosive approach fit well with the spirit of the times. Berkeley in the 1960s, like Chicago in the 1940s and 1950s, was one of the centers for the development of American sociology, and the impressive array of faculty and students, coupled with the protests and debates on campus, had a dramatic effect on Goffman, forcing him to question the very basis by which social actors come to understand and behave towards each other. This theme found its best expression in *Frame Analysis*. Goffman's predilection to view the world as an outsider found considerable support in a community such as Berkeley, an enclave that was self-defined as radical and alienated. Further, one might speculate that the rich and lively street culture found on and around the Berkeley campus provided an impetus for Goffman's analyses of the dynamics of public behavior, given expression in *Behavior in Public Places* and *Relations in Public*.

The University of Pennsylvania was not quite the same intellectual center that Chicago and Berkeley had been, despite the presence of important figures (e.g. Phillip Rieff, Marvin Wolfgang, E. Digby Baltzell); yet even there Goffman was able to create a social environment that supported and enhanced his work. As a Benjamin Franklin Professor, Goffman did not have any specific department responsibilities, and his contacts ranged far afield from the Department of Sociology, incorporating scholars at the Annenberg School of Communication, the Department of Anthropology, and the Department of Linguistics. Indeed, for many of his early years at the University of Pennsylvania, Goffman had only a distant relationship with many colleagues in the Department of Sociology. Perhaps most significant in terms of his social and intellectual development was Goffman's contact with the sociolinguists William Labov and Dell Hymes. Much of Goffman's later work, notably *Gender Advertisements* and *Forms of Talk*, was heavily influenced by communications theory and sociolinguistics.

While it is plausible to contend that Goffman's intellectual eminence would likely have revealed itself in any circumstances, the fact that for much of his career he was surrounded by first-rate scholars in communities of intellectual and social ferment surely contributed to the development of his idiosyncratic vision.

THE INTELLECTUAL CONTEXT

As noted above, the Department of Sociology at the University of Chicago was small, but intellectually central to the vitality of the discipline. During Goffman's early years as a student in the department, only seven full professors were on staff: Ernest Burgess, Louis Wirth, Herbert Blumer, William F. Ogburn, Robert Hauser, Everett Hughes, and W. Lloyd Warner. Yet, despite the size of the unit, the faculty was remarkably active on a number of important projects. While there was not a mentorship relationship between faculty and students during this period, many students worked with faculty on various projects. Everett Hughes was particularly active in these projects, and worked closely with numerous students (although not, apparently, with Goffman himself). These collaborations produced, among others, studies of the process of aging and medical training (resulting in *Growing Old: the Process of Disengagement* and *Boys in White*). The presence of the National Opinion Research Center (NORC) on campus, having recently moved from the University of Denver, provided a noninteractionist context for large-scale survey research (for other examples of the intellectual context and activities of Chicago in this period see Lopata, 1995, pp. 366–72).

Goffman is a part – a central, defining part – of that group of young scholars who were trained at the University of Chicago in the decade after the Second World War: the "Second Chicago School" (Fine, 1995). These scholars included such subsequently influential and notable figures in the discipline as Joseph Gusfield, Howard Becker, Ralph Turner, Fred Davis, Helena Lopata, and Kurt and Gladys Lang, to name a few. Together, these scholars took a skeptical stance toward the dominant functionalist and quantitative perspective of mid-century American sociology, postulating an alternative, if somewhat hazy, vision. This period represented the flowering of interpretive sociology: a group of scholars that more than their interactionist predecessors were relentlessly empirical, producing a powerful set of detailed, descriptive analyses not found in the substantive analyses of Robert Park, Herbert Blumer, and Everett Hughes. These younger scholars, each in his or her own way, revealed an interest in the power of sudden, dramatic change, a concern with totalitarian control, and a concern with the basis of both community and conformity. The development of theories of collective behavior, race and ethnicity, work and occupations, and deviance, grounded in empirical analyses, set an agenda for research in these areas for decades (see, for example, Snow and Davis, 1995; Wacker, 1995; Galliher, 1995).

At Berkeley, intellectual debates concerned political analysis and language studies. Goffman's mentoring of Gary Marx and John Lofland falls into the first category, his teaching of the future conversational analysts Harvey Sacks, David Sudnow, and Emanuel Schegloff into the second category. Political themes, never explicitly developed in Goffman's own writing, find their echoes in the metaphors of concentration camps in *Asylums*, of passing in race relations in *Stigma*, and in the discussion of espionage in *Strategic Interaction*.

The years at the University of Pennsylvania broadened Goffman's interests in sociolinguistics, nonverbal communication, and the role of implicit meaning in communication systems. Goffman's (1979) analysis of the role of gendered visual communication in magazine advertisements in *Gender Advertisements* could only have been developed in an intellectual context in which the content analysis of media sources was intellectually central and academically legitimate. It is surely not incidental that Goffman's reunion at Annenberg with his early mentor at the University of Toronto, Ray Birdwhistell, certainly was an impetus for his attempt to understand body language. In a similar vein, the sociolinguistic essays found in *Forms of Talk* and in "Felicity's Condition" result from Goffman's interactions with linguists at the University of Pennsylvania. This built on his earlier dialogues, particularly with John Searle, at Berkeley in the early 1960s.

Although it is difficult to trace precisely the intellectual forces that influenced Goffman's distinctive creativity, the intellectual currents at those institutions in which he studied and was employed had a considerable effect on the development of his sociology. Even such a distinctive voice as Goffman's was modulated by the other participants in his academic choruses.

GOFFMAN'S IDEAS

As noted, it is notoriously difficult to classify Goffman's style of sociology. Although he was a central figure in American sociology from the early 1960s until his death in 1982, and although he has been adopted by prominent European social theorists interested in the analysis of human agency, Goffman's ideas are difficult to reduce to a number of key themes. A "Goffman school" did not emerge before or after his death. Many sociologists acknowledge an influence, but few consider their work to be a continuation of Goffman's. As Hymes memorably put it, few sociologists have been prepared to pick up Goffman's "golden shovel" (Hymes, 1984, p. 625; quoted by Drew and Wootton, 1988, p. 2).

This observation has led some scholars (Smith, 1989; Williams, 1980) to posit a similarity between Goffman and Georg Simmel. Simmel likened his essayistic ideas to a cash legacy that can be spent or reinvested, with the result that the source is no longer evident in the product. Perhaps something similar has occurred with Goffman's legacy: contemporary sociologists have cashed in their "positions" on Goffman, transforming his work into their own visions. Understood in this way, Goffman emerges as a precursor to ethnomethodology, to structuration theory, to neo-institutionalism, and to both a modernist, critical social theory and a postmodern symbolic interactionism.

Two images of Goffman emerge from this discussion: Goffman can be seen as either a maverick or a transitional figure. Both images account for the absence of a Goffman school. As a maverick, Goffman produced a one-of-a-kind sociology, both stylistically and substantively. Schegloff (1996) recently commented that although several generations of sociologists have admired Goffman's work, there is little sense of what to do with it. As Goffman remarked about himself, his work resists pigeonholing.

Further, as Brown (1977), Atkinson (1989), Fine and Martin (1990), Manning (1991), Smith and Travers (1998), and others have shown, Goffman is a maverick in that his writings can be read as both literature and social science. Although literary figures such as Burke and Pirandello were important to his dramaturgical account of everyday life, Goffman's writing style probably owes more to Everett Hughes.

Not only did he cite literature as source material, Goffman also displayed a deft metaphorical touch. Goffman's work has a literary sensibility that is rare in modern sociology (see Abbott, 1997). Goffman's stylistic devices, however appealing, implicitly question orthodox methodological approaches. What is implicit in his style is often explicit in his prefaces, which defend a Hughesian methodology by criticizing what he sees as the pretensions of quantitative methodology (see, for example, the preface to *Relations in Public*).

Goffman can also be seen as a transitional figure. In this guise he appears as a bridge between generations of Chicago sociology and some of the varied concerns of contemporary sociology. Understood in this way, Goffman is a successor to both Park and Hughes. Particularly from Hughes, Goffman found similarities in apparent differences. Instead of focusing on the obvious differences between the career trajectories of, for example, lawyers and prostitutes, Goffman also looked for telling similarities. Goffman developed a passion for a comparative, qualitative sociology that aimed to produce generalizations about human behavior.

Goffman's ideas have become transitional elements in European theoretical ventures as well. Anthony Giddens (1984) has accorded Goffman a special place in the theory of structuration: seeing a recognition of the interplay of structure and interpretive agency in his analysis. To a lesser extent, Habermas has also attempted to incorporate Goffman into his theory of undistorted communication (see Chriss, 1995). Strong ties also exist between Goffman's and Bourdieu's writing. However, it is worth remembering that Goffman was suspicious of grand theoretical schemes, and his preface to *Frame Analysis* indicated his more modest ambitions. Nevertheless, it is certainly true that new generations are being exposed to Goffman, in some cases for the first time, through the work of these prominent social theorists.

Goffman's Work

We distinguish six components of Goffman's work: (a) his pre-dramaturgical writings, including his graduate work at the University of Chicago; (b) his extended metaphorical investigations, notably *The Presentation of Self* but also his contribution to the study of strategic conduct and game theory; (c) his mature ethnographic work, *Asylums*, and his analysis of the social aspects of mental illness; (d) his sustained inquiry into the organization of everyday behavior, referred to as the "interaction order"; (e) his later investigations into the "framing" of social encounters; and (f) his analysis of language and social interaction. This division is only roughly chronological. Although Goffman's dramaturgical work is linked to the early phase of his career, he retained this interest and it permeates his later work. Similarly, although Goffman is remembered for his early ethnography of St Elizabeths hospital, Goffman also conducted later ethnographic work in Las Vegas and in Philadelphia, where he studied a classical music radio station. Of course, the study of the interaction order is, as Williams (1980) and Manning (1992) point out, the aspect of his work that is present from his doctoral dissertation to his Presidential Address to the American Sociological Association. So, this sixfold classification of Goffman's work must be treated cautiously.

Pre-dramaturgical writings

Goffman's early writings (1949, 1951, 1952, 1953a, b) produced a nucleus of ideas to which he returned throughout his academic career. His master's thesis is a survey-based project concerning the audience response to a popular radio soap opera, *Big Sister.* In an attempt to extend the research of Lloyd Warner (Warner and Henry, 1948), Goffman interviewed fifty women from the Hyde Park area of

Chicago to discover the typical characteristics of a segment of the soap opera's audience. Goffman attempted to use the Thematic Apperception Test (TAT) to investigate the relation between personality and socioeconomic status. In the course of the research Goffman became critical of the ability of this test to measure responses, and a large segment of the thesis is spent criticizing his own methodology. Smith (1993, p. 11) argued that this line of criticism was essential to the development of Goffman's work:

> It is important to note that [in his master's thesis] Goffman is not engaged in a wholesale critique of positivistic research methods and analytical traditions, but rather [he] presents carefully-formulated criticisms of his own research methods in the light of his original objectives. Goffman shows how, adjudged in the light of its own criteria, the experimental logic of his variable analysis cannot succeed. These discussions also show that Goffman's later (see especially the preface of *Relations in Public*) sharply critical comments on experimental logic and variable analysis were not made in the abstract but have their source in Goffman's firsthand research experience of the deficiencies he describes.

Goffman's first two published papers are quite unlike his master's thesis: both present subtle, almost cynically detached, observations about human conduct. Both are self-consciously literary in their handling of metaphor. "Symbols of Class Status" (1951) explores instrumental manipulations of symbolic representations of class. These manipulations can occur because although symbols represent class status, they do not constitute it. Goffman pointed to the efforts of "curator groups" – or cultural gatekeepers – who protect their group's status symbols from misuse. In a strikingly pre-dramaturgical way, the "Symbols" paper examines the necessary conditions for a persuasive performance to take place. In "On Cooling the Mark Out" (1952), Goffman uses the language of the confidence trick to discuss everyday behavior, suggesting that the world can be understood as competing groups of "con artists" and "marks." The con artist must first steal from the mark, and then "teach" him or her to accept the loss philosophically, without public complaint (ibid., p. 452). This paper contributes to the "sociology of failure." Goffman suggested that people who have failed, by their own standards or those of their group, are "dead people" who nevertheless continue to walk undetected among the living successes (ibid., p. 463).

Goffman's doctoral dissertation, "Communication Conduct in an Island Community," analyzes forms of self-presentation and both verbal and non-verbal interaction among inhabitants of a small island in the Shetlands. The first part of the dissertation served both as an introduction to everyday life on a Scottish island in a community Goffman referred to as "Dixon" and as a justification for the work presented later. Goffman aimed for more than a case study: his goal was to use this material to generate a model of communication strategies in face-to-face interaction. Goffman emphasized that empirical material was not merely a foil for conceptual elaboration; rather, his conceptual elaboration was based on his ethnographic observations (Goffman, 1953a, p. 9).

The dissertation is largely concerned with the analysis of the intersection of ritual and context in everyday life. To this end, Goffman classified the analytic differences between various kinds of social occasion (ibid., pp. 127–35). This in turn enabled him to examine the ways in which people could pay ritual homage to the projections of self evident in all social situations. These rituals, many of which are simply small offerings of appreciation or admiration, make accommodation and integration possible. However, as Williams (1980, p. 231) has commented, accommodation alone may or not be a genuine reflection of concern, and beneath a veneer of politeness, social interaction may be understood as a kind of "cold war" (Williams, 1980, p. 231; Goffman, 1953a, p. 40).

In many ways, the key elements of Goffman's later sociology can all be found in this work: his interest in the interaction order of everyday life, his concern with ethnography and qualitative sociology, and his coolly ironic and self-consciously literary style are all evident (Williams, 1980, p. 210). The still unpublished dissertation remains a key resource for understanding the development of Goffman's ideas.

Metaphorical investigations

Goffman is justly famous for *The Presentation of Self in Everyday Life*, in which he outlined a theatrical, or "dramaturgical," vocabulary with which to describe everyday social encounters, such as eating in a restaurant, visiting friends, or attending a funeral. However, he used the same strategy, that of extended metaphorical description, in other projects, most notably where he analyzes game-like social situations, and hence it is appropriate to consider them as a single package.

The Presentation of Self expanded ideas outlined by Kenneth Burke's "dramatistic" approach (Burke, 1969). As Tom Burns (1992, p. 112) shrewdly observed, Goffman's achievement lay in his ability to pursue "the theatrical metaphor beyond the commonplace notion of 'putting on an act,'" so as to build an "analogical superstructure" that fully exploited the analytical resources of the theatrical metaphor. It is also important to note the work of Harré (1979, pp. 189–231), who has attempted to develop dramaturgical analysis by returning to Burke and retracing Goffman's steps. In so doing, Harré draws our attention to the connection between Goffman's earlier analysis of the social setting and his later analysis (in *Relations in Public*) of the *Umwelt* or surrounding social scene.

The Presentation of Self can be thought of as a "handbook" of action, containing six dramaturgical themes: the performance, the team, the region, discrepant roles, communication out of character, and impression management. These themes had been initially explored in Goffman's dissertation, where they were integrated into his ethnographic study of Dixon. In *The Presentation of Self* these themes have been repackaged as general features of social interaction. In a sense, Goffman used his observations of a small Scottish island as building blocks for an ambitious, general theory.

Goffman aimed to provide a persuasive description of familiar events. A person's performance is "given" if it is intended to influence other participants' understanding of the events at hand (Goffman, 1959, pp. 26, 32). Performances consist of elements designed to enhance the audience's sense of "realness." These include a "front": the stage props, appropriate expressions, and attitudes that allow a performer to conjure up a desired self-image. For example, part of what makes a lawyer convincing to a jury is not only the strength of his or her legal argument, but also a professional appearance and appropriate manner. The trial lawyer Fred Barlit reported that when he travels to try a case he is careful to wear different shoes to court every day, so that jurors can believe that he is a hometown lawyer (reported by Couric, 1988, p. 23). Details such as this are necessary for the "dramatic realization" of a performance. In either a discursive or a nondiscursive way, we are all dramaturgically savvy, and hence anxious to distinguish the "given" or "planted" elements of a performance from the unintended elements that were unwittingly "given off" by the performer. For example, a person who wishes to appear scholarly might prominently carry a copy of Wittgenstein's *Philosophical Investigations*. However, if he clearly pronounces the "W" of Wittgenstein, he gives off a rather different impression. As Goffman notes, the key to dramaturgical success is to control the audience's access to information, so that elements of performances that are given are such that audiences believe they were given off.

Goffman's dramaturgical analysis extends to the organization of physical as well as social space, as he describes the "front and "back" stages (or regions) of locations. A public performance is given on a front stage by a "team" of performers who construct a view of the world for the benefit of a public audience. However, in a back stage area, these performers may "knowingly contradict" (Goffman, 1959, p. 114) the impressions that had carefully been publicly presented. Goffman also indicates that these two regions are connected by a "guarded passageway" (such as the double doors found between the kitchen and dining room in many restaurants) so that the public performance cannot be shattered by an inadvertent view of the back stage. This aspect of Goffman's analysis is quite literal: it is more a footnote in the history of architecture than a metaphorical description of familiar experience. Goffman gave the following example: "If the bereaved are to be given the illusion that the dead one is really in a deep and tranquil sleep, then the undertaker must be able to keep the bereaved from the workroom where the corpses are drained, stuffed and painted in preparation for their final performance" (ibid., p. 116).

Manning (1992, pp. 44–8) suggests that Goffman's dramaturgical analysis is underpinned by a "two selves thesis." One self is a public performer with carefully managed impressions; the second self is a cynical manipulator hidden behind the public performance. Following Park, Goffman noted that the etymology of person is "mask." The two selves thesis explains the common belief that the dramaturgical perspective is a cynical view of social life which implies that all relationships are inauthentic and self-serving.

In other writings Goffman explored alternative metaphorical recastings, most notably a game-theoretic perspective. Although he was knowledgeable of the work in game theory by mathematicians and economists – and frequently cited the seminal text by Von Neuman and Morgenstern (1944) – Goffman's contribution to the field was heavily influenced by his friendship with Thomas

Schelling, whose own work is not mathematically sophisticated. Goffman's first efforts at game theory can be traced to his dissertation (Manning, 1992, pp. 64–71), and his ideas were developed most fully in two books, *Encounters* (1961) and *Strategic Interaction* (1969).

Although aspects of Goffman's work can be read as contributions to game theory (see, for example, Collins, 1980, pp. 191–9; Manning, 1992, pp. 56–71), Goffman generally preferred to emphasize the extent to which game theory is compatible with the legacy of Chicago Sociology and symbolic interactionism. He referred to this theoretical merger as "strategic interaction," and his discussion of it (Goffman, 1969, pp. 136–45) contains one of his few public reflections about the strengths and weaknesses of symbolic interactionism. Goffman's concern about the symbolic interactionism of Mead and Blumer is that its insights can dissipate into truisms about the importance of meaning and context. His hope for strategic interaction (which he understood as the addition of Schelling's work to the symbolic interactionist mix) was that a greater level of specificity could be achieved. Goffman explained this as follows:

> following the crucial work of Schelling, strategic interaction addresses itself directly to the dynamics of interdependence involving mutual awareness; it seeks out basic moves and inquires into natural stopping points in the potentially infinite cycle of two players taking into consideration their consideration of each other's consideration, and so forth. (ibid., p. 137)

Goffman is proposing to transform Blumer's (1969) seminal statement about the basic tenets of symbolic interactionism. Blumer's focus was on the individual, definitions of the situation, and the mediation of symbols. Goffman advocated a focus on the player, basic moves, and the rules governing face-to-face conduct.

Goffman believed that the distinction between a player and a party is often "easy to neglect" (Goffman, 1969, p. 87), with the consequence that important distinctions may be missed. Players (or actors) can play for others or for themselves. Players can be "pawns" to be sacrificed for the sake of the game. They can also be "tokens" who express a position. Goffman (ibid., pp. 87–8) pointed out that Western diplomacy distinguished between the "nuncio" who can represent a party but not negotiate for it and the "procurator" who can negotiate but not represent. To use a contemporary example, car showrooms contain nuncios who can transmit an offer from a procurator who does not negotiate openly with the opposing party, who wishes to purchase a car. The role of ambassador combines the duties of the nuncio and the procurator, but ceremonial constraints prevent ambassadors from commercial ventures.

According to Goffman (ibid., pp. 11–27), the basic moves of strategic interaction are the "unwitting," the "naive," the "covering," the "uncovering," and, finally, the "counter-uncovering" move. The unwitting move occurs when the player is not deliberately acting in the game, as when a person buying a car engages in small talk during which he reveals that he recently inherited a lot of money. A naive move is an unwitting move as judged by another player. For example, a landlord may judge the claim that a potential tenant dislikes pets as an unwitting move in the game of apartment-renting. A control move is one which will improve a player's standing in a game if accepted by other players. The possible effects of control moves are calculated: "What is essentially involved is not communication but rather a set of tricky ways of sympathetically taking the other into consideration as someone who assesses the environment and might profitably be led into a wrong assessment" (ibid., p. 13).

An example of a primitive control move is camouflage or concealment. More sophisticated control moves involve active misrepresentation (ibid., p. 14). In order to counteract a control move, a player may use an uncovering move. This can involve either spying or an examination of some kind, either of the player or of marks of his or her presence. The interrogator is by design and training the master of the uncovering move (ibid., p. 18). The final basic move is the counter-uncovering move. Goffman gave an instructive example here: instead of presenting an interrogator with a perfect alibi, a suspect may choose to offer one that is wanting and inconclusive, reasoning that a person with nothing to hide would be able to present only a partial alibi, not one that appears to have been specially devised for the contingency of being caught (ibid., p. 20).

Players and moves take place within games, or, as Goffman (1961b, pp. 84–8; 1983) put it, within social worlds or "situated activity systems." These worlds are governed by the normative constraints that govern the interaction order, the uncovering of which was a focus of much of his work. Early in his career, Goffman considered the merits of using Garfinkel's famous "breaching experiments" (Garfinkel, 1967) to identify these constraints, during which participants act in inappropriate ways in an attempt to make rules of conduct transparent. While acknowledging the strength of this approach (1961b, p. 18), Goffman focused instead on the discovery of "rules of irrelevance" which instruct participants about what they should and should not make the focus of their attention during interaction (ibid., pp. 18–31). Clearly, this early contribution signaled the interest in frames explored at length later (Goffman, 1974). Goffman understood throughout his work that social worlds are vulnerable, and that normative rules, though "flimsy," are responsible for our "unshaking sense" of social reality (Goffman, 1961b, p. 72).

Mature ethnographic work: asylums

In 1955 Goffman began fieldwork at St Elizabeths Hospital in Washington, DC, a large mental hospital with about 7000 patients. Installed as the assistant to the athletics director, Goffman was free to roam the hospital as he wished, without his presence causing undue attention. Only the Superintendent of St Elizabeths was aware of his true purpose.

The choice of St Elizabeths was propitious: the mental hospital provided Goffman with a setting in which he could associate with a sequestered and maligned group – a group that for his academic readers was exotic as well. This site provided him with the opportunity to side with the underdog. Goffman was positioned to snipe at institutionalized authority and, in a Hughesian way, invert traditional hierarchies. Goffman used the opportunity to explore the characteristics of "total institutions," settings in which the time and space of inmates are seemingly controlled completely by staff. Although prisons are the baseline example of the total institution (Goffman, 1961a, p. 20), St Elizabeths, like mental institutions in general, exhibited comparable features.

Hence, St Elizabeths allowed Goffman to collect data for a radically different ethnography. Manning (1998) has referred to *Asylums* as not simply an ethnography of St Elizabeths but an "ethnography of the concept of the total institution." Fine and Martin (1990) gesture to a similar observation when they point out that *Asylums* gives almost no information about the routine operations of St Elizabeths. Goffman does not describe the layout of the hospital; nor does he describe the personnel. There is not even an account of a typical day. Instead, Goffman conveys a "tone of life" – depicting, for instance, the mundane scrounging of cigarettes and food – and in so doing he presents an ethnography less concerned with description than with analysis (Fine and Martin, 1990, p. 93). Goffman's primary goal in *Asylums* is to understand the organization of total institutional life, of which St Elizabeths is an example. In this way, Goffman's aspirations exceed those of the traditional case study.

Asylums consists of four essays, each of which was published separately. Unsurprisingly, therefore, there is a certain amount of repetition, as Goffman reworked similar or identical material. The first three essays are interrelated, as they all examine the ordinary experiences of patients (or, as is often the case, inmates) in total institutions. The second essay also considers the "pre-patient" process leading to institutionalization. However, the final essay of *Asylums* is quite different, and sits uncomfortably with the other contributions. This paper is a theoretical examination of professional–client interaction. In it, Goffman isolates the unique elements of psychiatrist–client interaction, in order to show the "grotesque" predicament of the mentally ill (Goffman, 1961a, p. 186). One example Goffman gave of this concerned the treatment of unruly patients. Because staff were unable to punish them for actions that were understood to be linked to a disease, punishments became hidden behind misleading labels. This meant that "solitary confinement" was transformed from an undisguised punishment into a treatment option known as "constructive meditation" (ibid., 82).

Most of *Asylums* deals with the pre-patient and inpatient phases. In the second essay, Goffman offers a subtle account of the process whereby a person who behaves in an unusual way can become a candidate for institutionalization. Although he does not provide a clear account of the empirical basis for his argument, Goffman persuasively discusses the "betrayal funnel" through which unwitting pre-patients discover that the people in whom they have invested the most trust are the same people who report their actions to medical and other personnel. This is an especially painful time for pre-patients, because they witness their families and friends acting strangely around them, hanging up calls when they walk in the room, changing topics when interrupted, and meeting secretly. This informal network of concerned people benignly deceives the pre-patient, refusing to talk to him or her openly, often until they recommend to the pre-patient that a visit to a "doctor" might be helpful, unable even then to avoid this euphemistic reference to a psychiatrist. The unintended consequence of the behavior of concerned friends is that the old adage that "just because you're paranoid doesn't mean they're not out to get you" rings true. Ultimately, pre-patients are passed on to a "circuit of agents" – social workers, various officers of the criminal justice system, psychiatrists, and others – who then assess the viability and desirability of institutionalization. Goffman's analysis can be justly compared to Foucault's (1979) account of the "carceral society" in *Discipline and Punish*.

Once institutionalized, patients are exposed to "batch living" and the tightly controlled life typical of any total institution. The staff has extensive control of time and space, upheld with carefully planned schedules and surveillance devices (Foucault, 1979). The result is "civil death" (Goffman, 1961a, p. 25), or, as Goffman sometimes puts it, a "mortification of self" (ibid., p. 31). New patients at St Elizabeths were quickly transformed from civilian outsiders into hospital products: they were supplied with clothes, familiar names were dropped, and they were disciplined so as to accept the authority of staff members. At St Elizabeths, a "ward system" punished uncooperative patients by limiting them to poor living conditions, from which they could only move gradually to a ward which afforded a degree of comfort.

Over time, St Elizabeths, in common with other total institutions, offered "privileges" to patients who accepted their diminished roles. These consisted of minor rewards, such as cups of coffee or access to newspapers or television. As Goffman trenchantly explained, the consequence of the privilege system "is that cooperativeness is obtained from persons who often have cause to be uncooperative" (ibid., p. 54). An unintended consequence is that patients had a diminished sense of self-worth as they discovered that they were willing to accept trivial rewards in oppressive conditions. In this sense, the total institution had accomplished its mission to be a "forcing house" for changing persons, because outside its walls patients would have been unlikely to cooperate in return for rewards consisting only of taken-for-granted supplies and services.

In different ways and by different means, both the mortification of self and the privilege system undermine the patients' sense of self. In many total institutions, hospital patients, prison or concentration camp inmates, military recruits, neophyte nuns and monks all experience severe attacks on their core conception of self. To use Ralph Turner's (1968) vocabulary, the total institution is able to mount an attack on the person's self-conception, the sense that we have of who we "really" are.

In response to these severe infringements, patients learn to resist the pull of the total institution without directly confronting it, a strategy that, Paul Willis reports in *Learning to Labor*, is also used by rebellious high school boys. Goffman identified four strategies of resistance, which he referred to idiomatically as "playing it cool." The first strategy, "situational withdrawal," involves intensive daydreaming as a means of escaping or absenting oneself from the total institution. In *One Flew Over the Cuckoo's Nest*, Ken Kesey also recognized this practice, as he described patients on a ward pretending collectively to watch a football game on television, becoming for a while completely absorbed in the excitement of the imagined game. The second strategy is to establish an "intransigent line" which if breached triggers uncooperative behavior. This is a means whereby inmates demonstrate a measure of control over their lives by telling themselves (if no one else) that they can only be pushed so far. The intransigent line is always provisional and subject to revision. At its limit, it may involve a hunger strike. Goffman points out that staff members may try to break the intransigent prisoner – in a mental hospital this may take the form of electroshock treatment (ibid., p. 62). The third strategy is colonization, during which inmates play up whatever positive features they can identify in the total institution. Goffman indicates that for inmates with experience of several different total institutions it is simply a matter of reapplying familiar adaptive techniques whereby a home of sorts is made of a restrictive environment. The third essay of *Asylums* contains many examples of "secondary adjustments" – the inmates' ways of challenging institutional authority, thereby giving a human touch to an institutionalized world. The fourth strategy, conversion, involves the inmate's acceptance, or the pretense of acceptance, of the institution's ideology: "the inmate appears to take over the official or staff view of himself and tries to act out the role of the perfect inmate" (ibid., p. 63).

Goffman argued that the similarities between inmate experiences in different total institutions are both "glaring" and "persistent" (ibid., p. 115), such that the apparent antics of the institutionalized mentally ill are misunderstood as symptoms of underlying disorders but better understood as extensively practiced adjustments to trying and threatening circumstances. Goffman made this point forcefully:

> The impression may be given, therefore, that patients throughout the day fitfully engaged in childish tricks and foolhardy gestures to better their lot, and that there is nothing inconsistent between this pathetic display and our traditional notions of mental patients being "ill." I want to state, therefore, that in actual practice almost all of the secondary adjustments I have reported were carried on by the patient with an air of intelligent down-to-earth determination, sufficient, once the full context was known, to make an outsider feel at home, in a community much more similar to others he has known than different from them. (ibid., p. 266)

The interaction order

In his dissertation, Goffman (1953a, p. 343) used this term to characterize the web of normative beliefs that facilitate communication and social interaction. In this context, it has a functionalist basis and an empirical target. Goffman was not attempting to develop functionalist theory; instead, he wanted to promote the observational study of everyday behavior, and several premises of functionalism were useful for this purpose.

As a result, the concept "interaction order" is purged of an explicit functionalism and is used simply to refer to the study of face-to-face interaction. He then clarified this broad definition by stating that the organization of the interaction order can be understood as "ground rules for a game, the provisions of a traffic code or the rules of syntax of a language" (Goffman, 1983, p. 8). Drew and Wootton (1988, p. 7) remark that this commits Goffman to investigating the "procedures and practices through which people organized, and brought into life, their face-to-face dealings with each other."

Goffman's investigations of the interaction order involve the creation of a vocabulary with which to recast familiar experiences and an empirical inquiry into the applicability of this new vocabulary. However, this empirical inquiry has not been conducted using the mainstream social scientific framework of hypothesis-testing and quantification. In the preface to *Relations in Public*, Goffman acknowledged that his work does not meet the orthodox methodological standards of sociology. However, he was not repentant; instead he criticized sociologists whose work has the appearance of science but lacks explanatory power. Throughout his career, Goffman presented a diverse range of examples for comparison that conform to and exemplify his vocabulary. As a result, Burns (1992, p. 33) refers to Goffman's work as a "sociography" rather than as a sociology, to emphasize the classificatory focus of his research, and to downplay the extent to which it should be judged by the tenets of quantitative social science.

Goffman's exploration of the interaction order consist of four interrelated classificatory inquiries: (a) types of social event; (b) types of audience; (c) levels of commitment; and (d) self-presentation. Throughout his work, but most notably in *Behavior in Public Places*, Goffman classified the types of social event in the interaction order. This classification identified the range of variations in which people find themselves "copresent" with others. To this end, Goffman distinguished a "gathering," a "situation," and a "social occasion" (Goffman, 1963a, pp. 17–19). A gathering occurs when two or more people are in each other's immediate presence. A situation is the "full spatial environment" which begins with "mutual monitoring" (ibid., p. 18). A social occasion, such as a birthday party or a work day at an office, is bounded by space and time, likely to involve props or equipment, and is the background against which situations and gatherings are likely to take place.

In *Behavior in Public Places*, Goffman also analyzed audiences, distinguishing the acquainted from the unacquainted. In *Forms of Talk* (Goffman, 1981a), he also distinguished between a hearer and an overhearer. The acquainted are recognized either "cognitively," as being a particular person and not merely a category of person, or "socially," i.e. the acquainted are recognized in the sense of being welcomed and acknowledged (Goffman, 1963a, pp. 112–13). The acquainted need a reason not to initiate an encounter ("I can't stop, I'm late!"); the opposite holds true for the unacquainted. Goffman considered the circumstances whereby the unacquainted can approach each other. One set of circumstances concerns people who occupy "exposed" social positions, such as police officers, priests, and newsstand vendors, all of whom can be approached for information or even to exchange greetings (ibid., p. 125). There are also people who are considered so "meager in sacred value" that they can be addressed without explanation (ibid., p. 126). Goffman suggests that the old and the very young are examples: they are "open persons" who are exposed to public interaction by virtue of their status as persons and not because of their roles. A third circumstance facilitating interaction among the unacquainted occurs when someone is demonstrably out of role, as when someone is drunk or dressed in an unusual costume. Finally, there are those "non-persons," who are so lacking in social presence – servers of various kinds – that others can freely converse and act *as if* these figures were not present.

In different social events with these audiences, people display different levels of commitment. This commitment or involvement is the person's capacity to give "concerted attention" to the present engagement (ibid., p. 43). This changes during the day, producing an "involvement contour." Goffman distinguished "main" and "side" involvements: the former are claims on the person that he or she is obliged to acknowledge, the latter are activities that can coexist with but must not threaten the focus of the event. Main and side involvements complement each other, in the sense that they allow people to demonstrate respect for group activities while asserting an autonomy from them (Manning, 1992, p. 84).

Self-presentation issues are addressed throughout Goffman's early work, and dramaturgical ideas from his dissertation are recycled in *The Presentation of Self*. Later, in *Relations in Public*, Goffman reconsidered how people appear in social settings, analyzing the different "territories of the self" by which people mark out the space around them. He also considered the "tie-signs" (such as hand-holding) that distinguish groups as a "with" (Goffman, 1971, pp. 194–210; Fine et al., 1984).

Goffman's analysis of the interaction order classifies a broad range of everyday behavior, and draws attention to how people are sensitive to even minor variations to expected conduct. His analysis reveals the stickiness of the web of normative expectations governing mundane interaction. Goffman does not, however, provide anything more than a general account of rule-following practices or socialization processes. The absence of an account of this kind is surprising, especially given his fondness for quoting from etiquette manuals, which are explicitly "how to" guides to middle-class conduct. Goffman was amused by the writings of Emily Post and others, and drew on their work for examples for his own classificatory accounts.

The framing of social life

Goffman's *Frame Analysis* was published in 1974 after a decade of preparation. It was a project in which Goffman had invested a tremendous amount of time and effort, and the resulting 586-page book was meant to be a major statement of general sociological importance. Unfortunately, the reviews of *Frame Analysis* were mixed and even Goffman's supporters found the book excessively long and repetitive. Nevertheless, the core ideas struck a chord with social scientists and cognitive scientists.

A frame is a way of organizing experiences: it is one of the means whereby people identify the kind of activity that is taking place. For example, the act of kissing someone may be understood romantically, as a gesture of support, as a way of accepting an apology, as an unwanted advance, and so on. Following from the work of Gregory Bateson (1972), Goffman's analysis of frames tried to show how people distinguish these different kinds of activity. The implication is that the procedures to frame something so that it appears real or genuine are the same procedures used to mislead people. To this extent, frame analysis is an extension of Goffman's earlier dramaturgical work (Manning, 1992, p. 120).

Frame Analysis is in part a development of ideas from *The Presentation of Self*, but it also bears resemblance to Goffman's study of strategic interaction, particularly the essays in *Encounters* in which social interaction is analyzed as a set of "moves" between "players." Each move preserves or modifies the definition of the situation. This is apparent in Goffman's (1969) account of the work of espionage agents, who constantly evaluate whether their cover has been lost during a mission.

As with other projects, Goffman's frame analysis involves a classificatory vocabulary with which to redescribe the social world. "Frame analysis" is defined as the study of the "organization of experience," each frame of which is a principle of that organization (Goffman, 1974, p. 11). The most fundamental frames are "primary frameworks," which are either "natural" (involving physical events) or "social" (involving human intervention). In either case, the primary framework involves what "really" is happening: a transparent view of reality. For example, two people meeting for a picnic may be understood as using a social framework as a "date," but if the event is cut short by poor weather, the relevant frame is natural. Primary frameworks can be challenged in various ways: by astounding events, deceptions, and miscues that undermine the audience's sense of what is occurring (Goffman, 1974, p. 36). More importantly, primary frameworks can be "keyed" – that is, their meanings can be transformed into something patterned on but independent of the initial frame (ibid., p. 44). Actors recognize that a transformation has taken place, and that the key "unlocks" what is actually occurring. Thus, a key might show us that what appears to be a fight is really just play. These keyings can themselves be rekeyed in a way that requires careful analysis.

In addition to keys there are "fabrications." A frame is fabricated when it is organized so as to mislead others (ibid., p. 83). Fabrications are either "benign" (that is, for the benefit of an audience) or "exploitative" (that is, for the benefit of the fabricator). Keys and fabrications undermine our sense of social life, with the result that frames must be "anchored," so as to persuade people that what appears to be real is real.[2] Together these concepts provide for a construction of interpretations, grounded on, but not limited to, taken-for-granted meanings.

Language and social interaction

Although Goffman's analysis of talk is given extended treatment in *Forms of Talk* (1981a), similar ideas are aired in the later chapters of *Frame Analysis*, and before that in "The Neglected Situation" (1964). In these works Goffman outlined the general thrust of his argument concerning language and social interaction. Goffman (1964) emphasized that the activity of speaking is social and must be understood as an element of the situation and not as simply a linguistic construction. The appropriate connection between grammar and social interaction remains a fertile area for investigation. Talk cannot be understood merely as the linguistic component of social interaction and analyzed discretely; instead, it must be understood as an inseparable aspect of concerted and coordinated social action.

In the introduction to *Forms of Talk*, Goffman identified three themes of his work on language and social interaction: ritualization, participation frameworks, and embedding. Ritualization refers to the "movements, looks and vocal sounds" that accompany speaking and listening (Goffman, 1981a, p. 2). A participation framework identifies the relationship of each person in an event to that event. For example, a person who overhears an utterance stands in a different relationship to the event from the person to whom the comment was directed. Embedding is the ability to separate the person who speaks from the ownership of the words that are spoken: we can, for example, represent the beliefs of others or quote someone (ibid., pp. 2–4).

These themes are then examined in the five essays that follow. The main themes of this work are captured in one of the essays, concerning a person's "footing" (ibid., pp. 124–59). Goffman defines footing as something concerning a participant's projected self in social interaction. A change in footing occurs when a speaker begins a new alignment to the present interaction (ibid., p. 128). Goffman writes that a "change in footing implies a change in the alignment we take up to ourselves and the others present as expressed in the way we manage the production or reception of an utterance. A change in our footing is another way of talking about a change in our frame for events" (ibid., p. 128). This comment suggests continuity between Goffman's earlier analysis of both frames and the intersection between language and social interaction.

The discussion of footing was introduced with an almost literal example, as Goffman began by discussing an exchange between President Nixon and a female reporter, Helen Thomas. Just after signing a piece of Congressional legislation, Nixon commented on Thomas' clothing, specifically her wearing of "slacks." He asked her to model her clothing for him and the others present by making a pirouette. Then, after attempting to make jokey comments about the relative merits of slacks and "gowns," Nixon asked which was the cheaper item. Thomas replied that they cost the same and Nixon delivered his punchline: "Then change" (ibid., pp. 124–5).

This strip of social interaction exemplifies Goffman's themes. The gendered exchange involves a temporary change of footing in which small talk, with its own tone and content, is marked as a "time-out" from the official business at hand. At the end of the paper, Goffman returned to this example, suggesting that Nixon's change in footing is neither just a display about the "forces" of sexism and presidents nor just a bracketing device marking the end of a ceremony. Rather, Nixon's change in footing was an attempt to demonstrate to the press that he still retained a lively wit and a personal touch, that he was capable of being both the President and an engaging citizen. Goffman ended the paper by speculating that in this exchange Nixon actually lost his footing, because his presentation of self was too wooden and self-conscious, and that even though the members of the press laughed at the proper moment, they did so from Presidential respect and not out of admiration for the man.

Goffman leaves unanswered the question of how he could know that the press interpreted this incident in this way, suggesting only that it should be possible to identify a "structural basis" with which to analyze the cues and markers in the interaction that would confirm his interpretation. This reveals an important difference between Goffman and contemporary conversation analysts, for whom the interest is in precisely the details about which, in this example at least, Goffman only speculated.

GOFFMAN'S IMPACT

As noted above, Erving Goffman's impact on social theory has been both great and modest. The limits of Goffman's influence are evident in more than the relative absence of younger colleagues who can point to his direct mentoring. More significant is the absence of the style of research and writing that Goffman represented. The form of Goffman's work has not been easy to duplicate. In part this absence refers to the lack of attention that certain of Goffman's primary topics now receive. The analysis of behavior in public places, while it has not entirely disappeared, remains a small field, perhaps because of the perceived "triviality barrier." While creative work is conducted by contemporary scholars such as Lyn Lofland, Carol Brooks Gardner, and Spencer Cahill, the micro-examination of public life has not further developed a set of innovative and powerful concepts as was evident in Goffman's finest work. Likewise, the development of theoretical constructs, explicating the structure of interaction routines, has not advanced much beyond the dramaturgical models that Goffman proposed over a quarter century ago.

Part of these limits of Goffman's impact can be attributed to the daunting perception of his idiosyncratic brilliance. Few wish to place themselves in comparison with this master sociologist, particularly since his approach lacks an easily acquired method. How can one learn to do what Goffman did? Methodological guidelines do not exist. This has the effect of leaving the work both *sui generis* and incapable of imitation. The belief (and perhaps the reality) is that Goffman created a personalistic sociology that was virtually mimic-proof.

Yet this account of the limitations of Goffman's influence is misleading. Nearly all sociologists have been influenced by Goffman's insights. Certainly he had a profound impact in bringing micro-interactionist concerns into the mainstream of the discipline of sociology. As noted above, the important social theorists Anthony Giddens, Jürgen Habermas, Randall Collins, Jeffrey Alexander, and Pierre Bourdieu are all indebted to Goffman's writing, particularly in light of their attempts to create a "seamless" sociology that integrates societal and institutional structures with the agency of individual actors.

Other substantive arenas have also been influenced by Goffman's sensibility and analyses. Part of this importance is reflected in the increasing prominence of qualitative and ethnographic methods, as evidenced by qualitative journals and ethnographic articles in the flagship journals of the discipline. Even though Erving Goffman cannot be considered an exemplary ethnographer – his ethnographic writings were too casual (Fine and Martin, 1990) – the prominence of his writings made a claim that participant observation research could produce rich and persuasive theory. This is exemplified in Goffman's discussion of his research in the Shetland Islands, described in *The Presentation of Self*, and his more elaborate detailing of the strategies of patients in St Elizabeths hospital in *Asylums*. If these were not the most detailed or exemplary ethnographies of the period in methodological terms, they were, along with William Foote Whyte's 1943 *Street Corner Society*, the most influential and among the most widely read. Goffman demonstrated that a cogent example, coupled with a powerful turn of phrase, could encourage the sociological imagination. Further, Goffman's writing style has contributed to a loosening of the rules by which social scientists communicate (Fine, 1988; Fine and Martin, 1990). Goffman's sardonic, satiric, jokey style has served to indicate that other genres and tropes can be legitimate forms of academic writing.

In substantive arenas, Goffman's writings have had repercussions as well. Most notably, *Asylums* provided an impetus for the movement to deinstitutionalize mental patients and to eliminate the large state mental hospitals that often served as warehouses for those who stood outside of societal norms. Whether the massive deinstitutionalization of mental patients contributed to the problem of homelessness, it cannot be doubted that the movement to change the role of the mental hospital was given voice by the searing images found in Goffman's writings.

Goffman's influence is also evident in the usage that various sociologists have made of the concept of frame. The image of a frame as a means of exploring how individuals and groups come to define their environment has been particularly prevalent in the examination of social movements (Snow et al., 1986; Gamson, 1992). In this model, distinct from the usage of frame proposed by Goffman or Gregory Bateson, the actions of social movement participants depend on how they perceive the frameworks in which they are embedded. Frame represents the content of the story by which individuals and groups come to recognize their worlds. This usage does not suggest that a frame represents the kind of reality (an experiment, play, conning) that is being faced, but rather the meaning of the situation. Still, even if the definitions of frame do not accord exactly with that proposed in *Frame Analysis,* this cultural and interactional model of social movements was inspired by Goffman's writing.

Finally, we can trace the concern with the construction of meaning and the phenomenology of reality to Goffman's writings. The increase in interest in symbolic interaction and conversation analysis (the most influential offshoot of ethnomethodology) is in considerable measure an effect of Goffman's emphasis that social interaction is not a given, but is negotiated by participants (Maynard and Zimmerman, 1984; Manning and Ray, 1993). While Goffman was neither the first scholar to make this argument nor the most vigorous proponent of the position, his status as a major social theorist whose works were assigned to generations of graduate students had a unique influence. This constructionist perspective is now a taken-for-granted aspect of sociological thought, even by those whose own research is based upon the assumption that social perspectives converge sufficiently to permit statistical analysis.

VALUING GOFFMAN

This chapter is not intended to be a paean to a Goffmanian sociology. Yet we repeat, as we began, that Goffman is arguably the most significant American social theorist of the twentieth century; his work is widely read and remains capable of redirecting disciplinary thought. His unique ability to generate innovative and apt metaphors, coupled with the ability to name cogent regularities of social behavior, has provided him an important position in the sociological canon. Further, his sardonic, outsider stance has made Goffman a revered figure – an outlaw theorist who came to exemplify the best of the sociological imagination.

Although Erving Goffman's most influential work was published almost forty years ago, and he died nearly two decades ago, his analyses feel very contemporary: perhaps the first postmodern sociological theorist. Erving Goffman – and his former graduate student colleagues at the University of Chicago in the immediate postwar years – provided models that reoriented sociology. If sociology as a discipline has changed over the past several decades – and it clearly has done so dramatically – it is in considerable measure because of the directions that Erving Goffman suggested that practitioners pursue.

Acknowledgments

The authors wish to thank George Ritzer, Greg Smith, and Yves Winkin for their help in the preparation of this chapter.

Notes

1 As we note, Goffman was born in Canada, but his graduate training and employment was in the United States.

2 In an interesting empirical application of this argument, Goffman used a frame analytic perspective to analyze gender. In *Gender Advertisements* (1979) Goffman argued that some male–female rituals are best understood as a keying of parent–child rituals.

Bibliography

Writings of Erving Goffman

Some Characteristics of Response to Depicted Experience. 1949. Unpublished MA thesis, Department of Sociology, University of Chicago.

Symbols of Class Status. 1951. *British Journal of Sociology*, 11, 294–304.

On Cooling the Mark Out: Some Aspects of Adaptation to Failure. 1952. *Psychiatry*, 15(4), 451–63.
Communication Conduct in an Island Community. 1953a. Unpublished PhD dissertation, Department of Sociology, University of Chicago.
The Service Station Dealer: the Man and His Work. 1953b. Chicago: Social Research Incorporated.
The Presentation of Self in Everyday Life. 1959. New York: Anchor.
Asylums. 1961a. New York: Anchor.
Encounters: Two Studies in the Sociology of Interaction. 1961b. Indianapolis: Bobbs-Merrill.
Behavior in Public Places: Notes on the Social Organization of Gatherings. 1963a. New York: Free Press.
Stigma. 1963b. Englewood Cliffs, NJ: Prentice Hall.
The Neglected Situation. 1964. *American Anthropologist*, 66(6), 133–6.
Interaction Ritual: Essays on Face-to-face Behavior. 1967. New York: Anchor.
Strategic Interaction. 1969. Philadelphia: University of Pennsylvania Press.
Relations in Public: Microstudies of the Public Order. 1971. New York: Basic Books.
Frame Analysis: an Essay on the Organization of Experience. 1974. New York: Harper and Row.
Gender Advertisements. 1979. New York: Harper and Row.
Forms of Talk. 1981a. Philadelphia: University of Pennsylvania Press.
Reply to Denzin and Keller. 1981b. *Contemporary Sociology*, 10, 60–8.
The Interaction Order. 1983. *American Sociological Review*, 48, 1–17.
On Fieldwork. 1989. *Journal of Contemporary Ethnography*, 18(2), 123–32.

Further reading

Abbott, Andrew (1997) Of Time and Space: the Contemporary Relevance of the Chicago School. *Social Forces*, 75(4), 1149–82.
Abbott, Andrew and Graziano, Emanuel (1995) Transition and Tradition: Departmental Faculty in the Era of the Second Chicago School. In Gary Alan Fine (ed.), *The Second Chicago School?* Chicago: University of Chicago Press.
Atkinson, Paul (1989) Goffman's Poetics. *Human Studies* 12(1/2), 59–76.
Bateson, Gregory (1972) *Steps toward an Ecology of Mind*. New York: Ballantine.
Berman, Marshall (1972) Weird but Brilliant Light on the Way We Live Now. *New York Times Review of Books*, February 27, 1–2, 10, 12, 14, 16, 18.
Blumer, Herbert (1969) *Symbolic Interactionism*. Englewood Cliffs, NJ: Prentice Hall.
Brown, Richard (1977) *A Poetic for Sociology*. Cambridge: Cambridge University Press.
Bulmer, Martin (1984) *The Chicago School of Sociology*. Chicago: University of Chicago Press.
Burke, Kenneth (1969) *A Grammar of Motive*. Berkeley: University of California Press.
Burns, Tom (1992) *Erving Goffman*. London: Routledge.
Camic, Charles (1996) Three Departments in Search of a Discipline: Localism and Interdisciplinary Interaction in American Sociology, 1890–1940. *Social Research*, 62(4), 1003–33.
Chriss, James (1995) Habermas, Goffman, and Communicative Action: Implications for Professional Practice. *American Sociological Review*, 60(4), 545–65.
Clifford, James (1988) *The Predicament of Culture*. Cambridge, MA: Harvard University Press.
Clough, Patricia (1992) *The End(s) of Ethnography*. Newbury Park, CA: Sage.

Collins, Randall (1980) Erving Goffman and the Development of Modern Social Theory. In Jason Ditton (ed.), *The View From Goffman*. London: Macmillan.

Collins, Randall (1988) Theoretical Continuities in Goffman's Work. In Paul Drew and Anthony Wooton (eds), *Erving Goffman: Exploring the Interaction Order.* Cambridge: Polity Press.

Conrad, Peter and Schneider, Joseph (1980) *Deviance and Medicalization: from Badness to Sickness*. St Louis: C. V. Mosby.

Couric, Emily (1988) *The Trial Lawyers*. New York: St Martin's Press.

Davies, Christie (1989) Goffman's Concept of the Total Institution: Criticisms and Evasions. *Human Studies*, 12 (1/2), 77–95.

Delaney, William P. (1977) The Uses of the Total Institution: a Buddhist Monastic Example. In Robert Gordon and Brett Williams (eds), *Exploring Total Institutions.* Champaign, IL: Stipes.

Denzin, Norman and Keller, C. M. (1981) *Frame Analysis* Reconsidered. *Contemporary Sociology*, 10, 52–60.

Ditton, Jason (ed.) (1980) *The View from Goffman*. London: Macmillan.

Drew, Paul and Wootton, Anthony (eds) (1988) *Erving Goffman: Exploring the Interaction Order.* Cambridge: Polity Press.

Edmondson, Ricca (1984) *Rhetoric and Sociology.* London: Macmillan.

Fine, Gary Alan (1995) A Second Chicago School? The Development of a Postwar American Sociology. In Gary Alan Fine (ed.), *A Second Chicago School?* Chicago: University of Chicago Press.

Fine, Gary Alan (1996) Reputational Entrepreneurs and the Memory of Incompetence: Melting Supporters, Partisan Warriors, and Images of President Harding. *American Journal of Sociology*, 101, 1159–93.

Fine, Gary Alan and Martin, Daniel D. (1990) A Partisan View: Sarcasm, Satire and Irony as in Erving Goffman's *Asylums*. *Journal of Contemporary Ethnography*, 19(1), 89–115.

Fine, Gary Alan, Stitt, Jeffrey, and Finch, Michael (1984) Couple Tie Signs and Interpersonal Threat: a Field Experiment. *Social Psychology Quarterly*, 47, 282–6.

Fish, Stanley (1989) *Doing What Comes Naturally.* Durham, NC: Duke University Press.

Foucault, Michel (1979) *Discipline and Punish: the Birth of the Prison.* New York: Random House.

Galliher, John (1995) Chicago's Two Worlds of Deviance Research: Whose Side Are They On? In Gary Alan Fine (ed.), *The Second Chicago School?* Chicago: University of Chicago Press.

Gamson, William (1992) *Talking Politics*. Cambridge: Cambridge University Press.

Garfinkel, Harold (1967) *Studies in Ethnomethodology.* Englewood Cliffs, NJ: Prentice Hall.

Geertz, Clifford (1988) *Works and Lives: the Anthropologist as Author.* Stanford, CA: Stanford University Press.

Giddens, Anthony (1984) *The Constitution of Society.* Berkeley: University of California Press.

Giddens, Anthony (1987) *Sociology and Modern Social Theory.* Cambridge: Polity Press.

Glaser, Barney (1992) *Basics of Grounded Theory Analysis*. Mill Valley, CA: Sociology Press.

Glaser, Barney and Strauss, Anselm (1967) *The Discovery of Grounded Theory.* New York: Aldine de Gruyter.

Grimshaw, Allan (1983) Erving Goffman: a Personal Appreciation. *Language in Society*, 12(1), 147–8.

Gusfield, Joseph (1995) Preface: the Second Chicago School? In Gary Alan Fine (ed.), *A Second Chicago School?* Chicago: University of Chicago Press.

Hammersley, Martin (1992) *What's Wrong with Ethnography?* London: Routledge.

Harré, Rom (1979) *Social Being: a Theory for Social Psychology.* Oxford: Blackwell.

Heirich, Max (1970) *The Beginning: Berkeley 1964.* New York: Columbia University Press.

Hughes, Everett (1977) *The Growth of an Institution: the Chicago Real Estate Board.* Chicago: University of Chicago Press.

Hymes, Dell (1984) On Erving Goffman. *Theory and Society*, 13(5), 621–31.

Ignatieff, Michael (1983) Life at Degree Zero. *New Society*, January 20, 95–7.

Jameson, Frederic (1976) Review of Frame Analysis. *Theory and Society*, 13, 119–33.

Lopata, Helena Znaniecka (1995) Postscript. In Gary Alan Fine (ed.), *The Second Chicago School?* Chicago: University of Chicago Press.

Manning, Philip (1989) Resemblances. *History of the Human Sciences*, 2(2), 207–33.

Manning, Philip (1991) Drama as Life: the Significance of Goffman's Changing Use of the Theatrical Metaphor. *Sociological Theory*, 9(1), 70–86.

Manning, Philip (1992) *Erving Goffman and Modern Sociology.* Stanford, CA: Stanford University Press.

Manning, Philip (1998) Ethnographic Coats and Tents. In Gregory Smith (ed.), *Goffman's Patrimony: Studies in a Sociological Legacy.* London: Routledge

Manning, Philip and Ray, George (1993) Shyness, Self-confidence and Social Interaction. *Social Psychology Quarterly*, 56(3), 178–92.

Marx, Gary (1984) Role Models and Role Distance: a Remembrance of Erving Goffman. *Theory and Society*, 13(5), 649–62.

Platt, Jennifer (1994) The Chicago School and Firsthand Data. *History of the Human Sciences*, 7(1), 57–80.

Platt, Jennifer (1995) Research Methods and the Second Chicago School. In Gary Alan Fine (ed.), *The Second Chicago School?* Chicago: University of Chicago Press.

Schegloff, Emanuel (1996) Confirming Allusions: toward an Empirical Account of Action. *American Journal of Sociology*, 102, 161–216.

Smith, Gregory (1989) A Simmelian Reading of Goffman. Unpublished PhD dissertation, Department of Sociology, University of Salford, England.

Smith, Gregory (1993) Chrysalid Goffman. Unpublished manuscript.

Smith, Gregory (1994) Snapshots "Sub Specie Aeternitatis": Simmel, Goffman and Formal Sociology. In David Frisby (ed.), *Georg Simmel: Critical Assessments, volume 3.* New York: Routledge.

Smith, Gregory and Travers, Andrew (1998) Goffman's Project and Program: Framing a Sociological Legacy. Unpublished manuscript.

Snow, David A. and Davis, Philip W. (1995) The Chicago Approach to Collective Behavior. In Gary Alan Fine (ed.), *The Second Chicago School?* Chicago: University of Chicago Press.

Snow, David A., Rochford Jr, E. Burke, Worden, Steven K., and Benford, Robert D. (1986) Frame Alignment Processes, Micromobilization and Movement Participation. *American Sociological Review*, 51, 464–81.

Strauss, Anselm and Juliet, Corbin (1990) *Basics of Qualitative Research.* Newbury Park, CA: Sage.

Turner, Ralph (1968) The Self-conception in Social Interaction. In Chad Gordon and Kenneth Gergen (eds), *The Self in Social Interaction.* New York: Wiley.

Verhoeven, J. C. (1993) An Interview with Erving Goffman. *Research Language and Social Interaction*, 26(3), 317–48.

Von Neuman, John and Morgenstern, Oskar (1944) *Theory of Games and Economic Behavior*. Princeton, NJ: Princeton University Press.
Wacker, R. Fred (1995) The Sociology of Race and Ethnicity in the Second Chicago School. In Gary Alan Fine (ed.), *The Second Chicago School?* Chicago: University of Chicago Press.
Warner, W. Lloyd and Henry, W. E. (1948) The Radio Day-time Serial: a Symbolic Analysis. *Genetic Psychology Monograph*, 37.
Weber, Max (1949) *The Methodology of the Social Sciences*. New York: Free Press.
Williams, Robin (1980) Goffman's Sociology of Talk. In Jason Ditton (ed.), *The View from Goffman*. London: Macmillan.
Williams, Robin (1988) Understanding Goffman's Methods. In Paul Drew and Anthony Wootton (eds), *Erving Goffman: Exploring the Interaction Order*. Cambridge: Polity Press.
Willis, Paul (1977) *Learning to Labor*. New York: Columbia University Press.
Winkin, Yves (1988) *Erving Goffman: Les Moments et Leurs Hommes*. Paris: Minuit.
Winkin, Yves (1998) Erving Goffman: What Is a Life? In Gregory Smith (ed.), *Goffman's Patrimony: Studies in a Sociological Legacy*. London: Routledge.
Winkin, Yves (1999) Erving Goffman: a Biography. Unpublished manuscript.

3

Richard M. Emerson

Karen S. Cook and Joseph Whitmeyer

The Person

Growing up in Utah within the confines of Mormon culture and community at the base of snow-capped mountains exerted a profound, but little acknowledged, influence on the life and work of Richard Marc Emerson. The mountains he seemed to have always loved were his escape from the closed and somewhat stifling nature of the town in which he was raised. Two themes that emerged subsequently in his work as a sociologist can be traced to these roots: (a) the idea that dependence upon another (or a group) grants them power over you; (b) the notion that the very uncertainty of success brings its own form of motivation. In many ways he was also drawn eventually to sociology by his deep personal understanding of the role of norms, community pressure, hierarchical power relations, and what being an outsider meant in a close-knit town. The lure of the mountains that took hold at a very early age also fed his sociological imagination, and he became an astute first-hand observer of group performance under stressful situations as he joined many mountaineering expeditions during his career, including the first successful American attempt to climb Mount Everest in 1963.

During the last few years of his life he and his wife, Pat, who had studied anthropology and South East Asia, made many trips to Pakistan to live with and study the remote mountain villages to which their treks and mountain expeditions had taken them over the years. Having lost a son, Marc, at the age of 17 in a tragic mountain climbing accident, Dick and Pat had returned on a sabbatical to the mountains of Pakistan to come to terms with their loss and to gain the support of the mountain people they had come to love. In their joint work and in some of his final papers Emerson examined more deeply the nature of these communities, their historical roots as outposts of the vast English empire, and the authority and power relations that had defined these communities in relation to the emergent nation state over time.

A web of intricate social and organizational arrangements made each expedition into the remote mountain villages of Pakistan a job of enormous proportions, especially for lengthy sojourns. Such challenges engaged the full range of talents and skills of Richard Emerson, from the academic and intellectual to the intensely physical. As a member of the elite mountaineering company of the Army during the Second World War, he was able to advance the considerable technical skills he had begun to develop in the mountains of Utah and Wyoming during his youth. He completed his undergraduate degree in sociology with a minor in philosophy at the University of Utah. Later he did graduate work at the University of Minnesota, where he received his MA in 1952 and his PhD in 1955. He was admitted for graduate training at both Harvard and Berkeley, but neither offered the financial assistance that Minnesota did. His master's thesis was entitled " Deviation and Rejection: an Experimental Replication," and was co-directed by Don Martindale, his advisor in sociology, and Stanley Schachter, then a faculty member in psychology at the University of Minnesota.

He was trained in both sociology and psychology, and his PhD thesis was an extensive field and experimental study of the determinants of social influence in face-to-face groups. The field study included an investigation of boy scout troops in what was to be one of his few empirical examinations of social influence outside of the laboratory. Perhaps it was precisely because of the difficulties of collecting data on these boy scouts that he returned to the more controlled environment of the experimental laboratory in much of his subsequent empirical work.

Another significant empirical adventure came when he stepped out of the lab into the "real world" to study social influence, though this time it was to conduct a unique study of group performance among mountain climbers on the 1963 Everest expedition. This research was supported by a National Science Foundation grant entitled "Communication Feedback in Groups under Stress." During this historic expedition, Dick Emerson, one of the strongest team members physically, also served as a field researcher, conducting both experimental and observational research on his colleagues during what amounted to highly complex maneuvers, often at very high altitudes. His mountain climbing friends still complain about the journals they had to keep and even more about the negative feedback they received (in one condition), often during a difficult traverse or climbing exercise. For this unusual and pathbreaking work Richard Emerson received the Hubbard Medal on behalf of the National Geographic Society. The medal was awarded to him at the White House by President Kennedy in 1963 upon his return to the United States from the expedition.

While many academics of his generation moved around during their careers, Emerson served only two institutions during his lifetime. His first job was at the University of Cincinnati, where he joined the faculty in 1955 and was awarded tenure in 1957. He left Cincinnati in 1965 to become a member of the Sociology Department at the University of Washington. His Seattle home overlooked the

Cascade Mountains, where he often climbed with friends and colleagues, the same mountains that later claimed the life of his teenage son. It was at the University of Washington that he completed his first major theoretical papers on social exchange theory, written in 1967 and later published (1972) in a volume on sociological theories in progress. While this work came to fruition at the University of Washington, the earliest seeds of the theory were evident in his PhD thesis and in two of his most influential pieces, on power–dependence relations, published in 1962 and 1964, just before he left the University of Cincinnati. The 1962 paper, entitled "Power–Dependence Relations," became a citation classic in 1981 due to its enormous influence. We trace some of the influence of this work on the social sciences in the section on the intellectual impact of his work.

The tragedy of his life, which began with the death of his son, Marc, followed him throughout his life. He and Pat endured the loss of friends and loved ones, most associated with the tight-knit community of mountain climbers in the Pacific Northwest or with their friends in the remote villages of Pakistan, where the deaths of sherpas were common, but never easy to accept. Willie Unsoeld, close friend, fellow mountaineer, and colleague at the Evergreen State University in Washington, was killed in an avalanche on Mount Rainier. The Unsoelds lost a daughter, Devi, to the mountains and had endured the long recovery of a son who received serious head injuries from a fall while mountain climbing. Despite the certainty of tragedy in the lives of mountain climbers, Emerson continued to climb until his untimely death in 1982. In fact, during the last year of his life he was deeply engaged in planning for a return trip to Pakistan for a long sojourn in remote mountain villages with his wife. In many ways he was just reaching the peak of his career when he died suddenly on the evening before his daughter, Leslie, was to be married in their living room, with the Cascades looming in the background. Cancer surgery a year earlier had taken its toll, but his death was unexpected.

For a career cut short by premature death, the impact of his work can be judged as even more impressive. His collaborative work with Karen Cook at the University of Washington was just beginning to show fruits, and the graduate students they jointly trained, including Mary Gillmore and Toshio Yamagishi, among others, were just beginning their research careers. It is clear that the impact of his work in the social sciences would have been even greater if he had not died in his late fifties.

One gets a clear image of the heart and soul of Richard Emerson in a passage he wrote in the early stages of his career for a book entitled *The New Professors*, by Bowen (1960). In this chapter he writes about his love of mountains:

> Some of the things I appreciate most for sheer beauty are high alpine mountains, their winding valley glaciers, and foreboding corniced ridges. I love to feel them beneath my feet, when climbing, as well as view them as a painter might. . . . As I ascend the mountain, I can . . . read from its contours its past and its future, and my climb is placed in grand context. In fact, through the whole experience I am placed in context! And, mind you, people ask me why I climb mountains.

If he had not become a sociologist, he would have become a sculptor, he once admitted. But, whatever his chosen vocation, he would have never given up the mountains he loved and that had been the primary source of his self-worth even as a child.

In this chapter we focus on his academic work and its impact. For the record, he was also a formidable photographer, whose stark photos of sheer mountain ridges, snow-capped peaks at the top of the world, and close-up shots of the mountain people he loved and their villages are mainly unpublished, except for some that appear in various Sierra Club publications. This black and white legacy of unique pictures that chronicle various expeditions and social reality in remote locations may one day also prove to be a significant contribution to social science. Several of these photos hang in the Commons Room in the Department of Sociology at the University of Washington. Before discussing more fully the impact of his scholarly work, we will comment briefly on the social and intellectual context which influenced both the style and content of his research.

THE SOCIAL AND INTELLECTUAL CONTEXT

Richard Emerson was one of the large number of men who entered academia after the Second World War, supported by the GI Bill, and many in this cohort of scholars are now retiring. As with most of his contemporaries, his graduate training was influenced by the Second World War and the research that had been funded during and following the war. As Cartwright (1979) notes in his review of the development of the field of social psychology, the Second World War had an enormous impact upon the social sciences as researchers attempted to come to terms with the rise of Hitler and the events that precipitated the war. Common topics of research were authoritarianism, styles of leadership, group solidarity, loyalty, conformity and obedience, nationalism, and power. Emerson was influenced by these trends in his own graduate training, which spanned the disciplines of sociology and psychology. In his early career he studied leadership and social influence.

While at the University of Cincinnati he was jointly an assistant professor of sociology and a senior research associate in psychiatry, where he collaborated on a variety of projects on family relations. In this role he developed the Cincinnati Family Relations Inventory. He also participated with many other influential social psychologists in the leadership training that was offered at the National Training Laboratory at Bethel, Maine. Here he was trained not only in the science of leadership, but also in the practice of developing leadership skills. This laboratory was established with funding after the war to determine the factors that promoted the development in society of good leadership. In part, all these efforts nationwide were derivative of the deep political concerns that had emerged during the war over the rise of Hitler, a man who was able to lead a nation to tolerate genocide in the name of nationalism.

For over two decades after the Second World War, the field of social psychology can be said to have been in its heyday. Funding poured into universities, research and training centers in order to produce a science of human behavior and social dynamics. Much of the funding came from military-related sources like ARPA and the Navy (ONR). NIMH and NSF were also strong funding sources for social science of this type. This stream of research carried the academics trained right after the war through the early stages of their careers, which coincided with the expansion of university education in the United States. During the 1950s and 1960s most universities and colleges were in expansionist mode and departments hired many of the PhDs that had been produced as a result of the GI Bill and other efforts to induce students to obtain graduate degrees and become college teachers. This growth was also fueled by the need to educate the "baby-boom" children, the largest cohorts of children the United States had known. The earliest boomers, born just after the war in 1946 and later, began entering higher education in the early 1960s. Emerson's career spanned these events.

Another significant component of the social/intellectual context in which Emerson's work was carried out was the strong emphasis upon sociology as a science and social psychology, in particular, as a scientific subdiscipline. Logical positivism was making inroads into the social sciences in the late 1950s and the early 1960s, with the rising popularity in some sociological circles of the work of Popper (1961), Kuhn (1963), Hempel (1965), and others. This work emphasized the general theoretical strategy of deductive theorizing, the formulation of abstract theoretical principles that could be used along with clearly defined concepts to derive predictions that could be tested empirically. Emerson's training in sociological theory and experimental work in psychology made this form of theory development natural for him. It is most evident in his major theoretical pieces, "Exchange Theory, Parts I and II," written in 1967 and published subsequently in 1972. This formulation is described in greater detail in the section below. Here we will comment only on the general intellectual climate in the social sciences that influenced his work at the time this work was produced. Of course, not all sociologists trained during this same time frame were drawn to deductive theorizing.

Other more specialized influences on his substantive work can be traced to his mentors and the work of his colleagues at Cincinnati and Washington. At Minnesota, Martindale introduced Richard Emerson to general sociological theory and the significant philosophy of social science debates of the time. Stanley Schachter, one of his MA thesis advisors, trained him in experimental methods and the empirical investigation of hypotheses derived from theoretical propositions. As mentioned above, he also worked at Cincinnati on the development of various tools for empirically investigating family relations (i.e. the inventory and computer-based scoring system he helped to develop), and here he was exposed to small groups and leadership training. His contacts with social scientists outside of sociology at the University of Cincinnati were also influential in the development of his theoretical work on power. Alfred Kuhn, an economist at the University of Cincinnati, once informed Karen Cook that he and Richard Emerson had had many productive conversations about theoretical work in the social sciences, the philosophy of science, and general theories of power and exchange as colleagues. Kuhn's major work, *The Study of Society: a Unified Approach*, published in 1963, gives evidence of this cross-fertilization.

At the University of Washington, Emerson was influenced by his colleagues in the sociology department, especially those who were involved with him in the social psychology program, one of the most nationally visible programs in this subfield. The faculty involved with this program included Frank Miyamoto, Otto Larsen, Phillip Blumstein, Robert Leik, David Schmitt, and Robert Burgess. Long conversations over coffee about behaviorism with Bob Burgess and Dave Schmitt drew Emerson's attention to the developments in the empirical investigation of human behavior from a behaviorist perspective. During the 1960s behaviorism was growing as a result of the influence of B. F. Skinner (see especially *About Behaviorism*, 1974) and others who were charismatic and very optimistic about the development of a science of behavior. This theoretical development coincided with the growth of interest in the philosophy of social science and with the debate over the importation of natural science models and modes of theorizing into the social sciences. Together, these developments generated widespread optimism in the potential for producing a science of human behavior. It was against this backdrop that Emerson formulated his own theory of social behavior while at the University of Washington.

Certainly Homans was the first social exchange theorist to explore the implications of behaviorism for the study of social interaction, but Emerson is noted for his more extensive treatment of behaviorism as the natural foundation for a theory of social exchange. These principles were spelled out in his chapter entitled, "Exchange Theory, Part I. A Psychological Basis for Social Exchange." This piece reflects both the formal deductive theorizing he had come to value and his attempt to provide a more developed micro-level theory of behavior based on the scientific principles of behavior being produced at that time by behaviorists like his colleague Robert Burgess. This informal influence, noted in a footnote in Emerson's chapter, was more formally acknowledged in a paper published by Emerson in a collection of readings on human social behavior edited by Burgess and Bushell (1969). Burgess and Emerson also co-taught for a while the undergraduate lecture class on social psychology at the University of Washington, which stimulated further cross-fertilization of ideas.

In 1972, Karen Cook joined the Department of Sociology at the University of Washington, attracted to the department by the strength of the social psychology program and the opportunity to work with Richard Emerson, whose work she had been exposed to in her own graduate training at Stanford University, where she was influenced by mentors Joseph Berger, Bernard P. Cohen and Morris Zelditch, who also emphasized training in formal theory, deductive models, and experimental methods. In 1973, Cook and Emerson collaborated in the development of a long-term program of research funded by the National Science Foundation to empirically test propositions derived from Emerson's theory of social exchange, focusing special attention upon the development of a theory of the distribution of power in exchange networks. In addition, Cook and Emerson developed the first computer-based laboratory in sociology for the study of social exchange. This work is described more fully in the theory section. This fruitful collaboration continued until Emerson's death in 1982. Karen Cook continued this program of research with the help of several former students and collaborators, including Mary Gillmore (University of Washington), Toshio Yamagishi (Hokkaido University), Karen A. Hegtvedt (Emory), and, more recently, Jodi O'Brien (Seattle University), Peter Kollock (UCLA), and Joseph Whitmeyer (University of North Carolina-Charlotte).

The collaboration with Karen Cook led to the introduction of more cognitive concepts to the theory of social exchange that Emerson had developed, and a gradual move away from the behavioristic model that had been the hallmark of his original theoretical work. In addition, her work on equity and distributive justice influenced the research by introducing into their joint theoretical work concerns over fairness and equity, returning to some of the normative aspects of social exchange addressed only briefly by Homans and more extensively by Blau. The more behavioral formulation has been subsequently developed and advanced significantly by the work of Linda Molm, trained at the University of North Carolina, primarily by Jim Wiggins, a behaviorist. She has developed a systematic theory of exchange based explicitly upon the behavioral principles originally developed by Emerson, and in a very intensive program of experimental research she has explored the use of power in what she terms "non-negotiated" exchanges. In the development of social exchange theory it is clear that social networks linking the investigators and their collaborators and students have had significant influence. A more complete analysis of the ties among the various actors who subsequently developed Emerson's work is beyond the scope of this chapter. However, it is important to acknowledge that a large part of the social and intellectual context in which a theorist works is social relations, including those with colleagues and students who influence his or her work.

Jonathan Turner (1986) has done a nice job of articulating the specific nature of Emerson's contributions and the intellectual significance of his landmark pieces on power–dependence relations (1962, 1964) and social exchange theory (1972, parts I and II). In his evaluation of exchange theory in the late 1980s Turner argued that Emerson had resolved one of the key difficulties in developing exchange theory to apply across levels of analysis, with the introduction of the idea of connected exchange relations forming networks of exchange. For Turner, this obviated the need to develop ever more complex conceptions of exchange as the nature of the social unit shifted from an individual to a group, organization, or larger social system. In Emerson's theory the "actors" could be individuals or corporate actors involved in networks of exchange (see Cook and Whitmeyer, 1992).

THE THEORY

Scientists know that, no matter how brilliant their theories, no matter how accurate their explanations, eventually their work will be improved upon and even superseded, no longer consulted directly. The most important scientists have impact not so much through the particular content of their theories, but through changing other scientists' perspectives. They introduce new concepts or reconceptualize old ones in new ways. They fashion new perspectives or ways of looking at familiar phenomena, raising a host of new questions which lead to the rapid development of new theoretical formulations. Their legacy is an approach, concepts, questions.

Richard Emerson is such a scientist, and he contributed much in the way of theory and explanations, but, even more importantly, presented a new way of conceiving and studying an old concept, social power. His approach to social power and social exchange has led to a large program of research and theory development within sociology, and at the same time has informed and enhanced analysis in a variety of substantive areas of social science. Of his specific theoretical formulations, some are still used, some have been modified, and some have been superseded. However, his approach will always be an essential part of social theory.

Emerson's legacy to social theory can be divided into three areas: theoretical approach, theoretical substance, and methodological approach. As with most scientists, during his life he and his collaborators and colleagues were occupied primarily with the second of these, theoretical substance. He worked to develop theories that offered explanations for particular social phenomena, to test these theoretical formulations, and to improve them, based on empirical research. However, in retrospect his legacy in the other two areas has been equally important. Naturally, these three areas – approach, substance, and methodology – are intertwined in his work, and so they are in our description of it.

Emerson's most important contribution is his approach to social power. This approach is distinctive for several reasons. First, he believed that power could be quantified and measured and thus analyzed rigorously, even mathematically. As a result, his analytic theory of power could be tested through experiments. Second, he argued that a theory of power must be based on a conception of the nature of the social relations in which power is embedded. Third, the theory of power should include a behavioral model of the actor. These features of his perspective can be applied more generally than just to social power, but are key to Emerson's approach to power.

Social power is a useful concept. It has been employed by major social thinkers for centuries: Machiavelli, Marx, and Weber, to name just three. Lay people commonly use the term to explain certain social outcomes, whether on the scale of countries or within small informal groups. Nevertheless, its scientific use had been hampered by its lack of formalization and quantification. George Homans, co-pioneer with Peter Blau and Richard Emerson of the exchange perspective in sociology, also discussed power in a deductive framework. However, Emerson took the crucial step of defining power as a quantifiable, measurable concept. This had two beneficial consequences. Theory could become formal and mathematical, with a gain in precision and power over purely verbal reasoning and deduction. In addition, empirical measures of power could be devised so that theoretical inferences could be tested.

The step of formalizing social power was taken in Emerson's 1962 article, "Power–Dependence Relations." The power of actor *A* over actor *B* is equated to the dependence of actor *B* on actor *A*:

$$Pab = Dba \tag{1}$$

The dependence of *B* on *A* in turn is a positive function of the "motivational investment" of *B* in "goals mediated by" *A* and a negative function of the "availability of those goals" to *B* outside the *A–B* relation (Emerson, 1962, p. 32). In this early work, it appears that Emerson takes equation (1) to be a theoretical postulate, with power and dependence considered as at least conceptually distinct, rather than as a definition of power. The fact that Emerson (1964) experimentally tests this equation suggests this as well. However, by 1972, apparently Emerson considered equation (1) to be a *definition* of power ("*Power* is redundant and unnecessary in this scheme, given our conception of dependence"; Emerson, 1972, p. 64). Some subsequent researchers, such as Pfeffer and Salancik (1978) and Molm (1997), likewise have taken equation (1) to be a definition and a measure of power.

Two crucial aspects of equation (1) are that power is a property of a *relation* and that power is a *potential*. A more precise way of stating the first aspect is that an actor's power is not simply a property of that actor, but rather it has a referent, namely the other actor. The second aspect means that power exists prior to behavior and behavioral outcomes. It can therefore affect those outcomes. Moreover, power itself can be affected by other factors, such as aspects of social structure and characteristics of the actors (status, gender, etc.). The analysis of what causes and affects power is separate from and analytically prior to analysis of how power and other factors affect behavior.

An important and influential part of Emerson's power–dependence theory is his identification of *balancing operations*. He calls an exchange relation in which power (and dependence) is unequal *unbalanced*. Then, in view of the two variables that affect dependence, Emerson suggests four possible balancing operations; that is, processes that will make power more equal in unbalanced relations. Suppose *A* is more powerful than *B*; that is, $Pab > Pba$ and $Dba > Dab$. To balance this relation: (a) *B* can reduce the level of motivational investment in goals mediated by *A* ("withdrawal"); (b) *B* can come up with alternative sources (e.g. actor C) for those goals mediated by *A* ("network extension"); (c) *B* can attempt to increase *A*'s motivational investment in goals *B* mediates (e.g. through "status-giving"); and/or (d) *B* can work to eliminate *A*'s alternative sources for the goals *B* mediates (e.g. by engaging in coalition formation with other actors, in particular, other suppliers).

It should be noted that Emerson's approach to social power as developed in his 1972 theoretical formulation entails conceiving of social interaction as exchange. Thus this theory falls into two traditions in social science, the study of social power and what is sometimes called exchange theory. In fact, Emerson terms his general approach *social exchange theory*. As Emerson (1972, p. 39) notes, "My initial reason for beginning the work set forth in these two chapters was to formulate a more encompassing (and hopefully enriching) framework around previous work on power–dependence relations."

Emerson then took the methodological step, largely unprecedented in sociology for research on social power, of testing his theoretical propositions with laboratory experiments using human subjects. Such experiments test theory by testing hypotheses derived from the theory for the particular conditions of the laboratory experiment. Laboratory experiments may not be suitable for testing explanations of naturally occurring phenomena (for development of this argument see Zelditch, 1969). However, just as in the physical sciences, they are ideal for *theory*-testing because factors exogenous to the theory can be controlled. Support for hypotheses derived from theoretical principles for specific experimental conditions usually provides unambiguous support for those principles. This is difficult to achieve outside the laboratory, since social processes are rarely isolated in any social context, and thus findings obtained using other methodologies often have alternative interpretations or somewhat ambiguous meaning. (Of course, this can also happen in poorly designed experimental studies.)

Experimental tests of power–dependence theory were possible for two reasons. First, the mathematical definition of dependence allowed it to be created and measured in the laboratory. Second, by conceiving of social interaction as exchange, it was possible to test the theoretical propositions by creating a setting for exchange through experimental design. The theory explicitly applies to exchange with reference to any goals or resources. Thus, experimentally convenient exchange could be used (see also Molm, 1997, on this point). Emerson published his first experimental tests supporting power–dependence theory in 1964.

In a two-part work written in 1967, but published only in 1972, Emerson builds his social exchange theory by extending his analysis of power and dependence in exchange relations in two directions. Part I presents a basis in behavioral psychology for power–dependence theory. In his earlier work, Emerson did little more than assert the relationship between dependence and motivational investment in mediated goals and the availability of alternatives, respectively. Here he derives those relationships from the principles of behaviorism.

"Exchange Theory, Part II: Exchange Relations and Network Structures" contains the crucial extension from exchange relations to exchange networks that is the basis for most of the remaining work of his career. A few definitions are important. An exchange relation is conceived in part I as a "temporal series" containing opportunities for exchange, which, he argued, evoked initiations of exchange that in turn produced or resulted in transactions. An *exchange network* is a set of actors linked together directly or indirectly through exchange relations. An actor is then conceived as "a point where many exchange relations connect" (Emerson, 1972, p. 57). More specifically, two exchange relations between actors *A* and *B* (represented as *A–B*) and between actors *B* and *C* (*B–C*) are *connected* at actor *B* if they share actor *B* and if transactions in one relation are somehow related to transactions in the other relation. Note that this is a specialized definition: a connection exists not between actors but between exchange relations. A connection between two exchange relations is either *positive* or *negative*. Suppose two exchange relations are connected. If exchange in one relation is positively related, in frequency or magnitude, to exchange in the other relation, the connection is *positive*. In this case if *A–B* and *B–C* are positively connected exchange relations, for example, an increase in the frequency of *A–B* exchange could result in an increase in the frequency of *B–C* exchange. If exchange in one relation is negatively related, in frequency or magnitude, to exchange in the other relation, the connection is *negative*. In the case in which the *A–B* and *B–C* relations are negatively connected, an increase in the frequency of *A–B* exchange could result in a decrease in the frequency of *B–C* exchange. An example is the situation in which *A* and *C* are alternative dating partners for *B*. Finally, a negatively connected exchange network is *intracategory* if the resources any network member provides could substitute for the resources any other network member provides (such as friendship in a friendship network). A negatively connected network that is not intracategory is *cross-category* (such as a network of heterosexually dating people).

Ironically, given current developments, Emerson considered a move toward economic theory as the basis for his version of exchange theory, which was the strategy Blau had adopted, but he dismissed this idea by arguing that operant psychology provided a more "social" micro-level basis for the theory. The primary reason was that he viewed the social relation as the major focus of the theory (and the social structures created through the formation of exchange relations). That is, the focus was the relatively enduring interactions between particular actors rather than what he viewed as the dominant focus in economics, the transaction in which actors were perfectly interchangeable.This fit with the primary task of developing an approach in which social structure was the major dependent variable. In part I, Emerson (1972, p. 41) states clearly that his purpose is to "address social structure and structural change within the framework of exchange theory."

Before presenting descriptions of what he termed prototypical exchange network structures, Emerson developed several key concepts which define the factors that are significant in understanding exchange relations. These include reciprocity, balance, cohesion, power and power-balancing operations. Reciprocity, for Emerson, was little more than a description of the contingencies intrinsic to all human social exchange, not an explanation. Norms of obligation emerge to reinforce this feature of social exchange, but they are not necessary as an explanation of continued exchange. The reinforcement principles and their link to initiation of exchange provide sufficient explanation for the continuity or extinction of exchange relations in this framework. Balance in an exchange relation is reflected in any difference in initiation probabilities. An exchange relation is balanced if $Dab = Dba$. That is, the relation is balanced if both parties are equally dependent upon the other for exchange (i.e. for resources of value). The concept balance is critical, since it sets the stage for understanding the "balancing operations" Emerson develops to explain changes in exchange relations and networks.

Cohesion represents the "strength" of the exchange relation or its propensity to survive conflict and the costs associated with the impact of what Emerson calls "external events." Relational cohesion is represented in the 1972 chapters as the average dependence of the two actors in the relation. Subsequently, Molm (1985) and others (e.g. Lawler et al., 1988) have come to refer to this concept as average total power (or simply total power). The concept represents how much is at stake in the relation (not the relative power of each actor within the exchange relation, which is treated separately in further developments in the theory). Power is defined straightforwardly in this work as based on dependence, as indicated above, and this definition becomes the basis for specifying the various possible "balancing operations" available to actors in imbalanced exchange relations.

To conclude the 1972 work, Emerson uses these definitions together with the theoretical apparatus he has built involving power, dependence, and balancing processes to predict changes in exchange networks. Examples are as follows. Actors who are weak because they are rivals in a negatively connected network will tend either to specialize or to form a coalition. If they specialize they develop what is effectively a new division of labor. If they form a coalition they have merged to form a "collective actor" in the network, which then must operate as one. Intracategory exchange networks (or networks in which only one dominant type of resource is exchanged, such as approval) will tend to change until they are closed, meaning that social circles get formed and the boundaries are maintained. Such closed social circles, like socially exclusive clubs, are often difficult for new members to penetrate. Under certain circumstances, intracategory networks will tend to become stratified, with closed classes. Here Emerson's theory becomes quite speculative in an effort to examine how networks become stratified, forming classes differentiated by resource magnitude. Both intraclass exchange and interclass exchange are investigated as elements in the emergence of stratified exchange networks. Tentative theoretical principles are developed to explain, for example, the tendency for initiations to "flow upward" in interclass exchange and for transactions within such relations to be initiated from above. Many of these theoretical insights embedded in the text of part II of Emerson's formulation have never been fully developed theoretically or investigated empirically, nor have the rudimentary notions of norm formation and groups as exchange systems been elaborated (an exception is the work of Stolte, 1987).

In 1978 and 1983, Emerson and his colleague Karen Cook, together with former students Mary Gillmore and Toshio Yamagishi in the case of the 1983 paper, published two papers that extend the theory to the analysis of exchange networks and present experimental tests of those extensions (Cook and Emerson, 1978; Cook et al., 1983). From power–dependence theory it follows that, all else being equal, actors who have more alternatives for obtaining their goals will be less dependent on individual partners and thus have more power. Thus, in a negatively connected network, actors who have more partners with whom they can engage in full exchange will have more power. Theoretically, in such cases access to alternatives increases the availability of the resources of value (or goals to be obtained through exchange).

Assuming that to have power is to use it (Emerson, 1972), this proposition can be tested by measuring power use. Use of power in an exchange relation entails obtaining terms of exchange more favorable to oneself. Therefore, the more powerful actor in an exchange relation should obtain more favorable terms of exchange. Exchange as operationalized in the 1978 and 1983 experiments consists of negotiating the terms of trade between two parties (or more) for resources of value which are converted into monetary payoffs at the end of the experiment. Assuming actors use their power, the more powerful actor in an exchange relation should obtain a larger share of the valuable resources to be exchanged; that is, receive more points than the partner.

The two experiments in the 1978 paper involve four-actor, fully linked networks. That is, each actor has exchange opportunities with the other three. In the experiment on the balanced network, all linked pairs were equivalent: all could obtain resources of similar value in exchanges with their trading partners (i.e. no actor had resources of greater value than the others). In the experiment on the unbalanced network one of the four actors offered a more valuable resource and thus was the more desirable exchange partner (the transaction was worth a total of 24 units of profit); exchanges between the other actors proffered resources of similar, but lower, value (these transactions were worth a total of eight units of profit). In the unbalanced network, the actor with the more valuable resource was the best alternative for each of his or her partners, thus giving that actor the most power according to the theory. This prediction was supported. Not only did the powerful actor gain significantly more points than his or her partners, but he or she also gained significantly more points than any of the positionally equivalent actors in the balanced network.

The 1983 article is a natural extension of the theory to larger networks, but at the same time enters a new domain. In the 1978 article, the four-actor exchange network was simply the context for tests of predictions from power–dependence theory. In the 1983 article, network structure has become an interesting factor in its own right. The network studied consists of five actors, no longer fully linked, but linked in a ring, so that each actor has only two potential trading partners (see figure 3.1). One of the five exchange relations is not very profitable (the transaction total is worth only eight points, as opposed to a total of 24 units of profit in each of the other four potential trading relations). If we ignore that low-profitability relation (which connects F_1 and F_2), we have a line (sometimes called "Line 5") of five actors and four exchange relations, F_1–E_1–D_1–E_2–F_2. Previous theory on social networks had supposed that positional centrality in a network confers the most power, and thus that D_1 would be most powerful. However, the authors of this study use power–dependence theory to predict that if such a network is negatively connected, actors E_1 and E_2 will emerge as the most powerful actors.

The power–dependence reasoning is as follows. In each exchange relation, a partner with no alternatives will be more dependent and therefore less powerful than a partner with more alternatives (or technically a greater availability of resources). Thus, the *F*s will be less powerful than the *E*s. D_1 has two alternatives, but since they have weak alternatives from whom they can obtain favorable outcomes, D_1 is more dependent on them than they are on D_1. As a

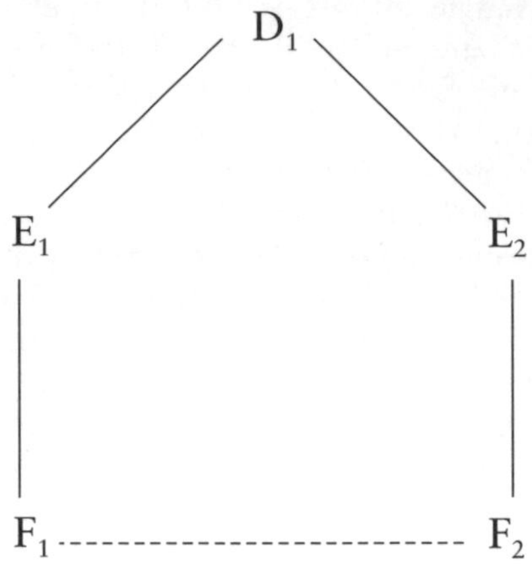

Figure 3.1

result, D_1 is forced to reduce offers (or demands) down to the level of the *F*s in order to compete. Experimental results supported these general hypotheses.

Note that, as is common in scientific investigation, the experiments reported in the 1978 and 1983 articles were designed to provide clear tests of theory, not to be instances of substantively important exchange phenomena. As a result, many of the substantive features of these experiments are not theoretically crucial. They are operationalizations of theoretical concepts, for which theory therefore makes predictions, which in turn can be evaluated as tests of theory. Thus, exchange is operationalized as coming to agreement on a trade of resources (or profit points); "motivational investment" is operationalized as conversion of points to money (at a constant rate); and negativity is operationalized by allowing each actor only one exchange per round. Many of these aspects of experimental design are not common in natural situations (e.g. one exchange per round), but they instantiate the theoretical concepts in ways easy to control and measure, and therefore permit clear tests of the theory. Thus tested and supported, the theory can then be applied to more complicated natural situations of exchange and exchange networks.

The 1983 paper also inaugurated two general trends in research on exchange networks. First, it presents computer simulation results for four networks: the Line 5, and networks with seven, ten, and thirteen actors. Note again that in order to test the theory of exchange networks, exchange network experiments are designed to focus actors on a single goal: profit maximization. It is easy to embody this goal in simulations by incorporating simple procedures by which simulated actors pursue it. Simulations can thus show whether many actors simultaneously following these procedures produce the results that the theory of exchange networks predicts. Simulation results will thus be valid to the extent that the incorporated procedures match those followed by natural actors.

Second, the paper presents an algorithm for determining the distribution of power in a negatively connected exchange network directly from the network structure. This algorithm is grounded loosely in power–dependence theory. However, application of the algorithm involves only analysis of the network structure and does not use power–dependence theory or models of actor behavior explicitly. This particular algorithm quickly came to be perceived as inadequate. However, many researchers have followed the lead of this paper in seeing it as desirable to have such a structural-level algorithm, and have devised others (see the section on impact for citations to this work).

Emerson's last paper, which he did not complete but which was published in 1987 in an incomplete state, is entitled "Toward a Theory of Value in Social Exchange." However, as he notes and italicizes, "A theory of value must be a theory of actors" (Emerson, 1987, p. 14). This paper attempts to present a more complete model of the (human) actor than that used in his theoretical work of 1962 and 1972. Here he is filling in important remaining lacunae in those theories, just as in his 1972 work he went back and filled in a deductive basis for his 1962 work on power–dependence theory.

Value – that is, the relative importance actors place (behaviorally) on obtaining certain goals or resources – is crucial to both power–dependence theory and its extension into the theory of exchange networks. For example, the first and third of the four balancing operations in a relationship of unequal dependence involve changes of value. Suppose *B* is more dependent on *A* than the reverse. *B* can decrease the value of the goals *A* mediates or attempt to increase the value to *A* of the goals *B* mediates. The values of network members are also integral to the categorization of different types of networks. A *negative* exchange connection exists when two members value a divisible resource provided by a common partner, or when they provide resources that are substitutable to the common partner (a characteristic of the partner's values) and on which the partner satiates. An intracategory network is one in which all network members place similar value on resources available from the other network members.

However, in these theories two important simplifications are made concerning human actors – or, to put it differently, the scope of these theories is limited in two ways. First, the theories of power dependence and exchange networks concern actors interested in only one or perhaps a few goals. Yet human actors are complex, having a variety of different things (goals) they value to different extents, with those values interrelated in complicated ways. A theory of social exchange and social power will become more useful to the extent that it can relax those restrictions and apply to situations in which a fuller panoply of goals is relevant.

Second, in these theories the values of different actors are simply given, without being explained. In 1972 Emerson wrote, and italicized, "In this chapter we will not presume to know the needs and motives of men," followed by "We will see how far we can go on this skimpy basis" (Emerson, 1972, p. 44). Clearly, filling out some of this skimpiness would add to the scope and power of the theory. Understanding how value is created and changed clearly would inform understanding of how and when the first (withdrawal) and third (e.g. status-giving) balancing operations are likely to occur. It would also provide at least partially for a theory of formation and change in the various types of exchange networks.

THE IMPACT OF EMERSON'S WORK

Emerson's influence on contemporary social science falls into two main areas: work stemming from his original formulation of power–dependence theory, and research based on his work on social exchange and exchange networks.

Emerson's work on power and dependence itself has been carried forward in two directions: theoretical investigation of power and more substantive studies of a wide variety of social phenomena. First, his approach has been incorporated into the development of general theory concerning social power. Many power theorists take a more general view, either conceiving of power more broadly or considering social processes in addition to exchange. Thus Emerson's exchange perspective, in which power exists through dependence in an exchange relation, is included alongside other processes, such as persuasion and legitimate authority (see, for example, Wrong, 1988; Coleman, 1990; Friedkin, 1993b).

Second, Emerson's approach has found application in studies of a wide variety of social phenomena. Interactional dynamics in all types of settings frequently involve exchange and power. To the extent that power and power use is responsible for outcomes, Emerson's approach proves useful in analysis and explanation. Substantive areas of study in which it has been applied successfully include marriage and family dynamics, marketing, legal studies, geopolitics, and especially the study of organizations.

Power–dependence theory is a cornerstone of one of the dominant perspectives in organizational studies, known as the *resource dependence* perspective (e.g. Pfeffer and Salancik, 1978). According to this perspective, organizations need a variety of resources from both outside and within the organization. Those entities – individuals, subunits, or other organizations – that exclusively provide the most needed resources will have the most power over or in the organization. This key postulate comes directly from the principle embodied in equation (1), although resource dependence theorists point out that for power actually to be exerted, other elements are also necessary.

Since organizations are not self-sufficient they must engage in exchanges with other organizations and entities in their environments to assure survival. Organizations thus spend much of their time and energy involved in efforts to manage these "strategic dependencies." As Scott (1992, p. 115) argues, "One of the major contributions of the resource dependency perspective is to discern and describe the strategies – ranging from buffering to diversification and merger – employed by organizations to change and adapt to the environment." An early treatment of these strategic options was presented in the work of James D. Thompson (1967) in his influential book, *Organizations in Action*. The application of power–dependence theory to the analysis of organizational exchange and interorganizational relations was pursued by Cook (1977) and subsequently by Cook and Emerson (1984). This work is reflected in more recent developments within the field of organizations. Many of the strategies available to organizations to manage their critical dependencies can be understood in terms of the balancing operations spelled out in power–dependence theory, since the goal is to acquire necessary resources without increasing dependence. Such strategies include, under different circumstances, joint venture, long-term contracting, specialization, consolidation, reduction in production arenas, and vertical integration of various types, among others. As Scott (1992, p. 193) puts it, "Unequal exchange relations can generate power and dependency differences among organizations, causing them to enter into exchange relations cautiously and to pursue strategies that will enhance their own bargaining position."

The work of Emerson and his colleagues has continued to inform research and theory development following the resource dependence perspective on organizations. For example, a recent study (Seabright et al., 1992) of auditor–client relationships found that as the fit between auditor and client declined, the likelihood of this relationship dissolving increased, as the resource dependence perspective predicts. However, the tendency for the relationship to dissolve was attenuated by the development of attachment between the individuals – a development predicted by Emerson and his collaborator Karen Cook. Thus the authors of the study conclude, "We . . . argue, following theoretical work on social exchange such as Cook (1977) and Cook and Emerson (1978), that attachment is a distinct attribute of interorganizational relationships" (Seabright et al., 1992, p. 153).

Power–dependence theory, as well as its descendent, the theory of exchange networks, has also contributed to the network perspective on organizations. Using power–dependence theory (Emerson, 1962; Cook and Emerson, 1978), Mizruchi (1989) expects and finds that economic dependence and interdependence among businesses leads to similarity in their political behavior. Knoke (1990) points out the parallel between network structures studied in the laboratory and network structures both within and between organizations. He suggests that this parallel should allow theory on exchange networks to help explain power and outcomes in organizational networks, but notes that the complications of the naturally occuring networks have hindered application of the theory thus far.

More recently, various organizational theorists have extended the analysis of networks to the study of organizations and the role of networks more broadly in the economy (see especially Lincoln et al., 1992; Powell, 1990; Sabel, 1991; Gerlach, 1992). Networks are examined as they affect labor practices, informal influence, ethnic enterprises, the organization of business groups, and the networking of companies across national boundaries (see Powell and Smith-Doerr, 1994, for a review). Central to these efforts is the attempt to analyze the relative power of the economic actors in the network and the strategies used to enhance network-wide power or to alter the distribution of power within the network. The focus of attention is on the structural location of the actors in the network and how that influences strategy. Exchange theory and the resource dependence perspective (e.g. Pfeffer and Salancik, 1978) based on power–dependence arguments are commonly used as the framework for analysis in these investigations of economic impact. Other topics of investigation include strategic alliances, collaborative manufacturing enterprises, vertical integration of firms, interlocking directorates, network diffusion of innovative practices, and mergers.

In the field of marketing too, theory has been developed by applying the theoretical ideas of Emerson, Cook, and colleagues to organizations. Cook and Emerson (1978) themselves pointed out the relevance of exchange networks to marketing, noting, for example, that vertically integrated markets and channels of distribution in fact are positively connected networks. A recent example is the work of Anderson et al. (1994), who discuss *business networks*, defined as two or more connected relations between businesses, each business conceived as a collective actor. One of their key propositions is that each firm in a network will develop a *network identity*. This identity has three dimensions: an orientation toward other actors, competence, and power. The last of these, power, is a function of an actor's resources and its network context, following Emerson, Cook, and colleagues. In their examination of two case studies, Anderson et al. note contrasting effects of positive and negative exchange connections. They also point out that connections may switch between positive and negative through time, or even may be simultaneously positive and negative, a point also noted in theoretical work following Emerson and colleagues (Whitmeyer, 1997b). Further exploration of these cases leads Anderson et al. to suggest mechanisms, typically involving network identity, of changes over time in relations and connections in business networks.

In the area of family studies, power–dependence theory has contributed to an understanding of the dynamics of relationships both within families and between family members and outsiders. For example, a recent study of adoption processes analyzing the relationship between birth mothers, adoptive parents, and adoption facilitators suggests that birth mothers may have more power because all other parties are dependent on their decision (Daly and Sobol, 1994). In the study of dating couples, partners, and married people various authors have applied exchange concepts to the analysis of the longevity and quality of such relationships despite the argument that an exchange "logic" does not work in close, personal relations. Michaels et al. (1984), for example, find that exchange outcomes are a more important predictor of relationship satisfaction than are equity concerns. In addition, Sprecher's (1988) research indicates that relationship commitment is affected more by the level of rewards available to partners in alternative relations than by fairness or equity considerations, though there is also evidence in various studies that fairness does matter (see review by Hegtvedt and Cook, forthcoming). A major focus of much of this research is the perceived fairness of the exchanges that occur over time and the symmetry or asymmetry in mutual dependence on the relationship.

Cook and Donnelly (1996) applied the concepts of longitudinal exchange and generalized exchange relations to intergenerational relations both within the family and within the society at large. Relations between generations can be examined as implicit exchange relations in which each generation must determine how to allocate its resources to the next generation, and on what basis. Reciprocity, trust, dependence, power, fairness, and asymmetry in exchange benefits all play a significant role in these determinations. These dynamics are important within families and relate to social issues like long-term care, child care, elder abuse, health care, and the transfer of wealth. Many of these issues also arise at the aggregate level for the society at large in terms of the nature of the relations between the generations, with implications for property law, taxation, welfare policy, social and health services, and education.

Applications of exchange theory in fields like health care are less common, but interesting. Shortell (1977), for example, used exchange theory to analyze the nature of physician referrals under the standard fee-for-service funding regime in place in the health care system at that time. More recently, Grembowski et al. (1998) have examined physician referrals under managed care using an exchange-based model of the nature of the decisions to refer and the network of providers involved in the delivery of health services under different degrees of "managedness." Issues of power and dependence are addressed in this literature at various levels, including the physician–patient relation, the relations between various categories of providers (e.g. physician to physician, primary care provider to specialist, physician to alternative health care provider, and physicians to hospital administrators or other managers within the health care system), and relations between organizational units with involvement in delivery of services (insurance carriers, suppliers of goods and services, other health and community agencies, etc.). Research based on models of exchange and power–dependence principles in the arena of health care holds the promise of providing a more general theory of the processes involved than is currently available. The major shifts that have occurred over the past decade in the delivery of health care have involved significant changes in the distribution of power among the key players in that organizational system (i.e. the shift in power from relatively autonomous physicians to the hospitals in which they practice and the insurers that pay them).

Finally, power–dependence theory has been applied in the geopolitical realm, to relations between states. For example, Jonathan Turner (1995) proposes that ongoing exchange relations between states lead to balancing operations, as suggested by Emerson (1962, 1972). When dependence between states is unequal – that is, trade is imbalanced – the more dependent partner will take steps to reduce the imbalance, perhaps even resorting to coercion.

Emerson's fruitful extension of theory and research into exchange networks has led to the experimental investigation of exchange networks, which has spawned a large body of subsequent research leading in a number of directions. Some of the research looks at social processses in addition to those Emerson investigated. For example, Linda Molm (e.g. 1997) has developed an extensive research program on exchange networks in which network members not only can reward (i.e. confer resource gains on) each other, but also can punish (i.e. impose losses on) each other. As operationalized, punishment consists of taking points away from partners. She also has varied the exchange process by looking at reciprocal exchange, in which partners take turns rewarding or punishing (or not) each other, rather than negotiated exchange, in which partners must come to an agreement about who gets what before the transaction is completed. Emerson's experimental research and much of the work that followed the lead of Cook and Emerson (1978) was restricted to negotiated exchange, though the theoretical formulation Emerson developed was not restricted in this manner.

This point is most clearly demonstrated in the interesting work of Linda Molm (1981, 1987, 1990, 1994, 1997) on reciprocal (or "non-negotiated" exchange).

In her most recent extensive treatment of coercive power in social exchange, Molm (1997) presents the results of a ten-year program of experimental research which indicates the nature of the effects of coercive power in exchange relations. The surprising finding she addresses in this work is the result that coercion is rarely used even by those in positions of power advantage. The primary reason is that the use of punishment power imposes losses upon the exchange partner and raises the cost of the use of power, in terms of both opportunity costs (time better spent in active pursuit of other rewards) and the potential for retaliation. As Molm (1997, p. 138) puts it, in an exchange relation in which one partner uses coercive power to increase exchange benefits, "the coercer pays a price for the rewards obtained." Her work has initiated a more complete examination of the dynamics of exchange processes and the role of strategy in determining the outcomes that were viewed primarily in Emerson's work as structurally induced.

Edward Lawler (e.g. Lawler and Yoon, 1993, 1996), along with colleagues, and others have pursued research that explores in greater depth the notion of an exchange *relation*; that is, a situation of ongoing rather than one-time-only exchange. Lawler builds on the notion, from Emerson's work (1962, 1972; Cook and Emerson, 1978) on power–dependence theory, of *cohesion*, defined as the total dependence (of both partners) in an exchange relation. To this he adds emotional processes, and develops a theory of *commitment* in exchange relations. Not only does this research build on Emerson's work, but it is consistent with the spirit of that work, in its emphasis on an exchange relation as more enduring, and more meaningful for its members, than a simple economic opportunity. A key feature of Lawler's theory of relational exchange is the idea that instrumental exchange relations become transformed over time (based on the nature of the exchange dynamics) in such a way that the relation itself becomes a valued object worthy of commitment. In his studies of gift-giving he examines this transformation and measures it in terms of the emergence of commitment between exchange partners. A second feature that makes this work interesting is that it explicitly incorporates emotions into the theory, an aspect that is distinctly missing in Emerson's early work on exchange, but much less so in the work of the anthropologists who studied more primitive forms of exchange (e.g. Mauss and Malinowski).

Another variant on exchange processes in exchange networks is *generalized exchange*. Under rules of generalized exchange, actors reward actors who are different from the actors who reward them. The prominent existence of such exchange systems in some societies has been described by anthropologists. Inspired by these descriptions, Emerson (1981) himself suggested investigation into generalized exchange, but never had the opportunity to pursue it. It was left to his colleagues and former students (e.g. Gillmore, 1987; Cook and Yamagishi, 1993) to conduct the first experimental investigations of this type of exchange network. One interesting feature of many systems of generalized exchange is that they produce *social dilemmas* through the incentive structures they create for network members. Namely, members do better as individuals by not giving to their partners, but if all refuse to give, they all do worse than if they all gave. Thus, we see investigation of exchange networks extended into the domain of social dilemmas, which is a vast area of research in its own right (see Yamagashi, 1995).

Finally, a considerable body of research continues the experimental study of the effect of network structures on power distributions in exchange networks. Since the late 1980s much of this effort has gone into the development of models to predict accurately the distribution of payoffs among network members given a particular network structure. Most notably, David Willer, Barry Markovsky, John Skvoretz, and their colleagues have developed a series of algorithms for making such predictions for a wide variety of experimental exchange networks, under a variety of experimental rules (e.g. Markovsky et al., 1988, 1993). Nevertheless, this work claims a theoretical basis different from power–dependence theory. It is based on what Willer (1981, 1987) refers to as "elementary theory." Thus, we will not discuss it in further detail in this piece on Emerson's legacy. Another approach to predicting outcomes, called the *expected value model*, has been developed by Noah Friedkin (1992, 1993a). This approach incorporates the notion of actors behaving according to their dependence, and thus has stronger ties to Emerson's approach. As with other algorithms, however, the primary aim of Friedkin's approach has been the accurate prediction of experimental outcomes.

Presumably the rationale behind such model-building efforts is the idea that a model that accurately predicts outcomes somehow must capture the essential processes involved. Nevertheless, this research probably has not moved in the direction Emerson might have anticipated. Recall that Emerson came up with an experimental operationalization of exchange networks as a way of testing analytically derived theory. The concentration on predictive models entails a shift from considering experimental exchange networks simply as an operationally convenient way of testing theoretical points, to considering them as objects of interest in their own right. This shift also means, however, that less attention has been paid to continuing the analytic development of theory concerning power, exchange, and network structure which would be more generally applicable.

One continuation of Emerson's theory of exchange networks that does concentrate on developing more general theory not tied specifically to experimentally operationalized networks is the recent use of microeconomic theory to analyze exchange networks. Cook and Emerson (1978) note the relevance of microeconomic theory for exchange processes, but suggest that equity theory and power–dependence theory provide a more precise analysis of the social interactions in an exchange *relation*. However, in the past few years, theorists have begun to use sophisticated microeconomic theory, in particular game theory and general equilibrium analysis, to analyze the effects of network structure and other factors in exchange networks. In essence, microeconomic models underlying the theory replace the behavioristic models Emerson used to describe basic processes.

Game theory was used to analyze exchange networks first by Bienenstock and Bonacich (1992). Game theory is appropriate for this task, since it is a theoretical apparatus derived for situations in which actors interact strategically in order to maximize some clearly defined interests. A key game theoretic concept is the *core*, defined as the set of all possible outcomes that cannot be improved upon by any coalition of actors, including individual actors and the set of all actors. Bienenstock and Bonacich suggest the *core* as an appropriate solution for exchange networks. One implication is that under many circumstances network structure in negatively connected networks may lead to only a range of power distributions rather than a single power distribution. A subsequent article by Bienenstock and Bonacich (1997) discusses another game theoretic solution concept, the *kernel*. They point out its strong similarity to the concept of *equidependence*, developed from Emerson's theory as a tool for predicting exchange network outcomes by Cook and Yamagishi (1992). According to Bienenstock and Bonacich, one reason to use game theoretic concepts such as the kernel explicitly is that theorists then can take advantage of the large body of work in game theory. For example, they note that the failure of restrictions on information to affect results in some experiments is what would be expected if the kernel describes the experimental subjects' strategies.

General equilibrium analysis is a fundamental tool of modern microeconomics that has been adapted for application to exchange networks by a number of researchers (Marsden, 1983; Whitmeyer, 1994, 1997b; Yamaguchi, 1996). Unlike game theory, which applies to situations involving few actors who thus can act strategically, assumptions of general equilibrium analysis make it most appropriate for market situations; that is, situations involving many actors, all of whom have competitors (Whitmeyer, 1997a). Nevertheless, for analyzing exchange networks it has the merit of yielding a *single* power distribution, which moreover lies within the range of power distributions identified by game theory. Often this single point is sufficient for supporting qualitative theoretical predictions.

Yamaguchi (1996), for example, adapts general equilibrium analysis to exchange networks by assuming that actors are interested not in goods possessed by their partners, but in exchange with those partners itself. A key concept in his approach is that of the *substitutability* of an actor's alternative partners. This is incorporated into his general equilibrium model as the *elasticity of substitution*, denoted s. Thus, the model can treat both positively and negatively connected networks, since for $0 < s < 1$ an exchange connection is positive, while for $s > 1$ an exchange connection is negative. Through estimation of s, the model can approximate results from experimental networks, both positive and negative. Moreover, the model allows Yamaguchi to explore causes of *centralization*, defined as "agreement between the positions of power and the positions of global centrality." In particular, he is able to develop hypotheses concerning effects of substitutability on centralization.

For the most part, Emerson's deductions concerning balancing operations and thus change in exchange networks have been ignored in subsequent research on exchange networks (with the exception of some work on coalition formation; e.g. Gillmore, 1987; Cook and Gillmore, 1984). This stands in contrast to applications of power–dependence theory in other areas of study, such as organizations, where Emerson's theory of balancing processes has proved useful. This is perhaps because research on exchange networks almost without exception has used experimental exchange networks of short duration and restricted exchange. That is, for reasons of control and logistics, experimental exchange networks have lasted not more than one or at most two hours, and have restricted interaction and domains of exchange. Under such constraints, it is not likely that network members will be able to use balancing processes. However, this may be an area of future research and theoretical development. Other topics currently being investigated include the role of emotions in exchange, the relationship between fairness assessments and strategy in negotiated and non-negotiated exchange, the nature of commitment and solidarity processes, and the emergence of trust in generalized exchange.

Assessment of Emerson's Legacy

Most social theorists die before the full impact of their work is revealed. Emerson was no exception to this rule. While he was alive in 1981 to learn that his 1962 paper on power–dependence relations had become a citation classic, he did not live long enough to accept the invitation to write about this contribution in his own words. This essay completes this unfinished business. Fifteen years after his untimely death it is easier to assess the nature of the impact of the work Emerson began in the early 1960s. In a few words his 1962 and 1964 pieces fundamentally altered the social science view of power. Power viewed as a relational construct based on dependence is now the common view. It is the way we talk about power in most contexts (short of pure violence) at the individual, organizational and societal levels. This is reflected in work on power in friendships, marital partnerships, families, organizational sub-units or departments, organizations and interorganizational relations, governments in relation to citizens or other entities, and international relations. Examples of applications in some of these arenas have been provided in the section on the influence of Emerson's work.

Related to the impact of his work on power is the extent to which theories about social exchange within the field of sociology now draw upon his conception of exchange networks. He was the first exchange theorist in sociology to extend the theory to apply to networks of connected exchange relations. Homans's theoretical work remained primarily at the dyadic and group level. Blau developed an exchange framework that extended into the macro-realm of social life and more complex forms of association, but he did not propose networks as the basis for the extension of exchange concepts beyond the micro-level, as Emerson subsequently did. The significance of this theoretical move, reflected in Turner's assessment discussed earlier in this chapter, is that it connects exchange theory directly to developments in the analysis of social networks (a field that has also expanded greatly in the past two decades) and to the analysis of new forms of organization (see especially Powell and Doerr-Smith, 1994).

Bibliography

Writings of Richard M. Emerson

Power–Dependence Relations. 1962. *American Sociological Review*, 27, 31–41.

Power–Dependence Relations: Two Experiments. 1964. *Sociometry*, 27, 282–98.

Operant Psychology and Exchange Theory. 1969. In R. Burgess and D. Bushell (eds), *Behavioral Sociology*. New York: Columbia University Press.

Exchange Theory, Part I. A Psychological Basis for Social Exchange. Exchange Theory, Part II. Exchange Relations and Network Structures. 1972. In J. Berger, M. Zelditch and B. Anderson (eds), *Sociological Theories in Progress, volume 2*. Boston: Houghton Mifflin, pp. 38–87.

Structural Inequality: Position and Power in Network Structures (with John F. Stolte). 1977. In R. Hamblin and J. Kunkel (eds), *Behavioral Theory in Sociology*. New Brunswick, NJ: Transaction, pp. 117–38.

Power, Equity and Commitment in Exchange Networks (with Karen S. Cook). 1978. *American Sociological Review*, 43, 721–39.

Social Exchange Theory. 1981. In Morris Rosenberg and Ralph Turner (eds), *Social Psychology: Sociological Perspectives*. New York: Basic Books, pp. 30–65.

The Distribution of Power in Exchange Networks: Theory and Experimental Results (with K. S. Cook, M. R. Gillmore, and T. Yamagashi). 1983. *American Journal of Sociology*, 89, 275–305.

Exchange Networks and the Analysis of Complex Organizations (with Karen S. Cook). 1984. In Samuel B. Bacharach and E. J. Lawler (eds), *Perspectives on Organizational Sociology: Theory and Research, volume 3*. Greenwich, CT: JAI Press, pp. 1–30.

Toward a Theory of Value in Social Exchange. 1987. In Karen S. Cook (ed.), *Social Exchange Theory*. Newbury Park, CA: Sage, pp. 11–46.

Further reading

Anderson, James C., Håkansson, Håkan, and Johanson, Jan (1994) Dyadic Business Relationships Within a Business Network Context. *Journal of Marketing*, 58, 1–15.

Blau, Peter (1964) *Exchange and Power*. New York: John Wiley and Sons.

Bienenstock, Elisa Jayne and Bonacich, Phillip (1992) The Core as a Solution to Negatively Connected Exchange Networks. *Social Networks*, 14, 231–43.

Bienenstock, Elisa Jayne and Bonacich, Phillip (1997) Network Exchange as a Cooperative Game. *Rationality and Society*, 9, 37–65.

Bowen, R. O. (1960) *The New Professors*. New York: Holt, Rinehart & Winston.

Cartwright, Dorwin (1979) Contemporary Social Psychology in Historical Perspective. *Sociometry*, 42, 250–8.

Coleman, James S. (1990) *The Structure of Social Theory*. Cambridge, MA: Harvard University Press.

Cook, Karen S. (1977) Exchange and Power in Networks of Interorganizational Relations. *Sociological Quarterly*, 18, 62–82.

Cook, Karen S. (1987) *Social Exchange Theory*. Newbury Park, CA: Sage.

Cook, Karen S. and Donnelly, Shawn (1996) Intergenerational Exchange Relations and Social Justice. In Leo Montada and Melvin J. Lerner (eds), *Current Societal Concerns About Justice*. New York: Plenum Press, pp. 67–83.

Cook, Karen S. and Gillmore, M. R. (1984) Power, Dependence and Coalitions. In Edward J. Lawler (ed.), *Advances in Group Processes, volume 1*. Greenwich, CT: JAI Press, pp. 27–58.

Cook, Karen S. and Whitmeyer, Joseph W. (1992) Two Approaches to Social Structure: Exchange Theory and Network Analysis. In Judith Blake and John Hagan (eds), *Annual Review of Sociology, volume 18*. Palo Alto, CA: Annual Reviews, pp. 109–27.

Cook, Karen S. and Yamagishi, Toshio (1992) Power in Exchange Networks: a Power–Dependence Formulation. *Social Networks*, 14, 245–66.

Daly, Kerry J. and Sobol, Michael P. (1994) Public and Private Adoption: a Comparison of Service and Accessibility. *Family Relations*, 43, 86–93.

Friedkin, Noah E. (1992) An Expected Value Model of Social Power: Predictions for Selected Exchange Networks. *Social Networks*, 14, 213–29.

Friedkin, Noah E. (1993a) An Expected Value Model of Social Exchange Outcomes. In Edward J. Lawler, Barry Markovsky, Karen Heimer, and Jodi O'Brien (eds), *Advances in Group Processes*. Greenwich, CT: JAI Press, pp. 163–93.

Friedkin, Noah E. (1993b) Structural Bases of Interpersonal Influence in Groups: a Longitudinal Case Study. *American Sociological Review*, 58, 861–72.

Gerlach, Michael L. (1992) *Alliance Capitalism: the Social Organization of Japanese Business*. Berkeley: University of California Press.

Gillmore, Mary R. (1987) Implications of Generalized Versus Restricted Exchange. In Karen S. Cook (ed.), *Social Exchange Theory*. Newbury Park, CA: Sage, pp. 170–89.

Grembowski, David, Cook, Karen S., Patrick, Donald, and Roussell, Amy (1998) Managed Care and Physician Referral: a Social Exchange Perspective. *Medical Care Research and Review*, 55, 3–31.

Hegtvedt, Karen A. and Cook, Karen S. (forthcoming). Distributive Justice: Recent Theoretical Developments and Applications. In Lee Hamilton and Joseph Sanders (eds), *Justice, volume 1*. New York: Plenum Press.

Hempel, Carl (1965) *Aspects of Scientific Explanation*. New York: Free Press.

Homans, George C. (1961) *Social Behavior: Its Elementary Forms*. New York: Harcourt, Brace and World.

Knoke, David (1990) *Political Networks: the Structural Perspective*. Cambridge: Cambridge University Press.

Kuhn, Alfred (1963) *The Study of Society: a Unified Approach*. Homewood, IL: Irwin-Dorsey.

Kuhn, Thomas (1964) *The Structure of Scientific Revolutions*. Chicago: University of Chicago Press (2nd edn 1970).

Lawler, Edward J., Ford, Rebecca, and Blegen, Mary A. (1988) Coercive Capability in Conflict: a Test of Bilateral Deterrence versus Conflict Spiral Theory. *Social Psychology Quarterly*, 51, 93–107.

Lawler, Edward J. and Yoon, Jeongkoo (1993) Power and the Emergence of Commitment Behavior in Negotiated Exchange. *American Sociological Review*, 58, 465–81.

Lawler, Edward J. and Yoon, Jeongkoo (1996) Commitment in Exchange Relations: a Test of a Theory of Relational Cohesion. *American Sociological Review*, 61, 89–108.

Lincoln, James R., Gerlach, Michael, and Takashi, Peggy (1992) Keiretsu Networks in the Japanese Economy: a Dyad Analysis of Intercorporate Ties. *American Sociological Review*, 57, 561–85.

Markovsky, Barry, Willer, D., and Patton, T. (1988) Power Relations in Exchange Networks. *American Sociological Review*, 53, 220–36.

Marsden, Peter V. (1983) Restricted Access in Networks and Models of Power. *American Journal of Sociology*, 88, 686–717.

Michaels, James, Edwards, John N., and Acock, Alan C. (1984) Satisfaction in Intimate Relationships as a Function of Inequality, Inequity and Outcomes. *Social Psychology Quarterly*, 47, 347–57.

Mizruchi, Mark S. (1989) Similarity of Political Behavior Among Large American Corporations. *American Journal of Sociology*, 95, 401–24.

Molm, Linda D. (1981) The Conversion of Power Imbalance to Power Use. *Social Psychology Quarterly*, 16, 153–66.

Molm, Linda D. (1985) Relative Effects of Individual Dependencies: Further Tests of the Relation between Power Imbalance and Power Use. *Social Forces*, 63, 810–37.

Molm, Linda D. (1987) Linking Power Structure and Power Use. In Karen S. Cook (ed.), *Social Exchange Theory*. Newbury Park, CA: Sage, pp. 107–29.

Molm, Linda D. (1990) Structure, Action and Outcomes: the Dynamics of Power in Exchange Relations. *American Sociological Review*, 55, 427–47.

Molm, Linda D. (1994) Is Punishment Effective? Coercive Strategies in Social Exchange. *Social Psychology Quarterly*, 57, 75–94.

Molm, Linda D. (1997) *Coercive Power in Social Exchange*. Cambridge: Cambridge University Press.

Molm, Linda D. and Cook, Karen S. (1995) Social Exchange and Exchange Networks. In Karen S. Cook, Gary A. Fine, and James S. House (eds), *Sociological Perspectives on Social Psychology*. Boston: Allyn and Bacon, pp. 209–35.

Pfeffer, Jeffrey and Salancik, Gerald R. (1978) *The External Control of Organizations: a Resource Dependence Perspective*. New York: Harper and Row.

Popper, Karl (1961) *The Poverty of Historicism*. London: Routledge & Kegan Paul.

Powell, Walter W. (1990) Neither Market nor Hierarchy: Network Forms of Organization. In L. L. Cummings and Staw (eds), *Research in Organizational Behaviour, volume 12*. Greenwich, CT: JAI Press, pp. 295–336.

Powell, Walter W. and Doerr-Smith, Laurel (1994) Networks and Economic Life. In Neil Smelser and Richard Swedberg (eds), *The Handbook of Economic Sociology*. Princeton, NJ: Princeton University Press/New York: Russell Sage Foundation, pp. 368–402.

Sabel, Charles F. (1991) Moebius-strip Organizations and Open Labor Markets. In P. Bourdieu and J. S. Coleman (eds), *Social Theory for a Changing Society*. Boulder, CO: Westview Press, pp. 23–54.

Scott, W. Richard (1992) *Organizations: Rational, Natural, and Open Systems*, 3rd edn. Englewood Cliffs, NJ: Prentice Hall.

Seabright, Mark A., Levinthal, Daniel A., and Fichman, Mark (1992) Role of Individual Attachments in the Dissolution of Interorganizational Relationships. *Academy of Management Journal*, 35, 122–60.

Shortell, S. M. (1974) Determinants of Physician Referral Rates: an Exchange Theory Approach. *Medical Care*, 12, 13–31.

Skinner, B. F. (1974) *About Behaviorism*. New York: Vintage Books.

Skvoretz, John and Willer, D. (1993) Exclusion and Power: a Test of Four Theories of Power in Exchange Networks. *American Sociological Review*, 58, 801–18.

Sprecher, Susan (1988) Investment Model, Equity, and Social Support Determinants of Relationship Commitment. *Social Psychology Quarterly*, 51, 57–69.

Stolte, John F. (1987) Legitimacy, Justice and Productive Exchange. In Karen S. Cook (ed.), *Social Exchange Theory*. Newbury Park, CA: Sage, pp. 190–208.

Thibaut, John W. and Kelley, Harold H. (1959) *The Social Psychology of Groups*. New York: John Wiley and Sons.

Thompson, James D. (1967) *Organizations in Action*. New York: McGraw-Hill.

Turner, Jonathan H. (1986) *The Structure of Sociological Theory*. Homewood, IL: Dorsey Press.

Turner, Jonathan H. (1995) *Macrodynamics: toward a Theory on the Organization of Human Populations*. New Brunswick, NJ: Rutgers University Press.

Whitmeyer, Joseph M. (1994) Social Structure and the Actor: the Case of Power in Exchange Networks. *Social Psychology Quarterly*, 57, 177–89.

Whitmeyer, Joseph M. (1997a) Applying General Equilibrium Analysis and Game Theory to Exchange Networks. *Current Research in Social Psychology*, 2, 13–23.

Whitmeyer, Joseph M. (1997b) The Power of the Middleman – a Theoretical Analysis. *Journal of Mathematical Sociology*, 22, 59–90.

Willer, David (1981) The Basic Concepts of Elementary Theory. In David Willer and Bo Anderson (eds), *Networks, Exchange and Coercion: the Elementary Theory and Its Applications*. New York: Elsevier.

Willer, David (1987) The Location of Power in Exchange Networks. *Social Networks* (Special Issue), 10, 187–344.

Wrong, Dennis H. (1988) *Power, Its Forms, Bases, and Uses*. Chicago: University of Chicago Press.

Yamagishi, Toshio (1995) Social Dilemmas. In Karen S. Cook, Gary A. Fine, and James S. House (eds), *Sociological Perspectives on Social Psychology*. Needham Heights, NY: Allyn and Bacon, pp. 311–54.

Yamagishi, T. and Cook, K. S. (1993) Generalized Exchange and Social Dilemmas. *Social Psychology Quarterly*, 56, 235–48.

Yamagishi, T., Gillmore, M. R., and Cook, K. S. (1988) Network Connections and the Distribution of Power in Exchange Networks. *American Journal of Sociology*, 93, 833–51.

Yamaguchi, K. (1996) Power in Networks of Substitutable and Complementary Exchange Relations: a Rational-choice Model and an Analysis of Power Centralization. *American Sociological Review*, 61, 308–22.

Zelditch, Morris (1969) Can You Really Study the Army in the Laboratory. In A. Etzioni (ed.), *A Sociological Reader in Complex Organizations*. New York: Holt, Rinehart and Winston, pp. 428–539.

4

James Coleman

Siegwart Lindenberg

Introduction

James Coleman is at present widely considered to be the most prominent sociologist worldwide[1] since Talcott Parsons and Robert Merton. He was born in 1926 in Bedford, Indiana. After a brief interlude as a chemist, he studied sociology at Columbia University in New York from 1951 to 1955, mainly with Merton and Lazarsfeld. Lipset was his thesis advisor. His own assessment of the influence of these three is succinct: "I worked *with* Lipset, worked *for* Lazarsfeld, and *worked to be like* Merton" (Coleman, 1990a, p. 31). "To Robert K. Merton, my teacher" reads the dedication of Coleman's major book, *Foundations of Social Theory.*

After his studies, he became an assistant professor in Chicago for three years and settled as an associate professor for the next fourteen years at the Department of Social Relations of Johns Hopkins University. From 1973 on to his death in 1995, he was professor of sociology at Chicago.

When one presents an author rather than a problem and a problem solution, I believe that it is essential to find a generative key to the work that is being discussed; to find a particular well from which the work, including possible inconsistencies, springs.

There can be more than one key to unlock someone's work but probably there is only a limited number of keys that fit. Coleman's work is so vast and diverse that it is no trivial matter to find one of those fitting keys. He wrote and edited close to thirty books and wrote over 300 articles. How can one find a spring from which it all emerged? If we look at what he said about his own interests and use a considered overview over his work in order to select the most pertinent statements, we can glean two major concerns. First, "a deep concern I have had, since my own high school days, with high schools and with ways to make possible their better functioning" (Coleman, 1961, p. vii). Although this statement was made early on in his career, "the deep concern" stayed within him all his life and drove a good deal of his work. Second, "my major interest is in the way social systems (or subsystems) function."[2] In a subtle way, Coleman indicated by this statement that the functioning of systems was even more important to him than high schools and their improvement. His "major interest" dominated his "deep concern." He even objectified this major interest into sociology's major concern. One year before his death he wrote: "The most formidable task of sociology is the development of a theory that will move from the micro level of action to the macro level of norms, social values, status distribution and social conflict" (Coleman, 1996, p. 348). Lest we miss the message that this task is all about system functioning, he also told us what it was all about: "to discover in real social systems implicit rules and norms, constraints and goals, and the way in which the actions they generate combine and interact to produce system functioning" (ibid.).

For a complete theory of system functioning, we need an equal concern for the macro-to-micro link. Coleman was fully aware of this but, as can be gleaned from his claim about "the most formidable task of sociology," the macro-to-micro link was secondary or at least not as interesting to him. He was quite consistent in this attitude throughout his life as a sociologist. By 1964 (Coleman, 1964a, pp. 37ff) he had distinguished between "explanatory" and "synthetic" theories. The former answer why-questions, whereas the latter answer what-consequence-questions, meaning questions that address the consequences of actions for social phenomena. Even then, in his view, sociology (i.e. his sociology) was (and should be) mainly concerned with synthetic theories.

The combination of his two major interests resulted in a third preoccupation: policy research and institutional innovation, especially in the field of education. The wish to improve the functioning of high schools, combined with the "synthetic" approach, led Coleman to put a great deal of effort into debating how policy research should be done and into theory-driven practical suggestions on how to improve the functioning of the educational system.

An overview of Coleman's work thus falls naturally into these three groups: his work on education, his work on the micro–macro link, and his work on policy research. In all three, the generation of society plays an important role. Education was for him one of the major vehicles for generating an adaptive and just society. The micro–macro link traces the mechanisms by which society is generated; on this basis, policy research helps to create the tools for the purposeful generation of certain societal effects. In my discussion, I will first present Coleman's major contributions in the field of education; then I will turn to his view on policy analysis; finally, I will discuss his "foundations," which mainly deal with the micro–macro link.[3]

EDUCATION

Coleman's research on education can be divided into three phases. The first phase comprised *The Adolescent Society*; the second phase consisted of the vast research which led to *Equality of Educational Opportunity*; the third phase consisted of his research on private schools and social capital. I will present each phase in some detail.

The Adolescent Society

The first book Coleman ever wrote on high schools was at once one of his most successful books: *The Adolescent Society* (1961). He investigated 39 classes in ten high schools from communities of different size. The book already combined the three major themes of his overall work: education, system functioning, and policy research. How does a high school function from the students' point of view and what can be done to improve its functioning? The particular puzzle, though, only came out during the research itself, and it is much more specific. In industrial societies, education is of utmost importance and only schools can dampen or erase the effect of accidents of birth by creating equality of opportunity. The major goal of schools is thus to teach children knowledge and cognitive skills. This major goal should be reflected in the value system of schools and in the activities that are rewarded. However, in most schools, from the male students' point of view, it is athletics and, for girls, social success (especially with boys) rather than scholastic achievement that dominate the value system and the social rewards, channeling effort away from scholastic pursuits. While there are important differences between schools concerning value and reward systems, the similarity in values and social rewards is striking, especially in the consistency with which the scholastic achievements rank below non-scholastic characteristics and pursuits. The question which Coleman then asked was: how can this be? Why does the value and reward system of teachers and of the larger society with regard to the major function of schools not find its way into adolescent society in schools?

Although *The Adolescent Society* remains well known even today, many of its most poignant findings have been forgotten. What lingers in the literature is the question of whether Coleman did not overestimate the importance of peer groups and underestimate the importance of the family. I will return to this point below. This overview of Coleman's work gives me the opportunity to refresh the reader's memory with regard to findings and explanations in this book which in my judgment have not lost their importance over time.

Question to the student: "If you could be remembered here at school for one of the three things below, which one would you want it to be? Brilliant student, Athletic star (boys), Leader in activities (girls), Most popular." The answers to this question were compared to the answers by parents to a comparable question ("If your son or daughter could be outstanding in high school in one of the three things listed below, which one would you want it to be?"). Table 4.1 shows the results.

There is a glaring disparity between what parents would like their children to be and the students' own ideal. The difference is most pronounced in the category "brilliant student." For boys, 77 percent of the parents would like them to stand out as a brilliant student, while 68 percent of the boys find their ideal in athletics and in being popular. For the girls, parents are more modest in

Table 4.1 How boys and girls want to be remembered and how their parents want them to be outstanding in school (percentages)

	Boys	*Parents (for boys)*	*Girls*	*Parents (for girls)*
Brilliant student	32	77	28	54
Athletic star (boys)	45	9		
Leader in activities (girls)			38	36
Most popular	23	14	34	10

Source: compiled from Coleman's *The Adolescent Society.*

their academic expectations, but still a majority would like their daughters to be brilliant students most of all. Girls themselves think differently: 72 percent opt for leader in activities or popularity.

The low standing of academic achievement in the adolescent's value system is corroborated for both boys and girls by the questions about what it takes to belong to the leading crowd and what it takes to be popular. This does not mean that good grades do not contribute to elite standing or to popularity. Rather, it indicates that in most schools investigated, good grades only add to standing when a student also excels in other things. This fact is important because even though it prevents an overall negative correlation of academic success and popularity in school, it means that a good deal of the energies of those who could get high grades are distracted into non-scholastic activities.

There are mainly two things Coleman wants to explain with regard to these findings. First, what determines the value system in schools? A value system for him is the consensual relative evaluation of certain kinds of activities and achievements (sports, scholastic achievement, stirring up excitement, etc.). In particular, what interests him is the rank order of athletics versus scholastic achievements. Second, he wants to explain relevant individual outcomes, i.e. self-esteem and grades.

THE THEORY OF THE LEADING CROWD His explanation of the value system is quite ingenious. He focuses on the importance of social rewards and punishments, which he identifies as popularity, respect, acceptance into a crowd, praise, awe, support, and aid on the one hand, and isolation, ridicule, exclusion from a crowd, disdain, discouragement, and disrespect on the other hand. These rewards and punishments operate in the community at large and inside the school. In order to understand how they work in school, Coleman uses the concept of "the leading crowd." Adolescents in schools form a community, and Coleman argues that every community has a leading crowd. Social rewards are tied to the criteria of membership in the leading crowd and thus the crucial question is: what does it take to get into the leading crowd?

GIRLS For reasons to be explained later, Coleman offers separate explanations for girls and boys. Let me begin with the *girls*. Coleman's general assumption is that the criteria for membership in the leading crowd depend *not* so much on the values parents hold for their children (such as scholastic versus social achievement) but on the parents' status system. An all-important difference is whether the status of most parents in the community is or is not well established and what criteria the parents use in their own status competition. Where the status of the parents is well established (as in the small town in this study), most students are familiar with the community status system and will more or less reproduce it in school. As a consequence, the leading crowd will largely be a reflection of this status system. If the community is clearly stratified, then family background will play an important role as criterion for membership in the leading crowd. If the status differences are not so large (as in a small farming community), then the criteria of membership in the leading crowd are more based on popular interests of the student body. If the status system of the parents puts considerable emphasis on social achievement for women, then girls in school will also put a great emphasis on social achievements, rather than good grades. There may still be a positive correlation between family background and grades (because of the higher educational level of the elite parents), but high grades will not help to make a girl more popular within the leading crowd. Where parents consider education to belong to the status criteria (also for women), good grades will also belong to the criteria of membership in the leading crowd. In this case, grades will correlate even more highly with family background than in the previous case.

The picture is quite different for communities with high mobility in which the status of parents is not generally known and has to be demonstrated (in the study, these are the larger communities). There are basically two ways for parents to do this, both involving the demonstration of visible status characteristics. First, parents try to demonstrate their status by indications of material success, through ostentatiousness in consumption and the handling of money. Second, parents demonstrate their status by the way they act. Since there is no stable traditional community to reward acting according to traditional norms, status can be demonstrated by acting with self-assuredness and social skill. In such mobile communities, the criteria for membership in the leading crowd in school will then also reflect ostentatiousness, self-assuredness and social skill. Coleman stresses an irony here. Self-assuredness and social skills (in the absence of clear traditional norms) are meant to demonstrate independence, initiative, meeting challenges, and the ability to fascinate other people. Such behavior in school is quite incompatible with doing what you are told. Students in the leading crowd thus have to demonstrate their independence from parents and teachers, take initiative, and "stir up excitement." The irony is that the strong influence of peers on the behavior of students derives from the strong influence of the (mobile) community on the status criteria in school.

BOYS In principle, there is no reason to assume that these processes hold only for girls. However, for *boys*, family background is generally much less important a criterion for belonging to the leading crowd than for girls. Why is this so? Coleman's answer to this question also deserves much more attention than it has gotten hitherto. He argues that it is the *system of interscholastic competition* in sports that overshadows the status effect of the community on the membership criteria of the leading crowd. When students compete for grades, they do so individually, so that one student's good grades are a threat to the other students' good grades. However, it is a completely different matter if there is an interscholastic competition where excelling also increases the status of those who do not excel. Interscholastic competition allows the *combination* of an internal status differentiation with status equality toward the outside, and it allows the person high on the internal status system to increase everyone's status on the external status system (the one in which the entire school is pitted against other schools or communities). In such a system, the good athlete may be rewarded in three ways for his effort. He is high on the internal status system, he is popular (i.e. others do not begrudge his high status, they like him, and they approve of what he is doing), and he may be high with his school team on the external status system. For this very reason, interscholastic competition offers many more social rewards than scholastic achievement, and drains effort away from the latter. In this way, athletic status can successfully compete with other criteria for membership in the leading crowd and reduce their importance.[4]

REMEDY Coleman's suggestion of pushing scholastic achievement higher up the rank order of students' priorities is typical of someone interested in the functioning of systems. He suggests that students be pushed not to achieve better in school individually but to affect the criteria for membership in the leading crowd. Since the school should cut through ascribed criteria of family background and religion, the remedy should be strong enough to cut through these influences. Based on his own research, he could think of no stronger instrument than using the motivating power of interscholastic competition for this purpose. If this competition could be devised to pertain to scholarly matters rather than to sports, then scholarly achievement would become a major criterion for membership in the leading crowd. Coleman thereby also rectifies the bad image competition has in the public eye as a means to spur learning. It is only individual competition cut loose from intergroup competition which has negative effects, especially when it is tied to arbitrary judgments by teachers who reward the quiet little girl in the front row for always providing the "right" answer. Coleman specifically suggests the construction of knowledge-related *games*, especially computer games (in 1961!), which could be played between schools. Even if the games were not played between schools but only within schools they would at least remove the often arbitrary judgment by teachers on scholastic achievement. Not much has happened with these suggestions so far, but with present-day information technology, the possibility of introducing interscholastic competition on scholastic matters has come a lot closer at hand. What Coleman did not consider was the possibility that competition in scholastic matters might ultimately not bring what sports did even if it involved competition between schools. Scholastic completion may not require *joint* efforts to the same degree that team sports do. One very clever student may win a competition in scholastic matters for the entire school without involving anyone else in the preparation or the competition itself. In team sports, many have to cooperate well and do their best to win the competition. In addition, the entertainment value of sports is likely to be considerably higher for a broad range of people than that of scholastic competition.

Equality of Educational Opportunity

Based on the success of *The Adolescent Society* (TAS), Coleman was a few years later asked to conduct a large-scale study which resulted in the *Equality of Educational Opportunity* (EEO, 1966). The concern in this study was again with the possibility of the school preparing the student for the requirements of modern society, irrespective of the student's family background (especially his or her racial background). But the focus this time was not on the functioning of the school or part of the school as a system, but on finding facts relevant for social policy: to what extent do schools overcome the inequalities with which children come to school? Do school resources (teacher quality, class size, equipment, expenditure per pupil, etc.) play an important role? The study was truly huge. It involved more than 600,000 students in more than 3,000 elementary and secondary schools. Family background and attitudes of students, the composition of student bodies, and school resources were among the important independent variables, and school achievement (verbal and math scores) was the major dependent variable.

There were many results of this study, but three of them aroused national interest, controversy, and policy changes for quite some time. First, the family background of the students (especially regarding race) plays (statistically speaking) the most important role for student achievement. Second, school inputs have no large effect on student achievement. Third, there is an *asymmetric context effect* on student achievement: weaker students do better among better students but better students are not pulled down by the presence of weaker students. The first and second findings combined constituted a large blow to the expectation that the school operates as the great equalizer of inequalities in opportunity. Family background (mainly race) was much too important and school inputs were much too unimportant for this equalization to occur. These findings also cast some doubt on the meaning of equality of opportunity for both input- and output-based measures of the concept. Because these findings went so much against the grain of equality expectations, they were challenged time and again, leading to various reanalyses. Below, I briefly examine the major criticism.

The third finding was the most consequential and controversial of all. Because most schools were race-segregated, the finding of an asymmetric context effect could be used by advocates of race-integrative policies to suggest bussing black children daily into white schools. There, the asymmetric context effect would do its job and increase the achievement of the black minority students. In this way, the weight of the first and second findings could be partially lifted, and some equality of opportunity could be achieved through schools after all.

Whereas the EEO study deviated greatly in approach from his earlier study on schools, it did show considerably continuity in the substantive findings, even if the focus was different. For example, the research in TAS focused on the question of under what conditions the influence of family background weakens, in favor of peer influence. But this did not imply that family background was deemed unimportant in TAS. To the contrary. Coleman stressed in TAS that, generally speaking, the influence of parents was stronger than that of peers (if measured by the question of whose disapproval would be more difficult to accept: parent's or peer's).[5] This influence was also evidenced in the reproduction of the community status symbols within the school. The strong influence of family background in EEO is thus not in contradiction to TAS, as often assumed.[6] Coleman's theory of community in TAS implied that, unless there are strong countervailing forces at work, inequality in schools is mainly a matter of the status system of the community, including the cumulation of advantages in middle- and upper-class families. Interscholastic sports competition was such a strong countervailing power, but it distracted from scholarly pursuits and thus did not contribute much to the reduction of family and community influence on cognitive achievement.

A similar continuity in findings can be found with regard to the influence of school expenditure on achievement. Coleman claimed in TAS that school expenditure (teachers' salary, school buildings, laboratory equipment, and libraries) does not make a large difference, just as he found years later in EEO.

Where, then, lay the difference between TAS and EEO that is most relevant for the understanding of Coleman's work? In later years, Coleman identified EEO as a "detour" in his own research (Coleman, 1996, p. 19). He was quite dissatisfied, and it is instructive for the understanding of his later development to see why that was so. Uncharacteristically for his earlier approach, Coleman had used a conventional sociological inductive approach in the search for "factors" and their relative weight for the determination of the dependent variable. Thereby, he failed to study the social system of schools and also failed to look at the goals, interests, and constraints of those involved. In short, he did not use an *actor orientation*, as he had done in TAS ("getting inside the lives of those who pass through the schools"); nor did he pay much attention to parents and teachers as actors (something he had done at least to some degree in TAS). In his own terms, EEO, "by largely ignoring the social system of the school, and taking the administrative perspective of the school as delivering services individually to students, may have missed the most important differences between the school environments in which black and white children found themselves" (Coleman, 1996, p. 20). He realized through further research in the 1970s that, even if there was an asymmetric context effect (and that was not sure), it would not work as predicted for bussing because white families fled from urban areas to the suburbs in order to escape the bussing, thereby increasing racial segregation. As a result, he turned against bussing policies and was bitterly attacked for doing so by the advocates of this policy, who had so depended on his prior findings for their own political purposes. In the social context of the 1970s, the social sciences were highly intertwined in political battles, and research on education most of all. If results were politically unacceptable for certain vocal groups, they would be denied and the researcher pursued by these groups. As we will see below, it is this kind of situation that led Coleman to adopt a view on policy research wholly based on revealing mechanisms which could not be easily dragged into a political process of finding the truth. A mechanism-revealing approach must pay close attention to what actors do. The way he had done the EEO research was decidedly not mechanism-revealing, and thus fell prey to a great deal of political controversy.

The failure to take an actor orientation is also responsible for the most cutting and lasting criticism of his study. Had he taken an actor orientation, he would have realized that all three of his major findings may have been strongly affected by the *selection effects* of parents' decision to send their children to certain schools and to be in the company of certain peers.[7] I believe that it was his negative experience with this kind of inductive factor-finding study which cemented his belief that one has to study the functioning of systems, and do so by taking the perspectives of the actors involved. As I discuss below, he spent the last ten years of his life developing analytical tools for this kind of approach.

Refinement of the theory of community–school relations: social capital

In TAS, Coleman distinguished between two kinds of community: first, the traditional community, with dominant values and a consensual status order; second, the mobile community, without dominant values and without consensual status order. In the latter, status has to be demonstrated by ostentatiousness with regard to consumption and financial power, and by self-assuredness and social skills. Each kind of community affects schools differently, but as a general trend, the first kind of community is vanishing, leaving the dynamics of status achievement of mobile communities and the cumulated advantages of families as the major sources of inequality in school achievement, unless there are strong countervailing forces. Until this point, Coleman had only thought of interscholastic competition as a countervailing force. Now, driven to pay attention to selection effects, Coleman discovered that the strong family influence could itself be a countervailing force.

As part of a study on achievement in public versus private schools (Coleman et al., 1982; Coleman and Hoffer, 1987), Coleman refined the theory of community impact on schools on the basis of what he learned from the critique of the EEO study: that one should not forget that parents often choose schools and that they often do so in order to *increase* the impact of family background on what happens in schools. This kind of choice leads basically to two kinds of communities. A *functional community* "is a community in which social norms and sanctions, including those that cross generations, arise out of the social structure itself, and both reinforce and perpetuate that structure" (Coleman and Hoffer, 1987, p. 7). When parents interact with one another and with their children and when the parents' interaction includes concern for their children, then a functional community will arise. A school becomes part of a functional community when parents of such a community select a particular school for their children and when their children are in the majority in this school. The school, then, is not an "agent" of society (as it is for public schools) but an agent of a community of families. In TAS, Coleman assumed that the only functional communities possible are the traditional (residential) communities, and he observed that they are vanishing. Now he revised this view in the sense that he discovered that special kinds of non-residential communities do not vanish. Religious communities *with common worship* form such a special functional community. The reason status effects do not completely overshadow the value effects in these communities is the very fact that they are not residential communities and thus lack the major locus of status competition between families. The parents may live in very different neighborhoods but they interact through the institution of the church, which creates some closure and dense, at times intergenerational, contact, including contact concerning values, education, and aspirations in life.

Similar values are clearly not enough to create a functional community. Parents who share similar values (including educational philosophies) but do not interact do not come to common evaluations, do not reinforce each other's norms and sanctions and do not have the relevant information for comparative judgments concerning their own children. When these parents choose to send their children to a particular kind of school the school is an agent of the parents and their values, rather than an agent of society at large or an agent of a (functional) community. Teachers and parents have the same values and thus teachers are likely to represent these values. But the effect of this for education is limited by the fact that the only links among parents and between parents and the school are the common values. Parental involvement in the school itself is not subject to social pressure from other parents of the community, and there is generally no reinforcement of the norms and sanctions that come from the community itself. Coleman calls this kinds of community a *value community.*

In sum, Coleman assumes that the traditional residential (functional) community vanishes and that what are left are non-residential religious functional communities, value communities, and the great mass of adults not related to either. For the last, work has become the relevant context of interaction, but it is not intergenerational and thus does not constitute a community that can reach into schools, other than by the effects of cumulated (dis)advantages and status dynamics. In the USA, three kinds of schools can be identified. First, there are religious private schools involved in functional communities. The most frequent of these in the USA is the Catholic school. Second, there are private schools, some religious, some not, involved in value communities (Montessori, Quaker schools, military academies, etc.).[8] Third, there are public schools not involved in any community (heterogeneous parents). The last are by far the largest group of schools in the USA. What relevance do these different types of school have for the achievement of students, and what does this have to do with community?

It is appropriate to answer these questions, especially for children from disadvantaged families, because it is here that the school can make the biggest difference by counteracting the accident of birth. As Coleman had stated in TAS, the traditional functional community creates inequality of achievement inside the school because the parents' status structure will be more or less reproduced in the school and teachers are influenced by it in their attention to and evaluation of students. Teachers follow parents' values more than society's values (if there is a conflict); parental involvement will be relatively high and norms and sanctions are reinforced. However, because of this, status and stigmas from the local community will carry over into school, thus reinforcing the effects of family background that reproduce the community status order in terms of achievement. Children from disadvantaged families are thus confronted with the fact that their lack of support at home is not compensated but matched by the school. By contrast, in religious functional communities, things are different because the community is established mainly on the basis of religion. Because of this, there is a much smaller influence of parental status on the status of the child in school. Given that religious values are both universalistic and achievement-oriented, and that the reinforcement of values and sanctions coming from parents' interaction pertains to these values (i.e. to academic demands), one would predict that children from disadvantaged families would do much better in religious functional community schools than in traditional functional community schools.

How do value communities affect school achievement? Because parents in such communities have made a conscious choice to send their children to a particular school, they are likely to be concerned about how the school functions, and because teachers act as agents of the parents there is no hostility between teachers and parents. Coleman calls common values and norms *social capital*, and thus value communities have some social capital. However, they have only a low level of social capital because the common norms and sanctions are not reinforced through interaction. Thus, in contrast to functional communities, value community schools have few social resources for realizing high academic demands, especially for those who have no parental support in meeting these demands (i.e. for children from disadvantaged families).

TEST A proper test of this theory of community influence on schools is not possible for Coleman because the data were basically known before the theory was formulated. The test of hypotheses should thus be interpreted as a *post hoc* consistency test with the question: is the theory able to make sense of the data? If social capital works the way this theory of community–school relations assumes, then we should find, specifically with regard to the workings of social capital, the following for pupils from disadvantaged families:

1. Schools which are part of a functional community should show systematically higher parental involvement in school than value community schools, which, in turn should show a higher rate of parental involvement than public schools (social pressure argument).
2. Social capital of parents and schools should have a positive effect on achievement if scholastic achievement is a value (norm and sanction reinforcement argument).
3. Even within a functional community school, achievement of pupils should correlate positively with the amount of social capital of the parents (norm and sanction reinforcement argument).

4 Universalistic values and achievement orientation alone will not suffice to counteract the negative effect of the community status order on the achievement of children from disadvantaged families. Only when these values are linked with the social capital of a religious functional community will this impact of the community status order be significantly reduced or eliminated (norm and sanction reinforcement argument).

RESULTS Let us have a brief look at the results. Coleman divided the schools into three groups corresponding to the theoretical differentiation made: Catholic schools (generally functional community schools, high social capital), other private schools (generally value community schools, low social capital), and public schools (no intergenerational community, no social capital). The first hypothesis fit. Coleman found parental involvement was highest for Catholic schools, somewhat lower for other private schools, and low for public schools. The second hypothesis is corroborated by a clear superiority of Catholic schools with regard to verbal and math achievement, and also by a good show of verbal achievement in value community schools. Public schools scored the lowest on these measures of achievement. For the third hypothesis, we have to remember that the characteristic feature of the religious functional community (as compared to the value community) is that there is intergenerational interaction via the church. This interaction in turn reinforces norms and sanctions. For this reason, the frequency of the student's church attendance should correlate positively with school achievement, especially if the student is in a functional community school. This hypothesis also fits with the findings. Catholic students who attend church often do considerably better in verbal and math achievement than Catholic students who do not. Conforming to the expectations regarding social capital, this effect is twice as strong for Catholic students in Catholic schools as for those in public schools. The hypothesis was also corroborated in terms of dropout rates. Here the difference is quite dramatic. Of the frequent Catholic church attenders in Catholic schools, only 2.7 percent dropped out. Of the Catholic students who rarely or never attended church and went to a public school, more than 21 percent dropped out of school.

The fourth hypothesis was the most crucial for Coleman's refinement of the theory of the relation between community and school. Common values of teachers and parents are not enough to reduce the impact of the community's status order on achievement. For this effect, it is also necessary that parents and school form a functional community. In order to check this hypothesis, Coleman interprets the Catholic values as universalistic and achievement-oriented, and – together with the social capital assumptions about the Catholic church community – he thus comes to expect students from disadvantaged (i.e. black and Hispanic) families to do much better in Catholic schools than in other private schools (and, of course, in public schools). This is consistent with the findings. If one looks at "deficient" families (especially single-parent families, families with working mothers, families without much communication between parents and children) one finds a result very similar to that for disadvantaged families. Values alone are thus not enough to support high academic demands, especially for children of disadvantaged or deficient families. The reinforcement of norms and sanctions through interaction among parents themselves, among parents and their children, and among parents and teachers makes the crucial difference in whether enough strength is given to values to counteract the effect of the community status order.[9]

Because the test of this social capital theory of community influence on schools was *post hoc*, and because the crucial assumptions on church interaction and on universalistic and achievement-oriented values of Catholics were not directly tested, there is ample room left for empirical work and theoretical refinement of this theory. Indeed, Coleman's studies have spawned considerable research interest in private schools and in social capital.[10] No firm judgment is possible yet.

Policy Research

Coleman had very outspoken views on policy research, and they are well worth going into in some detail. For a good understanding of these views, it is necessary to see how they depend on his conception of social change in the Western world.

The Asymmetric Society

As we have seen, in TAS Coleman's analysis of the relation of community to schools is based on a view that the relevant social change in the Western world is driven by the vanishing of traditional residential communities. Later he qualified this view by pointing to the existence of religious functional communities. But, despite this addition, he kept hammering on the classical theme of a change from *Gemeinschaft* to *Gesellschaft*, and he used this theme to work out the role of sociology in society. On this basis, he then elaborated both his views of policy research and his view of the need for fundamental research.

The theory of change that was underlying his analyses from early on was embellished and elaborated over the years and appeared as a book called *The Asymmetric Society*, which he published in 1982. The major thesis of the book and of later elaborations[11] is an interesting twist on the *Gemeinschaft–Gesellschaft* theme. The crucial distinction in this respect for Coleman is the one between a natural person and a legal person. In many ways, a legal person is constructed in analogy to a natural person before the law. It can own assets, it can have rights, responsibilities, and liabilities, it can enter into contract, it can appear before court, be a plaintiff or a defendant, and it can have legally recognized interests. In short, a legal person is in many ways an actor like a natural person, but it is not of flesh and blood but "corporate." This new kind of actor first appeared in the thirteenth century. Towns became such corporate actors, the church became a corporate actor, trading companies became corporate actors with limited liability, etc. The most serious consequences of its invention for the functioning of society took a long time to show themselves clearly. It was only in the twentieth century that the enormity of the impact of this invention came into full view.

Two developments greatly increased the role of corporate actors in society. First, over time, more and more corporate actors came themselves to be composed of positions rather than of natural persons. Positions can also be seen as legal persons of sorts, but their leeway is limited by the fact that they act as agents of a corporate actor: their rights, obligations, interests, etc., are derived from a corporate actor. Of course, like corporate actors, positions can act only through natural persons, but the legal consequences of acting as an agent of a corporate actor (i.e. as occupant of a position) or as a natural (i.e. private) person are quite different.

The second relevant change had to do with the change in balance between natural persons and corporate actors of the new (i.e. positional) sort. The latter increased greatly in numbers. For example, profit-making corporations in the United States increased by more than 500 percent between 1916 and 1968. This increase outdistanced the increase in natural persons. After the Second World War, corporate actors also greatly increased in size. In addition, corporate and semi-corporate actors of the old style (i.e. those composed of natural persons, such as the family and residential communities) decreased in importance. Productive activity has progressively moved from the family into the modern corporate actor, and thus it also moved away from a neighborhood of families (i.e. residential community). As a consequence, the household and the neighborhood lost much of their importance as foci of social interaction, whereas the corporate actor gained in importance as a focus.

This social change created and continues to create a number of important problems, which are due to the increasing asymmetry between corporate actors and natural persons, especially in terms of power. First, natural persons are increasingly affected by the actions of large corporate actors, but there is little they can do to change the balance of power in their favor. This changed the kind of risks natural persons are exposed to. "Old" risks were mainly due to externalities among natural persons (such as communicable diseases). They are on the decline. The "new" risks are due to behavior of powerful corporate actors that are little concerned about possible negative consequences of their action for natural persons (such as pollution). Second, due to their resources, large corporate actors are able to influence knowledge production and the distribution of information.

This has various consequences. It further reduces the ability of natural persons to take on corporate actors when their interests collide. Via the corporate actors' influence on the mass media and on the content of advertising, there is also an increased inconsistency of norms. For example, in market societies, large corporations stress the legitimacy and importance of spending money on yourself and of self-indulgence in general, which clashes with familial and community norms of caring for others and opposition to self-indulgence.

Third, corporate actors are responsible for only certain aspects of persons, say their learning in school or their safety as employee. They are not responsible for a person as person and thus not concerned with whether the various partial responsibilities add up. Because families and communities become less important, there developed a growing vacuum of responsibility for persons.

As a response to these problems, the state has grown considerably, taking the role of central corporate actor and assuming responsibility for reducing the asymmetry between corporate and natural actors, and for filling the vacuum of responsibility by welfare institutions. This increasing paternalism of the state creates a perverse effect. It decreases the power asymmetry between natural persons and corporate actors, but it increases the power aggrandizement of the state itself.

The tasks and preconditions of policy research

Against this background, policy research takes on quite a definite profile.[12] First, there is an increasing demand for various kinds of policy research. Corporate actors are purposefully constructed. With their growth, there is an increasing demand for research on the construction of corporate actors, dealing with their proper functioning, their efficiency, their interrelations, etc. Sociology in its various guises (either as sociology proper or under the name of business administration or organization studies) grows in response to this demand. Also, the state, acquiring ever more responsibilities to deal with power imbalances and dependencies, creates a demand for knowledge on how to deal with these responsibilities (sociology, public administration, welfare economics).

Second, the very diagnosis that leads to an understanding of the need for policy research also suggests normative guidelines for what should be done and how it should be done. The guiding normative stance is that policy research should help to redress the asymmetry between corporate actors and natural persons rather than reinforce it, and it should help to suggest how the vacuum of responsibility can be filled.

1 Because of the power balance, it is likely that corporate actors can afford policy research in their favor. Therefore, the information generated by policy research should always be distributed not only to the sponsor of the research but also to the people at whom the policy is directed.

2 Whether or not corporate actors sponsor it, there are some topics of research that should be covered anyway. Policy research should cover the potential perverse effects of state paternalism. How can the interests of natural persons be protected without strengthening the power of the state? This includes research on how to make corporate actors more responsible. Policy research thus includes prominently risk assessment and research into the possibilities of collective decision-making. Policy research should also be done on possible substitutes for the "old" corporate actors (family, church, community). This prominently includes research on socialization and education, on the possibility of age-balanced organizations, on social capital.

3 Most important for the way policy research should be done is Coleman's analysis of the relationship between policy research and legitimacy. Policy research is often used to legitimize a certain political aim. Whoever has the most resources can have research done to support his political aims. For this very reason, it can easily contribute to the asymmetry rather than redress it. Coleman comes to the conclusion that the only way out of the dilemma that

research can be "bought" to bolster a particular political position is that the research itself is done in such a way that it is considered legitimate by conflicting parties. This can only be achieved if the research does not only deal with factors and effects, but also reveals mechanisms by which the factors produce the effects. There can be much controversy about correlations and the significance of coefficients in regression models. But there can be much less controversy when the researcher traces the mechanism leading from certain causes to certain effects under certain conditions. The upshot of this view is that policy research can only be guarded against disabling politicization by being explicitly linked to fundamental research, and a certain kind of fundamental research at that. Here, Coleman's interests in policy research and in the functioning of systems come together. This, then, was one important reason for him to write a book on the foundations of social theory (Coleman, 1990b), i.e. the *foundations of social science as a mechanism-revealing science* in the service of policy research. In the last section of this chapter, I turn to this book, which is very important for rational choice sociology. Before that, I sketch the context within which rational choice sociology developed and the place Coleman took in this development.

Rational Choice Sociology

In his research on education, Coleman had been very much interested in detecting the mechanisms by which schools and communities work. However, this research did not focus on making a contribution to the conceptual tools with which a "mechanism-revealing" social science could build its substantive theories. His work on these tools was a separate strand. However, all three strands – education, tools for constructing social theory and policy research – had come together early in Coleman's construction of academic games.[13] As he had found out in TAS, games can create social environments which channel energies devoted to the improvement of knowledge and skills. By introducing the right kind of games one could use them as instruments of social intervention in schools. At the same time, games create a simulated social system and in their construction one would have to anticipate the system's functioning. In addition, by observing games in action, one can discover links between the elements of the games (rules, communication structure, group formation, etc.) and the collective outcomes. Thus games are at once tools for social policy and tools for the detection of system functioning, analogous to experiments in psychology. Coleman was a pioneer in this use of simulation games (see Boocock, 1996). The construction of a system in order to understand it has remained the basic approach throughout his theoretical development.[14] This approach also fed Coleman's development as a rational choice sociologist. How did this paradigm develop?

In the 1960s, the hegemony of functionalism in sociology waned and sociologists began to battle for the successor to the throne. Symbolic interactionism, conflict sociology, exchange theory, systems theory, in their various versions, attacked each other and greatly weakened the prestige sociology had achieved over the years. In addition (or maybe even because of it), a number of economists had broken through the traditional division of labor between sociology and economics and had begun to move into "non-market" areas, especially with regard to the question of how collective decision-making was possible (how one could aggregate individual preferences) and what kinds of institutions would optimally solve problems encountered in collective decision-making. This included studies on voting, political party competition, and coalition formation, constitutions, the supply of public goods, interest groups, bureaucracy, property rights, public policy, and finance. At times this work has been collectively called "the new political economy" or "modern political economics" (see Frey, 1978). The work of Arrow, Downs, Buchanan and Tullock, Hayek, and North is of particular relevance here, but soon political scientists such as Riker (see Riker and Ordeshook, 1973) followed suit. In 1965, the economist Mancur Olson published his *The Logic of Collective Action* and introduced the free-rider problem to the analysis of group behavior, greatly affecting the way interest groups and social movements would be studied from then on.

Through these developments, game theory finally became useful for the analysis of social phenomena on a wider scale, and quickly spread into political science, and later also to sociology and social psychology, especially concerning the study of social dilemmas. As far as sociology was concerned, this "onslaught" by rational choice via economists and political scientists was at first mainly restricted to the area of political sociology, but it exerted considerable pressure on the traditional dividing line between economics and sociology (see Lindenberg, 1985).

From early on, Coleman had followed these developments and was keenly interested. He had come to this interest on account of Homans (see Coleman and Lindenberg, 1989), who made a strong point for viewing social behavior as exchange. But unlike Homans, Coleman did not try to explain exchange behavior by psychological learning theories. He was persuaded that learning theories would not be very useful for the reconstruction of system functioning, whereas a microeconomic approach would. The latter is purposive and has proven its usefulness for the analysis of systems of exchange; the former focuses on conditioning and has been restricted to the analysis of small groups.

In 1964, Coleman published an article that can be seen as the analytical result of his interest in games and the mechanics of system functioning, and, at the same time, as the beginning of the long strand of developing tools for the analysis of social systems. It had the simple title "Collective Decisions" and it dealt with the question of how the economic theory of exchange could be used to explain social order. He argued that sociologists usually take as their starting point social systems in which norms exist. In turn, these norms govern individual behavior. But that says nothing about why there are norms to begin with and how social order can emerge when there are no norms. For this reason, he argued for what he considered to be the opposite, but possibly more fruitful, error: to start with man wholly free, "unsocialized, entirely self-interested, not constrained by norms of a system, but only rationally calculating to further his own self interests" (Coleman, 1964b, p. 167). He held on to this starting point all the way to his *Foundations of Social Theory.*

After 1964, the exchange theory which traces the creation of social order, including norms, rights, systems of authority, and concentration of power, was further worked out in many articles and a number of books. In 1973, he published the book *Mathematics of Collective Action*. One year later, the book *Power and the Structure of Society* appeared. At that time, Coleman's "rational choice" approach remained very much within the realm of what non-market economists did: collective decision-making.

During the early 1970s, the "new political economy" also influenced a number of European sociologists who had earlier been heavily influenced by Homans, most notably Albert, Hummell, Opp, Vanberg, Wippler, and Lindenberg. They developed various versions of rational choice sociology under different names: for example, "individualistic sociology" (see Vanberg, 1975), "structural-individualistic approach" (see Wippler, 1978), "individualistic social science" (see Opp, 1979), "the economic tradition" (see Albert, 1979), and related solutions to the micro–macro problem (see Lindenberg, 1977). In France, Raymond Boudon had been influenced by Lazarsfeld and by Coleman's work on education, and he adopted a rational actor orientation in his research on inequality in education (Boudon, 1974). A number of years later, he developed this into a full-fledged approach to rational action sociology (Boudon, 1981). Substantively, the European versions of rational choice (or rational action, as it was sometimes called) sociology were less formal and more concerned with truly sociological topics than was Coleman's concern with collective decision-making.

In the early 1980s the two developments began to merge. Coleman visited Europe and met with the European rational choice sociologists in a great number of symposia (beginning in 1980 with a symposium on solidarity and trust in Groningen, the Netherlands, and in 1981 with one in Berlin on the micro–macro problem). By then, rational choice sociology was institutionalized in a number of Dutch universities and through the Dutch national science foundation. In 1982, a Dutch–German delegation organized the first rational choice sessions of the International Sociological Association's Meeting (in Mexico), beginning the international institutionalization of rational choice sociology (see Raub, 1982).

Back in the United States, Coleman influenced a number of American scholars, who, quite independently of each other, developed versions of rational choice sociology, including Anthony Oberschall (1973) and Michael Hechter (1983).[15] Hechter also profited from the direct influence of the economic historian Douglas North, who was more sociologically interested than most economists.

The year 1983 was very important for further development. A conference organized by Coleman in Chicago brought many rational choice sociologists together and confronted them with non-market economists and with theorists who were critical of rational choice sociology. The conference papers were later published, along with the heated discussions that followed each presentation (see Lindenberg et al., 1986). This meeting was very important for the establishment of rational choice sociology as a generally recognized approach. Gary Becker, the economist who had done much to push the economic approach into non-market areas, participated at this conference and was asked a few months later by

Coleman whether he would consider a joint appointment in sociology. He accepted and both he and Coleman started in that year a joint faculty seminar on rational choice that became famous far beyond the circles of Chicago academia.

In 1984, a sizable conference on the micro–macro problem followed in Germany (see Alexander et al., 1987), and a few years later, at another rational choice conference in Germany on social institutions (see Hechter et al., 1990), the plan for a journal on rational choice sociology was born. Coleman was willing to carry the burden of editing the journal, and the first issues of *Rationality and Society*, as the journal was called after long deliberation on an appropriate name, appeared in 1989. In the academic year 1991–2, Coleman was president of the American Sociological Association (ASA) and used the ASA meetings of that year as a general forum on the importance of actor-oriented sociology. By then, his magnum opus had appeared and rational choice sociology had changed the discourse among sociologists, even among many of those who would not call themselves rational choice sociologists.

The Foundations of Social Theory

In 1986, Coleman collected his most relevant articles on collective action and published them under the title *Individual Interests and Collective Action*. The widening of his rational choice sociology into a general approach, however, had to wait until 1990, when his *magnum opus*, *The Foundations of Social Theory*, appeared.

The Foundations of Social Theory is a heavy tome of almost a thousand pages. The various bits and pieces Coleman had worked out earlier are here joined into one architecture. After an introductory chapter on "metatheory," the book presents five parts: I, "elementary actions and relations" (with, among others, a section on actors and resources, interest, and control); II, "structures of action" (with, among others, sections on authority, collective behavior, and norms); III, "corporate action" (with, among others, sections on constitutions and social choice); IV, "modern society" (with, among others, sections on the new corporate actors and on the new social science, akin to arguments from *The Asymmetric Society* but more focused on the relation between policy research and fundamental research); and V, "the mathematics of social action" (with, among others, sections on dynamics of the linear system of action, corporate actors, and collective decisions). This last part is a mathematical treatment of many of the theoretical points made in the book.

Because I have presented the major argument of part IV above, and because it is impossible to go into the mathematics of social action in this review, it is parts I to III which interest us the most. They reflect the "tool" character of the book. Simple tools are developed first, and they help to build more complex tools for the analysis of social systems later. Still driven by the primacy of intervention as the ultimate goal of the social sciences,[16] and, conversely, true to the idea that you only understand a social system if you can construct it, he builds up from micro to macro, from actors to exchange, to systems of exchange and all the way to corporate action. What is the gist of this development?

The *essential elements of actors* considered by Coleman all have to do with what drives interaction among actors, given that each actor strives to increase the realization of his or her interest. Because Coleman is mainly concerned with the micro to macro link, he does not want to assume things which he ultimately wants to explain. Thus, he uses the highly simplified model of microeconomics. "I will use the conception of rationality employed in economics" and "begin with norm-free, self-interested persons as elements of the theory" (Coleman, 1990b, pp.14, 31).

Given this theory of action, Coleman can pinpoint the well from which all social interaction is generated. The basic idea is quite simple, and it represents a reformulation of the classical economic *theory of exchange* (already used by Adam Smith): the natural state is interdependence among actors and this state is a condition of life which keeps returning even though actors keep reducing it. A slightly more technical way to say this is that actors have interests and they control some resources and events, but their world is imperfect because they are not fully in control of those resources and events that can increase the realization of their interests; some of these resources and events are partially or wholly under the control of others. Thus, in order to improve their situation, actors have to exchange control over resources and/or events, i.e. they have to exchange control over things which are of little interest to them for control over things that are of great interest to them. Such voluntary exchange by definition improves the situation of both actors.

Social systems are often generated by the need to facilitate the exchanges which reduce the individual interdependencies (even though such measures may increase the collective interdependencies).[17] What problems does exchange encounter? What solutions to these problems constitute the most important social systems? These two questions guide us easily through the bulk of Coleman's book.

Control over actions

RIGHTS TO ACT When two people exchange apples for oranges it seems that they exchange physical entities. Often, this view is sufficient. Upon closer inspection, however, it turns out that people do not exchange physical entities, but rights to carry out certain actions. In one society, the exchange implies that each party has the right to use the fruits as he or she sees fit: to consume them or to dispose of them. In another society, the fruits may be subject to certain religious restrictions and therefore the exchange implies only, say, the right to consume, not the right to plant their seeds, or to resell them. For intangible goods this point is even more obvious. To see that not goods but rights are being exchanged is an old but important way to analyze exchange. It presupposes, though, that there are rights. What are they and where do they come from? Here Coleman has developed an original and far-reaching conception. For him, the heart of the matter is *rights to act* in a certain way. To have control over something means that one has the right to do certain things with it.[18] What exactly the control entails depends on the right involved. Ownership of a resource can mean very different things, depending on what rights to act with regard to this resource are connected to it. A local government may not allow a house owner to rent his rooms without permission, a person may not be allowed to sell one of his organs, etc. There are other rights not ordinarily associated with ownership, such as the right to smoke, free speech, or freedom of movement. Rights may change, and thus can be lost and gained without them being exchanged. How can they change? Many rights are legal rights created in the political process. But that process ultimately rests on the broad area of rights not covered by law. For Coleman, such rights rest on consensus, especially the consensus of relevant others. Who are the relevant others? They are those who are powerful enough collectively to enforce a right. Quite contrary to the vast normative discussions on consensual allocation of rights (say by Rawls and Nozick), Coleman puts *given power differences* at the heart of consensus. When one considers power-weighted consensus (as one should, in Coleman's eyes), the question of how rights ought to be distributed is generally unanswerable and only meaningful *within* a system of action in which interests and relative power between actors are given (Coleman, 1990b, p. 53). Thus, rights have a social base, including the power distribution of such a base. But because the allocation of rights to act is so important, and because consensus is often not spontaneously generated, societies will develop structures that deal with the generation and change of such rights and with conflict arising from their allocation.

INALIENABLE RIGHTS AND AUTHORITY There is one particular class of rights which create special problems and special solutions. Individuals may or may not have the right of control over a particular class of their own actions. For example, a child may not have the right to decide when to go to school. Conversely, if people have rights of control over many of their own actions, then they can exchange them for something else. The special problem is that actions are inalienable: they remain a part of the person even if the right to control them has been given away. It is through this circumstance that *authority* relations come into existence. To have authority over X is to have the right to control a particular class of X's actions. Because X's actions are inalienable, authority can only exist if X grants the right to control to someone else (provided X has the right to control his own actions, including the right to transfer this right).

An important distinction with regard to authority relations is that between conjoint and disjoint authority. When I grant authority to someone over a certain class of my actions, it may be in a context where I presume the other (for example, a charismatic leader) acts in my interest. This is *conjoint* authority. There is a fundamental limitation to such authority relations, according to Coleman. For an individual, it is not easy to determine for what classes of action authority should be granted. Often, a leader is likely to ask more and an individual is likely to grant more control to the leader than is in the individual's own interest, especially when many other individuals do the same. It may not be easy to fine-tune such decisions and issues of the protection of the individual arise, creating a special problem of asymmetry, as we have seen in the discussion of *The Asymmetric Society*.

In a formal organization, I am likely to grant authority without the presumption that the superordinate acts in my interest. This is *disjoint* authority. Here, I need to be reimbursed for granting this right (say, by wages or salary) because the superordinate has no particular interest in my interests. The defect of this kind of relation, according to Coleman, is, conversely, that the subordinate has no particular interest in the outcome the superordinate wants to achieve. Although he gave away the right to control a certain class of his actions, he is still the one who has to perform these actions. Unless the actions over which control is granted can be closely monitored, individuals are likely to let those actions be governed by their own interests rather than by the outcome desired by the superordinate. This is well known in economics as the *principal–agent problem*. The superordinate, in turn, will try to extend his control over actions of the individual which have not been included in the original exchange. Unless the classes of actions can be very clearly specified, he will probably succeed and this success is likely to lead to the development of structures to protect both principal (superordinate) and agent (subordinate).

Time asymmetry and trust

Not all exchanges take place instantaneously. Often, a transaction is drawn out in time, such that one party must invest resources (i.e. give away control over resources) long before the other party returns the benefit. For example, in a conjoint authority relation, the control is given away at one point in time and the stream of benefits is drawn out over a longer period of time. Or a company may have to build special machines to make the product that the client wants. If the client pays ahead of time, he does not know whether he will get what he paid for, and if he pays afterwards, the company does not know whether it will recoup its investment. Exchanges which involve such *time asymmetries* involve a special kind of risk: the risk that depends on the performance of another actor. Coleman proposed to use the word *trust* to denote this special kind of risk. It can be expressed in a handy formula. Let p be the probability that the trustee is trustworthy (and $1 - p$ that he is not), let L be the potential loss if he is untrustworthy, and let G be the potential gain if he is trustworthy. Then I will trust the trustee (i.e. I will take the risk of unilateral transfer of control) if $p/1 - p > L/G$.

Many interesting questions are generated by this concept of trust. For example, information on p, L, and G will have a great impact on whether or not trust is placed, with p often being the least well known quantity. People are likely to have a standard estimate of p which holds for everyone in their system of action about whom they have no particular information. When L/G is large, then a person will trust only if p exceeds the standard estimate, and that may take considerable observation time. Trusting (i.e. close) friendships build up slowly because, in such relationships, the potential loss is quite high compared to the gain, and thus p must be high. A confidence man may achieve very quick trust by convincing someone that he has little to lose and much to gain, i.e. by making L/G appear very low, so that even a slight reduction of the standard estimate of p will still lead to placing trust. Research that has been generated by this conception of trust is growing.[19]

As with the other problems concerning exchange which have been discussed so far, this problem of trust is likely to lead to social structures in which it is to the potential trustee's interest to be trustworthy.

The impact of size: from relations to structures

As Simmel realized long ago, new problems arise if we move from a dyad to a triad, and new problems arise if we move from a small group to a large group. Heedful of this difference, Coleman moves from dyadic exchange to systems of exchange, from authority relations to systems of authority, from trust relations to systems of trust. The problems arising for the dyads are here confounded by the problems arising from size. I will briefly go into each one of them.

SYSTEMS OF EXCHANGE There may be more than one person offering or demanding a particular good for exchange. In that case, we get competition and indirect exchange; in short, we get markets. One of the major problems of establishing a market is the requirement of pairwise coincidence of wants: B wants something that A has and vice versa. If there is a medium of exchange, this coincidence of wants is not necessary for the exchange and a market can grow. For example, money allows exchange without this coincidence. Coleman discusses some media in non-economic systems of exchange, such as status. However, interesting non-economic systems of exchange can also exist without a particular medium of exchange if the goods exchanged are highly limited in number. The innovative twist he brings to the analysis of these kinds of systems is his particular theory of exchange, which allows a fairly sophisticated analysis of non-economic exchange systems.

The relevant elements of his theory of exchange are two individual-level characteristics (interests and control) and two system-level characteristics (power and value). An example will help. Actors have interests (say, a student wants good grades and free time; the teacher wants serious effort from the student) and they have control over certain resources (say, a student has initial control over his or her own time and effort; the teacher has initial control over grades). Effort can be defined as the proportion of total time a student spends on homework. In a school, there is then an exchange system in which effort is exchanged for grades. This exchange takes place with certain exchange rates. In a perfect market these exchange rates converge to one exchange rate which defines the relative values of effort and grades (values at equilibrium). Note that the exchange rate is a system-level concept; it does not represent the average individual ratio of effort to grades. Power is here conceived of as the value of the resources an actor controls. Thus, although power is assigned to an individual and not to a relation, it is a system-level concept because the value depends on all the others' interest. If the teacher values the effort of some students higher than that of other students, the market is imperfect and the exchange rate is not identical for all students. As a result, the power of students also differs. The power of the teacher is the value of grades. In part V of the *Foundations*, Coleman works out the mathematics of this kind of analysis (and for this example) and I will not go into this here.

Coleman focuses here on the analysis of non-economic exchange systems but, contrary to his treatment of authority and trust, he does not go more deeply into an analysis of problems of exchange systems themselves. Still, his approach to exchange systems has been quite influential. It has been applied in political science (for example, Marsden, 1981; Pappi and Kappelhoff, 1984; König, 1998) and it has helped the development of sophisticated models of influence in collective decision-making (Stokman and Van Oosten, 1994; Yamaguchi, 1996).

AUTHORITY SYSTEMS When authority relations are stacked, we get a multi-level authority system. Coleman's concept of rights is very useful here for pointing to a fundamental difference in the way authority systems are organized and function. In a *feudal* authority structure, the layers are indeed stacked. Each subordinate has vested authority in the direct superior. Household members were subject to the authority of the head of the household, the head was subject to the authority of a lord, who, in turn, was subject to the authority of a higher lord, etc., all the way up to the king. The advantage of this structure is that in each link the principal–agent problem is solved by personal loyalty, in which the subordinate identifies with (part of) the interests of the superior. However, the disadvantage is that the span of control is very small. A lord has no authority over members of someone else's household, even though he has authority over the head of the household.

By contrast, a *modern* authority structure involves two important innovations. First, not just one but two rights are transferred to the superior: the right to control a class of actions of the subordinate and the right to delegate this control to someone else. Thus, the boss can delegate authority to a supervisor, so that in fact the subordinate is supervised by someone in whom he or she has not vested authority. This removes all the constraints on the span of control, greatly increasing the power of an organization to act. However, now the principal–agent problem is considerable. If A delegates authority to B, how can she keep B from exercising authority over C mostly for his own interests rather than A's interests? This leads to the second innovation. Rather than authority being vested in individuals, it is vested in positions. The rights and resources belonging to the authority are the property not of a person but of a position.

As a consequence of this combined change from direct to delegated authority and from person to position, a new kind of actor evolved, in whom authority is vested by individuals and who delegates authority to the positions: a *corporate actor*. The importance of this change can – in Coleman's eyes – not be overestimated. We have seen that Coleman's view of policy research is governed by the asymmetry between natural and corporate actors. Modern society cannot be understood without understanding this asymmetry.

SYSTEMS OF TRUST The important point about trust is that it is often the decisive factor in the decision to go through or not to go through with a potentially advantageous exchange between two parties. Without trust the transaction will not go through, and because it would have been potentially advantageous for both, failure to go through is a loss for both. In transaction costs economics, such situations are well analyzed in terms of credible commitments (see Williamson, 1985) through which the probability of default becomes very small. Coleman chose to focus on another mechanism. When these two parties cannot place trust in each other, there may be intermediaries who are trusted by both and who can create an indirect link. Coleman discusses three such links: the advisor, the guarantor, and the entrepreneur. An example of the *advisor* is a lobbyist in Washington, DC, who introduces interested parties (potential trustees) to public officials (potential trustors). The public official trusts the judgment of the lobbyist that he or she has something to gain by being willing to listen to the potential trustee, and therefore he or she is willing to invest some time in the meeting. The *guarantor* is someone who is willing to bear the risk the trustor would otherwise face. The *entrepreneur* is someone who is able to combine the resources of various trustors and deploy them among various trustees. Examples are an investment bank or a political entrepreneur who is able to generate votes for a legislative proposal. Society can be seen as being shot through with such overlapping systems of trust, at times based on special institutions (such as an investment bank), at times based on reputation. These systems of trust are only just beginning to attract wide attention (see, for example, Klein 1997; Hofman et al., 1998).

Coleman also deals with larger systems. In particular, advisory trust can create large systems of trust which characteristically fluctuate in expansion and contraction. In academia such systems are well known. Let there be some well placed advisors who speak highly of X. Others, who trust the judgment of the advisors, repeat their assessment without admitting that they have not formed their own opinion on direct inspection of the performance (say, the publications). Such a reputation can expand quickly and generally lower the requirements for evidence of excellence for jobs, stipends, and research monies. However, this system is precarious. One well placed advisor who asks "Have you really read something by X and found it good? Can anyone really find this work outstanding?" may start a quick process of reputational contraction. A similar process can also be observed for charismatic leaders. Such processes can be analyzed as widespread transfers of control of belief, akin to processes of collective behavior.

Collective behavior, such as an escape panic, a bank or stock market panic, a hostile crowd, a rash of sightings of flying saucers, or other fads and fashions, seems to be far removed from rational action. But Coleman analyzes such seemingly irrational group behavior as situations in which many group members transfer large portions of control over their actions (or beliefs) to the various other members and wait for some action of these other members in order to determine what they themselves would do. Coleman discusses different kinds of this behavior and, in my judgment, the analysis is very original and perhaps one the most convincing examples of the usefulness of the concept of transfer of control.

The role of externalities

When two parties exchange, their actions may generate positive or negative effects on third parties who are not involved in the exchange. Such externalities may also be generated by someone's unilateral actions. Coleman follows the analysis by Ullmann-Margalit (1977) by assuming that it is situations of externalities which create a demand for norms (see also Lindenberg, 1977, 1982). As Ullmann-Margalit did, Coleman focuses mainly on negative externalities. However, he expands on the analysis of norms in a number of ways. First, he defines norms in his own framework as the socially established transfer of the right to control certain of one's own actions to others. A norm concerns some focal action. The most interesting cases involve a focal action which creates a conflict of interest between a target who performs the focal action and others who experience negative side-effects of this action, say from dropping a banana peel on the sidewalk. Norms which regulate such situations Coleman calls "essential norms" (as opposed to "conventional" norms, which coordinate action). The norm takes the right away from the target to do as he pleases and gives the right to control a certain class of his actions to the beneficiaries collectively (of whom the target may or may not be a member). The beneficiaries' right to sanction the target is nothing but the exercise of their right to control (which had been taken away from the target). This transfer of rights to the collectivity of beneficiaries is an important turning point in the construction because it marks the creation of collective actors.

Second, externalities create control interests in the "focal" action among those who experience the externalities. This does not create demand for a norm yet. A control interest only turns into a demand for a norm if (a) an action has similar externalities for many others and (b) no exchanges in rights among dyads can solve the problem (i.e. no individual can acquire the rights of control and a market in rights of control of the action cannot be easily established).

Third, demand for a norm does not mean that a norm will come into existence. What, then, is required for a norm to come into existence? The crucial point is sanctions. If the potential beneficiaries of a norm do not have the capability to apply effective sanctions against the focal action, they cannot really control the focal action of the target. For this reason, Coleman focuses on the conditions for establishing effective sanctions as conditions for the generation of norms. Briefly stated, these conditions come down to the ability to overcome the free-rider problem involved in sanctioning. In turn, this ability depends on social relationships, especially the closure of networks which can create rewards (say approval) for sanctioning which outweigh the costs of sanctioning. Closure provides the strength of consensus necessary for the legitimacy of and the strong approval of sanctioning. In this sense both the social structure and the norms that it can generate can be viewed as social capital, especially when the norms are "conjoint," i.e. when the targets and beneficiaries are the same persons.

Above I discussed the importance of corporate actors in Coleman's view of what drives the most serious problems within modern Western societies and gives direction to policy research. In the *Foundations*, Coleman brings the analysis of *corporate actors* into the general architecture of the micro-to-macro approach. When, due to size or other reasons, a group of individuals has a demand for norms but not the ability to create effective sanctions (and thereby lacks the ability to govern behavior by norms), it may be able to create a *formal constitution* in which the right to control certain classes of actions of individuals is transferred to a collectivity which, in turn, is then clearly identified as a corporate actor with vested authority. There are clear normative consequences of this conception. Constitutions which are established by force are likely to comprise individuals with very heterogeneous power and interests regarding the actions of the corporate actor. In all likelihood, the corporate actor has more authority over some individuals than they would voluntarily grant it. As a response, one could argue that the optimal constitution would be the "conjoint" one, in which targets and beneficiaries are the same individuals. However, Coleman argues, the whole point of this kind of an analysis is that under different circumstances different kinds of constitutions are optimal, since not consensus *per se* is important, but consensus weighted by the power of the actors involved. "A constitution is optimal if in the system that results, rights for each class of actions are allocated in accordance with the interests of those who, postconstitutionally, have power-weighted interests that are stronger than the opposing power-weighted interests" (p. 355).

In this consideration of power for the establishment of constitutions, Coleman's approach is unique, and it is not a matter of taking the side of the strong against the weak but a matter of the criterion used. Coleman rejects collective welfare criteria which are not based on individual choice, and he rejects criteria, such as Pareto optimality, which do not consider interpersonal comparison of utility. The more powerful has a stronger weight in the formation of consensus because others recognize his larger interest in a certain solution. In a way, power has an important effect even without its being used to coerce. Coleman's conceptions of interests, control value, and power lead him directly to the concept of relative power as the characterization of interpersonal comparison and the need for the consideration of interpersonal comparison for the micro-to-macro transition. Constitutions cannot arise and be maintained without reflecting relative power, because the ability to sanction is part and parcel of any collectively held right.

SUMMARY AND CONCLUSION

The key to Coleman's work can be found in two major concerns and their combination. First, he was concerned with high schools and with ways to improve their functioning. Second, and even more importantly, he was very interested in the development of theory on the functioning of social systems, which for him meant a theory that will move "from the micro level of action to the macro level of norms, social values, status distribution and social conflict." The combination of his two major interests resulted in a third preoccupation: policy research and institutional innovation, especially in the field of education. This review covers all three interests and, for reasons of space, I cannot summarize them here. Suffice it to mention a few highlights. His research on education resulted in interesting theories on the relation of community and social capital to what is going on in schools. It also resulted in the conviction that only an actor-oriented approach can handle the analysis of such complex phenomena as schools and school achievement. The same conclusion drove his view on policy research. In order to keep policy research from being dragged into political battles, it is absolutely necessary to analyze mechanisms which supposedly generate the effect from given conditions. Only such a mechanism-revealing social science can hope to gain enough consensus to stay out of the direct political interests. His *magnum opus*, then, was meant as the foundation for such a mechanism-revealing social science.

There can only be a rough *evaluation* of his work in such an overview. Coleman's work is vast and covers many different areas and, of those, only a few highlights can be mentioned here. His substantive theories of lasting interest are in my view his theory of community, his theory of the asymmetric society, including his elaborations of the concepts of social capital and of trust, and his theory of collective behavior (panics, crazes, etc.). In addition, his insistence that every theory using consensus should consider power-weighted consensus is probably one of the most far-reaching of his substantive suggestions and, at the same time, at present one of the least recognized. His work on rational choice sociology gave a considerable boost to this kind of approach, and it systematized a great number of known pieces into a new architecture.

Of course, there are also some *limitations*. Here, too, I will mention only a few which in my view are of particular importance. First, although many of his substantive theories have been developed in the context of empirical research, they are by and large not well tested yet. Either he developed theory in order to interpret his own findings or he developed it outside the context of empirical research altogether. There is thus ample room left for empirical work on his ideas. Second, his particular kind of rational choice theory led him at times into forced constructions. The insistence on using the "naked" model of rational choice of microeconomics, and the attempt to see all social processes in light of exchanges and the transfer of the right to act, at times severely hampered Coleman in working out his substantive theories. For example, he was of the firm opinion that the design of institutions which could replace the lost functions of primordial orders is one of the prime tasks of policy research. Yet it is hardly possible to describe the functions of primordial orders in the language of his framework, let alone come up with substitutes (see Lindenberg, 1993, 1996, for details). Third, his particular approach to the macro–micro–macro links focuses almost exclusively on the micro–macro connection and pays little attention to the macro–micro link. For this reason, Coleman's theoretical analyses are very much in need of complementary efforts by others. Fourth, his approach only considers exchange. For him people never jointly produce anything. For this reason, the dynamics of cooperation in joint production remains outside his analysis of trust and of the internal and external functioning of corporate actors.

All told, his considerable achievements dwarf the limitations and in my opinion Coleman's place among sociologists of the second half of the twentieth century is likely to remain unequalled.

Notes

1 This claim can be substantiated by the fact that Coleman in his later life was quoted more than any other living sociologist (see volume 19 of the *International Encyclopedia of the Social Sciences*, 1994). Merton is still alive and active at present but the major period of his contribution to sociology was in the 1940s to the 1960s.
2 Coleman transcript I, p. 361 (in Clark, 1996).
3 Clark's (1996) collection of papers on Coleman is very useful to flesh out many of the aspects covered in this review.
4 Coleman also sees a direct influence of community on the importance of athletics in the fact that adults use interscholastic competition as community entertainment.
5 Boys and girls answered almost identically: 54 percent found parents' disapproval, 43 percent peers' disapproval, and a mere 3 percent teachers' disapproval most difficult to accept; see TAS, p. 5.
6 The difference in research problem in TAS and EEO may have fostered the mistaken idea, often found in the literature (see Kandel, 1996), that Coleman "discovered" the influence of family background in EEO, against his earlier "exaggerated" view of peer influence in TAS.
7 This was forcefully driven home by a number of critics, most notably by Hanushek (1972). See Heckman and Neal (1996) for the broader context of these selection issues in Coleman's study.
8 Within this category, Coleman distinguishes a special subgroup of high-performance schools. I will not go into this finer-grade distinction here.
9 Coleman also finds that the social capital of parents and the school has a bigger impact on achievement of children from disadvantaged families than the per pupil expenditure of that school.
10 For example, Bryk et al. (1993), Schneider and Coleman (1993), Dijkstra and Peschar (1996), and Hofman et al. (1996).
11 Coleman later embellished the arguments in this book in various chapters of his *Foundations of Social Theory*, especially with regard to policy research.
12 There is a great number of publications by Coleman on policy research, but the arguments are most clearly brought together in part IV of his *Foundations of Social Theory*.
13 He is also quite explicit about the importance these games played for his own theoretical development: "It was the development and use of such social-simulation games which led me away from my previous theoretical orientation, of a Durkheimian sort, to one based on purposive action" (Coleman, 1990b, p. 11).
14 The reason computer simulation did not interest Coleman very much is, in his own words, that such simulation draws too much attention to the theory of action and distracts too much from the construction of social theory.

15 Somewhat later, Douglas Heckathorn came to develop an interesting game-theoretic approach to rational choice sociology.
16 The quality criterion of explanations is thus pragmatic: "The explanation is satisfactory if it is useful for the particular kinds of intervention for which it is intended" (Coleman, 1990b, p. 5).
17 This looks like a purely functional (black box) argument, but it is not. Coleman is fully aware that mechanisms need to be specified which translate a demand or need into a structure or rule. When I discuss the emergence of norms below, this point will become clear.
18 At times, Coleman speaks, somewhat confusingly, of the "right to control something," meaning that one has undisputed control over that something.
19 See, for example, Raub and Weesie (1990), Snijders (1996), and Buskens (1999).

Bibliography

Writings of James Coleman

The Adolescent Society. 1961. Glencoe, IL: Free Press.

Introduction to Mathematical Sociology. 1964a. Glencoe, IL: Free Press.

Collective decisions. 1964b. Reprinted in J. S. Coleman, *Individual Interests and Collective Action.* Cambridge: Cambridge University Press (1986), pp.15–32.

Equality of Educational Opportunity (with E. Q. Campbell, C. J. Hobson, J. McPartland, A. M. Mood, F. D. Weinfeld, and R. L. York). 1966. Washington, DC: US Government Printing Office.

The Mathematics of Collective Action. 1973. London: Heinemann Educational Books.

The Asymmetric Society. 1982. Syracuse, NY: Syracuse University Press.

High School Achievement: Public, Catholic, and Private Schools Compared (with T. Hoffer and S. Kilgore). 1983. New York: Basic Books.

Individual Interests and Collective Action. 1986. Cambridge: Cambridge University Press.

Approaches to Social Theory (edited with S. Lindenberg and S. Nowak). 1986. New York: Russell Sage.

Public and Private High Schools: The Impact of Communities (with T. Hoffer). 1987. New York: Basic Books.

In Memoriam George Homans (with S. Lindenberg). 1989. *Rationality and Society*, 1, 283ff.

Robert K. Merton as teacher. 1990a. In J. Clark, C. Modgil, and S. Modgil (eds), *Robert K. Merton.* London: Falmer Press, pp. 25–32.

Foundation of Social Theory. 1990b. Cambridge, MA: Harvard University Press.

Parents, Their Children and Schools (with B. Schneider). 1993. Boulder, CO: Westview Press.

Reflections on Schools and Adolescents. 1996. In J. Clark (ed.), *James S. Coleman.* London/Washington, DC: Falmer Press, pp.17–31.

Further reading

Albert, H. (1979) The Economic Tradition, Economics as a Research Programme for Theoretical Social Science. In K. Brunner (ed.), *Economics and Social Institutions.* Boston, the Hague, and London: Nijhoff.

Alexander, J. C., Giesen, B., Münch, R. and Smelser, N. J. (eds) (1987) *The Micro Macro Link.* Berkeley: University of California Press.

Boocock, S. S. (1996) Games with Simulated Environments: Educational Innovation and Applied Sociological Research. In J. Clark (ed.), *James S. Coleman*. London and Washington, DC: Falmer Press, pp. 133–46.

Boudon, R. (1974) *Education, Opportunity, and Social Inequality*. New York: Wiley.

Boudon, R. (1981) *The Logic of Social Action*. London: Routledge & Kegan Paul.

Bryk, A. S., Lee, V. E., and Holland, P. B. (1993) *Catholic Schools and the Common Good*. Cambridge, MA: Harvard University Press.

Buskens, V. (1999) *Social Networks and Trust*. Amsterdam: Thesis Publishers.

Clark, J. (ed.) (1996) *James S. Coleman*. London and Washington, DC: Falmer Press.

Dijkstra, A. B. and Peschar, J. L. (1996) Religious Determinants of Academic Attainment in the Netherlands. *Comparative Education Review*, 40, 47–65.

Frey, B. (1978) *Modern Political Economics*. Oxford: Martin Robertson.

Hanushek, E. (1972) *Education and Race*. Cambridge, MA: Ballinger Press.

Hechter, M. (ed.) (1983) *The Microfoundations of Macrosociology*. Philadelphia: Temple University Press.

Hechter, M., Opp, K.-D., and Wippler, R. (eds) (1990) *Social Institutions*. New York: Aldine de Gruyter.

Heckman, J. J. and Neal, D. (1996) Coleman's Contributions to Education: Theory, Research Styles and Empirical Research. In J. Clark (ed.), *James S. Coleman*. London and Washington, DC: Falmer Press, pp. 81–102.

Hoffman, P. T., Postel-Vinay, G., and Rosenthal, J.-L. (1998) What Do Notaries Do? Overcoming Asymmetric Information in Financial Markets: the Case of Paris, 1751. *Journal of Institutional and Theoretical Economics*, 154, 499–530.

Hofman, R., Hofman, W. H. A., Guldenmond, H., and Dijkstra, A. B. (1996) Variation in Effectiveness between Private and Public Schools: the Impact of School and Family Networks. *Educational Research and Evaluation*, 2, 366–94.

Kandel, D. (1996) Coleman's Contribution to Understanding Youth and Adolescence. In J. Clark (ed.), *James S. Coleman*. London and Washington, DC: Falmer Press, pp. 33–46.

Klein, D. B. (ed.) (1997) *Reputation: Studies in the Voluntary Elicitation of Good Conduct*. Ann Arbor: University of Michigan Press.

König, T. (ed.) (1998) Special Issue on Policy Networks. *Journal of Theoretical Politics*, 10(4).

Lindenberg, S. (1977) Individuelle Effekte, kollektive Phänomene und das Problem der Transformation. In K. Eichner and W. Habermehl (eds), *Probleme der Erklärung sozialen Verhaltens*, Meisenheim: Anton Hain, pp. 46–84.

Lindenberg, S. (1982) Sharing Groups: Theory and Suggested Applications. *Journal of Mathematical Sociology*, 9, pp. 33–62.

Lindenberg, S. (1985) Rational Choice and Sociological Theory: New Pressures on Economics as a Social Science. *Journal of Institutional and Theoretical Economics*, 141, 244–55.

Lindenberg, S. (1993) Rights to Act and Beliefs. *Journal of Institutional and Theoretical Economics*, 149, 233–9.

Lindenberg, S. (1996) Constitutionalism versus Relationalism: Two Versions of Rational Choice Sociology. In Jon Clark (ed.), *James S. Coleman*. London and Washington, DC: Falmer Press, pp. 299–312.

Marsden, P. V. (1981) Introducing Influence Processes into a System of Collective Decisions. *American Journal of Sociology*, 86, 1203–35.

Oberschall, A. (1973) *Social Conflict and Social Movements*. Englewood Cliffs, NJ: Prentice Hall.

Olson, M. (1965) *The Logic of Collective Action.* Cambridge, MA: Harvard University Press.

Opp, K. D. (1979) *Individualistische Sozialwissenschaft.* Stuttgart: Enke.

Pappi, F. and Kappelhoff, P. (1984) Abhängigkeit, Tausch und kollektive Entscheidung in einer Gemeindeelite. *Zeitschrift für Soziologie*, 13, 87–117.

Riker, W. H. and Ordeshook, P. C. (1973) *An Introduction to Positive Political Theory.* Englewood Cliffs, NJ: Prentice Hall.

Raub, E. (ed.) (1982) *Theoretical Models and Empirical Analysis.* Utrecht: Explanatory Sociology Publications.

Raub, W. and Weesie, J. (1990) Reputation and Efficiency in Social Interactions: an Example of Network Effects. *American Journal of Sociology*, 96, 626–54.

Snijders, C. (1996) *Trust and Commitment.* Amsterdam: Thesis Publishers.

Stokman, F. N. and Van Oosten, R. (1994) The Exchange of Voting Positions: an Object-oriented Model of Policy Networks. In B. Bueno de Mesquita and F. N. Stokman (eds.) *European Community Decision Making. Models, Applications, and Comparisons.* New Haven, CT: Yale University Press, pp. 105–27.

Ullmann-Margalit, E. (1977) *The Emergence of Norms.* Oxford: Clarendon Press.

Vanberg, V. (1975) *Die zwei Soziologien.* Tübingen: J. C. B. Mohr (Paul Siebeck).

Williamson, Oliver E. (1985) *The Economic Institutions of Capitalism.* New York: Free Press.

Wippler, R. (1978) The Structural–Individualistic Approach in Dutch Sociology. *Netherlands Journal of Sociology*, 14, 135–55.

Yamagushi, K. (1996) Power in Networks of Substitutable and Complementary Exchange Relations: a Rational-choice Model and an Analysis of Power Centralization. *American Sociological Review*, 61, 308–32.

5

Harold Garfinkel

Anne Rawls

The Theory

Since the publication of *Studies in Ethnomethodology* in 1967, Harold Garfinkel has come to be known as the "father" of "ethnomethodology." Garfinkel's theory and corresponding research program have had a widespread influence in the United States, Canada, the UK, Europe, Australia, and Japan. However, despite its acknowledged influence, there remains considerable debate and misunderstanding about what Garfinkel actually meant by ethnomethodology.

For instance, ethnomethodology has often mistakenly been associated with a focus on the individual; Garfinkel is thought to be concerned with the values and beliefs of individual social participants. Another widespread misunderstanding is that Garfinkel's research consists primarily of "breaching experiments" in which persons violate social expectations in order to demonstrate the existence of underlying rules governing social behavior. Others have associated ethnomethodology with a sort of social indeterminacy similar to Baudrillard's postmodernism. Ethnomethodology, however, is not a single research program, nor does it focus on a single social phenomena, whether individual or collective. Ethnomethodology, as elaborated by Garfinkel, involves a complete theoretical reconceptualization of social order and a corresponding multifaceted research program.

The word "ethnomethodology" itself represents a very simple idea. If one assumes, as Garfinkel does, that the meaningful, patterned, and orderly character of everyday life is something people must work constantly to achieve, then one must also assume they have some methods for doing so. If everyday life really exhibits a patterned orderliness, as Garfinkel believes it does, then it is not enough to say that individuals randomly pursuing shared goals will do similar things enough of the time to manifest trends, or patterns, of orderliness in society. Garfinkel argues that members of society must in fact have some shared methods for achieving social order that they use to mutually construct the meaningful orderliness of social situations.

One way of understanding this is by analogy with the idea that in order to make sense by speaking in a language persons have to speak the same language, using the same meanings for words and the same grammatical forms. Another analogy is with the idea that in order to play a game persons have to play by the same rules. It is not possible to play baseball by running downfield with a football. The essential rules of baseball are in important respects constitutive of the game of baseball. Constitutive means that the rules define recognizable boundaries and practices of the game.

There are problems with these analogies because Garfinkel does not think of members' methods in terms of rules or grammars, which are themselves over-simplified conceptualizations of the constitutive features of social practices. In fact, according to Garfinkel the idea that social order is a result of following rules is responsible for many of the classic problems with social theory. But the analogies, nevertheless, help to illustrate what it means to say that the methods used by persons to create the orderliness of ordinary social occasions are constitutive of those occasions.

Ethnomethodology, then, is the study of the methods people use for producing recognizable social orders. "Ethno" refers to members of a social or cultural group and "method" refers to the things members routinely do to create and recreate various recognizable social actions or social practices. "Ology," as in the word "sociology," implies the study of, or the logic of, these methods. Thus, ethnomethodology means the study of members' methods for producing recognizable social orders.

Ethnomethodology is not itself a method. It is a study of members' methods based on the theory that a faithful dedication to the details of social phenomena will reveal social order. The word ethnomethodology itself does not name a set of research methods any more than the word sociology designates a specific set of research methods. Ethnomethodologists have done their research in many and varied ways. The object of all these research methods, however, is to discover the things that persons in particular situations do, the methods they use, to create the patterned orderliness of social life. Not all research methods are capable of revealing this level of social order. But there are many that can.

Ethnomethodologists generally use methods that require total immersion in the situation being studied. They hold the ideal that they learn to be competent practitioners of whatever social phenomena they are studying. This ideal is referred to by Garfinkel as "unique adequacy." When the subject of research is something that most persons participate in regularly, like ordinary talk, the game of tic tac toe, driving, walking, etc., then unique adequacy can usually be assumed. However, with regard to practices with specialized populations, unique adequacy can be very hard to achieve. An ethnomethodologist pursuing unique adequacy within a specialized population may spend years in a research site becoming a competent participant in its practices, in addition to collecting various sorts of observational, documentary, and audiovisual materials. Ethnomethodologists have taken degrees in law and mathematics, worked for years in science labs, become professional musicians, and worked as truck drivers and in police departments, in an effort to satisfy the unique adequacy requirement.

Ethnomethodology involves a multifaceted focus on the local social orders that are enacted in various situations. The individual persons who inhabit these situations are, as individuals, uninteresting, except in so far as personal characteristics, such as blindness, reveal something about the competencies required to achieve the recognizable production of the local order that is the object of study.

The mistaken identification of ethnomethodology with a specific methodology, and in particular with "breaching experiments," may be due to the fact that in teaching ethnomethodology Garfinkel found it helpful to develop what he refers to as "tutorial exercises," so that students could have first-hand experience of the "phenomenal field properties" of socially constituted phenomena. These tutorial exercises generally involved disrupting the orderly achievement of intelligibility in some way. Students were assigned tutorial tasks which revealed the work involved in the individual and bodily mastery of the various practices constitutive of local orders. For instance, they might be asked to perform ordinary tasks wearing headgear that distorted their vision. The idea was that various tasks and situations that problematize everyday life actions would make students aware of the need for the constant achievement of the social orderliness of local settings. Without an actual experience that revealed the work involved in enacting social reality, Garfinkel found that students had great difficulty in grasping the point of ethnomethodology. The "breaching experiments" were not intended primarily as a research program, although some early research was conducted in this manner, but as a tutorial exercise for students.

Garfinkel's own early research was presented primarily in *Studies in Ethnomethodology.* "Studies," as the 1967 volume has come to be called, consisted of a collection of papers, each of which demonstrated a different theoretical and/or methodological facet of ethnomethodology: accountability, commitment to shared practices, social construction of identity, and the documentary method of interpretation, among them.

"Good Reasons for Bad Clinic Records" reported on a field study of a psychiatric outpatient clinic. The researchers had originally been interested in coding the clinic files. Instead they found that the files were for their purposes "hopelessly incomplete." What interested Garfinkel, however, was that the incompleteness of the files was not random. It reflected a combination of internal clinic practices and concerns for the accountability of those practices to outside agencies. Garfinkel argued that, because of the need for institutional accountability, clinic workers had to carefully manage the information contained in the files. Therefore, it could not be assumed that clinic files and the statistics they generated represent an accurate record of patient histories. They were not designed to do so. Rather, they were designed to meet the institutions' need for internal and external accountability.

Garfinkel's point is not only negative. While the statistical records produced by the clinic cannot be treated as an accurate account of cases, they can be used to show how clinic workers keep the files and why they keep the files the way they do. To a traditionally trained social scientist the clinic files are "bad" files. But they are not bad files from the clinic workers' point of view. They provide just those materials clinic workers need to produce the orderly routines of the clinic day and then account for those routines to the outsiders to whom they are accountable. For the clinic workers there are "good" reasons for these "bad" records. For the ethnomethodologist, the records provide important information regarding the way in which the social order of the clinic is achieved.

In the "Trust" paper Garfinkel elaborated the view that members' methods must be distinguished from the traditional notion of rules. Members' methods remain unspecified and unspecifiable in ways that distinguish them from rules. That is one reason why Garfinkel has objected to the analogy between members' methods and game rules or grammars. Rules and grammars are conceptual simplifications of constitutive features of actual social practices. Members' methods, while instructable and instructably observable, are, according to Garfinkel, not specifiable. Because members must use the same methods in order for recognizable local orders to be produced, there is a certain level of trust about shared methods that is necessary in order for mutual intelligibility to be achieved. This bears a resemblance to Habermas's argument that persons must assume a set of foundational assumptions before they can sit down and reason publicly with one another. The difference is that Habermas refers to a hypothetical set of commitments to the reciprocity of the situation. Garfinkel, on the other hand, underlines the need for all participants to "really" use "just the same" methods for producing recognizable actions.

For instance, if persons find themselves at a particular movie theater where people line up in a particular way, then they must figure out what methods for lining up are being used and line up that way too. Otherwise, they may find out after a great deal of waiting that they have not in fact been in line. That is, they have not been recognizably waiting in line, and the others in the theater will not accept their claim that they have been waiting in line. There will be a moral censure of their activities – "Hey you don't cut in line" – with all the anger and moral outrage that accompanies moral censure. If persons do not produce "just those" actions that are recognized as appropriate for the place they find themselves in, they will find that others do not recognize their actions.

The "Agnes" paper, which explored the practices involved in achieving a recognizable gendered image, has been the subject of much debate. In this paper Garfinkel presents a detailed account of his discussions with a young person who was seeking (and eventually received) a sex change operation. The critics have generally argued over whether or not Garfinkel and the doctors were "taken in" by Agnes, who claimed to be a young woman mistakenly labeled a young man. The question of whether Garfinkel was able to observe Agnes from an "objective" research standpoint, or whether his own beliefs and values influenced what he observed, seems to dominate the discussion.

However, this debate misses the point. What interested Garfinkel was the idea that gender must be socially managed. If Agnes, in being a man who was really a woman, or a man who was pretending to really be a woman, or a woman who had the biology of a man, etc., had to recognizably reproduce actions, expressions of emotion, posture, etc., that were recognizably female, then by watching and talking to Agnes it might be possible to discover the essential features of recognizable actions involved in the social construction of gender. If Agnes was "fooling" anyone, then the performance would, from Garfinkel's standpoint, be *more* valuable as a subject of research, not *less* valuable.

Critics often assume that gender is something biological and that Agnes either "really" had the biology or did not. Garfinkel was assuming something much more radical; that gender is a social production, such that persons who are said to be biologically male can produce recognizably female actions and thereby make the claim that they are female and be believed. The question Garfinkel raises is not the indeterminate biological one of whether Agnes is "really" male or female. The question is how, and in exactly what way, Agnes used members' methods to recognizably reproduce herself or himself socially as a female in each and every particular situation.

Garfinkel's research, understood in this way, is very illuminating. Unlike most of us, Agnes needed a high degree of awareness of how he or she achieved recognition as a gendered being. Agnes is in fact able to talk to Garfinkel at great length about the various ways in which he or she reproduced a recognizably feminine gender. This is one of the earliest discussions of gender as an entirely social phenomenon. Garfinkel could not be "wrong" or "taken in" concerning Agnes's gender, since for Garfinkel gender consists of the ability to produce recognizable social acts, emotions, and bodily forms. The questions of Agnes's "true" biology, or when and whether drugs were involved, make no difference. The point is that Agnes learned what he or she had to do in order to be accepted as "really" female and tried to do those things. Therefore, Agnes is an important source of information about how it is that women reproduce themselves as gendered beings in everyday life.

In the paper "Documentary Methods of Interpretation," Garfinkel argues that persons in everyday life construct carefully documented accounts that gloss the details of social practices in order to warrant claims they make about the orderliness of social events. Garfinkel argues that this common everyday life practice parallels the practices of formal analytic theorizing, which also proceed via documentation and bibliographies. In the very same ways that the everyday life practice of documentary reasoning glosses over the details of practices in producing a documented account, formal analytic reasoning glosses those practices as well.

Garfinkel argues that the documented accounts of both common-sense reasoning and formal analytic theorizing treat conceptual schemes as more important than the contingent details of practices. Because, in his view, social life is organized by the production of recognizable practices, the details of those practices are critical to the understanding of society. Yet the conceptual schemes involved in documented accounts gloss over these details. Therefore, formal analytic theorizing, based as it is on documented accounts, inevitably misses the essential orderliness of society. Where scientific sociology places the clarity of concepts at the heart of its science, Garfinkel blames this same reliance on clear concepts for the "loss of the phenomenon."

Using documentary accounts persons are always able to retrospectively reconstruct a plausible explanation of why something happened that appears to have predictive power. What Garfinkel argues, however, is that such retrospective documented accounts bear little or no relationship to how and why events actually unfolded prospectively in the way that they did. Therefore, when such accounts are used to predict future social behavior the results are notoriously inaccurate. In order to know why something happened, Garfinkel argues, one has to have a carefully detailed prospective account of practices as they unfold.

Garfinkel's argument bears important similarities to C. Wright Mills's argument, in a paper entitled "Situated Actions and the Vocabulary of Motives," that institutions are not organized prospectively according to rules, but retrospectively according to shared vocabularies of motive. Garfinkel goes farther than Mills, however, in insisting that social order is constituted not only retrospectively through the enactment of a shared vocabulary of motives (or accounts), but also prospectively through the enactment of detailed sets of shared practices. Ethnomethodology seeks to describe the concrete witnessable details of enacted practices as they unfold over their course, thus avoiding the circularity of documented accounts.

Since *Studies in Ethnomethodology* swept the discipline in 1967, Garfinkel has published only five articles: "On Formal Structures of Practical Action" with Harvey Sacks in 1970, "The Work of a Discovering Science Construed with Materials from the Optically Discovered Pulsar" with Michael Lynch and Eric Livingston in 1981, "Evidence for Locally Produced, Naturally Accountable Phenomena of Order, Logic, Reason, Meaning, Method, etc., in and as of the Essential Haecceity of Immortal Ordinary Society" (hereafter referred to as "Parsons's Plenum") in 1988, "Two Incommensurable Asymmetrically Alternate Technologies of Social Analysis" with Larry Weider in 1992, and "Ethnomethodology's Program" in 1996. While few, the articles are very important and quite illuminating. The bulk of Garfinkel's research, which is extensive, remains unpublished.

The paper "On Formal Structures of Practical Action," the first to appear after "Studies," and co-authored with Harvey Sacks, stands as a statement of the joint theoretical interest of ethnomethodology and conversation analysis. Garfinkel and Sacks spent several years working closely with one another in the early 1960s when Sacks was developing what would become known as conversational analysis. "Formal Structures" presents the argument that even the most mundane of practical actions have formal, observable, structures. While the idea is necessarily pursued differently in studies of conversation *per se*, and studies of practical activities that involve other sorts of practice along with conversation, the principle is the same. In order for practices to be mutually intelligible they must be recognizably produced. This idea that all mutually intelligible ordinary actions have an observable structure is a distinctive characteristic of ethnomethodology and conversational analysis.

The "Parsons's Plenum" paper, the only mature statement of the relationship between Garfinkel's work and traditional sociology as represented by Parsons, stands as a summary statement of concerns that have preoccupied Garfinkel's later work. Garfinkel argues in that paper that there are two very different assumptions made about the nature of the social world by Parsons and himself. He argues that the assumptions define their respective research programs in essential respects.

According to Garfinkel, Parsons assumed a world in which individual persons, while possessed of a degree of freedom to act according to personal drives and motives, nevertheless come to realize that there are culturally accepted ways for doing most things. Thus individuals, in pursuing their individual interests, will attempt to choose courses of action that are socially acceptable. Furthermore, the very ways in which they interpret their feelings and even their physical needs will be socially constrained. For instance, individuals may have a drive to dominate others. In modern Western society, however, they will, if properly socialized, learn to interpret this drive as an impulse to achieve power or prestige in any of a number of socially acceptable ways.

Furthermore, membership in various subgroups can be expected to influence the choice of goals. For instance, people's religious backgrounds may influence their choice to sublimate an impulse to dominate others. Or the learning of gender roles may influence women to suppress a strong impulse to independence, or conversely influence men to suppress a strong impulse to dependence.

Certainly individuals are constrained by social values. However, if one accepts Parsons's proposal that social order is composed entirely of the relationship between individuals and social constraint, then social order will appear to be merely the net result of general tendencies to comply with norms. In the absence of concrete witnessable patterns of order, evidence of an "underlying social structure" that produces norms and values and constrains persons to follow them depends on the statistical manipulation of large aggregate data sets, as individuals are expected to vary in their degree of compliance. The result, according to Garfinkel, is "Parsons's Plenum": a theoretically constructed world in which order can only be discovered after and as a result of the application of a social scientific method.

Given this initial assumption, the sort of detailed study of particular places and social events advocated by Garfinkel makes no sense. Such studies could not yield evidence of a "plenum" which can only be revealed by large aggregate data sets. However, Garfinkel, for his part, makes the initial assumption that all socially recognizable actions must be produced in orderly and expected ways, and that they display their orderliness in their concrete details. Therefore, he argues, studying concrete practices in the situations in which they are produced gives the researcher immediate access to the process of constructing local orders.

The certainty that order is displayed in the concrete details of enacted practices is not only, or even first, a theoretical assumption, but also something one feels when observing empirically the patterned orderliness of certain social occasions. Social occasions and their practices are often recognizably orderly in ways that the Parsons's Plenum approach cannot account for. The experienced concrete orderliness of such occasions demands a theory that can account for it.

Garfinkel's concern is that the widespread focus of formal analytic theory and methods on aggregating data across large populations is preventing the discovery of the production of social order. The dominant approach in the discipline of sociology to the problem of social order, he says, obscures the very processes of social orderliness that are being sought: the "what more" there is to social order than formal analytic theorizing can ever find.

It is the Parsons's Plenum view of "structure" that leads to the characterization of nonstatistical approaches to sociology, and ethnomethodology in particular, as individualistic "micro" sociologies that are indifferent to the problem of social order. From Garfinkel's perspective, it is Parsons who failed to examine the most fundamental aspects of social order. How are persons able to recognize what the valued courses of action are? How much the same do actions have to be to be recognizable as the same? When persons do not choose valued courses of action how are they sanctioned? In Parsons's system a great deal of behavior that does not fit the norms is possible. For Garfinkel this explains neither the high degree of compliance experienced in everyday life, nor the routine achievement of intelligibility.

Garfinkel does not see himself as examining society at an "individual" or "micro" level, but rather as examining the great classical questions of social order. He interprets Durkheim's immortal society to refer to the local production of order which Garfinkel calls "Immortal Ordinary Society." Society, on this view, does not depend on the tendencies of individuals to more or less comply with social norms. Society is immortal, in that the patterned orderliness of situations outlives the particular persons who staff them. Persons knew, according to Garfinkel, "of just these organizational things that they are in the midst of, that it preceded them and will be there after they leave; the great recurrences of ordinary society, staffed, provided for, produced, observed and observable locally and accountably, in and as of an 'assemblage of Haecceities'."[1]

The classic way of looking at social order places the emphasis on the populations who staff the scenes and thereby appear to create those scenes. The classic demographic questions focus on the characteristics of the individuals who make up the population: gender, race, income, religion, education, etc. Garfinkel's focus on patterned orderliness places the emphasis on the scene and away from the population. From his perspective, the variables are in the scene and not in the population. Any population coming on a particular scene could only recognizably reproduce it by recognizably producing the practices that identify it as a scene of a particular sort. Reconstructing the actor's point of view thus involves taking into account the various contingencies faced by any actor in attempting to produce recognizable practice. It does not involve the perspective of any particular actors. The basic requirements of recognizability must be able to take on the endless contingencies of the actual recognizable reproduction of practices, not the contingencies of individual differences.

In shifting the emphasis from persons to scenes Garfinkel points out that the emphasis was only focused on populations in the first place as a result of looking at the construction of order in the traditional Parsons's Plenum way. Garfinkel claims that the sort of social order that classical thinkers like Durkheim sought does not lie in the characteristics of populations, but in the situated details of practice, and, therefore, cannot be rendered by studies, following Parsons's

Plenum, which create an analytic universe to replace the real one. Neither can they be revealed by traditional studies of the actor's point of view that focus on individual beliefs, values, and perspective. For Garfinkel, the key lies in detailed studies of those shared practices that are essential to the production of local orders.

According to Garfinkel, practitioners of formal analysis know about local orders. But, they don't know what to do with them. They "know" about them only in a special sense: as problems, recurrent irritations, and errors in "measurement" that need to be "controlled" for. They do not know them as social orders. Ethnomethodology recognizes these recurrent irregularities as the achieved orderliness of the "Immortal Ordinary Society." They are Durkheim's "social facts" conceived of not as external and coercive social norms, shared values, collective concepts, or goals, but as the achieved and enacted concrete detail of particular recognizable social practices and their occasions.

Garfinkel rejects the vision, common both to Parsonian structuralism and the poststructural critique, that chaos and contingency are the primary attributes of ordinary social scenes as individual actors struggle against institutional constraint. For Garfinkel, mutually intelligible actions must have recognizably recurrent features and are therefore necessarily orderly.

This insistence on the ongoing production of social order at all mutually intelligible points has been interpreted as evidence that his sociology is conservative because it does not allow the individual actor any room to rebel or create. But Garfinkel does not deny that the individual may have unique or nonconforming thoughts and impulses. In fact, Garfinkel's position allows for a great deal more "rebellion" against institutional values than Parsons, poststructuralism, or postmodernism.

Since formal institutions, and collective concepts and beliefs, have little to do with the production of order and intelligibility, in Garfinkel's view, it is at least theoretically possible for persons to avoid their constraints. It is at the level of enacted practices, or Interaction Orders, that persons must conform to expectations with regard to social practice: if individuals are to achieve mutual intelligibility, they must produce practices that are recognizable to others as practices of a particular sort. While unrecognizable practices may convey various meanings, or have meanings attributed to them, they do not convey a single mutually intelligible meaning. Mutual intelligibility requires the production of shared recognizable practices.

Garfinkel's argument does not deny the reality of institutional constraint. Rather, it adds to the notion of a vague and distant conceptual, or structural, constraint on goals and values an inescapable and ever present constraint on the empirical forms that recognizable concrete actions can take. The message is not that persons should not rebel against social inequities or that social inequality is not of concern to the analyst. The idea is rather that the possibilities for unique expression are even more highly constrained at the interactional level than has been realized. Far from believing that all is well with the status quo, Garfinkel has spent his career warning that many of the most trusted methods, methods presumed to be objective, are themselves shaped in essential ways by constraints on the social practices that constitute the essence of those methods, resulting in "critical" studies biased in favor of the status quo.

THE PERSON

Harold Garfinkel was born in Newark, New Jersey, on October 29, 1917. His formative years were spent in Newark during the Depression, where his father, Abraham Garfinkel, owned a small business selling household merchandise to immigrant families on the installment plan. The neighborhood in which he was raised consisted of a large Jewish community, at a time when ethnicity was important, and the problem of how to overcome poverty and disadvantage to succeed in the "chosen" country was a pressing one. Many extremely bright young men and women, second- and third-generation immigrants, were struggling not only to find a place in American society, but to formulate that place in their own terms.

For the elder Garfinkel, raising a son during the Depression, employment was the most important concern, and he wanted to be sure that his son learned a trade. Harold, on the other hand, wanted a university education. There was in the family an in-law who was not Jewish and was therefore credited with knowledge about what sorts of professions were viable in the world outside of the Newark Jewish community.

This in-law agreed to give advice with regard to Harold's future. One night at the dinner table he asked Harold what profession he would pursue at a university. Harold, who didn't really want to pursue a profession, recalls that he had been reading an article on surgeons in the *New York Times* and it sounded interesting. He answered that he wanted to become a surgeon. His in-law then told his father, "surgeons and lawyers are driving taxicabs." It was the middle of the Depression (1935). Thereupon, it was decided that Harold would go into the installment business with his father. Courses in business and accounting were germane to the business, however, so it was agreed that Harold would attend the University of Newark, an unaccredited program at the time, majoring in business and accounting during the day, and working in his father's installment business at night.

This early thwarting of the young Garfinkel's plans for a university education had some unpredictably happy results. The courses in accounting, in combination with friends made at the university, had an important and positive influence on the later development of his sociological theory and research. Because the program was unaccredited, the teaching was done primarily by graduate students from nearby universities. In the case of business courses at the University of Newark, the lecturers were quite often graduate students in economics from Columbia. This meant not only that courses were often taught by the best and brightest young minds in the country, but also that in business courses Garfinkel was apt to be taught the theory of business in place of procedure.

According to Garfinkel, his later work on accounts owes as much, or more, to a business course at the University of Newark called the "theory of accounts" as it does to C. Wright Mills and Kenneth Burke, whose social theories of accounts he also studied. The course dealt with double entry bookkeeping and cost accounting. From this course, Garfinkel came to understand that even in setting up an accounting sheet he was theorizing the various categories into which the numbers would be placed. Choosing, for instance, whether to place an item in the debit or assets column was already a decision. Furthermore, that decision was accountable to superiors and other agencies in a variety of complex ways. The course, although a course in accounting, didn't deal with mathematics. "How do you make the columns and figures accountable?" was the big question according to Garfinkel.

These accountants and economists weren't describing events, they were describing "indicators," and unlike the social theorists Garfinkel was to encounter later, they were very frank about it. They didn't pretend that their indicators constituted an underlying order. There are clear connections between this approach to accounting and Garfinkel's later work. The argument of "Good Reasons for Bad Clinic Records," focusing, as it does, on the ways in which clinic workers render the files accountable, is an obvious parallel. So is the much later argument of the "Parsons's Plenum" paper that formal analytic theorizing creates an orderly social world out of "indicators" aggregated across large data sets.

At the University of Newark Harold hung out with a group of Jewish students who were interested in sociology. The group included Melvin Tumin, Herbert McClosky, and Seymour Sarason. According to Garfinkel, Philip Selznick and Paul Lazarsfeld, who were at Columbia at the time, were also known to members of the group. In fact, he recollects that Lazarsfeld taught a course in social statistics at the University of Newark attended by Tumin, McClosky, and Sarason. Students at this unaccredited university were able to take courses, developed by ambitious graduate students, not yet available at more traditional universities.

Discussions with this group turned Garfinkel's interests toward sociology. All the members of the group, along with their friends from Columbia, were later to rise to prominence, a fact that had a very positive influence on Garfinkel's career. Tumin became prominent as an anthropologist at Princeton. McClosky went on to join the political science faculty at Berkeley and helped to introduce survey research to political science. Seymour Sarason went on to join the psychiatry faculty at Yale. Philip Selznick joined the sociology department at UCLA and later went on to Berkeley (where he supported the graduate careers of Sacks, Schegloff, and Sudnow). Lazarsfeld, unknown at the time, went on to establish scientific sociology at Columbia.

By the time Garfinkel graduated from the University of Newark in the summer of 1939 he knew that he could not go into the installment business with his father. He had a professor of insurance, Lawrence Ackerman, in whom he confided. Ackerman told him not to worry; he would help Harold to "get away." A Quaker, Ackerman arranged for Harold to attend a Quaker work camp that summer, building an earthdam for a rural community in Cornelia, Georgia. In that work camp, Garfinkel met a number of idealistic young people from Columbia and Harvard. By the end of the summer he knew he wanted to be a sociologist. At the camp, Morris Mitchell, from the Columbia School of Education, advised him that the sociology department at the University of North Carolina, which placed an emphasis on sociology as an effective means of furthering public service projects, was the place to go.

So, at the end of the summer of 1939 Harold packed his bags and hitchhiked directly from the summer camp in Georgia to the University of North Carolina at Chapel Hill. In the process, he had to make his way across Tennessee and much of Georgia and North Carolina. There were very few cars traveling the road and the trip was a long one. Garfinkel reports spending at least one night in a town jail because he had nowhere else to sleep and the locals generously offered him the jail for the night. Howard W. Odum was chair of the sociology department at North Carolina at the time, a man with a serious commitment to improving the plight of the underprivileged. When Harold showed up on his doorstep, with his bags in hand, he recalls that Odum said to him "You are a New York Jew who has come to the country. I'll support you." Odum admitted Garfinkel to the department on the spot and offered him a graduate fellowship.

At North Carolina Guy Johnson became Harold's mentor and introduced him to the work of W. I. Thomas, whom he says he couldn't stop thinking about. Johnson was a former student of Odum, and his particular expertise was in race relations. Very active in local community associations that dealt with issues of race, Johnson generously made his own early research on race and interracial homicide available to Garfinkel, suggesting that he pursue the subject for his master's thesis. Garfinkel now owned a car, purchased for him by his father, and his fellowship freed him from the need to work, so he was able to visit all the courthouses in a ten county area and dig the information he needed out of the courthouse records. The result was his thesis on interracial homicide.

At North Carolina Garfinkel was introduced to a broad range of theoretical perspectives that shaped the development of ethnomethodology in significant ways. In addition to W. I. Thomas, he studied Florian Znaniecki's *Social Actions*, which he refers to as a highly significant, though much neglected, theoretical work. He was also introduced to the theories of accounts and vocabularies of motive of Kenneth Burke and C. Wright Mills. He studied a broad range of phenomenological philosophy with a fellow student, James Fleming, with whom he discussed courses in the philosophy department that dealt with Husserl, Schutz, and Gurwitsch. Seymour Koch in the psychology department introduced Garfinkel to Lewin and Gestalt psychology. *The Structure of Social Action*, by Talcott Parsons, had been published in 1937 and Harold purchased a first edition from McGraw-Hill that first Christmas at North Carolina. He says that he can still remember sitting in the backyard fingering the book, smelling the newness of its pages. According to Garfinkel it was a "love affair" with sociology from the beginning.

While immersed in the study of sociology at North Carolina, Garfinkel was befriended by a group of five students at the university who challenged Odum's view of sociology. While it seemed to Harold that the great political and social questions of the day were being debated with great energy at North Carolina, these students felt that the "real" debate was going on elsewhere. While Odum was committed to a program of documenting southern folk society, which he believed was the key to generic stable society, the students from New York City and Chicago were dreaming of Parsons at Harvard and Lazarsfeld and Merton at Columbia. It was going to be a scientific sociology, with Parsons, providing for order in ordinary society with grand heroic theories, at its head.

According to Garfinkel, Lazarsfeld was seen as the emissary to the new scientific sociology from Germany. He promised that sociology would become scientific with the use of social statistics and within ten years would be entirely mathematical. The idea was that if economists could make economic affairs accountable with indicators that made up a time series, then a scientific sociology should be able to do the same thing for social behavior in general. Everyone was singing the same chorus of models and modeling, and quantitative methods were the *sine qua non* if you wanted to be taken seriously.

According to Garfinkel, the students "used to worship in the computer room" and could get a PhD by "winding" out associations between variables from a Marchant hand-wound calculator. Students put their numbers into the keyboard and then started to wind the crank. One obtained association took an enormous amount of handwork and, according to Garfinkel, was considered a justifiable numerical account of what was variable in the factors of measurement.

In the sociology department at North Carolina, however, there was one graduate student, James Fleming, who was not taken up with the pursuit of empirical scientific sociology. Fleming was engaged in reading "across the disciplines," looking for the actor's point of view. Znaniecki's book *Social Action*, not the study of the Polish peasant, was the canonical text with regard to the actor's point of view. The most important of Znaniecki's works at the time, according to Garfinkel, the book is now rarely read. As Garfinkel recalls, Fleming believed that there was no major social theorist across the social sciences who was not making provision for the actor's point of view.

The push for a scientific sociology based on statistics turned sociological interest away from the problem of action as Znaniecki had formulated it. According to Garfinkel, Znaniecki was the first to vociferously insist on the adequate description of social action, an issue which became a primary concern of Garfinkel's and remained so throughout his career. The problem facing Znaniecki's theory of social action, however, according to Garfinkel, was what an adequate description of action could consist of, given the ubiquitous insistence on the relevance of the actor's point of view.

Garfinkel's combination of the theory of accounts with the problem of the actor's point of view would provide a novel approach to this problem. His first publication, "Color Trouble," an early effort at an adequate description of accounting practices, exhibits the skeleton of his mature view. It was published in 1939, Garfinkel's first winter at North Carolina.

Garfinkel's graduate career at North Carolina was interrupted by the entry of the United States into the Second World War. After completing his master's thesis, Garfinkel was drafted and assigned to the airforce in 1942, taking with him, as he had into his master's thesis on interracial homicide, his thoughts on Parsons and Znaniecki and his theorizing with regard to accounts. He was by that time also familiar with Husserl, Schutz, and Gurwitsch, and the idea of multiple realities drawn from Schutz (1967). In the airforce, Garfinkel was assigned to designing and teaching strategies for small arms warfare against tanks and rose to the rank of corporal. It was also during the war that Garfinkel married his wife Arlene.

The task of training troops in small arms warfare against tanks was the most ironically appropriate assignment one can think of for the future "father" of ethnomethodology. Garfinkel was given the task of training troops in tank warfare on a golf course on Miami Beach in the complete absence of tanks. Garfinkel had only pictures of tanks from *Life* magazine. The real tanks were all in combat. The man who would insist on concrete empirical detail in lieu of theorized accounts was teaching real troops who were about to enter live combat to fight against only imagined tanks in situations where things like the proximity of the troops to the imagined tank could make the difference between life and death. The impact of this on the development of his views can only be imagined. He had to train troops to throw explosives into the tracks of imaginary tanks; to keep imaginary tanks from seeing them by directing fire at imaginary tank ports. This task posed in a new and very concrete way the problems of the adequate description of action and accountability that Garfinkel had taken up at North Carolina as theoretical issues.

After the war, Garfinkel went on to Harvard to study for his PhD with Talcott Parsons.[2] The relationship between Garfinkel's work and Parsons's social theory, as it developed at Harvard, is an important one. Garfinkel insisted on the adequacy of description and a focus on contingent detail. Parsons relied on conceptual categories and generalization. The clash between their positions would develop into one of the most important theoretical debates of the past several decades. In his doctoral thesis, Garfinkel took on Parsons more or less directly. However, Garfinkel later withdrew from the conceptual debate, maintaining that his position could be demonstrated only empirically, not theoretically.

While pursuing his degree at Harvard, Garfinkel taught for two years at Princeton University.[3] While at Princeton Garfinkel organized a conference with Richard Snyder and Wilbert Moore, funded by the Ford Foundation, called "Problems in Model Construction in the Social Sciences." The idea was to develop interdisciplinary studies in organizational behavior. Garfinkel sought out innovative theorists for this conference, inviting Herbert Simon, Talcott Parsons, Kenneth Burke, Kurt Wolff, Alfred Schutz, and Paul Lazarsfeld. Kurt Wolff was at that time at Ohio State University in a soft money unit called the "Personnel Research Board," a group of industrial psychologists with federal funding to support studies of leadership on submarines and airplanes. When Garfinkel left Princeton in 1952, after receiving his degree from Harvard, Wolff brought him to Ohio for a two-year position.

In Garfinkel's second year on this project the budget was cut, eliminating support for his last six months. At this point, Fred Strodbeck, another classmate from Harvard, who was at Wichita engaged in his jury study project, asked Garfinkel to join the studies he was conducting with Saul Mendlovitz. While Garfinkel was at Wichita the three reported on their work at the American Sociological Association meetings in the summer of 1954. In preparing for this talk, Garfinkel searched for what to call what they found so interesting in their discussions with the jurors. He examined the Yale cross-cultural survey and saw all the "ethnos" – ethnoscience, ethnobotany, etc. – and thought of the jury members' close reasonings with one another as "ethnomethods." The word "methods" was, according to Garfinkel, an extrapolation from Felix Kaufmann, a philosopher, who spoke of the term methodology as the theory of correct decisions in deciding the grounds for action and further inference. Together the two words seemed to apply to what the jurors were doing. Thus, the term "ethnomethodology" was born.

In the fall of 1954 Harold was asked to join the faculty at UCLA. Selznick's earlier move to UCLA turned out to be of particular importance to Garfinkel; it was Selznick along with Tumin who talked the then-chair at UCLA, Leonard Broom, into hiring Harold when Selznick moved from UCLA to Berkeley. UCLA was a joint sociology/anthropology department at the time, and the anthropologists appreciated Garfinkel's attention to interactional detail. This was an unexpectedly lucky move for Garfinkel, as UCLA, which was practically unknown at the time, quickly rose to become one of the top universities nationally. From the very beginning at UCLA Garfinkel used the term ethnomethodology, developed in Wichita, in his seminars.

At UCLA Garfinkel worked with a number of students and colleagues who became prominent proponents of ethnomethodology and conversational analysis. His relationship with Harvey Sacks, who went to UCLA and then to UC Irvine after completing his dissertation with Erving Goffman at Berkeley, was of particular importance. Sacks, along with Emmanuel Schegloff, also from Berkeley, and Gail Jefferson, outlined what has essentially become a new field of conversational studies, referred to as "conversational analysis," within the general parameters of ethnomethodology.

Garfinkel and his wife Arlene, married during the war, lived in Pacific Palisades, California, continuously from 1961. They raised two children and supported one another's intellectual endeavors during 52 plus years of marriage. Arlene Garfinkel's work as a lipid chemist inspired many of Garfinkel's insights into scientists' work. Garfinkel formally retired from UCLA in 1987 but remained active as an emeritus professor.

The Social Context

Garfinkel grew to maturity at a critical moment in American history. The Depression, the Second World War, and the immediate postwar period were times of sweeping social transition. This social context created a mood of both opportunity and criticism that turned Garfinkel toward an interest in social issues. The Depression was a particularly difficult time for the American working class, whose jobs were eliminated by the failure of industry. During the Depression a new spirit of democracy and anti-elite sentiment swept the nation, and the New Deal placed an emphasis on the problems of the American poor and working classes for the first time. These circumstances led to a heightened political awareness among the working class, and the young Garfinkel found himself caught up in debates over politics, economics, and the possibility of general social transformation going on in the community around him. He dreamed of a university education and a life outside of the Newark Jewish community. They were difficult dreams for a member of an ethnic minority at the time to pursue. Yet Garfinkel's path was criss-crossed by a significant number of others who shared his background. The Depression era had ushered in a time of great intellectual debate within the lower classes that would propel many into the academic, political, and professional realms of society.

With the onset of the Second World War, however, the situation began to change. There were now jobs to be had in industries related to the war effort. In white working-class communities the perception that all was well with America quickly replaced the anxiety of the Depression years. The great majority of the white working class was eager to parlay its new-found job security into upward mobility into the middle class. Race-based government housing and lending programs, begun during the Depression, fueled this interest, enabling the white working class to distance themselves from African-American and ethnic minority communities by building all-white suburbs.

This created a crisis within the working class. The gains made by the working class during the Depression were really very small. Political organs of the working class, like the UAW (United Auto Workers), which had been so strong during the depression, began to wither in the mid-1940s. Even in so strong a union town as Detroit the union was unable to elect a mayor after this period. According to UAW leaders, their political position was weakened by large numbers of the white working class, who simply pretended they had achieved middle-class status, voting middle-class interests.

This wholesale adoption of middle-class values did not penetrate to Jewish and other ethnic minority communities. While they did benefit to some extent from the increase in jobs, the preferential treatment of the white working class during the war and postwar period raised the level of debate over social issues in minority communities to new levels. African-American and Jewish leaders continued to talk about equality and social change throughout the war and postwar years.

Thus, at a time when the majority of white working-class Americans were becoming more politically conservative, the unions that represented the working class, and those Jewish, African American, and other ethnic minorities who were excluded by housing and other forms of discrimination from participation in this exclusive all-white group, became further politicized. Socialism became increasingly popular and labor unions during this time increasingly identified with a socialist or Marxist framework. While it was not the only factor, race and ethnicity played a key role in the determination of political awareness during this period.

This early exposure to the importance of race and ethnicity is reflected in Garfinkel's early writings, in his master's thesis on interracial homicide, and in his first publication "Color Trouble." Both deal with the social production of African-American inequality and demonstrate a clear concern for, and understanding of, the plight of African-Americans, a group whose tenuous relationship to the mainstream Garfinkel well understood. A critical attitude toward the institutions of mainstream American society, political, social, and intellectual, continued to characterize Garfinkel's later studies in ethnomethodology.

In addition to the general social upheaval of the period and the debate it fostered over social issues, the Second World War was a particularly significant time in which to be Jewish in America. Because of the conflict with Hitler's fascist antisemitism, the widespread discrimination against Jews in the United States came to be seen generally for the first time as a social problem. After the war, when Americans realized the extent of German atrocities, an unprecedented effort was made to confront antisemitism. This general sentiment was fueled by the publication of personal records such as the diary of Anne Frank, and first-hand accounts of their arrival at the camps by returning American soldiers. While these efforts may have been more rhetorical than actual, they nevertheless helped to create an atmosphere in which the problems of minorities, and those of the Jewish minority in particular, were discussed.

Within the Jewish community this combination of events created a highly politicized atmosphere, much as a new awareness of postwar segregation and inequality did in the African-American community. Young Jewish men and women, particularly in New York, earnestly discussed politics, the war, and the creation of a Jewish state. When Garfinkel attended the University of Newark, even as a business and accounting student, he found himself continually caught up in these discussions.

This atmosphere of discussion and debate, because of its emphasis on the transformation of the social and political system, resulted, for the first time, in a widespread interest in the discipline of sociology. The social theories of Karl Marx were widely read during this period of wartime antifascism and Marx's antibourgeois stance made his position popular with the working class. Sociology, the efficacy of New Deal social programs, and the future of capitalism were all seriously debated in the 1930s and early 1940s at a time when most universities did not yet have sociology departments. This interest influenced the career choices of many young students, including Garfinkel.

The resulting increase in the demand for courses in sociology forced many universities to open sociology departments, a trend that continued through the 1950s and 1960s. Undergraduate and graduate students alike turned to sociology as a discipline relevant to the social issues of the day. New academic positions were created for those, like Garfinkel, who were attracted to academic life by the social upheaval of the times. Sociology promised to provide solutions to many pressing social problems, and there was room in the thriving new discipline for many innovative young thinkers.

The Intellectual Context

Critical to an understanding of Garfinkel's work is the fact that he began his graduate education at the University of North Carolina at Chapel Hill prior to the Second World War. He belongs to a generation, educated before the war, who received broad theoretical and methodological training not constrained by scientific sociology as it developed during and immediately after the war.

A tendency to focus on Garfinkel's graduate training at Harvard, overlooking the years he spent at North Carolina, has led to the view that the genesis of his position can be traced to his conflict with Parsons. In fact, it is much more accurate to set the development of Garfinkel's ideas against the intellectual backdrop of the sociology department at North Carolina. Garfinkel went to Harvard with a set of well formulated ideas about the importance of the actor's point of view, the unavoidable character of reflexivity, the importance of adequate description, and a reinterpretation of Mills's theory of accounts, developed at North Carolina. It was the conflict between these already deeply held and well worked out ideas, and Parsons's teaching, that led Garfinkel to develop his mature views.

Sociology, as Garfinkel initially encountered it in the 1930s, was a multifaceted discipline, with many widely divergent theories and methods. The Chicago School, inspired by the work of Robert Park, W. I. Thomas, Charles Horton Cooley, George Herbert Mead, and Florian Znaniecki, was still a dominant force. The perspective of the actor and interaction were serious issues. The work of Karl Marx was actively debated, and Parsons and scientific sociology had not yet come to dominate the discipline.

When Garfinkel arrived at the University of North Carolina as a graduate student in the summer of 1939 he encountered a group of scholars committed to addressing issues of poverty, inequality, and race relations. Both theoretically and methodologically, the department reflected the eclectic nature of the discipline at that time. The graduate training that Garfinkel and others received during this period was broadly theoretical, with a social problems emphasis. Ethnography was an important and widespread methodological tool. Philosophical and epistemological issues concerning the perspective of the actor, the problem of reflexivity, and the validity of knowledge and perception were an important part of the sociological curriculum. There were rumblings about the development of a new scientific sociology, but it had not yet come to pass.

By the time Garfinkel reached Harvard after the war, however, there was a recognized dominant type of sociology considered by most people to be more scientific and valid than the types of sociology that preceded it. Parsons was its acknowledged leader. Znaniecki, the Chicago School, C. Wright Mills, phenomenology, and Marxist sociology all but disappeared for a number of years. Even Max Weber and Émile Durkheim, social theorists championed by Parsons, were for years only interpreted and studied in terms dictated by Parsons.

How and why a combination of statistical methods and Parsonsian structural functionalism came to define the notions of "scientific" and "objective" is an interesting issue. Marx, Weber, Toennies, Simmel, and Mead had not really made use of statistics. Even Durkheim, who introduced the idea that statistical trends might represent underlying social facts in his book *Suicide*, made only very limited use of them. However, by the 1950s the world had changed. The old social order had been, if not radically transformed, at least given that appearance. Miracle drugs, invented to fight infectious diseases, were widely available. The power of the atom had been unleashed on Hiroshima and Nagasaki. Scientific and mathematical challenges directly related to the war had spurred the development of computers.

Novelists in the 1940s and 1950s wrote about a world dominated by technical reason and rational planning, by engineers and their computers. The new technologies seemed to give humans mastery over the universe. In areas of science and philosophy that had yet to make significant "breakthroughs" the assumption was that logic and scientific objectivity were what was needed. The solution, it was said, lay in numbers and the clarity of concepts. When Paul Lazarsfeld moved to the United States from Germany, the social statistics that he advocated were just what an eager population of sociologists, committed to becoming more scientific, wanted.

Other forms of sociology continued to be practiced. Studies focused on interaction continued as a paradigm at the University of Chicago. But in the new intellectual context anything other than the new scientific sociology had to be justified by contrast to the prevailing view. From the early fifties until the late sixties "statistical" sociology with a functional orientation reigned almost unchallenged.

Although dissatisfactions with Parsons's version of scientific sociology emerged quickly – it seemed to present a narrow, politically conservative, view of social issues, incapable of providing the practical advice for solving social problems that young sociologists sought – an initial response to this dissatisfaction was to attempt to perfect the Parsonsian system. The assumption was that the shortcomings were caused by failures in the application of Parsons's system: the statistics were not pure enough, or the concepts not clear enough. For a time, sociology became even more scientific and statistically driven in an attempt to eradicate these problems.

It began to be clear, however, that there were deep theoretical problems involved in the notions of scientific and mathematical clarity when applied to the study of human society. Because human actions are meaningful and involve reflexivity, human intelligibility does not lend itself to "objective" mathematical study. The discipline faced a crisis and sociologists began to search for alternatives. Earlier trends in sociological theorizing, temporarily eclipsed by the new statistically driven scientific theorizing, regained some of their former popularity. Marxist and Weberian approaches to sociology enjoyed a newfound popularity in the 1960s and 1970s. Interactionism and symbolic interactionism became popular. Sociological perspectives influenced by phenomenological philosophy, existentialism, and the philosophy of Wittgenstein also began to gain ground.

Into this social climate stepped Garfinkel, with his emphasis on interactional detail and adequate description. For many young sociologists, Garfinkel provided the first introduction to phenomenology, philosophy, and a new and different appreciation of classical social theory. He was one of the first to argue that phenomenological texts were central to the sociological enterprise. Confronted by a discipline in crisis, Garfinkel and other interactionists, like Herbert Blumer, Erving Goffman, and Howard Becker, seemed for many to have arrived "just in time" to save sociology. Very few students in the 1960s were interested in understanding how to maintain the status quo. They were interested instead in change and challenge; in social movements and revolution; in new ways of thinking that were not so Western, logical, and middle class in emphasis.

Garfinkel challenged the prevailing criteria for adequate research: that studies could be considered scientific only if they aggregated numerically across clear conceptual classifications. In so doing, he challenged the very notion of technical reason that was the driving force behind scientific sociology. He believed that the processes of theoretical and mathematical justification required for acceptance by scientific sociology were logically incompatible with the phenomena of social order. Scientific sociology, as it had emerged in the 1940s and 1950s at Harvard and Columbia, was, according to Garfinkel, obscuring, rather than clarifying, the understanding of social reality.

Garfinkel believed that sociology should be engaged in explaining how phenomena of social order are achieved and recognized by participants in the first place. He assumed a world in which social order was actual, evident, and witnessable in its details. Therefore, the details of social order should be empirically observable without conceptual or theoretical mediation. He argued that social order was to be found in contingencies of local settings, not in generalizations, however conceptually clear.

Ethnomethodology stands as a direct contradiction to the faith in formalism, technical reason, and mathematicized representations of social behavior that came to define postwar sociology. Garfinkel argued that formalism depends on the enactment of social practices which remain unexamined. Even engineers and mathematicians do not work in a pure mathematical vacuum. They must speak to one another. They must create conceptual representations of the domain in which they work. Engineers must imagine the uses to which persons will put the various products they are engaged in producing. These activities involve the use of practices which are in essential respects constitutive of what science, mathematics, and engineering will turn out to be. In fact, according to Garfinkel, no domain of human endeavor is free from this requirement. Ironically, in order to succeed at endeavors based in technical reason, a detailed understanding of those ordinary practices through which persons regularly achieve recognizable and intelligible social practices is required.

Impact

Since the publication of *Studies in Ethnomethodology* in 1967, Harold Garfinkel's work has had an enormous influence on various disciplines in the social sciences and humanities worldwide. Shortcomings with the "scientific" study of human society derived from various interpretations of structural functionalism and positivism in the 1960s and 1970s fueled a search in many disciplines for a new approach. Garfinkel's arguments introduced aspects of the problem of social order and intelligibility that promised to address these concerns. Garfinkel sought to restore both the perspective of the actor and the validity of adequate description of the details of social action. He took seriously the problem of interpretation proposed by hermeneutic philosophy as the alternative to positivism. However, he also and at the same time insisted on the importance of adequate empirical description.

The promise of simultaneously addressing all these issues had great appeal. In addition, Garfinkel's demonstrations of the taken-for-granted constitutive features of members' methods oriented the discipline toward the observation of social practice in a deeper and more detailed way. There has been a subtle shift since the 1960s and 1970s in what counts as adequate description, and Garfinkel played an important part in creating it. The shift crossed disciplinary boundaries and many scholars who would not think of themselves as having been interested in ethnomethodology were nevertheless influenced by Garfinkel's emphasis on members' methods and adequate description.

Researchers began to look for the underbelly of society. Informal orders were discovered everywhere: in formal institutions, in scientific practice, in classroom instruction. Wherever researchers looked there were previously unsuspected levels of detail to be uncovered. While Garfinkel was joined by Goffman and others in leading the discipline toward a more detailed look at interaction and the Interaction Order, it was Garfinkel who moved beyond the problems of self and interpretation to take a serious look at the problem of intelligibility at its most fundamental level.

His argument that even scientific practices and scientific objects are recognizably constructed social orders inspired studies in the sociology of science. His criticisms of technical reason and formalism in the scientific workplace gave rise to studies of practices in mathematics and engineering and the application of computers and other technology in the workplace. Studies of conversation influenced by Garfinkel, Sacks, and Schegloff had an impact on communication studies, semiotics, linguistics, and studies of communication in applied areas such as doctor–patient interaction, intercultural communication, legal reasoning, and various institutional and workplace settings.

Studies of institutional accounting practices, inspired by Garfinkel's theory of accounts, have focused on the generation of records during plea bargaining, on truck drivers' log keeping practices, police record keeping practices, and coroners' decisions with regard to suicide. For many with an interest in social reform his argument pointed toward the organizational production of those statistics which are offered by scientific sociology as representations of the "real" world. If administrators, politicians, and institutional workers all have ongoing organizational reasons for manipulating the generation of statistics, then surely the generation of statistics should be an important topic for a critical social science.

Furthermore, the idea that a social institution that is believed to discriminate by class and race, such as the police, the courts, schools, or a workplace, should be allowed through its own worksite practices to generate statistical accounts that support its own claims not to be discriminating, and that those statistical accounts should be taken as undeniable scientific evidence of social structure, is, in Garfinkel's view, unthinkable. Yet even today the vast majority of the articles published in the *American Sociological Review* use secondary statistical data sets generated by institutional accounts.

From Garfinkel's position, a scientific sociology based on such data can never be politically disinterested. It can only confirm the prevailing views of those institutions that generated its data. That may explain its popularity. Ethnomethodology, on the other hand, generally represented as indifferent to issues of structure and politics, is indifferent only to institutionalized structures of accountability. Ethnomethodology cannot be indifferent to political, ethical, or theoretical critique because that is essentially what it is. Garfinkel seeks to reveal the methods persons use to create the appearance that various "facts" exist independently of those methods.

Ethnomethodologists have also undertaken studies of specific disciplinary methods, such as survey research and focus group interviews. In all these studies the emphasis has been on the practices used to achieve the results in question. How and why do the police arrive at their statistics? How and why do survey researchers code responses to telephone surveys? The details of local practices that comprise the answers to the questions "how" and "why" are, according to Garfinkel, what the resulting statistics and aggregated coding schemes "really" mean. They are the "what more" to social order that is obscured by traditional theory and research.

Garfinkel's insistence that researchers achieve the "unique adequacy" requirement of methods before they attempt to answer these how and why questions has generated many studies that could be considered practical or applied research. Such "hybrid studies," done by outsiders who are also insiders, have as their aim that practitioners in the speciality area being studied will be as interested in the studies as professional sociologists. These studies include research on technical legal reasoning, classroom instruction, the work of mathematical proving, the work of scientific discovery, survey research, policing, doctor–patient interaction, workplace technology, social service delivery, traffic controllers, and jazz musicians.

Many, in fact most, of those who have developed a serious interest in ethnomethodology have also used conversational analysis, developed by Sacks, Schegloff, and Jefferson, as one of their research tools. Many of the practices essential to the constitutive features of any social setting make use of conversation, and there are essential constitutive features of conversation to which practitioners at any worksite must attend. Thus, the constitutive features of talk are inexorably intertwined with the achievement of ordinary practices.

From small beginnings with a handful of graduate students at UCLA, ethnomethodology spread quickly around the world. While several of Garfinkel's students were influential in the spread of ethnomethodology, and colleagues like Sacks and Schegloff also played an important role in promoting the popularity of ethnomethodology, its spread depended heavily on the interest of sociologists who never studied with Garfinkel and who initially knew little about ethnomethodology. Their interest had its origins in a deep dissatisfaction with the state of theory and methods in the discipline.

In recent years an increasing number of sociologists, dissatisfied with the discipline's lack of response to these concerns, have turned to poststructural and postmodern alternatives. It is interesting that while Garfinkel's position offers an important alternative to poststructuralism, it is not generally seen in that light. It is sometimes seen as a counterpart to poststructuralism, with the same indeterminacy and contingency, but rarely as an alternative that addresses the same problems in more satisfactory ways. Ironically, poststructuralists and postmodernists tend to view structure in a Parsons's Plenum sort of way, accepting the individual versus structure dichotomy, while they reject the moral validity of structures. Thus, both sides in the contemporary debate share a conception of structure that Garfinkel rejected. Consequently, his arguments, even though they constitute a profound rejection of structuralism, are not seen as addressed to that debate.

Poststructuralism begins with the understanding that it is against structures that the shared meanings of everyday life are achieved. Meanings are defined in structural opposition either to one another – "up" can only be understood in contrast to "down"' and "black" to "white" – or to institutional structures, as when a person's actions in waiting for a bus to get to work are seen to be defined by the institutions of work, or one's gender role is seen to be defined by the conceptual structure of gender terms in a given society. The essential idea is that "structures," in some fashion or other, impart meaning to everyday language and action. Then, in order to "break out," persons have to "deconstruct" the structures.

The problem is that the result of deconstruction should be a meaningless infinite regress if all shared meaning (and most private meaning) really were produced by relations between persons (or actions) and formal structure. But, in fact, the operation is often quite meaningful and revealing. This is hard to explain from within either the poststructural or the postmodern position. For Garfinkel, however, there are an unlimited number of complex ways of constructing the intelligibility of social action at the local level. When persons rebel against structure, the rebellion is made possible by these underlying endogenously produced intelligibilities. In fact, something like what Garfinkel is articulating seems to be the only explanation for how persons can rebel against structure yet have their language and activities remain mutually intelligible.

From Garfinkel's perspective, the popularity of deconstruction as a method is easy to explain. Poststructuralism is another version of theorized reality. While it is in some respects new, it is also very familiar. It promises novelty without requiring changes in the basic theorized assumptions of sociology as a discipline. In the rush to deconstruct, the social world is once again being theorized, and the interactional practices which are actually constitutive of intelligibility are being overlooked again in favor of an institutionalized view of meaning. Poststructuralism is, from Garfinkel's viewpoint, merely the flip side of structural functionalism: both posit social order and meaning in terms of a constraining relationship between individuals and social structures which threatens individual autonomy. For Garfinkel, on the other hand, the relationship between individuals and social structure is only a secondary phenomenon that needs to be seen against the backdrop of the prior achievement of mutual intelligibility and mutually intelligible practices at a more fundamental level.

Critics often ask why Garfinkel did not himself engage in clarification with regard to issues that have been so consequential for the reception of his work. I believe that his silence is due to a belief that as an argument his position could only be demonstrated theoretically. In Garfinkel's view, theoretical demonstrations depend hopelessly on imagined orders of affairs. Given his commitment to an empirical demonstration of his claims, Garfinkel feels strongly that if the argument cannot be persuasive without being theorized, it must be because the empirical demonstrations still fall somehow short of adequate description. Thus, Garfinkel has consistently met theoretical criticism by attempting to deepen the level of empirical detail in his research, not via theoretical response.[4]

Because he felt that the generic and theorized terminology of mainstream sociology rendered social orders invisible, Garfinkel has been wary of using generic terms and generalizations in his own work. His invention of new words and phrases to express the empirical social relations discovered through his research is part of what makes his work so hard to read. In order to read Garfinkel successfully one must make a commitment to treat his terminology as essential to his argument. In this regard, Garfinkel's writing resembles that of Marx, who, in his attempt to avoid treating mutually dependent social processes as though they were independent entities, constructed sentences in which the subject is also the object of the same sentence. In Garfinkel's case, the attempt to avoid theorized generalities has led to an emphasis on words which attempt to specify the concreteness of things and at the same time to specify the contingency of the various positions in which things are found. Phrases like "as of which," which multiply the propositional relationships between "objects" and the occasions upon which they are socially constructed as such, are common.

The continual emphasis in Garfinkel's work on "just-thisness," "haecceities," "details," "order," and "contingencies" is an attempt not to lose the phenomena through generalization. Trying not to refer to local order phenomena in general terms is linguistically strange. However, the importance of the contingencies of local order phenomena to his argument justifies the attempt.

Garfinkel has opened the way for a new sort of theorizing. Theorizing more broadly conceived does not have to be of the generic, categorizing, plenum sort. There is no reason, in principle, why theorists cannot be faithful to the phenomena; no reason why they have to proceed in generic terms. Garfinkel has shown us the possibility of empirical theorizing and it is in these terms that I want to refer to Garfinkel as one of the great social theorists of the twentieth century. However, he is quite right that contemporary theory has, for the most part, proceeded in terms of categories and generic terms. If I call Garfinkel a theorist, there are sure to be sociologists who will want to reduce his arguments to categories and generic terms. It is essential to note that this understanding of social theory is entirely incompatible with Garfinkel's view.

ASSESSMENT

Garfinkel's relationship to the discipline of sociology has from the first been both highly significant and extremely ironic. Garfinkel dedicated his life work to uncovering the empirical details of orderly social practices. However, mainstream sociology defined scientific empiricism as the study of abstract conceptual representations of individuals and their normative values, represented in numerical form. Because Garfinkel's work did not fit this definition of empirical, it has been characterized by the discipline as a "micro" sociology focused on individual, contingent, and subjective matters, not on the collective empirical aspects of social structure and intelligibility.

Similarly, many micro sociologists accept a version of sociology that treats conceptual representations as the foundation of social order and meaning. Because they think of "practices" in terms of concepts and ideas, they also reject Garfinkel's claim that in studying concrete witnessable practices he is engaged in empirical research. They argue that Garfinkel is theorizing the relationship between individual concepts and shared symbolic meanings, not engaging in empirical research, as he claims. Consequently, they criticize him for ignoring the infinite regress entailed by representational accounts of meaning.

Because Garfinkel rejects assumptions fundamental to both micro and macro sociology, sociologists from both camps make opposing versions of the same criticism of his work. It is incorrect to assess Garfinkel's work as a conceptual or interpretive exercise. Garfinkel does not set up a relationship between hidden conceptual meanings and their symbolic representations. Ethnomethodology is a thoroughly empirical enterprise devoted to the discovery of social order and intelligibility as witnessable collective achievements. Nor is ethnomethodology indifferent to issues of social structure; only to issues of institutional structure as defined by mainstream sociology.

The keystone of Garfinkel's argument is that local orders exist; that these orders are witnessable in the scenes in which they are produced; and that the possibility of intelligibility is based on the actual existence and detailed enactment of these orders. Because these orders are actual, they can be empirically observed. Because these orders are collective enactments, a focus on individual subjectivity would obscure them.

The characterization of ethnomethodology as an individualistic "micro" sociology is equally wrong. With regard to sociology as a whole, the macro/micro dichotomy is dangerously misleading, tending to portray any approach to sociology that does not focus on aggregations of institutional constraint as trivial. However, with regard to the work of Garfinkel, the distinction is completely meaningless. The dichotomy assumes a distinction between institutionalized and individualistic forms of social behavior that Garfinkel has completely rejected. For Garfinkel, no *social* behavior is individualistic and social institutions only exist as, and are reproduced through, contexts of accountability. His position is neither micro nor macro.

The true irony is that Garfinkel focused on members' methods for achieving recognizable social phenomena because he *did* believe that empirically observable, collectively enacted, social structures existed and were being obscured by conventional methods of research, *not* because he wanted to study individuals. Mainstream sociology focused on statistical indicators of individual tendencies to orient toward normative goals because they *did not* believe that there were social structures that could be observed empirically. They thought they had to aggregate across general concepts to get rid of the details of particular settings and thereby reveal order as a general principle. Garfinkel, on the other hand, believed from the beginning that order was there already in the details of social settings, and that aggregating those details across general concepts was leveling the details of social order to the point of nonrecognition. Focusing on individual interpretation similarly obscures the concrete details of enacted practice.

The misinterpretations of Garfinkel have their origin in the fact that his position conflicts with basic assumptions about the institutional character of social order, and the symbolic and representational nature of meaning; assumptions essential to the macro/micro distinction, which have dominated the discipline since the mid-twentieth century. Parsons popularized an institutional view of social order that left no room for Interaction Order phenomena. In Parsons's wake, Jeffrey Alexander formalized the basic disciplinary assumptions about institutional order, arguing that sociology either took a formal institutionalized collective view (macro) or was individualistic and contingent (micro).

Prior to Parsons, the discipline did not have such a strong bias in favor of institutional order and aggregated indicators. At the end of the nineteenth century close observations of situated events played a central role in social theory and research. Classical sociologists were often exhaustive in their description and documentation of the social processes and practices they were trying to explain. Although there was a tendency to reduce observations to generalizations and ideal types, it was really only in the period after the Second World War, the heyday of positivism, when sociology, and Durkheim in particular, came under fire as idealist and unscientific, that the current situation developed.

Intellectual circles in the 1920s and 1930s were involved in a love affair with positivism and numbers. If sociology came to be considered idealist, it would lose what little institutional support it had achieved. Parsons took it upon himself to save the discipline from the charge of idealism by formulating a sociology amenable to complicated numerical generalizations. The resulting increase in institutional support for the discipline occurred at just the same time that social conditions were creating an interest in arguments and ideas that could properly be said to be sociological. Without Parsons that interest might have turned to existing departments of political science, philosophy, or economics, instead of leading to the creation of new departments of sociology all over the country.

In one sense, Parsons rescued sociology. However, once started, the demand for numerical justification began to drive the discipline. Sociology went from a concern with documenting the details of social order to a concern with becoming more mathematical and generalizable, in order to justify itself as a science.

Mid-century sociology became quite divorced from earlier concerns for adequate description and the accurate representation of the actor's point of view. The beginning of the century concern with the meaning of social actions was almost completely forgotten.

Garfinkel's position preserves those earlier concerns. The difference is that his approach to social order places the emphasis on constitutive local orders, while Parsons and classical sociologists had generally placed it on either institutional or conceptual (representational) orders. Garfinkel's argument is that there is a level of order, below (so to speak) the institutional, or theorized level of order, which constitutes the fundamental intelligibility of social action and language. This is not an order of individual interpretation or conceptual representation, but rather a constitutive order of witnessable enacted practice. Garfinkel and Parsons are talking about two different conceptions of social order, Interaction Orders versus institutional order. For Parsons, only institutional orders and individuals exist, leaving the explanation of social order without any underpinning of fundamental intelligibility. For Garfinkel, orders at the level of witnessable practice provide a foundation of intelligibility against which institutional contexts of accountability can operate.

Insisting that Interaction Orders are fundamental, or indispensable, to sociology has been one of Garfinkel's greatest contributions. As the postmodern crisis makes clear, without an explanation of underlying intelligibility, social orders cannot be given a valid explanation. Because he conceived of social order strictly in institutional terms, Parsons had to invent the plenum in order to display a tendency to orderliness in society. He had to build an elaborate mechanism for displaying a tendency to order, because he believed that society was at any given point not actually ordered. Furthermore, the emphasis he placed on generalization and aggregation obscured the concrete witnessable order of social occasions from his view.

In rejecting this view, Garfinkel does not sacrifice the study of social order. He argues that in focusing on the recognizable production of practices he is studying social order. Mainstream scientific sociology, from his perspective, is studying mathematicized representations of institutionalized typifications, or accounts, not social order. It is in mainstream sociology that individual subjectivity, in the form of operationalized variables, theorized accounts, and individually produced institutional accounts, is to be found, not in ethnomethodology.

For Garfinkel the earlier interest in the actor's point of view, re-emerging in contemporary sociology, was as much a dead end as the focus on institutions. Sociology could not solve its problems by connecting concepts in heads with external symbolic representations. As Wittgenstein argued, representational approaches to meaning are as problematic as trying to explain social order in terms of formal structures. As ethnomethodology developed, the external concrete witnessable details of enacted practice came to dominate Garfinkel's approach to the problem of intelligibility.

Garfinkel did not give up the actor's point of view, which initially fueled his debate with Parsons. But he transformed it substantially, locating the experiential and contingent features of action, originally thought of as belonging to the actor, in the regularities of actual practices. The actor's point of view was transformed into a concern with what populations did in particular settings to achieve the recognizability of particular practices. According to Garfinkel, a population is constituted not by a set of individuals with something in common, but by a set of practices common to particular situations or events: the crowd at the coffee machine, the line at the supermarket, the "gang" at the science lab, and so on.

Instead of talking about the phenomenal properties of experience, Garfinkel began talking about the phenomenal field properties of objects. Thus, in an important sense the actor's point of view and the achieved meaning of social action no longer had to be thought of in connection with individual actors. Because, in Garfinkel's view, intelligibility is achieved in and through the enactment of observable practices, not through interpretive processes in the minds of individual actors, empirical studies of observable practices could reveal the actor's point of view.

Critics argue that the study of local social orders is not sociological because it consists only of a description of what people do and ignores the real social (i.e. institutional) constraints within which those actions took place. The constraint argument is fundamental to sociology; part of the assumption that social order is institutional. The discipline of sociology was, in an important sense, founded on Durkheim's argument that social facts exist as external constraint, rather than as artifacts of the combined psychosocial or biological impulses of a large number of persons. Therefore, when Garfinkel is interpreted as having argued against the existence of external constraint, he is thought to have repudiated the idea of social facts and thus to have rejected sociology as a whole.

However, far from repudiating the idea of external constraint, Garfinkel has reconceptualized it so as to avoid the individual versus society dichotomy and other problems inherent both in the classical theoretical formulation of this issue and in contemporary attempts to reformulate it.

Other critics, from what is sometimes called the "left" of ethnomethodology, and from the postmodern position, argue that ethnomethodology is hopelessly conceptual and theorized, and thus falls victim to its own criticisms of mainstream sociology. Such critics, however, tend to set up a straw man argument. They attribute to ethnomethodology a representational theory of meaning, equating enacted practices with subjective interpretive procedures (often mistakenly equated with the documentary method), and generally render practices in terms of concepts and beliefs. As ethnomethodology treats practices as consisting of their concrete witnessable details, the attribution is incorrect. There is nothing circular in the argument that in order to convey meaning visible concrete actions must be recognizable to others as actions of a sort, and that the constitutive features of what counts and does not count as actions of a sort must therefore be witnessable to participants and available for empirical observation.

For Garfinkel, structure and order are primarily located in local practices, which constitute a primary constraint, with formal institutions acting as a constraint in limited and specific ways via institutional contexts of accountability. According to Garfinkel, "The instructably observable achieved coherent detail of the coherence of objects *is* the fulfillment of Durkheim's promise that the objective reality of social facts is sociology's fundamental principle."[5] Garfinkel has offered a version of external constraint as accountability. Persons are accountable both at the local level for a commitment to a local order of practices, and, at what sociology has generally termed the institutional level, accountable to what Mills (1940) referred to as a shared "vocabulary of motives." Mills argued that persons in institutions do not act by following rules, they act by accounting for what they have done in terms of vocabularies of motive and justification which only retrospectively reference the rules.

In Mills's view, institutional practices bear a peculiar relationship to institutional rules, with rules constituting a context of justification for action, rather than something followed in order to produce the action. According to Mills, social actors examine the desirability of proposed courses of action, asking themselves what people would say if they did a particular thing, or considering how they could explain, or account for, a particular course of action. If a satisfactory explanation can be generated from within the shared vocabulary of motives, then an action can be considered to be in accord with the rules, no matter what form it takes. Therefore, while the rules constrain the practices, in this peculiar way of constraining what will count after the fact as having been a case of following the rules, they are not constitutive of action in its course.

Garfinkel's treatment of accounts goes beyond Mills in proposing a complex network of contexts of accountability at various levels of social organization. In Garfinkel's view persons can be accountable to external institutions, such as government agencies or scientific disciplines, at the same time that they are accountable to the expectations of their colleagues with regard to normal workplace procedures. Persons are constantly accountable for their production of recognizable talk and movements, even while they are managing institutional levels of accountability. Finally, they can also and at the same time be accountable to the properties of natural phenomena, which may refuse to cooperate in producing an accountable display for colleagues.

By extending Mills's theory of accounts in this way Garfinkel is able to consider a wide range of theoretical issues. The theoretical line of argument which Garfinkel's inquiry into "rules" (i.e. instructed action) and accountability develops includes: the classic distinction between traditional and modern rational action (Durkheim, Weber, Toennies, Simmel); the seminal argument of Mills with regard to contexts of accountability; many of the Chicago School studies of organizations and bureaucracies, which revealed the paradox of rules and informal cultures within organizations.

His position also runs parallel to other arguments developed during the 1950s and 1960s regarding the relationship between rules and practice, including: Goffman's study of asylums (1961); similar studies in prisons and psychology by Sykes (1958) and Szasz (1961); labeling theory, which examines the relationship between institutional behavior, the institutional production of statistics, and the beliefs and practices of the populations which staff those organizations; the distinction in philosophy between constitutive and other rules (Warnock, 1958; Searle, 1968); and the extension of this argument into game theory.

Garfinkel's focus on intelligibility also extends a second line of inquiry: attempts by classical social theorists to frame epistemology and intelligibility sociologically (Durkheim, 1915; Weber, 1921; Rawls, 1996). It is important to understand that classical social theorists were philosophers who challenged the limits of their discipline on the issues of epistemology and intelligibility. If, for instance, one begins with Durkheim's theory of the social origins of the categories of the understanding (in *The Elementary Forms*), then one finds Garfinkel continuing the inquiry into the question of intelligibility raised by Durkheim, and extended by Mead, Husserl, Heidegger, Mills, and Schutz, but all but forgotten by both mainstream scientific sociology and its postmodern counterpart.

In the *Elementary Forms of the Religious Life* Durkheim took on the philosophical problem of knowledge. Addressing the differences between Kant and Hume over the origins of human reason, Durkheim argued that the categories of the understanding have their origins in certain concrete social settings. He argued that those social settings supply the concrete experience of general ideas that Hume found the natural world could not supply and Kant had argued must be innate.

Durkheim argued that even key ideas like time, space, force, and causality have a social and not a natural empirical or *a priori* origin. As Durkheim realized, this argument cast the problem of knowledge in an entirely new light. In locating the conditions for intelligibility in the concrete social surroundings of daily life, and in taking the problem of intelligibility as the central problem sociology must address before constructing a theory of social order, Durkheim stands as a direct precursor of Garfinkel. Garfinkel continues to search for the foundations of human intelligibility, reason, and logic in the details of collaborative social practice.

Garfinkel has from the beginning been blessed with a vision of social order that allowed him to see order being produced around him in ordinary events which the rest of us experience as finished products, but which Garfinkel experienced as events produced from patterned details over their course. This is brilliantly evident in his first paper, "Color Trouble." In this paper, we get a picture of Garfinkel as a young student taking a bus home from college. When black passengers are ordered to the back of the bus and won't go, Garfinkel sees something the rest of us would have missed. As the driver engages in his dispute with the black passengers, he is formulating his actions in terms of the excuse he will have to give for being late at the end of the line. He is accountable not for his morals, but for being on time. The longer the dispute takes, the more important will be the acceptability of the account the driver can give, and it will thereby come to pass that color will turn out to be one of the troubles with busses which account for their lateness on certain southern runs.

Garfinkel's description of this incident is masterful, and the essay won an award as one of the best short stories of 1939. More importantly, however, it demonstrates the continuity of vision which has characterized Garfinkel's career as a social thinker. We can imagine Garfinkel sitting in social theory classes at Harvard being confronted with generic categorizations. He recalls that in his first theory class at Harvard the students were told to make up a social theory. The thing was to be purely an invention, an exercise in logic and the generic use of categories. As a young man with a keen sense for the actual unfolding of social order in the everyday world around him, this sort of theorizing, which operated on the assumption that everyday social scenes were not inherently orderly, and that their details were irrelevant, rubbed the wrong way. He quickly realized that his vision of a stable constitutive order of practice stood in contradiction to the received and approved methods of formal analytic theorizing. Through the years Garfinkel has remained true to his vision.

Notes

1 Haecceities is one of many words that Garfinkel has adopted over the years to indicate the importance of the infinite contingencies in both situations and practices. He has also used the words quiddities, contingencies, and details in this regard. I believe that Garfinkel changes his terminology frequently so as to maintain the open and provisional nature of his arguments. As persons develop a conventional sense for a word he has used, he changes it.
2 His Harvard cohort included Gardner Lindsey, Henry Riecken, David Schneider, David Aberle, Brewster Smith, Duncan MacRae, Bernard Barber, Frank Sutton, James Olds, Fred Strodbeck, Marion Levy, Hans Lucas Taueber, and Renee Fox, any of whom became prominent sociologists and several of whom were instrumental in furthering Garfinkel's career.
3 The faculty at Princeton included Marion Levy and Duncan MacRae, who had been at Harvard with Garfinkel, and Wilbert Moore. Edward Tiryakian, an undergraduate at Princeton for whom Garfinkel served as senior thesis advisor, would later publish Garfinkel's paper, co-authored with Harvey Sacks, "On Formal Structures of Practical Action."
4 Unfortunately, most of these studies remain unpublished.
5 Personal communication.

Bibliography

Writings of Harold Garfinkel

Color Trouble. 1939. In Edward O'Brian (ed.), *Best Short Stories of 1939*.
Studies in Ethnomethodology. 1967. Englewood Cliffs, NJ: Prentice Hall.
On Formal Structures of Practical Action (with Harvey Sacks). 1970. In Edward Tiryakian and John McKinney (eds), *Theoretical Sociology*. New York: Appleton Century Crofts.
The Work of a Discovering Science Construed with Materials from the Optically Discovered Pulsar (with Michael Lynch and Eric Livingston). 1981.
Evidence for Locally Produced, Naturally Accountable Phenomena of Order, Logic, Reason, Meaning, Method, etc., in and as of the Essential Haecceity of Immortal Ordinary Society. 1988. *Sociological Theory*, 6(1), 103–9.
Two Incommensurable Asymmetrically Alternate Technologies of Social Analysis (with Lawrence Weider). 1992. In Graham Watson and Robert M. Seiler (eds), *Text in Context*. Newbury Park, CA: Sage, pp. 172–206.
Ethnomethodology's Program. 1996. *Social Psychology Quarterly*, 59(1), 5–21.

Further reading

Baudrillard, Jean (1975) *Mirror of Production*. St Louis: Telos Press.

Baudrillard, Jean (1993) *Symbolic Exchange and Death*. Thousand Oaks, CA: Sage

Becker, Howard (1963) *Outsiders: Studies in the Sociology of Deviance*. New York: Free Press.

Blumer, Herbert (1969) *Symbolic Interaction: Perspective and Method*. Berkeley: University of California Press.

Cooley, Charles Horton (1902) *Human Nature and the Social Order*. New York: Scribner's.

Durkheim, Émile (1912) *The Elementary Forms of The Religious Life*. Chicago: Free Press.

Goffman, Erving (1961) *Asylums*. New York: Anchor Books.

Goffman, Erving (1963) *The Presentation of Self in Everyday Life*. New York: Anchor.

Gurwitsch, Aron (1964) *The Field of Consciousness*. Duquesne, PA: Duquesne University Press.

Habermas, Jürgen (1981) *The Theory of Communicative Action*. Boston: Beacon Press.

Heidegger, Martin (1962) *Being and Time*. London: SCM Press.

Hume, David (1739) *A Treatise of Human Nature*. Oxford: Oxford University Press.

Husserl, Edmund (1962) *Ideas*. New York: Collier Books.

Kant, Immanuel (1929) *Critique of Pure Reason*. New York: St Martin's Press.

Kaufmann, Felix (1944) *Methodology of the Social Sciences*. Oxford: Oxford University Press.

Lewin, Kurt (1938) *The Conceptual Representation and the Measurement of Psychological Forces*. Durham, NC: Duke University Press.

Mead, George Herbert (1934) *Mind, Self, and Society*. Chicago: University of Chicago Press.

Mead, George Herbert (1938) *Philosophy of the Act*. Chicago: University of Chicago Press.

Mills, C. Wright (1940) Situated Action and the Vocabulary of Motives. *American Sociological Review*, 5, 904–93.

Parsons, Talcott (1937) *The Structure of Social Action*. Chicago: Free Press.

Rawls, John (1996) Durkheim's Epistemology: the Neglected Argument. *American Journal of Sociology*, 102(2), 430–82.

Sacks, Harvey, Schegloff, Emmanuel, and Jefferson, Gail (1977) The Simplest Systematics for Turntaking in Conversation. *Language*, 50, 696–735.

Scheff, Thomas (1966) *Being Mentally Ill: a Sociological Theory*. Chicago: Aldine.

Schutz, Alfred (1967) *The Phenomenology of the Social World*. Evanston, IL: Northwestern University Press (originally published in German in 1932).

Searle, John (1968) *Speech Acts*. Berkeley: University of California Press.

Sykes, Gresham (1958) *The Society of Captives*. Princeton, NJ: Princeton University Press.

Szasz, Thomas (1961) *The Myth of Mental Illness: Foundations of a Theory of the Social World*. New York: Harper and Row.

Thomas, W. I. (1927) *The Polish Peasant in Europe and America*. New York: Alfred A. Knopf.

Warnock, Geoffrey J. (1967) *The Philosophy of Perception*. London: Oxford University Press.

Weber, Max (1921) *Economy and Society*. New York: Bedminster Press.

Znaniecki, Florian (1936) *Social Actions*. New York: Farrar and Rinehart.

6

Daniel Bell

Malcolm Waters

Daniel Bell (born 1919) was probably the most famous sociologist of his generation. He was hailed as the prophet of the emergence of a new society, the postindustrial society, and as one of the leading conservative critics of contemporary culture. Bell has been a controversial figure since he suggested in the 1960s that ideological conflicts had disappeared from modern society, but his work has been the spur for a recent flood of writing on the "new society." Bell's intellectual biography begins with an engagement with questions of work, the labor movement, and American capitalism, flowing through to more detailed discussions of political extremism, the new postindustrial society, and the disintegration of culture associated with postmodernism The three works that made Bell famous were *The End of Ideology*, *The Coming of Postindustrial Society*, and *The Cultural Contradictions of Capitalism*.

Daniel Bell's theory is historical and substantive rather than formal and analytic. It proposes that society is organized in three realms. However, Bell is doubtless better known for certain big theoretical ideas about change within each of these realms: the postindustrial society, the end of ideology, and the cultural contradictions of capitalism.

The Theory

The three realms of society are the techno-economic structure (TES; sometimes the "social structure"), the polity, and culture. *Society* is itself one of three superordinate regions (that Bell, confusingly, also describes as "realms"), the others being *nature* and *technology* (Bell, 1991, pp. 3–33). Nature is "a realm outside of man whose designs are reworked by men" (ibid., p. 8). It has two components: the *Umwelt*, the geographical environment, the world of organic and inorganic objects that is open to human intervention; and *physis*, the analytic pattern of natural relationships. Technology is "the instrumental ordering of human experience within a logic of efficient means, and the direction of nature to use its powers for material gain" (ibid., p. 20). It clearly impacts on nature in so far as it opens up possibilities for the transformation of the *Umwelt*, but it also has profound implications for society, creating consumption-based mass societies, elaborately differentiated occupational systems, and synchronized cultures. Bell is a convinced social constructionist, for whom society is "a set of social arrangements, created by men, to regulate normatively the exchange of wants and satisfactions" (ibid., p. 29, italics removed). It is "a social contract, made not in the past but in the present, in which the constructed rules are obeyed if they seem fair and just" (ibid., p. 29).

However, Bell's subdivision of society into three realms is more important. There is some inconsistency in terminology: in *The Winding Passage* (1991, pp. 3–33), the three realms are nature, technology and society, while the three "dimensions" of society are "social" structure, polity, and culture (ibid., p. 31); but in *The Cultural Contradictions of Capitalism* (1979, p. 10), the "techno-economic" structure, polity, and culture are listed as distinct "realms." Further, in *Winding Passage* the latter trinity is said to be a feature of all societies but in *Cultural Contradictions* Bell is agnostic on whether the scheme can be applied generally and reserves it only for modern society (ibid., p. 10). In general though, apart from the single essay in *Winding Passage*, Bell uses the word "realm" for the less abstract societal trinity rather than the more abstract existential trinity, and this is the usage that will be employed here. We can also assume that the three realms are universal aspects of all societies but become separate and autonomous only in modern society.

The *techno-economic structure* (TES) is the realm of economic life, the arena of social arrangements for the production and distribution of goods and services. Such activities imply applications of technology to instrumental ends and result in a stratified occupational system. The axial principle of the modern TES is functional rationality. It consistently drives towards minimizing cost and optimizing output and is therefore regulated by the process that Bell calls *economizing*. So we assess the development of the TES in terms of its level of efficiency, productivity, and productiveness. Indeed, change proceeds along the path of substituting technological processes and social arrangements that are more productive and efficient for those that are less so. *Contra* Weber, who locates the development of bureaucracy in the emergence of the modern state, Bell argues that bureaucracy is the axial structure of the TES. The more that technological functions become specialized, the greater is the need to coordinate these functions and therefore the more elaborate and hierarchical become the organizational arrangements that human beings put in place to accomplish such coordination. The lifeworlds of the TES are, in a terminology that might be traced to Lukács (1968), "reified" worlds in which the individual is subordinated to roles specified in organizational charts. They are also authoritarian worlds that subordinate individual ends to the goals of the organization orchestrated by a technocratic management that recognizes the validity only of the functional and the instrumental (Bell, 1979b, p. 11; 1991, p. 31).

The *polity* is the set of social arrangements that frames a conception of justice and then regulates social conflict within that framework. Justice is elaborated within a set of traditions or a constitution. Regulation is accomplished by applications of power; that is, by the legitimate use of force and, in many societies, by the rule of law. It is therefore a system of societal authority involving the distribution of legitimate power in society. In a modern society, the axial principle specifies that power is legitimated by reference to the consent of the governed. Moreover, this axial principle is egalitarian in so far as it specifies that each person must have a more or less equal voice in providing this consent. Because equality of political participation gives expression to the material and cultural aspirations of all members of society, it extends into other areas of social life via the institution of citizenship that implies equality of access to legal, social and cultural entitlements. The axial structure is a system of representation that allows general consent to be expressed through organized arrangements – that is, political parties, lobby groups, and social movements – that can funnel claims to the center (Bell, 1979b, pp. 11–12).

Bell's version of *culture* is much narrower than the conventional sociological or anthropological definitions that specify it as the overall pattern or shape of life in a society. While recognizing that culture includes the cognitive symbolizations of science and philosophy (ibid., p. 12n), as well as the character structure of individuals (Bell, 1991, p. 31), he restricts his interest in culture to the arena of expressive symbolism: "efforts, in painting, poetry, and fiction, or within the religious forms of litany, liturgy and ritual, which seek to explore and express the meanings of human existence in imaginative form" (Bell, 1979b, p. 12). These expressive symbolizations must always address what Bell regards as the universal and irreducible fundamentals of human existence, the nature and meaning of death, tragedy, heroism, loyalty, redemption, love, sacrifice, and spirituality (Bell, 1979b, p. 12; 1991, p. 31). The axial principle of modern culture is self-expression and self-realization; that is, the value of cultural objects must be assessed against the subjective sentiments and judgments of those who produce and consume them and not against objective standards (Bell, 1979b, p. xvii). The axial structures of modern culture are arrangements for the production and reproduction of meanings and artifacts.

Bell explicitly asserts that, 'there are not simple determinate relations among the three realms' (ibid., p. 12). This is because the direction and the pattern, what he often calls the rhythm, of change in each of them is fundamentally different. In the TES change is linear or progressive, involving an upward curve in production and efficiency. There is no such rule in the polity, where the pattern of change consists in alternation between opposing configurations. People can alternate between the efficiencies of oligarchy and the equalities of democracy, between the expertise of elitism and homogenization of mass society, or between the unifying tendencies of centralization and the localism of confederate systems (Bell, 1991, pp. xx, 31). By contrast, cultural change is recursive. While retaining its past, culture can follow one of two paths in developing upon it. It can follow the additive, developmental and incremental path of tradition, building on well established genres but not stepping outside them. Alternatively, it can engage in indiscriminate mixing and borrowing from several diverse cultural traditions (syncretism).

Because the rhythm of change is different in each realm, each follows its own path through time and thus each has its own separate history. In certain periods of time the particular formations apparent in each of the realms will be synchronized and there will be an accidental unity among them. Bell identifies twelfth-century Europe and the "apogee" of bourgeois society in the last third of the nineteenth century as examples of such periods (ibid., p. xx). However at other times, perhaps at most other times, the realms will be disjunctive; that is, their normative specifications will contradict one another at the level of experience. Disjunction between the realms is a structural source of tension in society and therefore the fulcrum of change. In contradistinction to holistic theories of society, then, Bell's theoretical approach proposes not only that disjunction of the realms is a normal condition of society but also that it is the central feature of contemporary society in particular.

However, the initial pattern of modern society was one of unification between the realms in the formation known as "bourgeois society." It involved a conjunction between individual entrepreneurship and personal economic responsibility in the TES, liberal resistance to the constraints of an enlarged and active state in the polity, and an emphasis on expressing the self, rather than a set of issues prescribed by tradition, in culture. However, a radical hiatus rapidly developed between the TES and culture. At first it involved a contradiction between the disciplinary constraints of work and the quest for a personal sense of the sublime and for emotional excitement in cultural expression. The more the ethic of work disappeared and the more that human labor became subjected to an authoritarian hierarchy, the more cultural tradition was eroded. Social legitimation, as Bell puts it, passed from the sphere of religion to modernism itself, to the cultivation of the individual personality. The economy responded to this demand, mass producing cultural artifacts and images. Modernism turned into a restless search for titillation and novelty, a "rule of fad and fashion: of multiples for the *culturati*, hedonism for the middle classes, pornotopia for the masses. And in the very nature of fashion, it has trivialized the culture" (Bell, 1979b, p. xxvii).

Bell explores this disintegration of modern society through three more specific theoretical accounts, one for each of the realms, for which he is better known than for the general theory. Perhaps the best known of these is Bell's theory of social change called the "postindustrial society." It argues that contemporary societies are or will be going through a shift so that industrial society will give way to a new techno-economic structure that will be as different from industrial society as industrial society is from pre-industrial society. We can perhaps begin by considering the distinctions that Bell makes between these three (1976, pp. 116–19, 126–9). A *pre-industrial society* can be characterized as "a game against nature" that centers on attempts to extract resources from the natural environment. It involves primary-sector industries carried out in a context of limited land supply and climatic and seasonal variation. An *industrial society* is "a game against fabricated nature" centering on the manufacturing and processing of tangible goods by semi-skilled factory workers and engineers.

By contrast, a *postindustrial society* is "a 'game between persons' in which an 'intellectual technology,' based on information, rises alongside of machine technology" (ibid., p. 116). The postindustrial society involves industries from three sectors: the tertiary industries of transportation and utilities; the quaternary industries of trade, finance, and capital exchange; and the quinary industries of health, education, research, public administration, and leisure. Among these, the last is definitive because the key occupations are the professional and technical ones with scientists at the core (ibid., pp. 117–18).

Bell elaborates his ideal-typical construct of the postindustrial society in terms of five dimensions (ibid., pp. 14–33):

- There will be a unilinear progression between industrial sectors (primary through quinary) and a corresponding shift in the labor force toward a *service economy.* Accordingly, "the first and simplest characteristic of a postindustrial society is that the majority of the labor force is no longer engaged in agriculture or manufacturing but in services, which are defined, residually, as trade, finance, transport, health, recreation, research, education, and government" (ibid., p. 15).
- The pre-eminent, although not necessarily the majority of, occupations in the society will be *the professional and technical class*, whose occupations require a tertiary level of education. The core will be scientists and engineers and together they will become a knowledge class that displaces the propertied bourgeoisie.
- *Theoretical knowledge* is the defining "axial principle" of the postindustrial society. The organization of the society around knowledge becomes the basis for social control, the direction of innovation, and the political management of new social relationships. Bell stresses that in a postindustrial society this knowledge is theoretical, rather than traditional or practical, in character. It involves the codification of knowledge into abstract symbolic systems that can be applied in a wide variety of situations.
- The advance of theoretical knowledge allows the *planning of technology*, including forward assessments of its risks, costs, and advantages.
- The society is based on a *new intellectual technology*, the software and the statistical or logical formulae that are entered into computers.

In the paperback edition of this work Bell alters this list of dimensions. The planning dimension is eliminated and seven new characteristics are added (Bell, 1976, pp. xvi–xix):

- Work focuses on an engagement in relationships with other people.
- The expansion of the services sector provides a basis for the economic independence of women that had not previously been available.
- Scientific institutions and their relationship with other institutions are the essential feature of the postindustrial society.

- Situses replace classes. Major conflicts will occur between the four functional situses (scientific, technological, administrative, and cultural) and the five institutional situses (business, government, university and research, social welfare, and military).
- Position will be allocated on the basis of education and skill rather than wealth or cultural advantage.
- Scarcity of goods will disappear in favor of scarcities of information and time.
- Society will follow a cooperative, rather than an individualistic, strategy in the generation and use of information.

However, the core of his proposal is that that there are two "large" dimensions by which one decides whether a social structure has entered a postindustrial phase. These are the centrality of theoretical knowledge (including by implication, the employment of science as a means to technological change) and the expansion of the quinary service sector.

A curious feature of Bell's political sociology is that its central and most controversial idea is not of his own origination. Bell (1988, p. 411) himself notes that the phrase "the end of ideology" was first used by Albert Camus in 1946. It entered sociology in the hands of one of Bell's intellectual confidants, Raymond Aron, who wrote a chapter entitled "The End of the Ideological Age?" for his book attacking Marxism called *The Opium of the Intellectuals* (reprinted in Waxman, 1968, pp. 27–48). Bell selected the theme as the title for a collection of essays on class and politics first published in 1960, but addressed it explicitly only in an epilogue.

Ideology is for Bell a secular religion: "a set of ideas, infused with passion" that "seeks to transform the whole way of life" (Bell, 1988, p. 400). Ideology performs the important function of converting ideas into social levers. It does so precisely by that infusion of passion, by its capacity to release human emotions and to channel their energies into political action, much as religion channels emotional energy into ritual and artistic expression. Ideology was at least partly able to fill the "psychic" gap left by the secularization processes of the nineteenth century by emphasizing the continuity of collective triumph against individual mortality. The political ideologies of the nineteenth century were also strengthened by two important alliances: with a rising class of intellectuals seeking to establish status against lack of recognition by the business bourgeoisie; and with the positive values of science that could measure and indicate progress.

"Today," Bell (1988, p. 402) asserts, "these ideologies are exhausted." He gives three causes: the violent oppression carried out by ruling communist parties against their populations; the amelioration of the worst effects of the capitalist market and the emergence of the welfare state; and the emergence of such new philosophies as existentialism and humanism, which emphasized the stoic-theological ontology of humanity, against such romantic philosophies as Marxism and liberalism, which emphasized the perfectibility of human nature. Bell's conclusion is captured in the following passage:

> [O]ut of all this history, one simple fact emerges: for the radical intelligentsia, the old ideologies have lost their "truth" and their power to persuade.
>
> Few serious minds believe any longer that one can set down "blueprints" and through "social engineering" bring about a new utopia of social harmony. At the same time, the older counter-beliefs have lost their intellectual force as well. Few "classic" liberals insist that the State should play no role in the economy, and few serious conservatives... believe that the Welfare State is "the road to serfdom" ... there is today a rough consensus among intellectuals on political issues: the acceptance of the Welfare State; the desirability of decentralized power; a system of mixed economy and of political pluralism. In that sense too the ideological age has ended. (Bell, 1988, pp. 402–3)

Bell is not, it must be stressed, entirely triumphalist about this development. He mourns the spent passions of intellectualized politics and wonders how the energies of the young can be channeled into them. And he also pleads for the retention of utopias as focuses for human aspiration, because without them society is reduced to a meaningless materialism.

Doubtless the most sociologically influential of Bell's arguments about the disintegration of the realms of modern society is his analysis of its cultural contradictions (Bell, 1979b). His general typification of modern culture can be found within his analysis of modernity. He defines modernity thus: "Modernity is individualism, the effort of individuals to remake themselves, and, where necessary, to remake society in order to allow design and choice" (Bell, 1990a, p. 72). It implies the rejection of any "naturally" ascribed or divinely ordained order, of external authority, and of collective authority in favor of the self as the sole point of reference for action. Although not every sociologist would agree with him, Bell adduces that sociology frames five important propositions about modernity (ibid., pp. 43–4):

- that society is constructed out of a social contract between individuals;
- that human beings are dualistic, having an original self and an imposed social self, and therefore face the prospect of self-estrangement or alienation;
- that religion is a superstition that precludes self-awareness;
- that modernity involves an autonomization of the value-spheres of culture (art, morality and justice) which, in particular, involves the differentiation of economics from morality and art from religion;
- that human nature is not universal but that the character of any particular human being is determined by that person's location in social structure (by occupation, ethnicity, gender, etc.).

Under modernity there can be no question about the moral authority of the self. The only question is that of how the self is to be fulfilled – by hedonism, by acquisitiveness, by faith, by the privatization of morality, or by sensationalism.

If bourgeois Protestantism was the privatized–moralistic answer to this question, the shift to a more hedonistic response, Bell argues, could only be confirmed once modernizing changes had also taken place in the realm of social (techno-economic) structure. The transformation of modern culture is due, he now asserts, "singularly" to the emergence of mass consumption and the increased affluence of lower socioeconomic groups (Bell, 1979b, p. 66). The techno-economic changes that made mass consumption possible and desirable began in the 1920s. They were of two types, technological and sociological. A key technological development was the multiplication of human effort by the application of electrical power to manufacturing and to domestic tasks. Others took place in the areas of transportation and the mass media, the latter in the forms of the cinema and radio. The sociological inventions were, for Bell, even more profound. They were: the moving assembly line that reduced the cost of consumer durables, especially cars; the development of advertising and marketing systems that could cultivate consumer taste; and the extension of consumer credit through installment plans, time payments, personal loans, and the like. These spelt the end of Protestant bourgeois culture.

Bell's critique of modernity centers on the absence of a moral or transcendental ethic that is displaced by a mere individualized anxiety. In Puritan communities guilt was assuaged by repentance. In mass society anxiety is assuaged by psychotherapy, a process that for Bell is bound to fail because security of identity can only be accomplished within a moral context. This transformation is but one consequence of the contradictions that arise from the cultural developments of modernity. The primary contradiction lies between cultural norms of hedonism and social structural norms of work discipline. But there is also an enormous contradiction within the social structure itself: a good worker delays gratification but a good consumer looks for immediate gratification. Bell concludes that this means "One is to be 'straight' by day and a 'swinger' by night"; and then cannot resist an exclamatory protest: "This is self-fulfillment and self-realization!" (ibid., p. 72).

This brings Bell to "an extraordinary sociological puzzle," that of why the cultural movement of modern*ism* that repeatedly attacks and dirempts modern social structure and bourgeois culture should have persisted for more than a century in the face of this contradiction. He defines modernism as: "the self-willed effort of a style and sensibility to remain in the forefront of 'advancing consciousness'" (ibid., p. 46). This attempt can be expressed in terms of several possible descriptions. First, it can be described as *avant garde*, as rejecting elitist cultural traditions in favor of a reinsertion of life into art. Second, it is adversarial: "The legend of modernism is that of the free creative spirit at war with the bourgeoisie" (ibid., p. 40). Last, it is impenetrable within conventional understandings and requires intellectual gyrations to be appreciated: "It is willfully opaque, works with unfamiliar forms, is self-consciously experimental, and seeks deliberately to disturb the audience – to shock it, shake it up, even to transform it as if in a religious conversion" (ibid., p. 46). This gives modernism an esoteric appeal, as Bell intones slightly ironically, but it also denies its other claims to being adversarial and *avant garde* – an elitist indulgence can be nothing but privileged. In modernism content and form disappear in favor of medium as the central expression. In art the stress is on paint, its means of application, and substitutes for it; music stresses sounds rather than harmony; poetry emphasizes "breath" and phonemics; literature employs wordplay as against plot or genre; drama promotes action and spectacle at the expense of characterization.

The adversarial "legend," as Bell calls it, has now been extended to order of all kinds. The free, creative spirit of the artist is now at war with "'civilization' or 'repressive tolerance' or some other agency that curtails 'freedom'" (ibid., p. 40). This adversarial strategy has, in general, been highly successful. The modern cultural arena has divorced from the capitalist system that spawned it and has become self-referential. The "hierophants of culture" now construct the audience and in dominating and exploiting it have come to constitute a cultural class. They have grown sufficiently in number to establish group networks and not to be treated as deviant, and they have independent control of the material substructure of artistic expression – galleries, film studios, weekly magazines, universities, and so on. From this lofty salient they sally forth to mount their attacks on crusty tradition:

> Today, each new generation, starting off at the benchmarks attained by the adversary culture of its cultural parents, declares in sweeping fashion that the status quo represents backward conservatism or repression, so that in a widening gyre, new and fresh assaults on the social structure are mounted. (ibid., p. 41)

The emphasis-on-medium and the rage-against-order are two of the three dimensions of contemporary modernism that Bell isolates. However, the third dimension, what he calls "the eclipse of distance" (ibid., pp. 108–19), is the one to which he gives the most attention. The classical fine arts followed two central principles: they were rational in that they organized space and time into a consistent and unified expression; and they were mimetic in that they sought to mirror or represent life and nature. Modernism denies these externalities and emphasizes instead the interior life, rejecting the constraints of the world and glorifying expressions of the self. Bell repeats the terms sensation, simultaneity, immediacy and impact as the syntax of modernism. Against the contemplative character of classical art, each of the artistic modernist movements (Impressionism, post-Impressionism, Futurism, Expressionism, and Cubism) intends:

> on the syntactical level, to break up ordered space; in its aesthetic, to bridge the distance between object and spectator, to "thrust" itself on the viewer and establish itself immediately by impact. One does not interpret the scene; instead, one feels it as a sensation and is caught up by that emotion. (ibid., p. 112)

Bell finds similar syntactical and aesthetic patterns in literature and music. Modern literature seeks to plunge the reader into the maelstrom of the emotions, while music abandons structure in its entirety.

The theory of modernism connects with the three realms argument. The disjunctions between culture and social structure are sustained by a mutual divorce. The cognitive expressions that arise from the social (techno-economic) structure are rapidly reifying and rationalizing human experience: extreme levels of occupational differentiation separate persons from the roles that they occupy; the proliferation of knowledge subcultures prevents the formation of a single expressive tradition that can speak to all; and the mathematization of symbolic representations leaves society without a common cultural language. Modernism is itself complicit in this development because, in rejecting the possibility of a common style, it prevents any claim that it is a culture at all. Modernist culture is differentiating rapidly into a variety of "demesnes," it lacks authoritative centers, it focuses on the instantaneity of the visual, electronic media rather than the permanence of print, and it denies the rationality of the cosmos. The outcome of these dual forces is the diremption of culture as an idea. In an important sense, Bell regards modern society as a society without a culture.

However, if Bell is worried about the effects of modernism then he is positively horrified by the prospects implied by the rise of postmodernism. Bell regards postmodernism as an essentially modernist trend, but as one which carries modernist logic to extremes. Postmodernism substitutes instinctual and erotic justifications for aesthetic and humanistic ones. In the hands of Michel Foucault and Norman O. Brown, "It announced not only the 'de-construction of Man' and the end of the humanist credo, but also the 'epistemological break' with genitality and the dissolution of focussed sexuality into the polymorph perversity of oral and anal pleasures" (Bell, 1990a, p. 69). It legitimated both homosexual liberation and a hippie-rock-drug culture, the latter striking directly at the motivational system that sustains an industrial or postindustrial TES. In a jaundiced phrase, Bell notes that, "the culturati, ever ready, follow[ed] the winds of fashion" (ibid., p. 70), as artists and architects took up the slogan to attack the boundary between high and popular culture. Postmodernist art, architecture, and music emphasize pastiche and playfulness, in Bell's view, at the expense of creativity and genuine style.

> What passes for serious culture today lacks both content and form, so that the visual arts are primarily decorative and literature a self-indulgent babble or contrived experiment. Decoration, by its nature, no matter how bright and gay, becomes, in its finite and repetitive patterns, mere wallpaper, a receding background incapable of engaging the viewer in the renewable re-visions of perception. Self-referential literature, when both the self and the referent repeat the same old refrains, becomes a tedious bore, like Uno in the circus, showing that he can raise himself on one finger. A culture of re-cycled images and twice-told tales is a culture that has lost its bearings. (ibid., p. 70)

THE PERSON

Daniel Bell was born in 1919 in the Lower East Side of New York City. Most of his family had chain-migrated from the Bialystok area that lies between Poland and Belarus. His paternal grandfather sold coal in winter and ice in summer from a horse-drawn cart. The family name was Bolotsky, but this was probably an invention only a few generations old, constructed to avoid military service. His father died when he was eight months old and he spent much of his childhood, along with his mother and siblings, with other extended kin, usually maternal sisters. By the age of eleven Bell had a new legal guardian, his paternal uncle Samuel Bolotsky. Samuel was a dentist and upwardly mobile and the name Bolotsky did not fit such a career. So a group of cousins got together to choose new names – some became Ballin, some Ballot, and some Bell.

Not withstanding the latter developments, Bell experienced the full gamut of poor, immigrant Jewish experience: Yiddish as the first language; Hebrew school; ethnic street gangs; petty crime; racketeering; and the public poverty of waterfront shacks. By his own supposition, these experiences of poverty predisposed him to become a socialist. When he was thirteen he joined the Young People's Socialist League, one of a number of socialist groups that lived in an uneasy relationship with the Jewish garment-workers' unions. An enduring picture of Bell is that at that tender age he spent long hours in the Ottendorfer branch of the New York Public Library reading avidly on socialism, but also on sociology.

Bell entered the City College of New York as an undergraduate in 1935, majoring in classics. He chose to do so on the advice of a brilliant young communist instructor named Moses Finkelstein, who suggested that ancient history was the best preparation for sociology because one could there examine entire and coherent cultures. After Bell graduated in 1938 he spent a year in graduate school at Columbia University, but without any apparent result. He left, for reasons unexplained, and spent most of the next twenty years working as a journalist. Most of the years of the Second World War were spent at the *New Leader*, a vehicle mainly used by social-democratic supporters of the union movement, first as a staff writer and then as managing editor. From 1948 to 1958 he was a staff writer and then Labor Editor at *Fortune*, the voice of American big business.

Bell's academic career began in 1945, when he accepted a three-year appointment teaching social science at the University of Chicago. Later, during the *Fortune* years, he moonlighted as an adjunct lecturer in sociology at Columbia (1952–6). However, he moved out of journalism permanently in 1958 as an associate professor in the same university. He was awarded a PhD by Columbia in 1960 for a compilation of his published work and was promoted to full professor in 1962. He moved to Harvard in 1969 and was appointed to a prestigious endowed chair as Henry Ford II Professor of Social Sciences in that university in 1980.

Bell is a relentless publisher. By his own count he has written or edited fourteen or so books and a best guess would suggest about 200 articles of a scholarly nature. The articles tend not to be published in sociology journals. He has published an article in the *British Journal of Sociology* (the Hobhouse memorial lecture) but has published only reviews in the *American Journal of Sociology* or the *American Sociological Review*. His preferred outlets are non-refereed, general intellectual journals that are often associated with the New York circle, with other Jewish interests, or with learned societies, including *The Public Interest*, *Commentary*, *The Partisan Review*, *New Leader*, *Dissent*, *Daedalus*, and *The American Scholar*.

Bell has also made important contributions to public life. Most of his public service was devoted to insisting on a sociological contribution to planning for the future at the national level. He was *seriatim*: a member of the President's Commission on Technology, Automation and Economic Progress (1964–6) and co-chair of its Panel on Special Indicators; chair of the Commission on the Year 2000, which he founded under the aegis of The American Academy of Arts and Sciences (1964–74); American representative on the OECD's Inter-Futures Project (1976–9); a member of the President's Commission on a National Agenda for the 1980s and chair of its Panel on Energy and Resources; and a member of the National Research Council, Board on Telecommunications and Computers.

In the later years of his career, Daniel Bell has been the recipient of numerous honors, prizes, and visiting lectureships. The most prestigious of these include: Guggenheim Fellowships in 1972 and 1983; the Hobhouse memorial lecture at the University of London, 1977; Vice-President of the American Academy of Arts and Sciences, 1972–5; the Fels lecture at the University of Pennsylvania, 1986; the Suhrkamp lecture at Goethe University, Frankfurt, 1987; the Pitt Professorship in American Institutions and a Fellowship of King's College, Cambridge, 1987–8; the American Academy of Arts and Sciences Talcott Parsons Prize for the Social Sciences, 1992; an American Sociological Association Award for a distinguished career of lifetime scholarship, 1992; and no less than nine honorary doctorates.

THE SOCIAL CONTEXT

Two aspects of the social context of Bell's youth were to influence his intellectual development: immigrant poverty and the Jewish religion. The impact of the first is perhaps best described by Bell himself:

> I had grown up in the slums of New York. My mother had worked in a garment factory as long as I could remember; my father had died when I was an infant. All around me I saw the "Hoovervilles," the tin shacks near the docks of the East River where the unemployed lived in makeshift houses and rummaged through the garbage scows for food. Late at night I would go with a gang of other boys to the wholesale vegetable markets on the West Side, to swipe potatoes or to pick up bruised tomatoes in the street to bring home, or to eat around the small fires we would make in the street with the broken boxes from the markets. I wanted to know, simply, why this had to be. It was inevitable that I should become a sociologist. (Bell, 1981, p. 532)

Judaism needs no general description here, but Bell experienced it in transition from a traditional, victimized, European context to a somewhat tribal but nevertheless more mobile, secular, and egalitarian American one. Bell declared his own atheism to his Melamud (teacher) at the age of 13. However, throughout his life he has experienced all the torture of the contradiction between being a deep believer in the capacity of religion to provide meaning and simultaneously not being a practising member of any religion. This tension is, according to Bell's friend and mentor, Irving Howe, directly reflected in his sociological output.

> [W]e thought we should know everything. . . . Meyer [Schapiro], I would say, is the ultimate example of the whole idea of range and scope. On a more modest level somebody like Danny Bell lives by the same notion. Behind this is a very profoundly Jewish impulse: namely, you've got to beat the goyim at their own game. So you have to dazzle them a little. (Howe, 1982, p. 284)

Bell's attempt to dazzle was made in the context of a very different America in the post-Second World War period from the society that had preceded it. As Bell himself puts it, the USA "passed from being a nation to becoming a *national society* in which there is not only a coherent national authority, but where the different sectors of the society, that is economy, polity, and culture, are bound together in a cohesive way and where crucial political and economic decisions are now made at the 'center'" (Bell, 1966, p. 69; original italics). Such centralization implies fiscal management by the manipulation of taxation and interest rates. Alongside this national economy there also developed a national polity by the extension of citizenship rights into the socioeconomic arena. The New Deal of the 1930s had ensured that the federal government had begun to assume many of the powers that previously had been vested in the states and the city governments. This process was extended in the 1960s as the government sought to engineer social equality by means of civil rights, anti-discrimination and voter-registration legislation and its enforcement. Such moves were supported by an extension of welfare state provisions, including medicare, social security, welfare payments, housing, environmental protection, and education.

American participation in the global war of 1939–45 and the leading position that the USA took in the victorious alliance in that war had provided a major impetus to centralization. The fact that the USA remained alert to a perceived Soviet military threat during the succeeding "Cold War" created a large, permanent, and centralized military and intelligence establishment. It was accompanied by the development of a national culture centered on the universities and the capacity of their members to move in and out of Washington policy circles. Mass communications, especially television, also contributed to the emergence of a national popular culture in which the sentiments and emotions of a large proportion of the population could simultaneously focus on a single event or entertainment.

American culture was founded in ideas of achievement, "masculine optimism," and progress – the USA had won all its wars, was economically dominant, and had the "biggest" and the "best" of everything material. This led to the notion of American exceptionalism, the idea shared by many citizens of the USA that theirs was an uniquely great and special society, the summit of human evolution and the guardian of crucial human values. By the 1960s, however, unspoken commitment to the American state came under threat from extremisms of the left and the right that recognized threatening international developments: European economic performance began to outstrip America; the USA managed only a doubtful performance in the space race against the USSR; American military adventurism proved less triumphal than in the past, especially in Vietnam; and America was cast in the role of a neocolonial power.

These developments wrought turmoil in university education in the 1960s. It had expanded under the weight of the postwar baby boom and the students were of a generation that had experienced comparative affluence, freedom from exposure to major international conflict, and relative freedom of expression. Many young American men resisted or avoided conscription to military service in Vietnam and many students, especially in the major universities, became politically active. The consequent political mobilization spread over into wider issues, including civil rights and the democratization of universities.

It would be foolhardy to subject Bell's theory to a crude sociology-of-knowledge analysis. Nevertheless, it is difficult to ignore the temporal correspondence between end-of-ideology and the emergence of a consensus-organized national society, between postindustrial society and the rapid expansion of universities, and between cultural contradictions and the value and generational conflicts that appended the Vietnam War. Bell is a substantive theorist and, as an acute social observer, his theoretical development is bound to reflect the social context in this way.

THE INTELLECTUAL CONTEXT

On attending the City College of New York (CCNY) in 1939, Bell joined a socialist reading group called "Alcove No. 1." Other members, including Meyer Lasky, Irving Kristol, Nathan Glazer, and Irving Howe, were often Trotskyite in their political orientation (although many of these were later to become the core of the neoconservative movement). While finding the members of the group a convenient sounding board for his own democratic socialist commitment, Bell could not accept Trotskyism. Indeed, by 1947 he had rejected socialism entirely, abandoned a book he was writing on the capitalist state, and moved into a job at *Fortune*.

His personal rejection of ideology was linked to an academic interest in its societal rejection. His first monograph (1967), published in 1952, examined the failure of socialism in the USA, and he also worked on the collapse of ideological extremism on the right (1964b). The culmination, of course, was the end-of-ideology essay. This was originally produced for a conference of the *Congress for Cultural Freedom*, a London-based anti-communist intellectual group that, probably unknown to Bell, received some of its income from the CIA (Wald, 1987, p. 351).

However, the bonds of youth remained strong and later crystallized into part of what became known as the "New York Intellectual Circle": "These New York Jewish Intellectuals came together as a self-conscious group, knowing each other, discussing ideas they held in common, differing widely and sometimes savagely, and yet having that sense of kinship which made each of them aware that they were part of a distinctive socio-historical phenomenon" (Bell, 1991, p. 130).

They had a common Jewish immigrant experience, they often spent their early years as socialists if not communists, and they were educationally mobile, often through CCNY and Columbia. In its maturity, the tone of the Circle was distinctly illiberal, refusing to denounce McCarthyism or the American military engagement in Vietnam, opposing affirmative action for blacks and women, standing radically opposed to student protest, and endorsing unquestioning American support for the state of Israel. The Circle was important because it was the integrating point for the national intellectual elite – over 50 per cent of the American intellectual elite lived in New York City and about half of that elite was Jewish (Kadushin, 1974, pp. 22–3). There is little doubt that Bell was a key figure in the Circle, partly by virtue of his contacts with the inner group, and partly because of his editorship of some of the more influential periodicals. However, he has always rejected the label "neoconservative" that Michael Harrington invented for many of its members, even though such authors as Steinfels (1979) always include Bell in the category.

This general intellectual context blended with an emerging sociological intellectualism located in the rapidly expanding universities. At Chicago Bell experienced his first large encounter with academic sociologists. There he team-taught a common course in social science with "an extraordinary group of young thinkers" (Bell, 1991, p. xvii), including David Riesman, Edward Shils, Milton Singer, Barrington Moore, Morris Janowitz, and Philip Rieff. These scholars represent a tradition now, save Bell, largely lost in American sociology, of theorizing long-term societal transformations and the problems they pose for social organization; that is, of doing substantive, general theory that lies between the sterilities of grand theory and empiricism.

The subsequent move to Columbia can be seen as part of the return of the prodigal to Jewish roots. In fact though, the influences there were mixed. Columbia indeed housed the sociological wing of the "New York intellectuals": Philip Selznick, Seymour Martin Lipset, Nathan Glazer, Alvin Gouldner, and Bernard Rosenberg, most of whom were sometime graduate students of Merton and Lazarsfeld. But, for Bell, "the primary influences were Robert McIver and the Horkheimer group, as well as a neglected figure, Alexander von Schelting, who had written a book on Max Weber's *Wissenschaftslehre*, and gave a reading course in Weber's *Wirtschaft und Gesellschaft* that I took" (Bell, personal communication, August 30, 1993).These influences introduced Bell to the Weberian tradition, but it was Weber in the proper guise of historical sociologist rather than Weber as a Parsonsian action theorist.

If one were to seek to locate Bell in relation to the classical triumvirate of founding theoretical ancestors, then, one would say that he is closest to Weber, most opposed to Marx, and most neutral in relation to Durkheim, not withstanding labeling as a Durkheimian (e.g. O'Neill, 1988; Archer, 1990). Otherwise, he is perhaps most influenced by such sociologists of his generation as Aron, Shils, Riesman, and Dahrendorf. However, what really impresses when one reads Bell is not his knowledge of sociological writings in particular but the breadth of his familiarity with the canon of the Western intellectual tradition. He is influenced at least as much by Aristotle, Rousseau, Schumpeter, Nietzsche,

Veblen, Saint-Simon, and Kant, as well as members of the New York Circle, chief among whom he would probably count Howe, Kristol, Trilling, Glazer, and Hook.

However, Bell has seldom been in tune with any dominant sociological intellectual context. When he left Columbia in 1969, American sociology was mainly divided between two hostile camps: the grand theorists led by Talcott Parsons and the positivistic empiricists led by such figures as Hubert M. Blalock and Otis Dudley Duncan. Theoretically weak and empirically inexact, symbolic interactionism had managed to limp on in the sociological imagination, largely by dint of the iconoclastic efforts of such figures as Howard S. Becker and Erving Goffman; and Alfred Schutz had shepherded the influence of European phenomenology into American sociology, although in its new host it mutated into the bizarre and more influential form of ethnomethodology (see Garfinkel).

Bell rejected all these possibilities. He wanted to be a theorist and a generalizer but he found that he could not accept a holistic vision of society that would deny the possibility of contradictory processes and interests and of divergent historical trends. Acutely tuned to shifts in moods and ideas, he found Parsonsian thought to be as inflexible and incommodious in relation to contemporary developments as that of Marx, and he has seldom allowed himself to be impressed by sociological positivism.

Impact

Kadushin's (1974) research on the American intellectual elite in the late 1960s established its membership at about seventy. Daniel Bell was among the top ten of those seventy, along with Noam Chomsky, John Kenneth Galbraith, Norman Mailer, Susan Sontag, and Edmund Wilson (ibid., pp. 30–1). There was no other sociologist in the top ten, although Hannah Arendt and David Riesman were in the top twenty and Edgar Z. Friedenberg, George Lichtheim, Nathan Glazer, Seymour Martin Lipset, Robert K. Merton, Robert Nisbet, and Franz Schurmann could be found lower down, alongside W. H. Auden, Marshall McLuhan and Barrington Moore. The list included neither of the leading theoretical sociologists of the time, Alfred Schutz and Talcott Parsons, nor did it include the leading empirical sociologists, Otis Dudley Duncan, Erving Goffman, and Paul F. Lazarsfeld, or the philosophers of social science, Carl Hempel and Ernest Nagel. Put simply, Kadushin's research confirms the fair estimate that Daniel Bell was probably the most publicly famous sociologist of the postwar generation.

Bell became an important figure not merely because he was read widely but because he has an unusual capacity to bridge academic and public discourse, so that he finds respect and admiration not only among colleagues but also in the elite and the middle mass. Bell fulfills the role of the *Schriftsteller*, the public intellectual *par excellence*. Other sociologists have also fulfilled this role, including, in Bell's own generation, David Riesman, Nathan Glazer, and C. Wright Mills, and in the contemporary context one can identify such figures as Amitai

Etzioni, Anthony Giddens, and Ulrich Beck, but none has been as effective or as famous as Bell. The reason may simply be that Bell is entirely courageous and straightforward. The fame is not accidental but the result of a reflexive, self-conscious, Franklinian effort to compose the self that combines outstanding talent, voluminous reading, a supportive intellectual circle, and a capacity for self-salesmanship.

An assessment of Bell's influence in the academic arena, however, has to be a little more equivocal. In the second half of the twentieth century, sociology has thrown up two figures that can undeniably stand alongside its classical founding theorists. They are Talcott Parsons and Jürgen Habermas. While a fair appraisal of Bell would not unreservedly put him in the same league, he would certainly have a claim to be at the head of the next small group to be considered. Bell's central legacy to sociology is the role he played in fracturing, at the level of general theory, the holistic hegemony, the two variants of the dominant ideology thesis, Marxian and Parsonsian (see Abercrombie et al., 1980). The theory of the three realms is by no means fully developed, but it does provide a conceptual map of the terrain over which sociology stakes its intellectual claim. The leading edge of contemporary theoretical sociology bears a much greater resemblance to Bell than it does to, say, Marx or Parsons.

One of Bell's greatest strengths is his ability to sense shifts in the *Zeitgeist*, to locate them within the Western tradition and to recast them in a provocative and stimulating way. If one had to select the biggest of the big ideas, then it would have to be that of the postindustrial society, the primary example of this capacity and the idea that will always be associated with his name. As Bell himself says, almost with surprise, the phrase "postindustrial society" has passed quickly into the sociological literature (Bell, 1976, p. ix). The argument must be regarded as strongest in its stress on the emergence of the quinary service sector and the development of information as a resource, and perhaps weakest in its claims for a scientocracy and the centrality of universities. These strengths and weaknesses are perhaps reflected in the ways in which sociologists conventionally use the term. Every sociologist knows that "postindustrialization" means the displacement of manufacturing occupations by service occupations, and indeed the description of such jobs as "postindustrial occupations" is common parlance.

The current theoretical fascination is with "New Times," the issue of whether society is entering a new phase that might be after modernity or industrialism. Bell's was the first full-blown example of such theory and it influences much of the current crop and anticipates many of its components. For example, the end-of-ideology thesis anticipates many recent theories of "new" or post-materialist politics (e.g. Inglehart, 1990) because it specifies that politics will be detached from class milieux and refocused on values and lifestyles. Similarly, the idea of the "eclipse of distance" in modernist cultural expression, in which the stress is on simultaneity, impact, sensation, and immediacy, resonates closely with Harvey's (1989) analysis of the postmodern sensibility.

The key contribution of the cultural contradictions argument is an analysis of postmodernism written long before that topic became fashionable. Bell's interpretation is, of course, fundamentally different from those of, say, Lash and Urry

(1987), Harvey (1989), or Crook et al. (1992), in that he views postmodernism as an extreme, perhaps unintended, development of modernism. Nevertheless, each of these three arguments draws on Bell's view that postmodernism involves the disruption and involution of tradition and the cultivation of a mobile, self-gratifying psyche. The theory also anticipates contemporary theories of "detraditionalization" (Giddens, 1991; Beck, 1992) that propose that late modernity involves a recasting of modernization as "reflexive modernization." Here individuals are no longer the product of social situations, but are deliberately self-composing in a calculus that compares the self with an idealized goal structure derived from the mass media and expert systems.

Bell's theory of postindustrialization has been appropriated directly in several instances. Two are particularly important. Lyotard's (1984) influential analysis of the postmodern condition draws directly on Bell in so far as he claims that society is moving into a postindustrial age and culture into a postmodern age. However, in Lyotard, the two operate in tandem rather than in contradiction. Postindustrial developments see the commodification of knowledge through the application of new technologies. Lash and Urry's (1994) specification of reflexive accumulation also draws directly on Bell. Here, postindustrialization proliferates cognitive signs, symbols that represent information that becomes the central component of production, displacing material components.

Bell would put himself at some distance from other "New Times" theories. The caveats he places on the postindustrial society thesis, in which, nomenclature notwithstanding, he is not theorizing the emergence of a postindustrial *society* but only a postindustrial, techno-economic structure, and his insistence that postmodernism is only an extreme extension of modernism, confirm this view. But, like it or not, this is exactly where his work has been most influential. Paradoxically, those who reject the notion of New Times in proposing that the current context is best theorized as high modernity or late capitalism (e.g. Habermas, 1981; Jameson, 1984; Giddens, 1991) would find least in common with Bell. The original concepts of postindustrialism and postmodernism that Bell developed have taken on a life of their own. They now center a galaxy of theories that propose that a historical phase shift is under way. They could not be more influential, but it is unlikely that their author would subscribe to the ways in which they are now employed.

ASSESSMENT

The scale of Bell's impact, it must be stressed, is focused on his substantive commentary on political, societal, and cultural change. This has tended to restrict his reputation as a theorist *per se* because, at least during the twentieth century, successful sociological theorizing has tended to become defined as formal and abstract rather than historical and substantive. To assess Bell's impact as a *theorist*, then, we need to concentrate our assessment on the more formal and abstract elements of the work. These are contained in the three realms argument, which, curiously in view of its quality, is seldom the subject of much serious analysis. As Steinfels (1979, p. 168) avers, the three realms argument "probably deserves more attention from philosophers of social science and theoretically minded sociologists than it appears to have received." This assessment concentrates initially on the three realms argument, and in doing so asks several fundamental questions.

The first might be: "Is society really divided into realms?" It is clear that in complex societies there are quite pronounced boundaries between the networks of social units known as the polity or the economy that are recognized not only by social scientists but by participants, although elsewhere, as in, say, forager societies, the realms are best regarded merely as analytic aspects of a unified society.

A second question might be: "How many realms are there?" The economy and the polity are relatively unproblematic. However, matters become rather more confused when one seeks to categorize the rest, the areas of culture, socialization, leisure, religion, education, community, and kinship. Unlike many others, Bell confines culture to artistic expression and religion. However, in so doing, he omits a whole realm of social life that is focused on domesticity and community, and that both Schutz and Habermas call the lifeworld.

A third question might be: "Are the axes identified appropriately?" The axial patterns of culture are specified tautologically, but there is some confusion about the axes of the TES and the polity. In what has become something of a sociological orthodoxy, Weber locates bureaucratic rationality primarily in the state, but Bell places rationality, bureaucracy, and unequal power firmly in the TES, while addressing the state as the happy sphere of equality and democratic representation. As Weber shows, the primary feature of a state is that it is a system for the allocation of power in hierarchies and that this power can be exercised authoritatively and even arbitrarily.

The last question is: "Are the realms disjunctive?" The general difficulty is that Bell has fallen victim to what Holmwood and Stewart (1991, pp. 42–4) describe as a "horizontal" theoretical fallacy, a view that the contradictory elements of a theory are experienced separately in different parts of society. The contradictions enunciated by Bell lie not between the realms but between the different parts of his theoretical system, which, by implication, might be in need of revision. Society is always unified at the level of human experience. Indeed, modernity is surely one of the success stories of human history in terms of its capacity to survive, prosper, and expand to near-universality. If it was riven by fundamental contradiction it would long since have disintegrated.

Analytic imprecision also weakens the theoretical account of the postindustrial society. First, as Nichols (1975, p. 350) indicates, Bell denies any claim that he is theorizing an end to capitalism and class. However, throughout the book, and particularly in the sections on stratification, it is clear that, in Bell's view, neither society as a whole nor the TES alone will be structured by capital accumulation in the future. This formulation surely must be designed to deny the reality of business power in a claim that is perhaps a little too anti-Marxist. Second, Bell forecasts the development of an enlarged communal state as if it can only happen in some future society. In fact, liberal corporatist states have long existed elsewhere than in the USA that have frequently successfully managed to balance claims within a reasoned political philosophy.

Bell's analysis of culture is the theoretical jewel, a dazzling tour de force, a brilliant demonstration of his humanity, his intellect, his passion, and his sensitivity. The work is challenging, stimulating, informative, and, as one has come to expect from Bell, prescient. Although it has the familiar Bellian problems of repetition, conceptual looseness, and inconsistency, these apparent deficiencies seem to provide him with a freedom to range across the regions of culture with a facility that no other sociologist has remotely accomplished. Nevertheless, the argument is both theoretically and normatively problematic.

Part of the problem is that the theory of culture is an extension of the three realms theory. Everywhere Bell finds radical contradictions between developments that do not really contradict each other at all. The biggest disjunction apparently lies between a culture that celebrates the self and a TES that requires the subordination of the self to discipline. However, an alternative interpretation of these processes is possible. In such an interpretation, the TES requires not self-discipline but merely a non-internalized compliance with rules. It accomplishes this conformity by delivering material gratifications. The individual "economizes" the relative values of wages, promotions, meaningful work, leisure time, overtime, etc. The primary source of commitment in the TES is therefore a radicalized individualism that links firmly to the gratification of the untrammeled self. On this alternative view, the fit between the instrumental worker, the yuppie entrepreneur, the rapacious consumer, and a spectacular, de-hierarchized artistic arena is indissoluble.

Bell's explanation for the rise of modernism is that technology released the demonic self from its religious jail. Several full-blown alternative arguments suggest that the "self," demonic or otherwise, is a modern construction rather than a foundational reality. Foucault (1981), for example, argues that sexuality was not constrained under premodern conditions but was embedded within kinship. For him, bourgeois society "discovered" sexuality and defined its perversities so that it could control it, precisely by means of discipline. For Foucault, as for Giddens (1985), discipline and surveillance are central components of modern societies, institutionalized in schools, prisons, hospitals, universities, and the state as well as factories. Bell tells us that bourgeois culture had long since been defeated by the 1960s, so that there was nothing against which to rebel, but Foucault tells us that there remained a society replete with authoritarian practices, elitist imposts, and bureaucratic controls. If the self strains to express itself against such constraints it is surely a little dismissive to treat that effort as inauthentic or as mere opinionism.

Bell's value-stance on culture is not merely conservative but elitist. His derogations of popular culture and of postmodernism must be read as a claim for not merely authoritative but authoritarian cultural standards. The most liberal reading of Bell's argument would suggest that he is claiming only that cultural standards must be set by knowledgeable experts who have worked through the canon and drawn upon the accumulated wisdom of generations. Three counter-arguments might be offered. First, as a reading of Bourdieu (1984) suggests, expertise is intimately linked to structures of power and class. The operation of systems of expertise acts as a mechanism of closure on access to privilege. Second, while expertise may briefly have been a neutral arbiter of cultural worth, it has long since been commodified, along with that art on which it pronounces. Expert opinion is now directly translatable into monetary values, so that the quality of a cultural object reflects its price, and not vice versa. Third, it is arguable that expertise and a fixation on tradition tend to smother innovation and participation, rather than releasing them.

Perhaps even more than the great sociological theorists of the nineteenth century, Daniel Bell has been the prisoner of his time, his circumstances, and his value-commitments. He appears unable sufficiently to step out of specifically American sociohistorical developments to see his theory generalized and adopted widely. Moreover, this incapacity leads him into fundamental errors about power and class and about the relationship between general cultural standards and individual expression. Notwithstanding these errors, the three realms theory resonates fully into the great sociological traditions and offers a much more accessible and non-determinant framework for the analysis of society than most of the alternatives. A great deal of work needs to be done on the theory, but it would be an investment that would yield rich rewards.

Bibliography

Writings of Daniel Bell

Adjusting Men to Machines. 1947. *Commentary*, 79–88.

Twelve Modes of Prediction. 1964a. *Daedalus*, 93, 845–80.

The New American Right (editor) (New York, 1955). *The Radical Right: The New American Right Expanded and Updated*. 1964b. Garden City: Anchor.

The Disjunction between Culture and Social Structure. 1965a. *Daedalus*, 94, 208–22.

The Study of the Future. 1965b. *The Public Interest*, 1, 119–30.

The Reforming of General Education: the Columbia College Experience in Its National Setting. 1966. New York: Columbia University Press.

Marxian Socialism in the United States. 1967. Princeton, NJ: Princeton University Press.

Towards the Year 2000: Work in Progress (editor). 1968. Boston: Beacon.

Confrontation: the Student Revolt and the Universities (editor with I. Kristol). 1969. New York: Basic Books.

Quo Warranto? Notes on the Governance of the Universities in the 1970s. 1970a. *The Public Interest*, 19, 53–68.

Work and Its Discontents (Boston, 1956). 1970b. New York: League for Industrial Democracy.

Capitalism Today (editor with I. Kristol). 1970. New York: New American Library.

Religion in the Sixties. 1971. *Social Research*, 38, 447–97.

The Postindustrial Society – a Symposium (with F. Bourricaud, J. Floud, G. Sartori, K. Tominaga, and P. Wiles). 1971. *Survey*, 16, 1–77.

The Coming of Postindustrial Society: a Venture in Social Forecasting (New York, 1973). 1976. New York: Basic.

The Social Framework of the Information Society. 1979a. In M. Dertouzos and J. Moses (ed.), *The Computer Age*. Cambridge, MA: MIT Press, pp. 163–211.

The Cultural Contradictions of Capitalism (New York, 1976). 1979b. London: Heinemann, 2nd edn.
First Love and Early Sorrows. 1981. *Partisan Review*, 48, 532–51.
The Crisis in Economic Theory (editor, with I. Kristol). 1981. New York: Basic Books.
The Social Sciences since the Second World War. 1982. New Brunswick, NJ: Transaction.
The Deficits: How Big? How Long? How Dangerous? (with L. Thurow). 1985. New York: New York University Press.
The World and the United States in 2013. 1987. *Daedalus*, 116, 1–31.
The End of Ideology: On the Exhaustion of Political Ideas in the Fifties (Glencoe, 1965). 1988. Cambridge, MA: Harvard University Press.
American Exceptionalism Revisited: the Role of Civil Society. 1989. *The Public Interest*, 95, 38–56.
The Third Technological Revolution – and Its Possible Socioeconomic Consequences. 1990a. Tokyo: Shukan Diamond.
Resolving the Contradictions of Modernity and Modernism.1990b. *Society*, 27, 43–50, 66–75.
The Misreading of Ideology: the Social Determination of Ideas in Marx's Work. 1990c. *Berkeley Journal of Sociology*, 35, 1–54.
The Winding Passage: Sociological Essays and Journeys (Boston, 1980). 1991. New Brunswick, NJ: Transaction, 2nd edn.
The Break-up of Space and Time: Technology and Society in a Postindustrial Age. 1992. Paper presented at the American Sociological Association Annual Meeting, Pittsburgh.
Downfall of the Business Giants. 1993. *Dissent*, 316–23.

Further reading

Abercrombie, N., Hill, S., and Turner, B. (1980) *The Dominant Ideology Thesis*. London: Allen & Unwin.
Archer, M. (1990) Theory, Culture and Postindustrial Society. In M. Featherstone (ed.), *Global Culture*. London: Sage, pp. 207–36.
Badham, R. (1984) The Sociology of Industrial and Postindustrial Societies. *Current Sociology*, 32, 1–141.
Beck, U. (1992) *Risk Society*. London: Sage.
Bloom, A. (1986) *Prodigal Sons*. New York: Oxford University Press.
Bourdieu, P. (1984) *Distinction*. London: Routledge.
Brick, H. (1986) *Daniel Bell and the Decline of Intellectual Radicalism*. Madison: University of Wisconsin Press.
Chernow, R. (1979) The Cultural Contradictions of Daniel Bell. *Change*, 11, 12–17.
Clark, C. (1957) *The Conditions of Economic Progress*. London: Macmillan.
Cooney, T. (1986) *The Rise of the New York Intellectuals*. Madison: University of Wisconsin Press.
Crook, S., Pakulski, J., and Waters, M. (1992) *Postmodernization*. London: Sage.
Dittberner, J. (1979) *The End of Ideology and American Social Thought: 1930–1960*. Ann Arbor: University of Michigan Research Press.
Foote, N. and Hatt, P. (1953) Social Mobility and Economic Advancement. *American Economic Review*, 18, 364–78.
Foucault, M. (1981) *The History of Sexuality volume 1*. Harmondsworth: Penguin.
Frankel, B. (1987) *The Postindustrial Utopians*. Cambridge: Polity Press.
Giddens, A. (1985) *The Nation-state and Violence*. Cambridge: Polity Press.
Giddens, A. (1991) *Modernity and Self-identity*. Cambridge: Polity Press.

Habermas, J. (1981) Modernity vs. Postmodernity. *New German Critique*, 22, 3–14.
Habermas, J. (1983) Neoconservative Culture Criticism in the United States and West Germany. *Telos*, 56, 75–89.
Hagan, R. (1975) Societal Disjunction and Axial Theory: Review Commentary on the Social Theory of Daniel Bell. *Review of Social Theory*, 3, 40–4.
Harvey, D. (1989) *The Condition of Postmodernity*. Oxford: Blackwell.
Hill, R. (1974) The Coming of Postindustrial Society. *The Insurgent Sociologist*, 4, 37–51.
Holmwood, J. and Stewart, A. (1991) *Explanation and Social Theory*. Basingstoke: Macmillan.
Holton, G. (1962) Scientific Research and Scholarship. *Daedalus*, 91, 362–99.
Howe, I. (1982) The Range of the New York Intellectual. In B. Rosenberg and E. Goldstein (ed.), *Creators and Disturbers*. New York: Columbia University Press.
Inglehart, R. (1990) *Culture Shift in Advanced Industrial Society*. Princeton, NJ: Princeton University Press.
Jameson, F. (1984) Postmodernism: Or the Cultural Logic of Late Capitalism. *New Left Review*, 146, 53–92.
Jumonville, N. (1991) *Critical Crossings*. Berkeley: University of California Press.
Kadushin, C. (1974) *The American Intellectual Elite*. Boston: Little Brown.
Kivisto, P. (1981) The Theorist as Seer: the Case of Bell's Postindustrial Society. *Quarterly Journal of Ideology*, 5, 39–43
Kleinberg, B. (1973) *American Society in the Postindustrial Age*. Columbus, OH: Merrill.
Kuhns, W. (1971) *The Postindustrial Prophets*. New York: Harper.
Kumar, K. (1978) *Prophecy and Progress: the Sociology of Industrial and Postindustrial Society*. Harmondsworth: Penguin.
Kumar, K. (1995) *From Postindustrial to Post-modern Society*. Oxford: Blackwell.
Lash, S. and Urry, J. (1987) *The End of Organized Capitalism*. Cambridge: Polity Press.
Lash, S. and Urry, J. (1994) *Economies of Signs and Space*. London: Sage.
Leibowitz, N. (1985) *Daniel Bell and the Agony of Modern Liberalism*. Westport, CT: Greenwood.
Longstaff, S. (1987) Daniel Bell and Political Reconciliation. *Queen's Quarterly*, 94, 660–5.
Lukács, G. (1968) *History and Class Consciousness*. London: Macmillan.
Lyotard, J. (1984) *The Postmodern Condition*. Manchester: Manchester University Press.
Marien, M. (1973) Daniel Bell and the End of Normal Science. *The Futurist*, 7, 262–8.
Miller, S. (1975) Notes on Neo-capitalism. *Theory and Society*, 2, 1–35.
Nichols, T. (1975) The Coming of Postindustrial Society. *Sociology*, 9, 349–52.
O'Neill, J. (1988) Religion and Postmodernism. *Theory, Culture and Society*, 5, 493–508.
Pahl, R. (1975) The Coming of Postindustrial Society. *Sociology*, 9, 347–9.
Rejai, M. (ed.) (1971) *Decline of Ideology?* Chicago: Aldine.
Rose, M. (1991) *The Post-modern and the Postindustrial*. Cambridge: Cambridge University Press.
Ross, G. (1974) The Second Coming of Daniel Bell. In R. Miliband and J. Saville (eds), *The Socialist Register 1974*. London: Merlin, pp. 331–48.
Rule, J. (1971) The Problem with Social Problems. *Politics and Society*, 1, 47–56.
Simons, H. (1988) *Jewish Times*. Boston: Houghton Mifflin.
Stearns, P. (1973) Is There a Postindustrial Society? *Society*, 11, 11–25.
Steinfels, P. (1979) *The NeoConservatives*. New York: Simon & Schuster.

Tilman, R. and Simich, J. (1984) On the Use and Abuse of Thorstein Veblen in Modern American Sociology, II. *American Journal of Economics and Sociology*, 43, 103–28.

Turner, B. (1989) From Postindustrial Society to Postmodern Politics. In J. Gibbins (ed.), *Contemporary Political Culture*. London: Sage, pp. 199–217.

von der Ohe, W., Drabek, T., Hall, R., Hill, R., Lopreato, J., Marcus, P., and Phillips, M., with a reply by Bell, D. (1973) The Coming of Postindustrial Society: a Review Symposium. *Summation*, 3, 60–103.

Wald, A. (1987) *The New York Intellectuals*. Chapel Hill: University of North Carolina Press.

Waters, M. (1996) *Daniel Bell*. London: Routledge.

Waxman, C. (ed.) (1968) *The End of Ideology Debate*. New York: Simon & Schuster.

7

Norbert Elias

Richard Kilminster and Stephen Mennell

> But my whole conviction is that our image of and orientation in our social world will become very much easier once we realise that human beings are not economic in one of their pockets, political in another and psychological in another, in other words that no *real* divisions correspond to the traditional divisions.
>
> *Norbert Elias (1970b, p. 148)*

Introduction

Norbert Elias (1897–1990) is most celebrated for his classic work *Über den Prozess der Zivilisation*, first published obscurely in German in 1939, but little known in the anglophone world until the publication of a translation (*The Civilizing Process*) in 1978–82.[1] In this book, Elias traces long-term connections between changes in power balances in society at large and changes in the embodied habitus – or cultural personality makeup – of individual people, among the secular upper classes in Western Europe from the late Middle Ages to the nineteenth century. His work constitutes an endeavor – rare in the history of sociology – to bridge the gap between "micro" and "macro" sociology in a *theoretical-empirical*, rather than merely a conceptual, way. Although it was originally grounded in a study of European history, the theory of civilizing processes points to linked changes in power, behavior, and habitus which can be demonstrated to have been at work elsewhere and in many other periods. In later books and articles, Elias greatly extended the scope of the original theory.

Elias's work constitutes a radical rejection of many of the common assumptions of sociology in the second half of the twentieth century. He conceived of the discipline in the broadest terms, not as just "hodiecentric" (or "present-centered") nor as the study solely of "modern" societies, but as including the study of long-term processes over the whole course of the development of human society. He was hostile to the hegemony of philosophy and what he sometimes called in conversation "philosophoidal" modes of thought in sociology, and told his fellow sociologists to stop making obeisances to the philosophers. His own sociological work is grounded in a *sociological* theory of knowledge and the sciences, rather than in the traditional assumptions of mainstream philosophical epistemology and philosophy of science. This is one of the main ways in which he differs from contemporary "social theorists," who are generally more deferential to philosophy, such as Anthony Giddens, Jeffrey Alexander, and Jürgen Habermas. Elias referred to his way of doing sociology as "process sociology" – it is also commonly referred to as "figurational" sociology – and it involves the rejection of many of the "static polarities" and "false dualities" that pervade sociological thinking.

Life and Times

Perhaps the most striking fact about Norbert Elias's career is how extremely late in life he gained recognition. He published fifteen books, but all of them, except the little-noticed first edition of *Über den Prozess der Zivilisation*, appeared after he reached normal retirement age – indeed most of them when he was in his eighties and nineties. Someone who in 1928 appeared on the same panel of discussants as Ferdinand Toennies, Werner Sombart, and Alfred Weber (Elias, 1929a) – figures whose work we associate with the end of the nineteenth century – thus finally came to seem a very contemporary presence to sociologists at the end of the twentieth century.

Elias was one of the generation of Jewish scholars who fled Germany in 1933 when Hitler came to power. Some of them were immediately able to establish themselves in universities in English-speaking countries; we can only guess how many of them, having escaped with their lives, failed to re-establish themselves as academics. Elias was almost one of the latter group.

He was born on June 22, 1897 in Breslau, the only son of Hermann and Sophie Elias. His father was a businessman, in the textile trade. Although, since the frontier changes at the end of the Second World War, Breslau is now the Polish city of Wrocław, the city was then fully German. At the distinguished *Johannesgymnasium* there, Elias received a first-class, all-round education in the humanities and sciences; he was immersed from an early age in the classics of German literature, Latin and Greek (a reading knowledge of both of which served as a useful research skill into his old age), and French, as well as being given a good grounding in mathematics, physics, and chemistry. Asked in old age whether, as a child, he felt more a member of the Jewish community or of the wider German society, Elias (1994b, p. 10) said that the very question reflected events that have unfolded since then. He knew as a child he was both a German and a Jew, but at the time the two identities did not conflict. There were isolated incidents of anti-Semitic remarks, but anti-Semites were people to look down upon. While this may indeed be true of his perceptions as a child, research since his death has revealed that his protestations of never having been involved in politics were not entirely true: from his teenage years he was a leading light in the Zionist youth movement Blau-Weiß (Hackeschmidt, 1997). An early article on antisemitism in Germany (Elias, 1929b) has belatedly come to light.

In 1915, reaching the age when he became eligible for conscription, Elias enlisted in a signals regiment of the German army, and saw action on both the Eastern and Western Fronts in the First World War. He remembered the carnage, especially seeing a comrade killed nearby, and he probably suffered shellshock but could not remember the circumstances. How he came to leave the front and return to Breslau remained a blur, but he served out the war back in his home town as an army medical orderly, and recalled watching a famous surgeon amputating limbs. After the Armistice he enrolled at Breslau University, for some time managing to pursue courses in both medicine and philosophy. He completed the pre-clinical part of the medical training, and always considered that his experience in the dissecting room had left a lasting mark on his understanding of how human beings work as social animals. For nothing he observed – especially dissecting the brain and the musculature of the face – corresponded to the distinction taken for granted in philosophy between the "external" world and the "internal" world of "the mind." But then, to his father's disappointment, he recognized that he could not pursue both disciplines, and dropped medicine in favor of completing his doctoral degree in philosophy.

Elias's student years were a time of enormous political and social instability in Germany after its defeat in the war, the abdication of the Kaiser, and the establishment of the Weimar Republic. Armed left-wing and right-wing militias fought each other in the streets. One of Elias's school-friends, a mild and scholarly youth but apparently suspected of left-wing leanings, was among those killed by the *Freikorps*, a right-wing organization. A little later, Germany experienced the great runaway hyperinflation of 1922–3, which destabilized many aspects of society and in Elias's own case meant that he had for a time to take a job in industry (as export manager for a local manufacturer of iron goods) in order to help support his temporarily financially embarrassed parents.

So, even before the rise of Hitler, Elias had seen a great deal at first hand of war, civil unrest, violent death, and social instability. It is important to bear this in mind as an antidote to a once-common misapprehension about *The Civilizing Process*: Elias did not set out in that *magnum opus* to write a celebration of Western civilization in the popular sense, still less to depict it as the outcome of inevitable "progress." On the contrary, Elias was very conscious of how hard won was the outward show of "civilization," yet how brittle a veneer it remained. That is made abundantly clear at the very end of his life in *The Germans*, in which he describes himself thus: "Standing half-hidden in the background of the studies published here is an eyewitness who has lived for nearly ninety years through the events concerned as they unfolded" (Elias, 1996, p. 1).

Elias wrote his doctoral thesis at Breslau under the neo-Kantian philosopher Richard Hönigswald, from whom he acknowledged that he learned a great deal, even though the relationship ended in their estrangement. The thesis was entitled "Idea and Individual,"[2] and was eventually accepted in January 1924, after a delay of more than a year occasioned by a dispute between student and supervisor. Their dispute concerned a fundamental issue: whether there are any grounds for postulating a notion of truth that is transcendental and independent of human experience and human history. Although he could not then formulate his viewpoint with the precision and clarity that came later, Elias recalled that he had begun at this time to come to the conclusion

> that all that Kant regarded as timeless and given prior to all experience, whether it be the idea of causal connections or of time or of natural and moral laws, together with the words that went with them, had to be learned from other people in order to be present in the consciousness of the individual human being. (Elias, 1994b, p. 91)

Ever afterwards, Elias argued that the whole central tradition of modern Western epistemology, from Descartes through Kant to twentieth-century phenomenology, was misconceived. It was based on asking how a single, *adult*, human mind can know what it knows. Elias called this the model of *homo clausus*, the "closed person," and found it lurking in much of modern sociology (Elias, 1994a, pp. 200–15; 1978, pp. 119ff; Mennell, 1998, pp. 188–93; Kilminster, 1998, chapters 4 and 5). He argued that we must instead think in terms of *homines aperti*, "open people," and in particular of "long lines of generations of people" building up the stock of human knowledge. The crucial point, however, which he developed in *The Civilizing Process* and other later works, was that the image of *homo clausus* corresponded to a *mode of self-experience* that was *not* a human universal but was a social product, particularly of European society from the Renaissance onwards.

The dispute with Hönigswald appears to have influenced Elias's decision, after he had received his doctorate and when his parents' finances had recovered, to resume his studies in Heidelberg not as a philosopher but as a sociologist. Max Weber had died four years earlier, but his circle, centered on his younger brother Alfred and his widow Marianne, was still a dominant presence in Heidelberg. Elias presented his first sociological paper, on the sociology of Gothic cathedrals in France and Germany, at a meeting of Marianne's salon, on the balcony of the Webers' house. Elias had earlier interpolated a semester at Heidelberg (when he also attended a student Zionist conference) during his studies at Breslau, and there had met Karl Jaspers, who introduced him to the work of Max Weber and also encouraged him to write an essay on the notions of *Zivilisation* and *Kultur* in German thought (with special reference to Thomas Mann's essay "Civilization's Literary Man"[3]). Now Elias enrolled as a *Habilitation* student with Alfred Weber, and set out to write a thesis on Florentine society and culture in the transition from pre-scientific to scientific thinking. Alfred Weber was very interested in questions of "civilization" and "culture." He argued that culture could not be reduced to economic relationships or explained in terms of economic interests. It always had to be understood in terms of social behavior, but its pattern of development differed from that of economics, science, and technology; in these there was progress, but in art, religion, and culture in general there were no progressions or regressions – culture was rather to be seen as the self-realization of the soul of a people (Alfred Weber, 1998). Elias's later theory of civilizing processes may be understood as in part an attempt to demonstrate that, *pace* Weber, structured long-term processes can be discovered in "culture movements" too.

Around this time, Elias became friendly with a young *Privatdozent*, Karl Mannheim, four years his senior, who introduced him into the Weber circle. In 1929, when Mannheim became Professor of Sociology at the then quite new University of Frankfurt, Elias went with him as his academic assistant. There were mixed motives for the move: friction had developed between Mannheim and Alfred Weber, making it uncomfortable for Elias as the friend of one and *Habilitation* candidate of the other; and Mannheim promised Elias earlier *Habilitation* than Weber was able to do. And last but not least, as an academic assistant Elias at last received a salary!

At Frankfurt, Elias embarked on a new topic for his *Habilitationsschrift*: a sociological study of life at the court of France in the seventeenth and eighteenth centuries. All the stages of Elias's *Habilitation* – which would give him the rank of *Privatdozent* – were rushed through, except for the inaugural lecture, early in 1933, just as Hitler came to power and shortly before Elias fled into exile. But the thesis was not published until 1969. That is the book known in English as *The Court Society* (1983).

Mannheim headed the Department of Sociology and, as his assistant, Elias was particularly involved in in supervising doctoral dissertations. The department was housed in rented space in a building owned and occupied by the Institut für Sozialforschung – later celebrated as "the Frankfurt School" – of which Max Horkheimer was Director. Relations between the two groups seem to have been polite but distant, although Elias was on good personal terms with Theodor Adorno. There is a degree of thematic similarity between the problems addressed in *The Civilizing Process* and by Horkheimer and Adorno in their *The Dialectic of Enlightenment* (1979) – the relations between control of nature, control of society, and self-control – but also a strikingly symptomatic difference. Horkheimer and Adorno write from within a very traditional philosophical discourse, whereas Elias sets out to turn questions traditionally posed in philosophical terms into empirically researchable socio-historical questions (Bogner, 1987).

Elias stayed long enough in Frankfurt after the Nazis came to power to be able to observe later that the process through which they came to power contained both highly rational *and* very violent elements – the two are not opposites. But, having lost his post and salary in the Nazi takeover of the university, later in 1933 he went into exile in Paris. He then spoke excellent French but little

English. But he failed to secure academic employment. He invested what remained of the money his father had given him in a business making wooden toys. It was not a success; Elias lost all his money, and was effectively destitute. At the urging of his old friend Alfred Glucksmann, who had already emigrated to Cambridge, Elias moved to England in 1935, where he secured a meager stipend from a Dutch Jewish charity.

Although in later years he claimed that *The Civilizing Process* was written in the Reading Room of the British Museum, it is possible that the first volume at least was begun in Paris, where he may have first encountered Lucien Febvre's essay on the origins of the concept of "civilization" (1930), which is cited in *The Civilizing Process*. In the early 1930s he also read Freud's *Civilization and its Discontents* (1930), which he acknowledged as the greatest single intellectual influence on *The Civilizing Process*. Freud's book serves as a reminder that in the 1930s a concern with "culture" and "civilization" was by no means associated with a naive faith in "progress" and its benefits.

The two volumes of *The Civilizing Process* were completed in a white heat of inspiration in London, by 1938 at the latest. The problem was how they were to be published. Elias's parents visited him in London that year, and he tried to persuade them to join him in exile. They refused. All their friends were in Breslau and, said his father, "They can't touch me – I've never broken a law in my life." His father died in Breslau in 1940, and his mother in Auschwitz in 1941. But before that, his father had arranged for *Über den Prozess der Zivilisation* to be printed in Breslau. Before it could actually be published, however, the printer too fled the country. Hermann Elias then surreptitiously arranged for the unbound sheets to be exported to Switzerland, where they were bound and eventually published by Haus zum Falken in 1939. That year, as Bryan Wilson was later wryly to observe, was not the most propitious moment for the publication of a two-volume work, in German, by a Jew, on, of all things, civilization. Few people read it. Among those who did, appreciatively, were Thomas Mann and two prominent reviewers in the Netherlands, both of whom sadly committed suicide when the Germans invaded their country in 1940 (Goudsblom, 1977b, p. 61).

On the publication of *The Civilizing Process*, Elias was awarded a Senior Research Fellowship at the London School of Economics, which was evacuated to Cambridge during the war. He was briefly interned with other "enemy aliens" during 1940, but returned to Cambridge and worked for British Intelligence at the end of the war. Afterwards, he lived in near poverty, scraping a living by teaching extramural lectures. In the early 1950s, with his old friend S. H. Foulkes, he was one of the founders of the Group Analytic school of psychotherapy (Elias, 1969; Pines, 1997). These were years when Elias published almost nothing, however, and the trauma of his mother dying in Auschwitz may be at least part of the explanation for that. Only in 1954, when he was already 57, did he secure his first secure academic post, at the respectable but obscure University College Leicester, soon to be the University of Leicester. There, with Ilya Neustadt, he helped to build up one of the most distinguished departments of sociology in Britain; both Anthony Giddens and John Goldthorpe – among many other notable figures – gained their first teaching posts in the Leicester department. On his retirement in 1962 he served for two years as the first Professor of Sociology at the University of Ghana, and on his return continued to teach part-time at Leicester. These were the years when he published *The Established and the Outsiders* with John Scotson (1994) and began, with Eric Dunning (Elias and Dunning, 1986), to develop in new directions the existing area of the sociology of sport. In 1969, however, *Über den Prozess der Zivilisation* was republished, and in consequence he rapidly became an intellectual celebrity in Germany and the Netherlands (see Elias, 1970b). In the 1970s, he was in demand in both countries as a visiting professor, and gradually abandoned residence in Britain, first for Bielefeld, then for Amsterdam. The 1970s and 1980s were years of unparalleled productivity, in which books and articles that had been gestating for decades finally flowed from his pen. This productivity was considerably aided by the devoted editorial assistance of Michael Schröter. Elias died, still writing at the age of 93, on August 1, 1990.

INTELLECTUAL CONTEXT AND INFLUENCES

One of the problems which anyone introducing Elias immediately faces is that of situating his highly original work within the theoretical schools, paradigms, and sociological language familiar to mainstream sociologists. The difficulty of "placing" him in the European sociological tradition has always been, as Johan Goudsblom (1977a, pp. 60, 77ff) has pointed out, a problem for commentators. It is difficult to find a place for Elias's sociology of figurations within the paradigms of recent sociology, such as phenomenology, action theory, functionalism, structuration theory, Marxism, Weberianism, poststructuralism, critical realism, rational choice theory, or neopositivism. Elias seems to fall between all stools. Echoes of, and parallels and similarities with, the work of others abound in Elias's figurational sociology, as do concepts and problems common to other traditions of social science, but in a strange way Elias's contribution remains stubbornly unique. How? To answer that question we need to take a brief detour.

Elias did not assign much importance to delineating carefully his intellectual debts and situating himself in relation to other writers and schools, in the detail that we have come to expect and find in the writings of, say, Parsons, Habermas, or Giddens. All this interpretative work of debt assignment and influences in relation to Elias has had to be done by others much later, following up clues in his writings and interviews and drawing on broader knowledge of the state of sociology in Germany in the first quarter of the twentieth century. For many years Elias would avow only one significant intellectual debt. In a footnote to the first volume of *The Civilizing Process* (1994a, p. 249), he acknowledges how much the study owes to the discoveries of Freud, which, he says, is obvious to the reader anyway, so did not need to be pointed out in all instances. Even then, he explicitly stressed the "not inconsiderable *differences* between the whole approach of Freud and that adopted in this study" (our emphasis). Rather than "digressing into disputes at every turn," he continues, it seemed more important "to build a particular intellectual perspective as clearly as possible."

Later, Elias further complicated the issue by challenging the conventional assumption that an "influence" always had to come from a book: "I am extremely conscious of the fact that others have influenced me, that I have learned from others – though not only from books, but also from the events of my age" (quoted by Goudsblom, 1977b, p. 78). He also claimed that, at the time he was writing *The Civilizing Process*, his knowledge of those writers whom we think of today as our sociological ancestors was "extremely deficient" (quoted by Goudsblom, 1977b, p. 78). But this admission has to be taken with a pinch of salt. Even if he did not know these writers in quite the depth that we take for granted today, he nevertheless still participated in the particularly rich sociological culture of Weimar Germany, in which many of these ancestors had already been discussed, absorbed, and processed and areas of enquiry established (see Mannheim, 1953, pp. 209–28; Aron, 1957; Schad, 1972).

The problem-agenda of the generation of Weimar sociologists which included Elias was a remarkably fertile one, set by gifted people such as Max Weber, Simmel, Veblen, Freud, Alfred Weber, Sombart, prominent Marxists such as Lukács, and the more sociologically sympathetic phenomenologists and existentialists, such as Hannah Arendt and Karl Jaspers, in the aftermath of one European war and in the build-up to another. The origins of Elias's sociology lie in the complex political conflicts and alignments of the Weimar period, although the applicability of his insights goes well beyond that. If Elias's work can be placed anywhere it is as a development out of the German *Wissenssoziologie*, to which it bears a family resemblance (Kilminster, 1993).

Having said all that, the question remains: what is the uniqueness of Elias's sociology? Following Goudsblom (1977b, p. 79) again, our view is that the key to answering this question lies in grasping how Elias managed to integrate *through empirical research* many seemingly incompatible perspectives into a "workable synthesis," a single testable model of human interdependence. This enabled him to solve in a preliminary way problems shrewdly posed, but left in the air, by other writers such as those already mentioned. These problems had already been made available, so to speak, in the sociological culture in which Elias participated. To name just a few significant sociological themes, he found, ready-to-hand, discussions of and research into: the conspicuous consumption of elites; "two-front" strata; the monopoly of the means of violence; rationalization; social equalization; competition; social differentiation and integration; the internalization of what is external; the development of civilized self-restraint. All these, and many more, Elias integrated into his sociological synthesis, as concepts or problems requiring solution. In doing so, he did not undertake a great deal of conceptual work to demonstrate how his concepts differed from those developed by other writers in different traditions. For him, the integrity of the synthesis and its empirical extension were everything.

Elias polemicized relentlessly against *homo clausus*. He repeatedly stressed the importance of the long, intergenerational, process of knowledge accumulation that exceeds the scope of the individual knowing subject – the Ego so beloved of the philosophers. At the same time, as has often been pointed out (most recently by van Krieken, 1998, p. 76), he doggedly went his own way and for the most part refused to acknowledge the work of other sociologists. This feature of Elias's thinking and acting perhaps reveals that even he was not immune to one of the self-delusions associated with the *homo clausus* experience, that of self-autarky. As a person, he may have found it hard to admit, even to himself, the extent of his intellectual debts to others. A more charitable gloss on this feature of his character would be that Elias probably genuinely could not see why anyone should be interested in where he had gotten his ideas from – something which, on the other hand, assumes a burning significance for many sociologists today. He did talk about these matters a little, later in his life, in various interviews and in particular in his *Reflections on a Life* (1994b), although somewhat selectively. By and large, he seems to have assumed that people reading *The Civilizing Process* would see that the explanatory power of the "workable synthesis" was everything and would seek to test it further in their own research. Working directly from the sociological model to empirical areas and back again in this high-minded, but unorthodox, way was not without its dangers. It exposed Elias to the risk that readers would find in his books some apparent similarities with the ideas of other sociologists and philosophers but, failing to appreciate the *synthetic* character of his work, accuse him of unacknowledged derivation or lack of originality. Some of the controversy surrounding the belated recognition of his work has arisen from this feature of his approach and his failure to always make this aspect of his way of working clear to his readers.

There is a parallel here with the holistic approach to society found in the work of Elias's colleague and friend of many years, Karl Mannheim, which may illuminate this issue. Perhaps Elias's being out of step with the expectations of the sociological profession regarding the elaborate acknowledgment and documentation of sources of inspiration is also *organically* related to the character of his integrating research strategy. As Kettler and Meja (1995) point out, in his restless attempts to uncover the *Zeitgeist*, Mannheim was open to ideas and inspiration from many sources in his pursuit of a political synthesis. Although Elias's work was not moving in that particular political direction, he did share with Mannheim the idea that the significance of a social event, social grouping or cultural item lies in its relationship with other aspects of the developing social structure as a whole. Subject to the further caveat that Elias would have no truck whatsoever with any talk in a sociological context of spirit (*Geist*), the succinct description given by Kettler and Meja (1995, p. 318) of Mannheim's way of working with concepts and research materials resonates with that of Elias:

> [Mannheim] would subject key concepts to a "change of function." It was unnecessary to criticise others; it was enough to correct and balance what they said by drawing on something said by someone else. All participants were seen as sharing the same condition or expressing the same spirit.

Reading Elias

There are some further unusual features of Elias's writings which set his work apart from the dominant forms of professional sociology to which we are accustomed. It is worth briefly outlining them as an aid to understanding Elias.

1 For most of his long career, for reasons often beyond his control, Elias was on the periphery of the sociology establishment and thus distanced from it. He therefore felt few of the pressures of the institutionalized world of the academic social sciences. One consequence of this is that his works have an unfamiliar structure and character. The reader will not find the customary beginning with a review of the literature or contemporary debates about the problem or topic addressed. Elias did not work that way. Rather, he always went for the problem or object of inquiry (for example, symbols, scientific establishments, Mozart, time, violence, aging and dying, work, or psychosomatics – to name just a few of the subjects he investigated in his later years), which he would explore in his own way, in his own language of figurational or process sociology.

2 In the later writings in particular, Elias typically lists very few references; indeed, frequently there will only be one, perhaps to an obscure book published many years ago. If one complained to Elias that he had failed to address the contemporary literature, or suggested that he was out of date, he would reply that you had a fetish for the new, that just because a book is old it does not mean that it may not still be the best treatment of a problem. And, conversely, new books did not necessarily represent an advance simply because they were new. It was the intrinsic cognitive worth of the book that counted, not whether it was currently *à la mode* (see Elias, 1987, pp. 117–18). He worked within a very long scientific time scale, detached from current orthodoxies.

3 It is worth mentioning the style of Elias's writings. Wolf Lepenies (1978, p. 63) aptly described their qualities: "a jargon-free concern with clarity, a careful training in sociological observation and a thoroughgoing combination of theoretical discussions with often surprising references to details." Elias was very alert to the subtleties and associations of the language and concepts we employ in sociology. He writes about social processes in a controlled language carefully cleansed of all traces of reification and static metaphysics and highly sensitive to evaluative nuances. Elias will talk of party-establishments when others refer to "the political"; or economic specialists rather than "the economic sphere"; or social specialists for violence control instead of "repressive state apparatuses"; or means of orientation rather than "ideological practice."

4 The more one reads Elias, the more aware one becomes of how he convinces readers not so much by conventional "logical" arguments for this or that position, as by expressing issues (particularly in his articles) in such a way as to provoke people into reflecting upon the categories or assumptions that they routinely employ in dealing with them. As well as containing a theoretical model and empirical materials, *The Civilizing Process* embodies a mode of experiential persuasion which cannot be described as entirely rational. As we read through the picturesque extracts from contemporary documents about

farting, bedroom behavior, spitting, torture, the burning of cats, or whatever, we gain insight *through this experience itself* into our own feelings of shame, repugnance, and delicacy derived from the standards of our own society, representing a later stage of development. Our reactions themselves exemplify the rise in the thresholds of shame, embarrassment, and repugnance which Elias is demonstrating. This effect partly explains why the book is so memorable.

THE SOCIOLOGICAL IMPERATIVE

For an adequate understanding of Elias, it is essential to appreciate how his sociology developed out of the desire to transcribe philosophical discussions of knowledge, society, culture, and the human condition into a form amenable to empirical sociological investigation. This leaves the status of philosophy ambiguous and disputable. These questions included those traditionally grouped under epistemology, ontology, and ethics (that is, "evaluative" or "normative" questions), which reappear in Elias's works transformed into a sociological idiom. We cannot stress too much the robustly sociological character of Elias's world view. The failure of various commentators to understand this dimension of Elias's work has led to a number of misunderstandings. Readers of Elias need to be prepared for his controversial and uncompromising views about philosophy and his rather sweeping denunciations of its practitioners, which have not won him many friends. He considered that his work presupposed the supersession of philosophy and consistently questioned the authority of philosophers (see Kilminster, 1998, chapter 1).

On the subject of *epistemology*, from as early in his career as when he was a doctoral student under Hönigswald, there were indications in Elias's work that he was moving in the direction of developing a sociological epistemology to replace the traditional philosophical one (Kilminster and Wouters, 1995). This transformed epistemology would relate ways of knowing to the patterns of living together of human beings and remodel the traditional issue of validity (*Geltung*). This realization gathers momentum in his work to a point where he makes a complete break with philosophy, decisively turning his back on the tradition. The failure to grasp this feature of his thinking has sometimes led some commentators to try to pull Elias back into the philosophy from which his life's work was a sustained attempt at emancipation (see, for instance, Maso, 1995); or to criticize him from philosophical positions which he regarded himself as already having moved beyond (Sathaye, 1973).

The neo-Kantian philosophy in which Elias was initially schooled alerted him to key areas of inquiry, including the problem of the historical validity of knowledge, the issue of origins and status of universal categories of thought, and the prevalence of the model of the individual knowing subject in epistemology. The classical German philosophical tradition generally, and neo-Kantianism in particular, thus constituted a point of departure for Elias's transfer of his intellectual energies into a dynamic and historical sociology, which he believed could provide a more inclusive and adequate framework for the solution of those problems. Once Elias had begun to make this break, we would argue, his sociological inquiries became *structurally different* from philosophy, despite odd similarities of terminology. For example, philosophical speculations about the "objects" of the different sciences and the so-called "modes of being" postulated by fundamental ontologists and philosophical realists provided the stimulus for Elias to develop a *testable* theory of the levels of integration (physical, chemical, biological, social, etc.) of the social and natural worlds investigated by the different sciences (Elias, 1987). Similarly, discussions of values, value-relevance, and value-freedom in Rickert and Max Weber are recast by Elias as the theory of involvement and detachment, in which the conceptions of "autonomous" and "heteronomous" evaluations play a central role (Elias, 1987; more on this below). Generally, therefore, one finds in Elias a principled avoidance of philosophical concepts and the consistent substitution of sociological alternatives which are more amenable to empirical reference. More examples include: "truth" is recast as "reality congruence"; "part/whole" becomes "part-unit/unit"; and "abstractions" are transformed into "symbols at a high level of synthesis."

On the subject of "*evaluative*" or "*normative*" matters, Elias commented very early in his career that "Ethical questions are routinely and very wrongly separated from other scientific questions" (Elias, 1921, p. 140). Furthermore, Elias's total commitment to sociology as a "mission," which comes out clearly in his autobiographical *Reflections on a Life* (1994b), tells us something. He saw sociology as potentially able to assist human beings to orientate themselves in the figurations they form together and to help them to control the unintended social entanglements which threaten to escalate into destructive sequences, such as wars and mass killings. The figurational view of society, and Elias's theories of civilizing processes and established–outsiders relations, are implicitly underpinned by the perceived imperative of generating knowledge to help groups in achieving greater "mutual identification" and thus to live in controlled antagonism with each other. Writers who have failed to grasp this aspect of his work have tended, in their criticisms of Elias, to confuse the technical and normative dimensions of some of Elias's concepts – for example, "civilization" and "civilizing processes" (e.g. Leach, 1986; Bauman, 1988) – when Elias was aware of the normative issue right from the start and had already, to his own satisfaction anyway, transformed the issue and the relevant concepts into a sociological form amenable to empirical investigation (Fletcher, 1997, chapter 8).

It is worth filling in a little more of the background to this aspect of Elias's writings, since it is crucial for an understanding of the "moral" dimension of his work, which could all too easily – in view of the intense commitment of Elias and his followers to empirical research – be assimilated unreflectively into the mode of "value-free," sociological empiricism. The matter can be clarified through examining the links between Elias's thinking and Karl Mannheim's sociological program from the 1920s and 1930s, in the development of which Elias participated. He shared the spirit, if not the last letter, of this intellectual venture. In addition to advocating a "relational" or "perspectival" view of society (echoes of which we find in Elias – see Kilminster, 1993, pp. 88–92), Mannheim's program was at the same time intended to deal with questions normally gathered together under the umbrella of "ethics," "politics," or "evaluative" and "existential" questions. These pertained to the ways in which humankind might achieve greater happiness and fulfillment individually and socially within what Mannheim called "the forms of living together of man" (Mannheim, 1957, p. 43).

In Mannheim's scheme of things, when considering evaluative matters the investigator makes a theoretical move sideways, the intention of this method being to redefine the scope and limits of assertions by politicians, philosophers, and others about the possibilities of human freedom, democracy, and happiness, by showing them to be coming inevitably from differing ideological perspectives. It was only through these one-sided perspectives that access was even possible to knowledge of society, all knowledge being existentially bounded and perspectival. Objectivity is sought by "the translation of perspectives into the terms of another" (Mannheim, 1936, pp. 270–1). Having made these moves, the investigator is then potentially able to evaluate the feasibility or validity of "ethical" or "political" issues in the form in which they were originally raised by the particular politician, party, or ideology. Mannheim refers to this theoretical journey as attaining a new form of "'objectivity'... in a roundabout fashion" (ibid., p. 270). These analytic steps then reach a point where the process "becomes a critique" (ibid., p. 256).

Elias's version of the journey specifies that it is only by a "detour via detachment" that sociologists can hope to gain more adequate knowledge of the structure of social events in which they themselves are also emotionally caught up (Elias, 1987, pp. 105, 106). He integrated a psychoanalytic dimension into the basic perspectivistic insight. He shared the Mannheimian ambition to transcribe so-called ethical and evaluative matters into sociologically manageable terms and thus to put the questions raised philosophically or ideologically on to another level. This position constitutes the pith and marrow of Elias's whole sociological program and is observable sometimes even in the interstices of his work. Consider, for example, the following statement in *The Court Society* on the historians' fear that sociological research threatens to extinguish human freedom and individuality:

> If one is prepared to approach such problems through two-pronged investigations on the theoretical and empirical planes in closest touch with one another, rather than on the basis of preconceived dogmatic positions, the question one is aiming at with words such as "freedom" and "determinacy" *poses itself in a different way.* (Elias, 1983, p. 30, our emphasis)

This "evaluative" intention also pervades the empirical-theoretical presentations that are laid out in *The Civilizing Process*. Elias opens the first volume with a sociogenetic inquiry, typical of the sociology of knowledge, into the origins of the concepts of *Kultur* and *Zivilisation*, which, as we have seen, were both redolent of the covert ideological dimension of Alfred Weber's sociology and other highly charged ideological conflicts at the time over whether civilized behavior was the acme or the nadir of the human social achievement. Among other things, the tacit task of *The Civilizing Process* is to reframe the range, applicability, and realistic usefulness of these two key terms via the sociological inquiry into their genesis in the European civilizing process in general. Significantly, Elias returns to the concepts at the end of volume II (Elias, 1994a, pp. 506ff, 520–4) at a new level and *reposes* the questions about human satisfaction, fulfillment, and constraint embodied more ideologically in the antithesis which partly provided the starting point.

THE PRINCIPAL WORKS

Elias wrote his first book, which we now know as *The Court Society*, in the Frankfurt years, but it was not published in any form until 1969. It is a sociological study of aristocratic society in France in the century and a half before the Revolution. The reign of Louis XIV (1643–1715) was particularly crucial in completing the process of the "taming of warriors" and transforming some of them into courtiers devoid of independent military power and increasingly the creatures of the king.[4] The courtly nobility were a "two-front stratum" (Simmel's phrase), grouped between the king and the rich bourgeoisie. Elias shows how much of what seems to us the bizarre detail of court ritual can be understood as mechanisms through which the king could manipulate courtiers through tiny expressions of favor and disfavor. The "ethos of rank" became all-pervasive. He shows, for example, how rank determined the courtiers' expenditure, quite regardless of their *income*, and as a result many became impoverished. In an important corrective to the common assumption that bourgeois economic rationality (Max Weber's *Zweckrationalität* or the Frankfurt School's "instrumental rationality") is the characteristic and even unique form of Western rationality, Elias contends that although the extravagance of courtiers appears "irrational" from a bourgeois point of view, it was a manifestation of a "court-rationality" which itself involved a high degree of restraint on short-term effects for longer-term objectives; it was a form of rationality in which prestige and rank, rather than capital and income, were made calculable as instruments of power.

Within the hotbed of faction and intrigue that was the court, courtiers had to develop an extraordinary sensitivity to the status and importance that could be attributed to a person on the basis of fine nuances of bearing, speech, manners, and appearance. Observing, dealing with, relating to, or avoiding people became an art in itself. And self-observation was inextricably bound up in that: greater *self-control* was required. To later sociologists reared on Erving Goffman,[5] that may seem a universal characteristic of human society; in some degree it is – there is no zero-point, as Elias was fond of remarking in this and many other contexts – but Elias argued that this sensitivity was developed in court society to an exceptional *extent* through the competitive struggle for prestige, with vital interests at stake.

The courtly ethos of self-control, Elias argues, is reflected in the literature, drama, and even the French formal gardens of the period. But, above all, it is seen in the philosophy of Descartes and his successors. The image of the person as *homo clausus* so evident in "cogito ergo sum" is not just a philosophical idea but also the characteristic mode of upper class self-experience that had been developing in Europe since the Renaissance and the Reformation (Elias, 1991b). Elias saw his demonstration of the part played by court society in the development of this mode of self-experience as a supplement to, and not necessarily contradictory in all respects to, Max Weber's parallel account in *The Protestant Ethic and the Spirit of Capitalism*. What was needed was a more comprehensive theory of the development of the modern self-image and mode of self-experience, and that is what Elias set out to provide in *The Civilizing Process* and his later writings.

In this complex *magnum opus*, Elias speaks of civilizing processes on two levels.[6] The first is the individual level, and is rather uncontroversial. Infants and children have to acquire through learning the adult standards of behavior and feeling prevalent in their society; to speak of this as a civilizing process is more or less to use another term for "socialization," and ever since Freud and Piaget there has been little dispute that this process possesses structure and sequence. But the second level is more controversial. Where did these standards come from? They have not always existed, nor always been the same. Elias argues it is possible to identify long-term civilizing processes in the shaping of standards of behavior and feeling over many generations within particular cultures. Again, the idea that these standards *change* is not controversial; the controversy is about whether the changes take the form of structured processes of change with a discernible – though unplanned and by no means irreversible – *direction* over time.

The two volumes of *The Civilizing Process* often strike new readers as being about quite different subjects: the first dealing with the history of manners in Western Europe from the late Middle Ages to the Victorian period, the second advancing a detailed model of the process of state formation, again in Europe, since the Dark Ages. The basic idea, and the basic link between the two halves, is that there is a connection between the long-term structural development of societies and long-term changes in people's social character or habitus. (*Habitus* was in fact the word Elias used in German in 1939, but in the English edition of 1978–82 it was translated as "personality makeup"; the concept of "habitus" was later popularized among sociologists by Pierre Bourdieu, who, though a great friend and admirer of Elias's, seems more likely to have picked up the word in the first instance from other writers.) In other words, as the structure of societies becomes more complex, manners, culture, and personality also change in a particular and discernible direction, first among elite groups, then gradually more widely. This is worked out with great subtlety for Western Europe since the Middle Ages.[7]

Elias began the first volume of *The Civilizing Process* by reviewing the accretion of evaluative meanings around the notion of "civilization." The word was derived from *civilité* – the term used by courtiers to denote their own ways of behaving – but by the nineteenth century it had come to have a single general function, as a badge of the West's sense of superiority:

> this concept expresses the self-consciousness of the West.... It sums up everything in which Western society of the last two or three centuries believes itself superior to earlier societies or "more primitive" contemporary ones. By this term, Western society seeks to describe what constitutes its special character and what it is proud of: the level of *its* technology, the nature of *its* manners, the development of *its* scientific knowledge or view of the world, and much more. (Elias, 1994a, p. 3)

By the nineteenth century, the ways people in the West used the *word* civilization showed that they had largely forgotten the *process* of civilization. Confident of the superiority of their own now seemingly inherent and eternal standards, they wished only to "civilize" the natives of the lands they were now colonizing (or the lower orders of their own societies). They lost awareness that their own ancestors had undergone a learning process, a civilizing process, through which they *acquired* the characteristics now perceived as marks of an imagined *innate* superiority.

In order to retrieve an awareness of this forgotten process from the European past, Elias studied the development of social standards governing eating, nose-blowing, spitting, urinating and defecating, undressing, and sleeping. The reason for investigating these most "natural" or "animalic" facets of behavior was that these are things that by their biological constitution all human beings have to do in any society, culture, or age. Moreover, human infants are born in more or less the same emotional and physical condition at all times and places, and in every society they have to learn how to handle these matters. Therefore, if the way they are handled changes over time, it stands out rather clearly.

Elias's principal sources were French, German, Italian, and English manners books from the Middle Ages to the mid-nineteenth century. In earlier centuries these basic matters of behavior – discussion of which would later cause embarrassment, or at least the humorous sensation of a taboo having been broken – were spoken of openly and frankly, without shame. Then gradually, from the Renaissance, a long-term trend toward greater demands on emotional management in adults becomes apparent: the child has further to travel, so to speak, to attain the adult standard. Codes of behavior become more differentiated, and thresholds of shame and embarrassment advance. Many things become hidden behind the scenes of social life – and also repressed behind the scenes of conscious mental life.

Elias produces evidence to show that this long-term civilizing process cannot be explained away simply by reference to rising levels of material prosperity or to advances in scientific knowledge of health and hygiene, although these were still involved. Moreover, a similar civilizing curve can also be discerned in the development of social standards of self-restraint over resort to the use of *violence*. The explanation is found in the dynamic of social interdependencies. Over a period of many centuries in Europe, chains of social interdependence have grown longer and people have become more subject to more multipolar social constraints. In other words, "more people are forced more often to pay more attention to more other people" (Goudsblom, 1989, p. 722). In the course of this process, the *balance* of the controls by which individual people steer their conduct shifts from the preponderance of external constraints (*Fremdzwänge* –

constraints *by other people*) towards more internalized self-constraints (*Selbstzwänge*). Here the influence of Freud on Elias is evident. But it is not just a matter of *more* self-restraint: rather, the balance tilts toward self-constraint being more *automatic*, more *even* (volatility of mood becomes less than in medieval times), and more *all-embracing* (standards apply more equally in public and private, and to all other people, irrespective of rank, etc.).

In the second volume, Elias puts forward a detailed theory of state formation in Europe, implicitly beginning from Max Weber's definition of the state as an organization which successfully upholds a claim to binding rule-making over a territory, by virtue of commanding a monopoly of the legitimate use of violence. Elias, however, is more interested in the process through which a monopoly of the means of violence – and taxation – is established and extended. That innocent addition – *taxation* – is significant. Elias insisted that Marxist attempts to accord causal primacy to economic "factors" or "forces" or "modes of production" were misleading. The means of production, the means of protection (including attack), and the means of orientation could not be reduced to each other; moreover, in the period of which Elias was talking, the means of violence and the means of production were simply inextricable.

Elias does not regard state-formation as the sole "cause"; indeed, he rejects the use of that concept entirely in this context. State formation, he argues, is only one process interweaving with others to enmesh individuals in increasingly complex webs of interdependence. It interweaves with the division of labor, the growth of trade, towns, the use of money and administrative apparatuses, and increasing population in a spiral process. The internal pacification of territory facilitates trade, which facilitates the growth of towns and division of labor and generates taxes which support larger administrative and military organizations, which in turn facilitate the internal pacification of larger territories, and so on – a cumulative process experienced as a compelling force by people caught up in it. Furthermore, this has long-term effects on people's habitus:

> if in a particular region, the power of central authority grows, if over a larger or smaller area people are *forced* to live at peace with one another, the moulding of the affects and the standards of the demands made upon emotional management are very gradually changed as well (Elias, 1994a, p. 165, our emphasis; translation modified to reflect Elias's later terminology)

According to Elias, the gradually higher standards of habitual self-restraint engendered in people contribute in turn to the upward spiral – being necessary, for example, in the formation of gradually more effective and calculable administration.

LATER EXTENSIONS

The theory of civilizing processes has provoked much scholarly debate.[8] Meanwhile, Elias extended his original thesis in many directions. What follows is a brief account of a selection of what we judge to be the most important, major extensions and developments of his ideas which he himself undertook, in chronological order. (A number of other works, monographs, and lectures have been omitted.)

In *The Established and the Outsiders: a Sociological Inquiry into Community Problems*, written with John L. Scotson (1965; second edition, 1994), Elias develops, through a detailed piece of empirical research of three neighborhoods in a Leicestershire village, the theory of established–outsider relations, which has a wider application. This theory (which is foreshadowed in *The Civilizing Process* and in early writings such as Elias's 1935 essay on the Huguenots; see Elias, 1998) is designed to provide simpler but more inclusive concepts than class, status, and party, which have dominated Marxian and Weberian approaches to inequality. (These general considerations are set out most clearly in "A Theoretical Essay on Established and Outsider Relations," written by Elias in 1976 and included in the 1994 edition of the book by Elias and Scotson). For Elias, class relations are only one form of social oppression and we should not generalize from their features to all types. The theory of established and outsider relations is conceived as part of the theory of civilizing processes, being particularly useful for understanding the complex dynamics of *varieties* of group oppression and group ascent, and the effects of such social ascendance on social and behavioral codes. In Eliasian language, it enables us to grasp with one concept the changing patterns in the uneven balances of power between many different kinds of interdependent groups in a figuration. These power balances include – in addition to those between economic classes – the relations between men and women, homosexuals and heterosexuals, blacks and whites, parents and children (or, more generally, between older and younger generations), governors and governed, and colonizers and colonized.

According to the theory (which has been applied in a considerable range of empirical research: see works cited in Kranendonk, 1990, pp. 158–69; Mennell, 1998, pp. 125–39), when the power gradient between groups is very steep, outsiders are often stigmatized as unworthy, filthy, shifty, or perhaps childlike, as in the case of whites stigmatizing blacks as Sambo figures. At this stage, images of outsiders are highly fantasy-laden and the attitudes of established toward outsiders are extremely rigid. The differences between the behavior and attitudes of established and outsiders are frequently (wrongly) explained biologically. The "group charisma" of the established is such that power superiority is equated with human merit or the grace of nature or God. Outsiders take into their conscience the view of themselves that the established have formed, and so come to accept that they are unworthy, even inhuman. They come to internalize their own "group disgrace." There is an echo of Anna Freud's (1968, ch. 9), "identification with the aggressor" here, the difference being that rather than regarding the phenomenon *individualistically* as a constant in relations between parent and child, or leader and follower, Elias refashions it as symptomatic of a particular *stage* of the shifting power relations between specific interdependent *groups*.

Where the balance of power is becoming more equal, tilting more in favor of the outsiders, then one finds symptoms of rebellion and emancipation, as in the case of the relations between older and younger generations, men and women, homosexuals and heterosexuals, and blacks and whites in recent times. At this stage of the process, images of outsiders become less fantasy-laden and the attitudes of the established groups toward the outsiders more flexible and accommodating. Outsiders begin to develop their own "we-image" and to deny the one imposed by the established. In the early stages of an emancipatory phase there are often calls for separatism (both blacks and women have been through this) and self-help groups form to build new self-images for the rising group (the slogan "black is beautiful" epitomizes this part of the process). As the balance of power becomes *relatively more* equal (not entirely equal) compared with the earlier phase, and outsiders begin to merge with the established to form a new establishment, then more realistic mutual perceptions become possible between groups as the tensions between them diminish.

The three books *Involvement and Detachment* (1987), *Time: an Essay* (1992), and *The Symbol Theory* (1991a) represent major extensions of the theory of civilizing processes to the history of humanity as a whole in the context of biological evolution. These three later works form part of the cluster of Elias's writings on the sociology of knowledge (see, for example, Elias, 1971, 1972, 1974, 1982, 1984), to which he himself, in various interviews, assigned considerable importance. In all of them Elias's very long-term orientation is much to the fore. He also argues in these works, among many other things, that an adequate understanding of social development needs to be integrated into the overall evolutionary process. As he puts it in *The Symbol Theory*:

> The natural constitution of human beings prepares them for learning from others, for living with others, for being cared for by others and for caring for others. It is difficult to imagine how social scientists can gain a clear understanding of the fact that nature prepares human beings for life in society without including aspects of the evolutionary process and of the social development of humankind in their field of vision, (Elias, 1991a, p. 145)

In *Involvement and Detachment* (1987), and in various articles written in the 1970s, Elias developed a sophisticated sociogenetic theory of knowledge and the sciences.[9] In the perspective of the development of human knowledge over the whole history of the species, the "double-bind" relationship between the dangers people faced and the fears they experienced posed formidable initial obstacles to an escape from emotionally charged, fantasy-laden, and "involved" knowledge. Escape can never be complete, but control over social dangers and fears has lagged behind control over natural forces and the fears arising from the human experience of them; and by extension the social sciences remain *relatively* less autonomous and "detached" than the natural sciences. Elias argues that the predominant form of explanation gradually changes across the spectrum from the physical through the biological to the social sciences, with law-like theories becoming less important. The aim of the social scientist should be to construct "process-theories" in five dimensions: the three dimensions of space, plus time and *experience*. As always for Elias, his own substantive sociological investigations stand as exemplars of the pursuit of process theories resting on an image of humankind as "open people."

In *Time: an Essay* (1992) Elias argues that "time" refers not to any universal substance or capacity of the human mind, as philosophers have variously claimed, but to the human social *activity* of *timing*. This activity rests on the human biologically endowed capacity for memory and synthesis, for making connections through the use of symbols. More than any other creatures, humans are orientated by the experience not only of each individual but also of long chains of generations, gradually improving and extending the human means of orientation. It is simply a means of using symbols to connect two or more sequences of changes – physical, biological, or social – using one as a frame of reference for the others. Hence, "time" is not just "subjective"; it has evolved through experience in a long intergenerational learning process.

The social need for timing was much less acute and pervasive in earlier societies than in the more highly organized modern industrial states. Increased differentiation and integration of social functions mean that in modern societies many long chains of interdependence intersect within the individual, requiring constant awareness of time in the coordination of numerous activities. People have to adjust themselves to each other as part of an increasingly intricate mesh of contacts and social necessities, which requires a socially standardized, high-level symbol of timing to enable this to be done with accuracy and predictability. A particularly complex system of self-regulation and an acute individual sensibility with regard to time has developed. The individualization of social time-control thus bears all the hallmarks of a civilizing process.

The Symbol Theory (1991a), which turned out to be the last extended work to be completed for publication by Elias prior to his death in August 1990, is an inquiry into the survival value in the evolutionary process of reality-congruent knowledge made possible by the human capacity for symbol making. Part of the task of this book is to look at the human social and biological condition in a detached, non-reductionist, and non-religious way, so as to enable us to develop a more realistic model of humankind as being caught up in the evolutionary process on another level. For Elias, evolutionary theory is not to be identified solely with Darwin's version, which he regards as incomplete and representing an early stage of elaboration. Anticipating the accusations of evolutionary determinism or teleology, he draws the crucial distinction here, as in several other places in this group of writings, between largely irreversible biological *evolution* and potentially reversible social *development*. Unlike processes of biological evolution, it is possible for social processes to go into reverse and return to an earlier stage of their development. (It is in this sense that he acknowledged the possibility of civilizing processes going into reverse as processes of "*de*civilization": see below.)

Within this broad framework of socio-natural development, which he calls the Great Evolution (Elias, 1987, part III), Elias sees the technical human capacity for communication via symbols to be a unique consequence of the blind inventiveness of nature. Symbols, he insists, are also *tangible* sound patterns of human communication, made possible by the evolutionary biological precondition of the unique and complex vocal apparatus of humans. The capacity of humans to steer their conduct by means of learned knowledge gave them a great evolutionary advantage over other species, which were unable to accomplish this at all or only to a very limited extent.

The Germans: Power Struggles and the Development of Habitus in the Nineteenth and Twentieth Centuries (1996) is a late collection of essays and lectures on German social development and national character and the rise of the Nazis, originally published in German in 1989, exactly 50 years after *The Civilizing Process*. The later volume expands and develops the triangular comparison between Britain, France, and Germany which runs through the earlier work, through a detailed analysis of the German case. Elias focuses on the successive historical diminution, through the wars of 1866 and 1914–18, of German territory in the west and east, resulting in the hegemony of Prussia in the German Confederation. This meant that a centralized German nation-state did not emerge with the ease and speed of other European states, such as England and France. The character of the German habitus, personality, and social structure, which combined to produce the rise of Hitler and the Nazi genocides, is best understood in relation to this feature of Germany's past.

The comparatively late unification of Germany occurred under the leadership of the militaristic ruling strata of Prussia. This was a process in the course of which large sections of the middle classes abandoned the humanistic values which had hitherto predominated in their social circles, and adopted instead the militaristic and authoritarian values of the hegemonic Prussians. German society became orientated around a code of honor, in which dueling and the demanding and giving of "satisfaction" occupied pride of place. Elias argues that Germany's unification involved the "brutalization" of much of the middle classes. The code of behavior which they adopted was essentially a warrior code which emphasized the cult of hardness and obedience and unyielding attitudes of contempt for weakness and compromise. Along with these features of the emerging German habitus was a need to submit to a strong state authority and a decided decline in people's ability to empathize with others. Or, in Elias's words, there occurred a contraction in the scope of "mutual identification." Combined with the weakening of the state's monopoly of violence in the Weimar Republic and the consequent escalation of violence and social fears, these preconditions gave rise to a compelling sequential development (a likely, but *not inevitable*, process) which produced a society-wide process of "decivilization," accelerating during the Weimar Republic and culminating in the Second World War and the Holocaust (see Fletcher, 1997).

PRINCIPLES OF PROCESS SOCIOLOGY

The central recommendations of Elias's sociology, as a theoretical-empirical research strategy, are set out most systematically and succinctly in *What Is Sociology?* (1978). (The highly stimulating theoretical reflections contained in *The Society of Individuals* (Elias, 1991b) are a good supplement.) These recommendations grew out of a vast amount of research and reflection, some of which we have tried to summarize. Elias states that sociology is about studying real people in the plural in webs of social interdependencies. People are bonded to each other not only economically or politically, but also *emotionally*. (The latter dimension had been a central theme of his work since the beginning. He anticipated the contemporary specialisms of the sociology of emotions and of the body a very long time ago.) Figurational sociology is committed to studying people "in the round," simultaneously in *all* the ways in which they are tied to each other in their social existence. It is best summarized as a dynamic sociology of human bonding and the formation of individuals, which centrally stresses the role of power in human relationships. Primacy is given to the developing structure of the social interdependencies (including local, national, regional, and global dimensions) in which people are actually integrated, not to "the social system" in the abstract, nor to analytically distinguished "spheres" or conditions of social action. As Elias declared, in a polemic against Talcott Parsons: "Why put 'actions' in the center of a theory of society and not the people who act? If anything, societies are networks of human beings in the round, not a medley of disembodied actions" (Elias, 1970a, p. 277).

Since sociologists are part of the figurations which they are seeking to understand and to explain, one of the problems they face is controlling for their wishes, fears, and prejudices ("involvements" in Elias's terminology), which stem from their own enmeshment in the tensions generated by social interdependencies which comprise their society. This problem presents itself simply because there is no place outside the antagonisms and conflicts of the figuration from which to observe it. So, for Elias, the problem of achieving a greater degree of sociological detachment is integral to his theory of knowledge and thus to his sociology (Elias, 1987). It also means that at this stage of the development of the discipline, the cognitive status of sociological texts cannot but be bound up to some degree with the social perspective, location, or position of their authors, and so must be to some degree "involved." So, if standards of detachment and fact orientation ("autonomous evaluations" in Elias's terminology) are only relatively weakly institutionalized in sociology, it is likely that a great deal of sociological output will be more informed by extra-sociological involvements ("heteronomous evaluations"). In other words, under present conditions the inquiries of many sociological practitioners will tell us more about them than about the objects of their investigations. Or to put it another way, their involvement/detachment balance will be tilted towards the former pole.

In summary, Goudsblom (1977a, p. 6) and Mennell (1998, p. 252) have distilled from Elias four principles of process sociology. The fact that readers may initially be suspicious of the simplicity and obviousness of these points may be indicative of the expectations of sophistication and difficulty which sociologists commonly associate with the language of the discipline, particularly its theoretical side.

1. Human beings are interdependent in a variety of ways; they are inextricably bonded to each other in the social figurations they form with one another, including with people they do not know.
2. These figurations are continually in flux, undergoing changes, some rapid and ephemeral, others slower and more lasting.
3. The long-term developments taking place in human figurations have been, and continue to be, largely unplanned and unforeseen but are nonetheless structured.
4. The development of human knowledge (including sociology itself) takes place within human figurations and forms one important aspect of their overall development.

SUMMARY AND EVALUATION

The reception of Elias's work and his reputation have varied from country to country. In the Netherlands and Germany his intellectual standing and reputation are considerable, while in Britain, France, and the USA he is appreciated only patchily (Mennell, 1998, pp. 278–84).[10] One of the obstacles to the appreciation of Elias in the USA is that one of prerequisites for making a successful career in sociology today is the choice of a specialism, say medical, political, or urban sociology, or perhaps methods. Specialization has gone a very long way in sociology generally, but particularly far in the USA. With one or two exceptions, there has been a decline (on both sides of the Atlantic) of the sociological generalist who can cross specialisms and draw things together. This, however, is precisely the (unfashionable) strength of Elias's perspective.

In the face of the forces of specialization, the synoptic thrust of sociology has been diverted into the artificial field of "social theory," which tries to accomplish this aim on a purely conceptual terrain. As a result, "theory" itself has ironically become yet another specialism. Here, however, the holistic, generalizing, connecting impetus is not carried out in the substantive, theoretical-*empirical* fashion so typical of Elias. Furthermore, the expansion of social theory has tended to pull sociology back into philosophy, again something upon which Elias had firmly turned his back (see Kilminster, 1998, part II).

So, it seems, it is hard to find a fertile soil in which Elias's unique brand of sociology can grow. In the case of Britain, the pattern had already been established. Although Elias lived and worked there for about forty years, scarcely anyone seemed to have noticed; at any rate, very few took up his work. Like many other continental social-scientific émigrés, Elias encountered the inertia of the British traditions of social administration, Fabianism, and empiricism in the service of social reform (Kilminster and Varcoe, 1996, pp. 5–10). In contrast, the Dutch were from early on receptive to Elias's work. *Über den Prozess der Zivilisation* was well reviewed in the Netherlands in the months before the German invasion in 1940, and a major research school developed there from 1969 onwards under the intellectual leadership of Johan Goudsblom. The question of why precisely the Netherlands should have been so much more receptive than Britain or the USA has not yet been fully answered.

There are signs that Elias's intellectual standing generally will continue to rise in the next few decades, with his work carried forward on to a new level. The generation that "discovered" and championed Elias in the early 1970s in Europe is now in mid–late career or approaching retirement. They used Elias's ideas in a wide variety of empirical research (see, for example, Mennell, 1985; Wouters, 1988; Goudsblom, 1992; van Benthem van den Bergh, 1992; Kapteyn, 1996). But this generation of Eliasians, which includes the present authors, is also the embattled one which had to fight to secure his recognition against the social weight of sociology establishments, proliferating paradigm communities, philosophoidal social theorists and politically orientated groups of sociologists (Goudsblom, 1977a, b; Dunning and Mennell, 1979; Dunning, 1987; Korte, 1997; Kilminster, 1998; Mennell, 1998). Sometimes these polemics and defences gave the understandable, but misleading, impression that the Eliasians were a sect. But there are younger people coming up who do not have to fight those battles. As Robert van Krieken (1998, p. 171) has written, there is no further mileage left in "settling questions of whether Elias was right or wrong, or of coming up with the 'correct' interpretation" of aspects of his work. We believe that the next generation can take for granted the nuanced understanding of Elias's work established by the one which preceded them and bring it to bear, along with other perspectives, on the burning issues of their generation. There is evidence that these are emerging as: (a) gender, sexuality, and identity (Klein, 1992; Shilling, 1993; Falk 1994; Tseëlon, 1995; Waldhoff, 1995; Klein and Liebsch 1997; Mellor and Shilling, 1997; Burkitt 1998; Greco, 1998); and (b) the reorientation of a sociological theory specialism bogged down in dualisms and over-abstraction (Burkitt, 1989; Heilbron, 1995; Fletcher, 1997; van Krieken, 1998; also Kilminster 1998). On the latter area, Robert van Krieken has captured the mood:

> There is a powerful tendency among sociologists towards polarisation between structure and action, micro and macro approaches, between historical sociology and ahistorical studies, between rational choice theory and sociological determinism. All the features of Elias's approach – the emphasis on social relations, long-term processes, the interweaving of planned action and unplanned development, the importance of seeing humans as interdependent, the centrality of power in social relations, and the significance of the concept of "habitus" in understanding human conduct – have considerable potential for taking sociological theory beyond these dichotomies, which seem to have rather outlived their usefulness. (van Krieken, 1998, p. 173)

Elias often said that his work was unfinished, simply an early elaboration of problems to be taken further by others. He offered his synthesis as an invitation to others to work empirically and theoretically to confirm or to refute and thus to amend the basic propositions. Our view is that his work is a rich source of inspiration for the sociological imagination.

Acknowledgments

We are grateful to Eric Dunning, Michael Schröter, and Cas Wouters for comments and correspondence.

Notes

1 The German text was republished in 1969, and Elias's reputation in Germany and the Netherlands grew rapidly from then onwards. A French translation was published in the early 1970s, but the English version was long delayed and surrounded by confusion when it did appear. The first volume was published under the title *The History of Manners* in 1978. There was then a four-year gap before the appearance of the second, which appeared under two different titles: *State- Formation and Violence* in Britain and the unauthorized *Power and Civility* in the United States. As a consequence, many readers and some reviewers failed to appreciate that the two volumes were inseparable halves of a single work. In 1994, Blackwell published a one-volume edition under the title *The Civilizing Process*, to which it is best to refer, though it reproduces all the textual faults of the earlier English edition.

2 A translation of the first couple of pages of the thesis – enough to give merely the flavour of what Elias wrote – is included in Goudsblom and Mennell (1998, pp. 6–7).

3 See Mann (1983).

4 Elias argued that the taming of warriors was a process of significance not just in European history but in the development of human societies generally, and that it had been relatively neglected by sociologists.

5 Goffman cited the original edition of *Über den Prozess der Zivilisation* in *Asylums* (1961) and *Behavior in Public Places* (1963); that is quite remarkable, considering the obscurity of Elias's work in the early 1960s. (He was probably introduced to the book by Edward Shils in Chicago, where he was a graduate student in the late 1940s.)

6 In fact, especially in his more recent works, such as *Time: an Essay* (1992) and *Humana Conditio* (1985), Elias also spoke of civilizing processes on a third level, that of humanity as a whole. See Mennell (1998, pp. 200–24).

7 *The Civilizing Process* is based entirely on European evidence. It is not so much that it is Euro*centric* as that it is *about* Europe. Elias recognized that one of the most important gaps in his work, and one of the most interesting lines for further research, was the study of equivalent – but in detail no doubt different – civilizing processes in other historic cultures.

8 For a fuller discussion of the controversies, see Mennell (1998), especially chapter 10.

9 Two of his most important essays on knowledge and the sciences were brought together in *Involvement and Detachment* (1987). His many other essays in this field, however, remain scattered between various journals in German or English. For a full discussion, see Mennell (1998, chapters 7 and 8).

10 Two recent signs that American sociologists are coming to regard Elias as a sociologist of the first rank are the inclusion of a selection of his writings in the famous Heritage of Sociology series (Mennell and Goudsblom, 1998) and George Ritzer's extended discussion of his work in the fourth edition of his book *Sociological Theory* (Ritzer, 1996, pp. 511–25).

Bibliography

Writings of Norbert Elias

Vom Sehen in der Natur. 1921. *Breslauer Heft*, 8–10 (May–July), 133–44.

Contributions to Discussion on Karl Mannheim, Die Bedeutung der Konkurrenz im Gebiete des Geistigen. 1929a. In *Verhandlungen des Sechsten Deutschen Soziologentages von 17 zu 19 September 1928 in Zürich*. Tübingen, J. C. B. Mohr.

Zur Soziologie des deutschen Antisemitismus. 1929b. *Israelitisches Gemeindeblatt: Offizielles Organ der israelitischen Gemeinden Mannheim und Ludwigshafen*, December 13, 3–6.

The Established and the Outsiders (with John L. Scotson). 1965 (2nd edn 1994). London: Sage.

Sociology and Psychiatry. 1969. In S. H. Foulkes and G. Stewart Prince (eds), *Psychiatry in a Changing Society*. London: Tavistock.

Processes of State Formation and Nation-building. 1970a. In *Transactions of the Seventh World Congress of Sociology, Varna. Volume III*. Sofia: International Sociological Association (1972), pp. 274–84.

Interview met Norbert Elias. 1970b. *Sociologische Gids*, 17(2): 133–40. Reprinted as An Interview in Amsterdam. In Johan Goudsblom and Stephen Mennell (eds), *The Norbert Elias Reader: a Biographical Selection*. Oxford: Blackwell, 1998, pp. 141–51.

The Sociology of Knowledge: New Perspectives. 1971. *Sociology*, 5(2/3), 149–68, 355–70.

Theory of Science and History of Science: Comments on a Recent Discussion. 1972. *Economy and Society*, 1(2), 117–33.

The Sciences: towards a Theory. 1974. In Richard Whitley (ed.), *Social Processes of Scientific Development*. London: Routledge.

What Is Sociology? 1978. London: Hutchinson.

Scientific Establishments. 1982. In Norbert Elias, Herminio Martins and Richard Whitley (eds), *Scientific Establishments and Hierarchies*. Dordrecht: Reidel.

The Court Society. 1983. Oxford: Basil Blackwell.

On the Sociogenesis of Sociology. 1984. *Amsterdams Sociologisch Tijdschrift*, 11(1), 14–52.

The Loneliness of the Dying. 1985a. Oxford: Basil Blackwell.

Humana Conditio: Beobachtungen zur Entwicklung der Menschheit am 40. Jahrestag eines Kriegsendes (8. Mai 1945). 1985b. Frankfurt: Suhrkamp.

Quest for Excitement: Sport and Leisure in the Civilizing Process (with Eric Dunning). 1986. Oxford: Basil Blackwell.

Involvement and Detachment. 1987. Oxford: Basil Blackwell.

The Symbol Theory. 1991a. London: Sage.

The Society of Individuals. 1991b. Oxford: Blackwell.

Time: an Essay. 1992. Oxford: Blackwell.

The Civilizing Process. 1994a. Oxford: Blackwell.

Reflections on a Life. 1994b. Cambridge: Polity Press.

The Germans: Power Struggles and the Development of Habitus in the Nineteenth and Twentieth Centuries. 1996. Cambridge: Polity Press.

The Expulsion of the Huguenots from France. 1998. In Johan Goudsblom and Stephen Mennell (eds), *The Norbert Elias Reader: a Biographical Selection*. Oxford: Blackwell, pp. 19–25.

Further reading

Aron, Raymond (1957) *German Sociology*. London: Heinemann.

Bauman, Zygmunt (1988) *Modernity and the Holocaust*. Cambridge: Polity Press.

Bogner, Artur (1987) Elias and the Frankfurt School. *Theory, Culture and Society*, 4(2/3), 249–85.

Burkitt, Ian (1989) *Social Selves*. London: Sage.

Burkitt, Ian (1998) Sexuality and Gender Identity: from a Discursive to a Relational Analysis. *Sociological Review*, 46(3), 483–504.

Dunning, Eric (1987) Comments on Elias's "Scenes from the Life of a Knight." *Theory, Culture and Society*, 4(2/3), 366–71.

Dunning, Eric and Mennell, Stephen (1979) "Figurational Sociology": Some Critical Comments on Zygmunt Bauman's "The Phenomenon of Norbert Elias." *Sociology*, 13(3), 497–501.

Falk, Pasi (1994) *The Consuming Body*. London: Sage.

Febvre, Lucien (1930) *Civilization*: Evolution of a Word and a Group of Ideas. In John Rundell and Stephen Mennell (eds), *Classical Readings in Culture and Civilization*. London: Routledge (1998), pp. 160–90.

Fletcher, Jonathan (1997) *Violence and Civilization: an Introduction to the Work of Norbert Elias*. Cambridge: Polity Press.

Freud, Anna (1968) *The Ego and the Mechanisms of Defence*, revised edition. London: Hogarth Press (first English translation 1937; original German edition 1936).

Freud, Sigmund (1930) *Civilization and Its Discontents*. New York: W. W. Norton (1962).

Goffman, Erving (1961) *Asylums*. Garden City, NY: Doubleday.

Goffman, Erving (1963) *Behavior in Public Places*. New York: Free Press.

Goudsblom, Johan (1977a) *Sociology in the Balance*. Oxford: Basil Blackwell.

Goudsblom, Johan (1977b) Responses to Norbert Elias's work in England, Germany, the Netherlands and France. In Peter Gleichmann, Johan Goudsblom, and Hermann Korte (eds), *Human Figurations: Essays for Norbert Elias*. Amsterdam: Stichting Amsterdams Sociologisch Tijdschrift, pp. 37–97.

Goudsblom, Johan (1989) Stijlen en beschaving. *De Gids*, 152, 720–2.

Goudsblom, Johan (1992) *Fire and Civilization*. London: Allen Lane.

Goudsblom, Johan and Mennell, Stephen (eds) (1998) *The Norbert Elias Reader: a Biographical Selection*. Oxford: Blackwell.

Greco, Monica (1998) *Illness as a Work of Thought: a Foucauldian Perspective on Psychosomatics*. London: Routledge.

Hackeschmidt, Jörg (1997) *Von Kurt Blumenfeld zu Norbert Elias: Die Erfindung einer judischen Nation*. Hamburg: Europäische Verlaganstalt.

Heilbron, Johan (1995) *The Rise of Social Theory*. Cambridge: Polity Press.

Horkheimer, Max and Adorno, Theodor W. (1979) *Dialectic of Enlightenment*. London: New Left Books.

Kapteyn, Paul (1996) *The Stateless Market*. London: Routledge.

Kettler, David and Meja, Volker (1995) *Karl Mannheim and the Crisis of Liberalism: the Secret of These New Times*. New Brunswick, NJ: Transaction Publishers.

Kilminster, Richard (1993) Norbert Elias and Karl Mannheim: Closeness and Distance. *Theory, Culture and Society*, 10(3), 81–114.

Kilminster, Richard (1998) *The Sociological Revolution: from the Enlightenment to the Global Age*. London and New York: Routledge (paperback edn, 2002).

Kilminster, Richard and Varcoe, Ian (1996) Introduction: Intellectual Migration and Sociological Insight. In Richard Kilminster and Ian Varcoe (eds), *Culture, Modernity and Revolution: Essays in Honour of Zygmunt Bauman*. London: Routledge.

Kilminster, Richard and Wouters, Cas (1995) From Philosophy to Sociology. Elias and the Neo-Kantians: a Response to Benjo Maso. *Theory, Culture and Society*, 12(3), 81–120.

Klein, Gabriele (1992) *FrauenKoerperTanz: Eine Zivilisationsgeschichte des Tanzes*. Berlin: Quadriga.

Klein, Gabriele and Liebsch, Katherina (eds) (1997) *Zivilisierung des weiblichen Ich*. Frankfurt-am-Main: Suhrkamp.

Korte, Hermann (1997) *Über Norbert Elias: Das Werden eines Wissensschaftlers*, revised edition. Opladen: Leske & Budrich.

Kranendonk, Willem H. (1990) *Society as Process: a Bibliography of Figurational Sociology in the Netherlands*. Amsterdam: Sociologisch Instituut, Universiteit van Amsterdam.

Leach, Edmund (1986) Violence. *London Review of Books*, October 23.

Lepenies, Wolf (1978) Norbert Elias: an Outsider Full of Unprejudiced Insight. *New German Critique,* 15, 57–64.

Mann, Thomas (1983) *Reflections of a Non-political Man*. New York: Frederick Ungar.

Mannheim, Karl (1936) *Ideology and Utopia*. London: Routledge & Kegan Paul.

Mannheim, Karl (1953) German Sociology (1918–1933). In Karl Mannheim, *Essays on the Sociology and Social Psychology*. London: Routledge & Kegan Paul.

Mannheim, Karl (1957) *Systematic Sociology: an Introduction to the Study of Society*. London: Routledge & Kegan Paul.

Maso, Benjo (1995) Elias and the Neo-Kantians: Intellectual Backgrounds of *The Civilizing Process*. *Theory, Culture and Society*, 12(3), 43–79.

Mellor, Philip and Shilling, Chris (1997) *Re-forming the Body: Religion, Community and Modernity*. London: Sage.

Mennell, Stephen (1985) *All Manners of Food: Eating and Taste in England and France from the Middle Ages to the Present*. Oxford: Blackwell.

Mennell, Stephen (1998) *Norbert Elias: an Introduction*. Dublin: University College Dublin Press.

Mennell, Stephen and Goudsblom, Johan (eds) (1998) *Norbert Elias on Civilization, Power and Knowledge*. Chicago: University of Chicago Press.

Pines, Malcolm (ed.) (1997) Special Section: Centennial Celebration to Commemorate the Birth and Work of Norbert Elias. *Group Analysis*, 30(4), 475–529.

Ritzer, George (1996) *Sociological Theory*, 4th edn. New York: McGraw-Hill.

Sathaye, S. G. (1973) On Norbert Elias's Developmental Paradigm. *Sociology*, 7(1), 117–23.

Schad, Susanne Petra (1972) *Empirical Social Research in Weimar Germany*. The Hague: Mouton.

Shilling, Chris (1993) *The Body and Social Theory*. London: Sage.

Tseëlon, Efrat (1995) *The Masque of Femininity*. London: Sage.

van Benthem van den Bergh, Godfried (1992) *The Nuclear Revolution and the End of the Cold War: Forced Restraint*. London: Macmillan.

van Krieken, Robert (1998) *Norbert Elias*. London: Routledge.

Waldhoff, Hans-Peter (1995) *Fremde und Zivilisierung: Wissenssoziologische Studien über das Verarbeiten von Gefühlen der Fremdheit – Probleme der modernen Peripherie-Zentrums-Migration am türkisch-deutschen Beispiel*. Frankfurt-am-Main: Suhrkamp.

Weber, Alfred (1998) Fundamentals of Culture Sociology: Social Process, Civilizational Process and Culture-movement. In John Rundell and Stephen Mennell (eds), *Classical Readings in Culture and Civilization*. London: Routledge, pp. 191–215.

Wouters, Cas (1988) Etiquette Books and Emotion Management in the Twentieth Century: American Habitus in International Comparison. In Peter N. Stearns and Jan Lewis (eds), *An Emotional History of the United States*. New York: New York University Press, pp. 283–304.

8

Michel Foucault

Barry Smart

Introduction: Foucault as a Social Theorist

With all beginnings there is a temptation to simply accept the established discursive order of things, to submit to the agenda which presents itself. But in addressing the issue of Foucault's contribution to social thought – the question of his status as a social theorist and the place, distinctiveness, and significance of his work within social theory – to simply proceed without reflecting on the terms of reference, and the question of their appropriateness, even if only briefly, would be to fail to do justice to the critically reflexive analytic approach Foucault consistently employed in his various studies.

Any attempt to situate Foucault is likely to promote debate, and the identification of Foucault as a social theorist is no exception. As is the case with many of the figures who have been identified as contributors to the discourse of social theory, other claims may be made, other contributions recognized. For example, Marx, Weber, and Simmel are regarded as key social theorists, but their respective works also contribute significantly, in some instances more significantly, to other discursive fields, including political economy (Marx), economic history (Weber), and philosophy and cultural analysis (Simmel). In the case of Foucault, philosophy and history might be acknowledged to have first claim, although the significance for social and cultural analysis of his studies of madness and reason, discipline and punishment, and sexuality and subjectivity is now widely recognized and beyond dispute. In raising these concerns I am trying to draw attention to a number of issues. In reading the work of a particular analyst it is necessary to be aware of the tendency to invoke "the author as the unifying principle in a particular group of writings or statements" (Foucault, 1971, p. 14) and to consider the consequences of so doing. This is a matter on which it is necessary to reflect, a matter with which Foucault was concerned because it had implications for the sources or texts selected for analysis, as well as the "unity" accorded to both the totality of writings ascribed to a particular authorial figure and the individual "works" considered to constitute the author's corpus. In the case of Foucault's various analytic writings, designating the work as "social theory" is not without its problems, for while there is much in Foucault's work that bears significantly on the concerns that lie within the broad discursive field of social theory, there is no direct or sustained attempt to theorize "the social" and no attempt is made to theorize "society," although there are detailed studies of particular social practices. In addition, there are a number of other essays and texts on language, literature and painting which are not generally considered when the figure of Foucault the social analyst is invoked; for example, works on Roussel, Blanchot, and Magritte (Foucault, 1987a, b, 1983a).

When summoned to reflect on his various studies, to account for and order their features, Foucault (1982a) quite deliberately described his practices as "analytical work" rather than as "theory," and when responding to comments on his analysis of relations of power he remarked that it is "not a theory, but rather a way of theorizing practice" (Foucault, 1988d, p. 12). Again, when asked shortly before his death to write a(n) (auto)biographical sketch, he described his enterprise as a *critical history of thought* (Maurice Florence [an alias], 1988). The implication of these remarks is not that Foucault's work has no bearing on social theory, but that the critically reflexive manner in which he conducted his inquiries has significant implications for the practice of social theory, and for the reflective, biographically driven meta-theoretical exercise in hand.

Although, as Foucault remarks, the notion that a proposition derives its "scientific value from its author" has been in decline in the natural, physical, and biological sciences for a considerable time – in some fields since the seventeenth century – in other discursive fields the author function continues to be of importance. Foucault comments on the way in which in literature the author function seems to have become even more important – authors are required to "answer for the unity of the works published in their names;... [to] reveal, or at least display the hidden sense pervading their work;... [and] to reveal their personal lives, to account for their experiences and the real story that gave birth to their writings" (Foucault, 1971, p. 14). Notwithstanding Foucault's methodical attempt in *The Archaeology of Knowledge* (1974) to argue that there are analytically more appropriate principles of unification by which a group of statements may be recognized to warrant the status of a discursive formation than the author function, the latter remains very prominent within social theory.

One of the difficulties encountered in trying to achieve an overview of Foucault's work is his commendable inclination to be prepared to think differently, his readiness to reinterpret earlier studies in the light of subsequently different circumstances and preoccupations, and his willingness to reconstruct or refocus his analyses. Foucault offers a series of (re-)interpretations of the aims and objectives of his work, notable among which are critical reflections in *The Archaeology of Knowledge* (1974) on earlier "disordered" studies; the designation in an inaugural lecture (1971) of the analytic terrain within which his work is to be relocated; reconceptualization of the earlier studies of madness and reason and medicine and the clinic as implicitly posing the question of the articulation and "effects of power and knowledge" (1980), first explicitly addressed in *Discipline and Punish: the Birth of the Prison* (1977b); identification in a subsequent major essay of the question of the subject as "the general theme of my research (1982a, p. 209); and a final refocusing of his work in a preface prepared for the much delayed second volume of *The History of Sexuality*, published shortly before his death, as providing an analysis of the "historicity of forms of experience" through a consideration of "the modality of relation to the self" (Foucault, 1986, pp. 334, 338).

It is ironic that an analyst who sought to problematize the status of the author and who speculated on "the total effacement of the individual characteristics of the writer" (Foucault, 1977a, p. 117) should have so frequently attempted to redefine his work. Far from becoming a matter of indifference, the author-function remains significant and Foucault's tendency to reinterpret his analyses serves as confirmation that the writing subject has not disappeared; indeed, it might be argued that his own work has for some become "a kind of enigmatic supplement of the author beyond his own death" (ibid., p. 120).

The Theory: Questions of Method and Analysis

There is no sustained attempt in Foucault's writings to specify or address "the social" as such, but the wide range of questions he posed, the various complex issues and concerns he considered, and the way in which he sought to conduct his analysis of particular institutions and practices have led to his work being widely regarded as central to our understanding of prevailing social conditions. Foucault was certainly not a sociologist, but there is much of relevance and value to sociology in his writings. Equally, there is in his work a great deal that bears significantly on the concerns which lie at the center of contemporary social theory.

In *The Order of Things: an Archaeology of the Human Sciences* (1970), Foucault analyzes the formation of the human sciences within the modern epistemological configuration and identifies the distinguishing features of modern thought. This is one of the early works which is cited in support of the identification of Foucault with structuralism, but his relationship to the problematic unity "structuralism" is more tenuous than some critics have allowed. There is no attempt to uncover elementary structures, as there is with Claude Lévi-Strauss, and there is no conception of a universal unconscious structured like a language, as there is with Jacques Lacan. And while there is an element of potentially misleading structuralist terminology in the first edition of *The Birth of the Clinic*, the analytic superficiality of phrases like "a structural analysis of the signified" is revealed when they are replaced in the second edition by more appropriate references to "an analysis of discourses." If there is a degree of common ground between the early works of Foucault and the analyses of Lévi-Strauss, Lacan, Louis Althusser, and Roland Barthes, respectively, it derives from a shared antipathy toward humanism and existential phenomenology.

In *Madness and Civilization: a History of Insanity in the Age of Reason* (1965), *The Birth of the Clinic: an Archaeology of Medical Perception* (1973), and *Discipline and Punish: the Birth of the Prison* (1977b), respectively, the different ways in which the modern subject has been constituted as an object of knowledge (mad/sane, sick/healthy, delinquent/law-abiding) as a consequence of modern scientific practices such as psychiatry, clinical medicine, and criminal science are carefully documented. Finally, after having published an introductory volume which, among other things, maps out a series of intended studies of the power–knowledge relations constitutive of modern Western sexuality, Foucault reconsidered and then reconfigured the project in the second volume in the series *The History of Sexuality: The Use of Pleasure* (1987c), in order to focus on the ways in which subjects reflect upon and constitute themselves as objects for themselves, as, for example, when individuals "recognize themselves as subjects of pleasure [and]... desire" (Florence, 1988, p. 14).

In contrasting, yet complementary, ways, Foucault's various analyses offer what at one point he describes as a "history of the present" (Foucault, 1977b, p. 31); that is, critical analyses which effectively explore the complex formation of our modernity. For Foucault such a critical and effective history contributes to the transformation of the present by revealing "the accidents, the minute deviations – or conversely, the complete reversals – the errors, the false appraisals, and the faulty calculations that gave birth to those things that continue to exist and have value for us" (Foucault, 1977a, p. 146). By exposing the contingency of modernity, the disorder and heterogeneity of events and processes, and the fragments which have been mistaken for secure foundations, Foucault effectively shows "how that-which-is has not always been; i.e., that the things which seem most evident to us are always formed in the confluence of encounters and chances, during the course of a precarious and fragile history.... It means that they reside on a base of human practice and human history; and that since these things have been made, they can be unmade, as long as we know how it was that they were made" (Foucault, 1983b, p. 206). And to learn how things have been made – in particular, how forms of modern subjectivity have been constituted, and associated forms of conduct determined – Foucault argued that it was necessary to analyze not only what he termed "techniques of domination" – for example, the range of disciplinary technologies of power employed in institutions like the asylum, clinic, and prison, and explored in his earlier studies – but also "techniques of the self," that is to say the means by which individuals may exercise "operations on their own bodies, their own souls, their own thoughts, their own conduct, and this in a manner so as to transform themselves" (Foucault and Sennett, 1982, p. 10). In each instance, whether it is disciplinary techniques or what Foucault sometimes called "technologies of the self," it is the *government* of conduct that is analytically central; that is, the ways in which conduct is formed and shaped, guided and directed.

Before we turn in more detail to discuss key features of Foucault's analyses of the "art of governing people in our societies," a discussion that will include consideration of (a) forms of modern rationality, (b) relations of power, and (c) questions of subjectivity, clarification of the analytic methods employed by

Foucault is warranted. Foucault has described several of his earlier studies as archaeologies and he has been credited with making a major contribution to an "archaeology of modernity" (Huyssen, 1984). In some of his later lectures and writings he makes reference to genealogical research and describes how he "tried to get away from the philosophy of the subject, through a genealogy of the modern subject as a historical and cultural reality" (Foucault and Sennett, 1982, p. 9). What are we to make of the notions of "archaeology" and "genealogy" employed by Foucault?

A number of critics of Foucault's earlier studies of madness and reason, medicine and the clinic, and the formation of the human sciences have claimed to find traces of structuralism (White, 1973; Stone, 1983). In *The Archaeology of Knowledge*, a text which outlines the distinctive features of an archaeological method of analysis of discursive formations, Foucault engages with, and attempts to distance his analytic approach from, structuralism. In *The Archaeology of Knowledge* Foucault states that his "aim is not to transfer to the field of history, and more particularly to the history of knowledge (*connaissances*), a structuralist method that has proved valuable in other fields of analysis" (Foucault, 1974, p. 15). While there is an admission that aspects of the analysis of transformations in the field of historical knowledge may not be "entirely foreign to what is called structural analysis," Foucault is adamant that he does not employ the "categories of cultural totalities (whether world-views, ideal-types, the particular spirit of an age)," and that he does not impose on history "the forms of structural analysis" (ibid.). As the imaginary interlocutor introduced by Foucault comments towards the end of the text, "you have been at great pains to dissociate yourself from 'structuralism'" (ibid., p. 199). In *The Archaeology of Knowledge* the question of how social institutions are articulated with discursive formations seems to be put to one side as the analytic approach adopted proceeds to accord discourses autonomy in order to concentrate on demonstrating the rules through which they achieve internal self-regulation. The archaeological approach described has been subjected to criticism on a number of counts, but primarily for rendering virtually incomprehensible the influence that social institutions have on what appear as "autonomous" discursive systems. In so far as archaeology is presented as an end in itself, Foucault is also vulnerable to the charge of effectively foreclosing "the possibility of bringing his critical analyses to bear on his social concerns" (Dreyfus and Rabinow, 1982, pp. xx–xxi). It is with the advent of genealogical research that the call for a more explicitly politically engaged form of critical analysis appears to be answered by Foucault.

A marked shift of analytic focus away from the rules regulating discursive practices and toward the social practices with which discourses are articulated is first signaled in Foucault's (1971) lecture "Orders of Discourse." This text anticipates a subsequent relative marginalization of archaeological analysis and concomitant elevation of genealogy in Foucault's work by placing emphasis on the importance of an analytic (re)turn to the question of the *social* production of discourse and the articulation of discourse and power. In his seminal lecture Foucault delineates the rules of exclusion through which the production of discourse is "controlled, selected, organised and redistributed" (ibid., p. 8). These rules take the form of prohibition, division, and rejection, and the opposition between "true" and "false," and of these it is the last that becomes increasingly important as Foucault's genealogical research proceeds. The principle of exclusion which has increasingly been assimilating the others is that between true and false, an opposition or division with its own complex and uneven history. From classical Antiquity to the present there has been a division differentiating "true discourse from false," a division which Foucault suggests has "never ceased shifting." Instead of an orthodox linear developmental conception of the discovery of knowledge, Foucault promotes the idea that mutations and transformations in knowledge may be regarded as manifestations of forms of the will to truth, and he adds that "this will to knowledge, . . . reliant upon institutional support and distribution, tends to exercise a sort of pressure, a power of constraint upon other forms of discourse" (ibid., p. 11). Implicit in Foucault's remarks on the modern will to knowledge is a concern that subsequently achieves greater prominence in his genealogical researches, namely an analytic focus on the complex articulations between forms of knowledge and relations of power.

Genealogy uncovers the myriad events, "the details and accidents that accompany every beginning" (Foucault, 1977a, p. 144); reveals the dispersions, deviations, and discontinuities that are displaced in the traditional historical analytic pursuit of order, continuity, and secure foundations. Genealogical historical inquiry, what Foucault sometimes terms "effective" history, dispenses with constants and treats everything as having a history. Stability and continuity cannot be assumed; history "becomes 'effective' to the degree that it introduces discontinuity into our very being" (ibid., p. 154). Notwithstanding the emphasis placed on genealogy in Foucault's later writings, archaeology does not disappear; to the contrary, it continues to serve as a methodology for isolating and analysing "local discursivities" in a manner which is complementary to genealogy (Foucault, 1980). As one analyst has remarked, "from the perspective of the production of a knowledge of discursive formations, archaeology remains the indispensable methodology, from the practical polemical and strategic perspective of the use of historical analysis, genealogy holds the key. However, beyond the language of complementarity, genealogy is clearly dominant. It connects the empirical analyses . . . to concerns activated in light of particular contemporary struggles" (Dean, 1994, pp. 33–4).

Rationality

As stated above, one of the difficulties which arises in attempting to offer a brief overview of Foucault's work is that of giving sufficient attention to the various modifications and shifts of emphasis which affect his analysis. However, there is an associated risk, namely that too much significance may be attached to apparent theoretical shifts, and that evidence of forms of continuity, from what is regarded as the first major work, *Madness and Civilization*, through to the end of his output, may not receive sufficient critical attention. A number of possible lines of continuity in Foucault's work have been identified. A continuous thread extending from *Madness and Civilization* to *Discipline and Punish* has been argued to be present in the form of "an institutional epistemology which correlates the possibility of particular developments in systems of thought to the means of observation and registration afforded by special institutional sites and mechanisms" (Gordon, 1990, p. 12). Another is the "interconnection of questions of governmental rationality and questions of the social organization of subjectivity: the linkage... between the macrophysics and the microphysics of power" (ibid., p. 11). With differing degrees of explicitness, evidence of forms of continuity may be found throughout Foucault's work in a general analytic preoccupation with forms of rationality, relations of power, and the constitution of forms of subjectivity.

Whether addressing questions of rationality, power, or subjectivity, Foucault consistently sought to demonstrate that notions of linear development, "reassuring stability," and continuity were problematic. Such a perspective led Foucault to express doubts about the analytic value of "rationalization" conceptualized as a unitary process and to argue instead that "we have to analyze specific rationalities rather than always invoking the progress of rationalization in general" (Foucault, 1982a, p. 210; see also 1981c, p. 226). Foucault's studies of the experiences of madness, illness, death, crime, and sexuality serve as appropriate examples, as they present analyses of "different foundations, different creations, different modifications in which rationalities engender one another, oppose and pursue one another" (Foucault, 1983b, p. 202).

Analysis of prominent aspects of modern rationality constitutes an important element in the work not only of Foucault but also of a number of other theorists, including Max Weber, members of the Frankfurt School, and Jürgen Habermas. However, scope for comparison of the works of Foucault with those of other prominent social theorists is not confined to the question of modern rationality and its consequences. The respective works of Foucault and Weber may be compared on a number of additional counts, including "their studies of forms of domination and techniques of discipline,... their writings on methodology and intellectual ethics, [and] their interest in Nietzsche" (Gordon, 1987, p. 293). In turn, other analysts have sought to consider the similarities and differences between the works of Foucault, the Frankfurt School, and Habermas, for the most part in relation to their respective conceptions of relations of power and domination and the influence of Nietzsche's philosophical thought (Hoy, 1981; Dews, 1984; Ingram, 1986).

There are a number of texts in which Foucault has outlined a response to the question of his relationship to aspects of Weber's work and Critical Theory. While Foucault (1988c) has commented that his approach to historical inquiry needs to be differentiated from Weber's "ideal types" analysis, it has been argued that when consideration is given to their substantive historical works differences begin to diminish (Dreyfus and Rabinow, 1982; Gordon, 1987). For example, in the course of an analysis of "world religions" Weber acknowledges that "'rationalism' may mean very different things" and that "rationalization of life conduct... can assume unusually varied forms" (Weber, 1970, p. 293). References such as these to different types of rationalism appear to anticipate Foucault's preference for an "instrumental and relative meaning" for rationalization; that is, for an analytic focus on "specific rationalities" rather than on an assumed general process of rationalization.

Foucault has been interpreted within the tradition of critical theorizing as a critic of reason *in toto*. For example, in an analysis of Foucault's general contribution to our understanding of rationalization, Habermas cautions that "we must be careful not to throw the baby out with the bath water and take flight in a new irrationalism. Foucault visibly falls into that danger" (Habermas, 1986, p. 69). In response to this type of criticism advanced by Habermas and others, Foucault comments that his work provides an analysis of the fragile and precarious history of what "reason perceives as *its* necessity, or rather, what different forms of rationality offer as their necessary being" (Foucault, 1983b, p. 206). Foucault adds that this is not to say that these forms of rationality are irrational, simply that "they reside on a base of human practice and human history" (ibid.). Foucault does not take flight in irrationality, he simply has another agenda; his approach and the questions he poses are quite different from those of Habermas. Elaborating on his thinking about rationality Foucault comments that:

> the central issue of philosophy and critical thought since the eighteenth century has always been, still is, and will, I hope, remain the question, *What* is this Reason that we use? What are its historical effects? What are its limits, and what are its dangers? How can we exist as rational beings, fortunately committed to practicing a rationality that is unfortunately crisscrossed by intrinsic dangers?... In addition, if it is extremely dangerous to say that Reason is the enemy that should be eliminated, it is just as dangerous to say that any critical questioning of this rationality risks sending us into irrationality.... If intellectuals in general are to have a function, if critical thought itself has a function, and, even more specifically, if philosophy has a function within critical thought, it is precisely to accept this sort of spiral, this sort of revolving door of rationality that refers us to its necessity, to its indispensability, and at the same time to its intrinsic dangers. (Foucault, 1982b, p. 19)

Whereas for the Frankfurt School and Habermas the analytic focus tends to fall on the relationship between rationality and domination, in particular the repressive sociocultural and political consequences of the increasing prominence of instrumental, economic, and administrative reason, for Foucault the problem is posed in quite different terms. Foucault does not identify a particular moment at which "reason bifurcated" into instrumental and moral forms; to the contrary he refers to an "abundance of branchings, ramifications, breaks and ruptures" (Foucault, 1983b, p. 201), and places analytic emphasis on the historically specific forms of rationality through which human subjects became objects of forms of knowledge, and the theoretical, institutional, and economic consequences of subjects speaking "the truth about themselves." One of the ways in which Foucault explored concerns such as these was through studies of the articulation of forms of knowledge with relations of power.

Power

Although the term is scarcely, if ever, employed in his earlier studies, Foucault claimed in an interview given in 1977 that an analytic interest in the exercise of power, "concretely and in detail – with its specificity, its techniques and tactics" (Foucault, 1980, pp. 115–16) was present in his work all along. Some six years later Foucault sought once more to clarify his approach to the analysis of power relations, this time to correct the impression that he was constructing "a theory of Power." While apparently ready to accept a description of his work as a "microphysics" or an "analytics" of power, Foucault remarked that "I am far from being a theoretician of power. At the limit, I would say that power as an autonomous question, does not interest me" (Foucault, 1983b, p. 207). Notwithstanding such denials, Foucault does offer a series of general observations on power, but rather than attempting to answer the question "what is power and where does it come from," it is the means by which power is exercised and the effects of its exercise with which his analysis is primarily concerned.

Power is conceptualized as a complex strategic situation or relation which produces social realities, practices, and forms of subjectivity, rather than as a property or possession which excludes, represses, masks, or conceals. As Foucault argues in *Discipline and Punish*, power "produces domains of objects and rituals of truth. The individual and the knowledge that may be gained of him belong to this production" (Foucault, 1977b, p. 194). In a series of related texts, Foucault (1979a, 1980) elaborates further on his understanding of power, emphasizing that it is not to be equated with "the sovereignty of the state, the form of the law, or the over-all unity of a domination given at the outset"; instead, power is to be understood "as the multiplicity of force relations immanent in the sphere in which they operate" (Foucault, 1979a, p. 92). Exercised "from innumerable points," power relations are "intentional and nonsubjective" (ibid., p. 94). Relations of power for Foucault are synonymous with sociality. Power is held to be always present in human relations, "whether it be a question of communicating verbally...or a question of a love relationship, an institutional or economic relationship" (Foucault, 1987d, p. 122). Power relations are relations in which influence is exercised over the conduct of free subjects, and as Foucault (1982a, p. 221) puts it, "only in so far as they are free." In brief, subjects have the potential to block, change, overturn, or reverse the relation of guidance, direction, and influence. As I have argued elsewhere, there appears to be an implication here that the subject is, in part at least, responsible for his or her own fate, in so far as there is always the potential to transform a relation of power into an adversarial confrontation (Smart, 1995).

Foucault's clarificatory comments have not resolved matters and his analysis of power relations has remained a source of controversy. For example, Peter Dews (1984, p. 88) suggests that "if the concept of power is to have any critical political import, there must be *some* principle, force or entity which power 'crushes' or 'subdues,' and whose release from this repression is considered desirable. A *purely* positive account of power would no longer be an account of power at all, but simply of the constitutive operation of social systems." Dews proceeds to argue that Foucault does not provide a satisfactory answer to the question of the basis of resistance to power, and concludes by drawing attention to the absence in his work of normative foundations for political critique. A related line of criticism is developed by Charles Taylor (1984, p. 152), who remarks that "Foucault's analyses seem to bring evils to light; and yet he wants to distance himself from the suggestion that would seem inescapably to follow, that the negation of these evils promotes a good." Taylor outlines a range of criticisms in which Foucault's position is described as "incoherent," too ready to equate humanitarianism with a system of control, and too inclined to represent the emergence of new forms of discipline in terms of domination. After having developed further criticisms of Foucault's work for its oversimplification of the complexity of historical events and processes, Taylor argues that a notion of power "*does not make sense* without at least the idea of liberation" (ibid., p. 173). Comparable objections are articulated by Habermas, who asks of Foucault, "Why is struggle preferable to submission? Why ought domination to be resisted?" (Habermas, 1987, p. 284).

What are at issue between Foucault and his critics, what divide them and prevent effective communication and debate, are quite different conceptions, not only of power, but also of truth and freedom. For example, for Taylor, "unmasking" modern forms of power has as its purpose the rescue of "two goods," notably freedom and truth, where "truth... is subversive of power... [and] is on the side of the lifting of impositions" (Taylor, 1984, p. 174). However, the terms employed by Taylor – the equation of power and domination and the idea of a "move toward a greater acceptance of truth – and hence also in certain conditions a move toward greater freedom" (ibid., p. 177) – are not compatible with Foucault's analytics of power. Power is conceptualized as productive and relational by Foucault, it is literally regarded as a "set of actions upon other actions" (Foucault, 1982a, p. 220), and, as I have already noted, is not to be equated with domination. In turn, truth is conceptualized as a historically variable sociocultural "system of ordered procedures for the production, regulation, distribution, circulation and operation of statements," and is considered to be "linked in a circular relation with systems of power" (Foucault, 1980, p. 133). Finally, freedom for Foucault constitutes the (pre)condition for the exercise of power; indeed, he argues that "freedom must exist for power to be exerted" (Foucault, 1982a, p. 221); the freedom to resist must be present, if only as a potential. What is striking about the critical discussion which has developed around Foucault's analytics of power is how frequently criticisms miss their mark because critics have failed to come to terms with the distinctive features of Foucault's analysis (Patton, 1989).

The conception that emerges in *Discipline and Punish*, of the individual as both an effect of power and the element of its articulation, receives clarification and elaboration in Foucault's subsequent discussion, in *The History of Sexuality, Volume 1*, of the development of "bio-power." The two basic forms in which "bio-power," or power over life, is considered to be exercised are disciplines of the body, or an "anatomo-politics of the human body," and a regulation of the species body, or a "bio-politics of the population" (Foucault, 1979a, p. 139). Foucault notes an increasing political and administrative concern, starting in the seventeenth century, to optimize the body's capability, enhance its usefulness, and ensure its docility and integration "into the machinery of production" (ibid., p. 141), followed later by increasing regulation of the species body or population, through interventions in "propagation, births, mortality, . . . health, life expectancy" (ibid., p. 139) and associated factors and processes. The distinction between two basic forms in which power is exercised over life is developed further in Foucault's (1979b, 1981c) analysis of individualizing and totalizing forms of governmental rationality, an analysis which draws attention to the historical process of the "governmentalization of the state" and its complex consequences. In the course of a series of clarificatory comments on the specificity of power relations, Foucault suggests that the exercise of power consists in "guiding the possibility of conduct and putting in order the possible outcome" (Foucault, 1982a, p. 221) and that, in this respect at least, power constitutes a matter of government. Conceptualizing the exercise of power in these terms – that is, as action upon the actions of "subjects who are faced with a field of possibilities in which several ways of behaving . . . may be realized" (ibid.) – constitutes an oblique response to the charge that his analysis portrays relations of power as all-pervasive.

Clarification of the exercise of power in terms of government draws attention to the presence of "individual or collective subjects," and serves as an effective response to the criticism that there is a neglect, if not an effective denial, of the active subject, the subject capable of resistance. It is in this setting, namely of a series of responses to questions concerning power, freedom, and governmentality, that Foucault moves once more to reformulate the goal of his work, by stating that the central objective had "not been to analyze the phenomena of power . . . [but] to create a history of the different modes by which, in our culture, human beings are made subjects" (Foucault, 1982a, p. 208). Three modes of objectification through which human beings are constituted as subjects are identified, notably: (a) particular "human" sciences which objectivize the "speaking subject" (e.g. linguistics), the "productive subject" (e.g. economics), and the "sheer fact of being alive" (e.g. biology); (b) "dividing practices" which constitute subjects as mad/sane, sick/healthy, and criminal/law-abiding; and (c) self-governing practices or "technologies of the self," through which human beings turn themselves into subjects.

Subjectivity

It is within the final project on sexuality that the question of the subject and technologies of the self become the focus of analytic concern. After the publication of an introductory volume to a planned series on sexuality there is a radical shift of historical and analytic focus away from the Victorian era, the "repressive hypothesis," and a promised subsequent clarification of the modern deployment of sexuality, to a concern with the expression and regulation of pleasures in classical Antiquity, explored in two further, and, as it transpired, final volumes.

To achieve an effective analysis of the subject and subjectivity Foucault argued that a major theoretical shift was necessary, one which would allow the focus of analysis to fall on "the forms and modalities of the relation to self by which the individual constitutes and recognizes himself *qua* subject" (Foucault, 1987c, p. 6). The shift in question led to a radical reorganization of the project around "games of truth," technologies of the self, and the problematization of particular practices, around, that is, "the slow formation, in antiquity, of a hermeneutics of the self" (ibid.). Consequently, the focus in the final volumes on sexuality falls on the different games of truth and error through which human beings historically came to be constituted as desiring subjects, and reflexively experienced themselves as such. The key question articulated is why sexuality became a matter of ethical concern: "how, why and in what forms was sexuality constituted as a moral domain?" (ibid., p. 10).

With this late "abrupt theoretical shift" Foucault moves, according to Dews (1989, p. 39), to "articulate the concepts of subjectivity and freedom in such a way as to avoid any suggestion that such freedom must take the form of the recovery of an authentic 'natural' self." Such a shift of analytic focus to the world of the ancient Greeks also allows Foucault to call into question contemporary assumptions about the "necessary link between ethics and other social or economic or political structures" (Foucault, 1986, p. 350) by placing emphasis on practices of ethical self-construction. However, when the issue of the self-constitution of the subject through technologies of the self is addressed, Foucault is careful to add, by way of clarification, that "these practices are . . . not something that the individual invents by himself. They are patterns that he finds in his culture and which are *proposed, suggested, imposed on him by his culture, his society and his social group*" (Foucault, 1987d, p. 122, emphasis added). While such an observation may seem relatively uncontentious, it does leave open and unanswered the respect(s) in which subjects are, or can be, recognized as active and responsible. To be more precise, and to address directly one of Foucault's later preoccupations, is it really appropriate to talk of creating oneself, and if so on what basis does it become possible "to create oneself"? Foucault takes the view that "the self is not given to us . . . [and] that there is only one practical consequence: we have to create ourselves as a work of art" (Foucault, 1986, p. 351). It is through a process of reflection on similarities and differences between the Greek world and the modern West that the conclusion that the self is not given to us is reached, the argument being that some of our main ethical principles "have been related at a certain moment to an aesthetics of existence" (Foucault, 1986, p. 350). But the idea that there might not be any "necessary link" does not mean that the constitution of the self as a moral subject of action can be considered free of social, economic, or political structures. Foucault's own references to cultural practices which are proposed, suggested, and imposed draw attention to, but neglect to analyze, the social context(s) in which forms of subjectivity are constituted and subjects participate, along with others, in processes of mutual self-development. While the formation of the self through social interaction is briefly acknowledged in Foucault's work – for example, reference is made to individuals transforming themselves through the help of others, and attention is drawn to the importance in the development of care for self of the role of a counsellor, guide, friend, master, "who will tell you the truth" (Foucault, 1987d, p. 118) – no attempt is made to elaborate on or to explore the complex relationships with others that are at the very heart of social life. The analyses outlined by Foucault in *The Use of Pleasure* (1987c), *The Care of the Self* (1988a), and associated texts and interviews introduced another "different line of inquiry in which the modes of relation to the self took precedence" (Foucault, 1986b, p. 338) and the decision to pursue an analysis of "forms of relation to the self" led to questions of ethics becoming an increasingly prominent feature of Foucault's final works (Smart, 1995).

THE PERSON

The idea that we need to know about the author to understand the intellectual *oeuvre* is one to which Foucault took exception. To be consistent with Foucault's viewpoint it would be more appropriate to subscribe to a line of aesthetic thought traceable to Mallarmé and the modernist movement in the arts, a line of thought which promoted the idea of the autonomy of the work (Eribon, 1992). However, while Foucault (1988d, p. 16) remarked that "my personal life is not at all interesting," many of those interested in his work have been curious about the life of the man.

Foucault grew up in Poitiers, in the French provinces, in the 1930s and 1940s. His family was traditional middle class and nominally Catholic. In 1945, Foucault went to Paris, to one of the most prestigious schools in France, the Lycée Henri-IV, to prepare for the entrance examinations to the École Normale Superieure (ENS), and it was at the Lycée that he first briefly encountered Jean Hyppolite, translator of Hegel's *Phenomenology*, who helped the class to prepare for their philosophy examination, and was introduced to the work of Georges Dumezil. These intellectual figures, along with George Canguilhem, were subsequently acknowledged by Foucault to have exercised a formative influence on his work. Foucault described his time at the ENS as "sometimes intolerable," and accounts of his arguments with fellow students, his attempt at suicide, and his difficulty coming to terms with his homosexuality provide an insight into the difficulties with which he had to cope while pursuing his interests in psychology, psychoanalysis, and psychiatry, and reading the works of Bataille, Blanchot, and Klossowski on "transgression" or the "limit experience." The intellectual environment in which Foucault studied was dominated by phenomenology. However, for the students who attended ENS with Foucault in the years 1946–50 it was the philosophy of Hegel, not Sartre, that was of central importance, and only after reading Hegel, and writing a dissertation on his phenomenology, did Foucault move on to the works of Marx, Heidegger, and Nietzsche. Reflecting on this period in an interview conducted in 1984, Foucault explains the "philosophical shock" of reading Heidegger and subsequently the work of Nietzsche, "the two authors I have read the most" (Foucault, 1988d, p. 250).

On receiving the *agrégation* in 1951 Foucault left the ENS for the Fondation Thiers, where he spent a year doing research before going on to teach at the University of Lille in 1952. In Lille Foucault wrote a book, *Maladie mentale et personnalité* (1954), and a long introductory essay to Ludwig Binswanger's *Le Rêve et l'existence* (1954). In 1955 he left France for Sweden, to escape the constraints of French social and cultural life and to try to find greater personal freedom. Working as a French instructor in the Department of Romance Studies at the University of Uppsala, Foucault was to find intellectual and personal disappointment. From Sweden Foucault moved in 1958 to the University of Warsaw and then to the Institut Français in Hamburg, before returning to France in 1960 with a text, *Folie et déraison: Histoire de la folie a l'âge classique*, which had been researched in France but written in exile. It was a text which constituted the principal thesis for the award to Foucault of the most prestigious French degree, a *doctorat d'état*, the text with which the *oeuvre* associated with the figure of Foucault really begins.

Foucault remained mobile, moving from the University of Clermont-Ferrand, where he taught psychology and philosophy (1960–6), to a philosophy post at the University of Tunis (1966–8), on very briefly, literally a matter of weeks, to the University of Nanterre, and from there to the University of Vincennes, to a tenured professorship in philosophy (1968–70), finally being appointed in 1970 to a chair in the History of Systems of Thought at the most prestigious institution in France, the Collège de France in Paris, where he remained until his death in 1984.

The Social and Intellectual Context

With a thinker as complex as Foucault the task of briefly outlining the social and intellectual contexts in which intellectual interests and affinities developed is daunting. Foucault's intellectual and personal journey from the provincial setting of Poitiers to cosmopolitan Paris, including detours to Uppsala, Warsaw, Hamburg, and Tunis, and periods spent in Brazil, Japan, Canada, and the United States, and in particular California, exposed him to a variety of different cultural practices and a multitude of experiences. Various "events" have been identified as having contributed in different ways to the development of the man and his work – growing up in an "old traditional society," coping with being a student in Paris, living and working in a number of other countries, returning to France in the wake of May 1968 and becoming a prominent figure in the redefinition and extension of the political, to encompass questions of madness, sexuality, imprisonment, and identity, and, of course, learning to live with a sexual orientation that for much of his life necessitated discretion, until his discovery that homosexuality "was an open and visible way of life and culture in New York and San Francisco" (Eribon, 1992, p. 315; see also Macey, 1993; Miller, 1993).

There are traces of many influences in Foucault's analyses, but moving away from the works of particular individuals, it might be argued, as he acknowledged on more than one occasion, that the broader intellectual context in which his thinking initially began to take shape, and in critical response to which his work from *Folie et déraison* (the heavily abridged English translation *Madness and Civilization* was published in 1965) onwards developed, was one which consisted of "Marxism, phenomenology, and existentialism" (Foucault, 1987a, p. 174; see also 1983b). This study, Foucault's first major work, has been argued to be "animated by a critique of Western reason that was not entirely at odds with the anti-scientism of Sartre and Merleau-Ponty" (Poster, 1984, p. 3). However, more significantly, the study presents a form of analysis in which a theoretical shift away from philosophies of consciousness and idealist notions of the subject begins to emerge. As Foucault later remarked, "in *Madness and Civilization* I was trying... to describe a locus of experience from the point of view of the history of thought" (Foucault, 1986, p. 336), not from the analytic perspective of existentialism. As such, the text anticipates, albeit at times tangentially, later analytic themes and developments in Foucault's work, including the productive effects of relations of power and the operation of "carceral institutions" (Gordon, 1990).

Existentialism and phenomenology represented only one part of the intellectual context in which Foucault's thinking initially developed; Marxism also exerted a powerful presence. Indeed, in the early 1950s Foucault was a member of the Communist Party, and he is reported to have said that at this time "Marxism as a doctrine made good sense to me" (Eribon, 1992, p. 52). Notwithstanding the influence exerted by Louis Althusser over Foucault, his relationship to Marxism was always somewhat marginal and indirect. When called upon to discuss his intellectual formation in general, and his relationship to Marxism and communism in particular, Foucault remarks that it was through Nietzche and Bataille, rather than Hegelian philosophy, that he found communism – "Thus it was that without knowing Marx very well, refusing Hegelianism, and feeling dissatisfied with the limitations of existentialism, I decided to join the French Communist Party. That was in 1950. A Nietzschean Communist!" (Foucault, 1991, p. 51). Within a very few years Foucault's "feeling of discomfort and uneasiness" with Communist Party political practices caused him to leave the party and immerse himself in his studies, but his name continued to be associated with that of Althusser, and for that matter other major French intellectual figures such as Lévi-Strauss and Lacan, through a wide-ranging theoretical debate over "structuralism" which took place in France during the 1960s.

As I have already noted, Foucault had a rather disparaging view of the notion of structuralism. While there is an admission that some of his earlier works, particularly *The Birth of the Clinic*, might at times have made too "frequent recourse to structural analysis" (Foucault, 1974, p. 16), Foucault generally sought to dissociate himself from structuralism and to question whether those accorded the status "structuralists" had anything more in common than a shared antipathy toward "the theory of the subject" (Foucault, 1991, p. 58). The reservations articulated by Foucault about the idea of structuralism, and the subsequent trajectory of his work, have been cited in support of his inclusion in two other, no less controversially constituted, intellectual formations, notably "poststructuralism" and "postmodernism." While Foucault clearly had reservations about structuralism, and sought to distance his own work from it, there is an acknowledgment that the works considered to exemplify such an approach do at least share a common interest in the question of the subject. In contrast, Foucault has remarked, "I do not understand what kind of problem is common to the people we call post-modern or post-structuralist" (Foucault, 1983b, p. 205). Despite such protestations, Foucault's work has been increasingly identified as "postmodern" (Hoy, 1988; Best and Kellner, 1991).

I have alluded above to merely one aspect of the political context in which the intellectual figure of Foucault was formed; clearly there are other significant features and events to which reference might be made. For example, in terms of historical events which had an impact on theory and politics in France, "May 1968" has assumed considerable significance. Foucault did not participate in the political struggles which took place on the university campuses and in the streets of France during May 1968, as he was working at the University of Tunis at the time, but he has acknowledged that the transformations induced in the intellectual and political climate had a decisive influence upon his work – "it is certain . . . that without May of '68, I would never have done the things I'm doing today: such investigations as those on the prison, sexuality, etc., would be unthinkable" (Foucault, 1991, p. 140). As well as making possible the study of particular practices and institutions, the events of May 1968 contributed to Foucault's thoughts on the changing status of the intellectual, and the possibility of "reaching a new kind of relationship, a new kind of collaboration between 'intellectuals' and 'non-intellectuals' that would be completely different from the past" (ibid., p. 142).

The question of intellectual activity, or practice, and the associated issue of the role of the intellectual, are explored in a number of Foucault's texts. In a discussion on intellectuals and power which took place in 1972, Foucault argued that the notion of the intellectual as a representative consciousness, as able to speak for others – "to place himself 'somewhat ahead and to the side' in order to express the stifled truth of the collectivity" – could no longer be convincingly sustained. In contrast, the appropriate task for the intellectual identified by Foucault is "to struggle against the forms of power that transform him into its object and instrument in the sphere of 'knowledge', 'truth', 'consciousness', and 'discourse'" (Foucault, 1977b, pp. 207–8). In consequence, the responsibility of the intellectual is no longer assumed to be the provision of knowledge for others, for they are already considered to "*know* perfectly well, without illusion" (Foucault, 1977a, p. 207); rather, the central objective is to challenge the prevailing regime of the production of truth which disqualifies local forms of knowledge as illegitimate (Foucault, 1980).

The conception of the intellectual that emerges from Foucault's intellectual practices and reflections is that of the critical interpreter, a conception which contrasts starkly with the universalizing, legislative ambitions of the modern intellectual. Foucault's conception of intellectual practice has presented great difficulty for readers accustomed to turning to the writings of intellectuals for solutions to social, cultural, and political problems. In Foucault's work it is not solutions or programmatic statements that one finds, but the identification of problems, literally "how and why certain things (behavior, phenomena, processes) became a *problem*" (Foucault, 1988b, p. 16). Throughout his work the emphasis tends to be placed on how and why particular forms of conduct came to be classified, analyzed, and treated, in short problematized, as, for example, "madness," "crime," "sexuality," and so on. In this way Foucault (1988c) sought to question and erode "self-evidentnesses and commonplaces," to contribute to the transformation of existing "ways of perceiving and doing things," and in turn to draw attention to the possibility of constituting new forms of subjectivity.

A critical stand on contemporary issues is taken in Foucault's work, but it is a stand that lays no claim to a universal immanent foundation, a stand that deliberately rejects the legislative ambitions of the universalizing intellectual role for a critical, interpretive, and more specific intellectual practice (Bove, 1980; Smart, 1986). It is a practice which effectively constitutes an "ethic for the intellectual" (Rajchman, 1985, p. 124), "an ethic of responsibility for the truth one speaks, for the political strategies into which these truths enter, and for those ways of relating to ourselves that make us either conformists or resisters to those relations. It is a timely ethic which assists in reclaiming thought's moral responsibilities" (Bernauer, 1992, p. 271), a critical practice which aims to open up new ways of thinking and being.

IMPACT

In a late reflection on his work Foucault comments that his earlier studies of "asylums, prisons, and so on" deal with "only one aspect of the art of governing people in our societies" (Foucault and Sennett, 1982, p. 10), and that analyses of the government of others need to be complemented by analyses of technologies of self-government. Evidence of the growing significance of a "problematic of government" as an organizing principle and prominent analytic theme can be found in a number of Foucault's later texts, and it is in relation to this broad concern that his work is continuing to have a major impact.

It has been argued that a concept of government occupies a pivotal place in the later Foucault for two reasons: "because it designates a continuity between the micro- and the macro-levels of political analysis, and because it spans the interface between the exercise of power and the exercise of liberty" (Gordon, 1987, p. 296). From the introductory volume on *The History of Sexuality*, where the problematic of government serves to "disarticulate or unde(te)rmine determinate notions of power" (Keenan, 1982, p. 36), Foucault proceeds to use the notion of government as a "guiding thread" in courses of study which address the "formation of a political 'governmentality'," notably liberalism as a governmental technology employed by a state administration to direct the conduct of men (Foucault, 1981a, b), and, turning away from the state and introducing a broader sense of the term, the different modes by which human beings are made subjects; that is, "government of individuals by their own verity" (Foucault, 1982a, p. 240). The problematic of government allows Foucault to avoid the equation of power with the "problematic of the king" and to place emphasis on the direction and guidance of human conduct.

More controversially, it has also been suggested by Colin Gordon that an analytic interest in rationalities of government is not confined to Foucault's later work alone and that there are "complex correlations and precedents" in the earlier "regional histories of normalizing practices," the argument being that institutions of internment analyzed in *Madness and Civilization* constitute an "instrument of a police art of government," and "Bentham's Panopticon, examined in *Discipline and Punish*, is a liberal theorem of political security" (Gordon 1987, pp. 297–8). In the later works analysis of relations of power becomes analytically a question of government, a question of the techniques, procedures, and rationales for guiding, directing, or structuring conduct. In this context government is not to be equated with an institution, or conflated with the state, it is an activity, the contact point "where the way individuals are driven by others is tied to the way they conduct themselves" (Foucault quoted in Keenan, 1982, p. 38). In the broadest of senses the problematic of government encompasses the government of "children, government of souls or of consciences, government of a home, of a State, or of oneself" (ibid., p. 37), and as such it makes possible analysis of the articulation in modern power structures of "individualization techniques, and of totalization procedures" (Foucault, 1982a, p. 213).

In so far as the problematic of government "could concern the relation between self and self, private interpersonal relations involving some form of control or guidance, relations within social institutions and communities and, finally, relations concerned with the exercise of political sovereignty" (Gordon, 1991, pp. 2–3), it has stimulated the development of a rich seam of Foucauldian analyses (Procacci, 1987; Miller and Rose, 1990; Burchell, 1991; Dean, 1992; and the work of *The History of the Present* research network). However, the influence Foucault's work has exercised on contemporary social thought extends beyond the theme of governmental rationality to encompass a wide range of concerns in a growing number of fields of inquiry. If philosophy and history constitute the fields of inquiry closest to Foucault's concerns, his influence nevertheless extends to many other fields, including in particular sociology, anthropology, literary and cultural studies, and feminism. Analysts working in such diverse fields as education, accountancy, architecture, and law have also found in Foucault's project the tools necessary for a series of innovatory studies: for example, on the significance of disciplinary technology in the development of "rational schooling" (Hoskin, 1979) and accounting practices (Hoskin and Macve, 1986); and the "rules of the game" associated with the structuring of space in modern society (Teyssot, 1980; see also Wright and Rabinow, 1982); as well as photography and electronic communications media as potential means of surveillance (Tagg, 1980; Poster, 1990, respectively).

ASSESSMENT

The impact of Foucault's work on contemporary social thought has already been substantial, and the legacy is still in the making. Whether in relation to social analyses of sexuality, the body and identity, concerns about relations of power, the place and status of intellectual activity in late modern societies, or questions of analytic method and perspective, the influence of Foucault's work continues to be very significant. Foucault sought to problematize, to provoke, to disturb the existing order of things, to challenge the prevailing regime of truth. Without doubt his diagnosis of our modern times has radically transformed the way in which we think about ourselves and our way of life, and it has done so to an extent which bears comparison with the influence exerted by the classical founding figures of modern social thought. Whether future generations will continue to read Foucault and find his analytic tools of value in their attempts to critically understand the history of their present only time will tell, but as one analyst has remarked, "it is difficult to envisage Foucault's work losing its provocation, irrespective of changing critical modes or of the inevitable attempts to institutionalize it" (Bernstein, 1984, p. 15).

Bibliography

Writings of Michel Foucault

Madness and Civilization. A History of Insanity in the Age of Reason. 1965. New York: Random House.

The Order of Things: an Archaeology of the Human Sciences. New York: Random House.

Orders of Discourse. 1971 *Social Science Information*, 10(2).

The Birth of the Clinic: an Archaeology of Medical Perception. 1973. London: Tavistock.

The Archaeology of Knowledge. 1974. London: Tavistock.

Language, Counter-memory, Practice: Selected Essays and Interviews, edited by D. F. Bouchard. 1977a. Oxford: Blackwell.

Discipline and Punish: the Birth of the Prison. 1977b. London: Allen Lane.

The History of Sexuality. Volume 1, An Introduction. 1979a. London: Allen Lane.

On Governmentality. 1979b. *Ideology and Consciousness*, 6.

Power/Knowledge: Selected Interviews and Other Writings 1972–1977, edited by C. Gordon. 1980. Brighton: Harvester Press.

At the Collège de France (i): a Course Summary, translated with an introduction by James Bernauer. 1981a. *Philosophy and Social Criticism*, 8(2).

At the Collège de France (ii): a Course Summary, translated with an introduction by James Bernauer. 1981b. *Philosophy and Social Criticism*, 8(3).

Omnes et Singulatim. In S. M. McMurrin (ed.), *The Tanner Lectures on Human Values, volume 2.* 1981c. London: Cambridge University Press.

The Subject and Power. 1982a. In H. L. Dreyfus and P. Rabinow, *Michel Foucault: Beyond Structuralism and Hermeneutics.* Brighton: Harvester Press.

Space, Knowledge and Power: Interview. 1982b. *Skyline*, March.

Sexuality and Solitude (with R. Sennett). 1982. In *Humanities in Review, volume 1.* Cambridge: Cambridge University Press.

This Is Not a Pipe. 1983a. Berkeley: University of California Press.

Structuralism and Post-structuralism: an Interview with Gerard Raulet, *Telos*, 55, 195–211.

The Foucault Reader, edited by P. Rabinow. 1986. Harmondsworth: Penguin.

Death and the Labyrinth – the World of Raymond Roussel. 1987a. London: The Athlone Press.

Foucault/Blanchot. Maurice Blanchot: the Thought from Outside. 1987b. New York: Zone Books.

The Use of Pleasure. The History of Sexuality, volume 2. 1987c. London: Penguin.

The Ethic of Care for the Self as a Practice of Freedom – an Interview. 1987d. *Philosophy and Social Criticism*, 12(2/3), 112–31.

The Care of the Self. The History of Sexuality, volume 3. 1988a. London: Allen Lane.

On Problematization. 1988b. *History of the Present*, 4.

Questions of Method: an Interview. 1988c. In K. Baynes et al. (eds), *After Philosophy: End or Transformation?* Cambridge, MA: MIT Press.

Michel Foucault – Politics, Philosophy, Culture. Interviews and Other Writings 1977–1984, edited by L. D. Kritzman. 1988d. London: Routledge

(Auto)biography Michel Foucault 1926–1984 (written under the name Maurice Florence). 1988. *History of the Present*, 4.

Remarks on Marx – Conversations with Duccio Trombadori. 1991. New York: Semiotext(e).

Further reading

Bernauer, J. (1992) Beyond Life and Death: on Foucault's Post-Auschwitz Ethic. In T. J. Armstrong (ed.), *Michel Foucault Philosopher*. London: Harvester Wheatsheaf.

Bernstein, M. A. (1984) Street-Foucault. *University Publishing*, Summer.

Best, S. and Kellner, D. (1991) *Postmodern Theory – Critical Interrogations*. London: Macmillan.

Bové, P. (1980) The End of Humanism: Michel Foucault and the Power of Disciplines. *Humanities in Society*, 3, 23–40.

Burchell, G. (1991) Peculiar Interests: Civil Society and Governing "The System of Natural Liberty." In G. Burchill, C. Gordon, and P. Miller (eds), *The Foucault Effect – Studies in Governmentality*. London: Harvester Wheatsheaf.

Dean, M. (1992) A Genealogy of the Government of Poverty. *Economy and Society*, 21(3).

Dean, M. (1994) *Critical and Effective Histories – Foucault's Methods and Historical Sociology*. London: Routledge.

Dews, P. (1984) Power and Subjectivity in Foucault. *New Left Review*, 144.

Dews, P. (1989) The Return of the Subject in Late Foucault. *Radical Philosophy*, 51, 37–41.

Dreyfus, H. L. and Rabinow, P. (1982) *Michel Foucault: Beyond Structuralism and Hermeneutics*. Brighton: Harvester Press.

Eribon, D. (1992) *Michel Foucault*. London: Faber and Faber.

Gordon, C. (1987) The Soul of the Citizen: Max Weber and Michel Foucault on Rationality and Government. In S. Whimster and S. Lash (eds), *Max Weber, Rationality and Modernity*. London: Allen and Unwin.

Gordon, C. (1990) *Histoire de la folie*: an unknown book by Michel Foucault. *History of the Human Sciences*, 3(1), 3–26.

Gordon, C. (1991) Governmental Rationality: an Introduction. In G. Burchell, C. Gordon, and P. Miller (eds), *The Foucault Effect – Studies in Governmentality*. London: Harvester Wheatsheaf.

Habermas J. (1986) *Jürgen Habermas Autonomy and Solidarity Interviews*, edited by P. Dews. London: Verso.

Habermas, J. (1987) *The Philosophical Discourse of Modernity*. Cambridge: Polity Press.

Hoskin, K. (1979) The Examination, Disciplinary Power and Rational Schooling. *History of Education*, 8(2).
Hoskin, K. W. and Macve, R. H. (1986) Accounting and the Examination: a Genealogy of Disciplinary Power. *Accounting, Organizations and Society*, 11(2).
Hoy, D. C. (1981) Power, Repression, Progress: Foucault, Lukes and the Frankfurt School. *Tri Quarterly*, 52, 43–63.
Hoy, D. C. (1988) Foucault: Modern or Postmodern? In J. Arac (ed.), *After Foucault – Humanistic Knowledge, Postmodern Challenges*. New Brunswick, NJ: Rutgers University Press.
Huyssen, A. (1984) Mapping the Postmodern. *New German Critique*, 33.
Ingram, D. (1986) Foucault and the Frankfurt School: a Discourse on Nietzsche, Power and Knowledge. *Praxis International*, 6(3), 311–27.
Keenan, T. (1982) Foucault on Government. Translator's Afterword to Is It Really Important to Think? An Interview with Michel Foucault. *Philosophy and Social Criticism*, 9(1), 29–40.
Macey, D. (1993) *The Lives of Michel Foucault – a Biography*. New York: Pantheon Books.
Miller, J. (1993) *The Passion of Michel Foucault*. New York: Simon & Schuster.
Miller, P. and Rose, N. (1990) Governing Economic Life. *Economy and Society*, 19(1).
Patton, P. (1989) Taylor and Foucault on Power and Freedom. *Political Studies*, 37, 260–76.
Poster, M. (1984) *Foucault, Marxism and History: Mode of Production versus Mode of Information*. Cambridge: Polity Press.
Poster, M. (1990) Foucault and Databases: Participatory Surveillance. In *The Mode of Information: Poststructuralism and Social Context*. Cambridge: Polity Press.
Procacci, G. (1987) Notes on the Government of the Social. *History of the Present*, 3 (Fall).
Rajchman, J. (1985) *Michel Foucault: the Freedom of Philosophy*. New York: Columbia University Press.
Smart, B. (1986) The Politics of Truth and the Problem of Hegemony. In D. C. Hoy (ed.), *Foucault: a Critical Reader*. Oxford: Blackwell.
Smart, B. (1995) The Subject of Responsibility. *Philosophy and Social Criticism*, 21(4).
Stone, L. (1983) Comment on *Madness*. *New York Review of Books*, March 31, 42–4.
Tagg, J. (1980) Power and Photography – a Means of Surveillance: the Photograph as Evidence in Law. *Screen Education*, 36.
Taylor, C. (1984) Foucault on Freedom and Truth. *Political Theory*, 12(2), 152–83.
Teyssot, G. (1980) Heterotopias and the History of Spaces. *Architecture and Urbanism*, 121.
Weber, M. (1970) *From Max Weber: Essays in Sociology*, edited by H. H. Gerth and C. Wright Mills. London: Routledge & Kegan Paul.
White, H. (1973) Foucault Decoded: Notes from Underground. *History and Theory*, 12, 23–54.
Wright, G. and Rabinow, P. (1982) Spatialization of Power: a Discussion of the Work of Michel Foucault. *Skyline*, March 18.

9

Jürgen Habermas

William Outhwaite

Jürgen Habermas, who retired in 1994 from his post as Professor of Philosophy and Sociology at the University of Frankfurt, is the leading representative of the second generation of the neo-Marxist critical theorists often known as the "Frankfurt School" (see Jay, 1973; Bottomore, 1984; Wiggershaus, 1987). Habermas, who studied under Theodor Adorno and Max Horkheimer after their return to Frankfurt from exile in the USA, differs from them in some crucial ways. Like them, he rejected Marxist philosophies of history, in which an account of the development of capitalism and of the rise of the working class is taken to show that the collapse of capitalism and its replacement by socialism are inevitable, or at least extremely probable. Yet he also felt that Adorno and Horkheimer had painted themselves into a pessimistic corner, from which they could only criticize reality, without offering any alternative. Habermas has argued instead throughout his intellectual career for a return to interdisciplinary critical social science of the kind practiced before the Second World War in Horkheimer's Institute of Social Research.

Habermas's mature theory, as he has developed it from the early 1970s, can best be understood as what he would call a "reconstruction" of what is presupposed and implied by human communication, cooperation, and debate. In terms of orthodox academic disciplines, there is a theory of communication (linguistics), a theory of communicative action (sociology), and a theory (both descriptive and normative) of morality, politics (including political communication), and law. At the back of all this are substantial elements of a philosophy of science (including, though not confined to, a critique of positivistic social science) and an account of the development of human societies, and in particular of Western modernity, which culminates in a diagnosis of what he sees as the central political problems confronting the advanced capitalist democracies and the world as a whole.

The Theory

The centerpiece of Habermas's developed theorizing is a theory of communicative action grounded in the analysis of linguistic communication. His basic idea is that any serious use of language to make claims about the world, as opposed, for example, to exclamations or the issuing of orders, presupposes the claims that what we say makes sense and is true, that we are sincere in saying it, and that we have the right to say it. These presuppositions can be questioned by our hearers or readers. As Habermas (1981, volume 1, p. 306) shows with the example of a professor asking a seminar participant to fetch a glass of water, even a simple request, understood not as a mere demand but "as a speech act carried out in an attitude oriented to understanding," raises claims to normative rightness, subjective sincerity, and factual practicability which may be questioned. The addressee of the request may reject it as illegitimate ("I'm not your servant"), insincere ("You don't really want one"), or mistaken about the facts of the matter (availability of a source of water).

Only a rational agreement which excluded no one and no relevant evidence or argument would provide, in the last resort, a justification of the claims we routinely make and presuppose in our assertions. This idea gives us, Habermas claims, a theory of truth, anticipated by the American pragmatist philosopher C. S. Peirce, as what we would ultimately come to rationally agree about (Habermas, 1984, p. 107). Moreover, if Habermas is right that moral judgments also have cognitive content and are not mere expressions of taste or disguised prescriptions, it also provides a theory of truth for issues of morality and of legitimate political authority. Moral norms are justified if they are what we would still uphold at the end of an ideal process of argumentation. "When I state that one norm should be preferred to another, I aim precisely to exclude the aspect of arbitrariness: rightness and truth come together in that both claims can only be vindicated discursively, by way of argumentation and a rational consensus" (Habermas, 1984, p. 109). This consensus is of course an idealization; Habermas at one time described it as resulting from what he called an "ideal speech situation." Yet it is counterfactually presupposed, he argues, by our everyday practice of communication, which is made meaningful by the real or hypothetical prospect of ultimate agreement.

The analysis of language-use can thus, Habermas believes, be expanded into a broader theory of communicative action, defined as action oriented by and toward mutual agreement. In social-theoretical terms, this can be contrasted with the models of instrumental or strategic, self-interested action (the model of *Homo economicus* which also largely dominates rational choice theory), normatively regulated action (the model, familiar from functionalism, in which we orient our action to a shared value system), or dramaturgical action, in which our actions are analyzed as a performance, designed to optimize our public image or self-image (Goffman, Garfinkel and others). All these types of action, Habermas claims, can be shown to be parasitic upon communicative action, which incorporates and goes beyond each of them (Habermas, 1981, volume 1, pp. 82–101). The theory of communicative action, then, underpins a communication theory of morality, law, and democracy, and it is these aspects which have dominated Habermas's most recent work.

One of Habermas's best known books is a short and highly compressed text called in English *Legitimation Crisis* (Habermas, 1973a). Here, and in related essays, published in English under the title *Communication and the Evolution of Society* (Habermas, 1976a), he advanced a neo-Marxist theory of historical development and a critique of contemporary advanced or "late" capitalism. Habermas argued that historical materialist explanations of the development of the productive forces needed to be augmented by an account of the evolution of normative structures, understood in a wide sense to include, for example, family forms. In late capitalism, again, a traditional Marxist account of capitalist crisis which focuses on the economic contradictions of the capitalist system needs to be modified to account for the role of the modern interventionist welfare state and the resultant displacement of crisis tendencies from the economic sphere to the political and cultural domains. Instead of the economic crises which remain the fundamental problem, what we experience are incoherent state responses, leading to what Habermas calls rationality crises which weaken state legitimacy; these state interventions also lead to an erosion of individual motivation and a loss of meaning.

In Habermas's subsequent work, grounded in his theory of communicative action, he worked out in more detail both the historical thesis and the diagnosis of contemporary capitalist crises. *The Theory of Communicative Action* (1981) traces the conflict between the rationalization of world views in early modernity, expressed, for example, in secularization and formal law and in the erosion of appeals to traditional authority, and, on the other hand, the restriction of this newly attained sphere, open in principle to rational debate, as market and bureaucratic structures come to dominate the modern world.

Thus, where Max Weber had seen a single, however diverse, rationalization process working its way through economic, political, legal, and religious structures and world views, Habermas stresses the distinction between two kinds of rationalization process. He borrows and modifies the phenomenological philosopher Edmund Husserl's concept of the "lifeworld," the world as it immediately presents itself to us prior to philosophical or scientific analysis. For Habermas, the lifeworld is less a purely cognitive horizon than an environment made up both of attitudes and of practices – a realm of informal culturally grounded understandings and mutual accommodations. In modernity, the systematization of world views and the development of formal reasoning in the law and other spheres involves a rationalization of the lifeworld; the autonomous development of markets and bureaucratic systems represents what he calls its colonization (Habermas, 1981, volume 2, p. 196). In other words, no sooner are human social arrangements opened up to rational discussion with a view to their modification than they are rigidified into the autonomous subsystems analyzed but not criticized by sociological systems theory. In Habermas's model, the "uncoupling" of autonomous market and administrative systems means that the lifeworld becomes "one subsystem among others."

As Max Weber realized, these subsystems become like machines, running independently of their original sources in the moral and political structures of the lifeworld: "economic and bureaucratic spheres emerge in which social relations are regulated only by money and power" (Habermas, 1981, volume 2, p. 154).

Habermas's reconstructive theory of communicative action includes an account of the changing institutional forms which it takes in Europe and North America from around the eighteenth century. This is a two-sided process. On the one hand, more and more areas of social life are prised out of traditional contexts and subjected to rational examination and argument. On the other hand, the expansion of markets and administrative structures leads to what Habermas calls the colonization or hollowing-out of the lifeworld by autonomous subsystems which are removed from rational evaluation, except within their own highly circumscribed terms. Examples of this process can be found in the attempts by welfare state systems to extend legal regulation and monetary calculation right into the private sphere, at the cost of those traces of solidarity which remain; and solidarity, Habermas insists, is a resource which cannot be bought or constrained. More broadly, the differentiation, whose analysis goes back to Kant, of what he calls the "value-spheres" of science, morality, and art facilitates their individual development, but at the cost of their estrangement from each other and from culture as a whole.

Habermas thus follows the tradition of analysis developed by Marx in his theory of alienation, by Max Weber in terms of rationalization and disenchantment (*Entzauberung*), and in György Lukács's concept of reification (*Verdinglichung*). In the early Critical Theorists' critique of instrumental rationality as something inevitably linked to domination, all these motifs come together (Habermas, 1981, volume 1, p. 144). In Habermas's view, however, all these models are insufficiently complex. Marx focuses too one-sidedly on the rationalization of the forces and relations of material production; Max Weber sees societal rationalization too narrowly in terms of patterns of individual purposive-rational action. One needs instead to differentiate between "the rationalization of action orientations and lifeworld structures" and "the expansion of the 'rationality', that is, complexity of action systems" (Habermas, 1981, volume 1, p. 145). Habermas addresses, in other words, the big question of whether we could have had, or can now have, modernity without the less attractive features of capitalism and the bureaucratic nation-state. More tentatively, in *Between Facts and Norms* (1992b) and in more recent volumes of essays, he has begun to reformulate elements of his model of advanced capitalist crisis in the language of his more recent theories (Habermas, 1992b, pp. 384–7).

I have focused in this brief discussion on the theoretical model which Habermas developed from the mid-1970s. His earlier work, however, which he now tends to treat somewhat dismissively, also remains in my view of enormous richness and importance. This is particularly true of *Knowledge and Human Interests* (1968b), which I briefly discuss below, but also of much of the rest of his extremely creative oeuvre (see Müller-Doohm, 2000). In some ways, indeed, his most recent work on the state and the public sphere returns, as Habermas has noted himself, to concerns which he had addressed at the beginning of his career and which continue to be central to his thinking.

If Habermas had a single target of attack in his early work, it might best be termed technocratic politics. This he attacked from two directions. One was his influential analysis of the rise and fall of the bourgeois public sphere (Habermas, 1962). The partially realized ideal of independent discussion and rational critique of public affairs which developed in the eighteenth century in Europe and North America mutated in the twentieth century, Habermas argued, into a conception of public opinion as something to be measured and manipulated. These operations in turn relied heavily on an ideology and practice of positivistic social science which Habermas (1963, 1968b) subjected to a philosophical and historical critique; this critique finally underpinned his conception of critical social theory oriented to the critique of ideology.

What might form the basis of this model of critical social science? Habermas (1963) was initially attracted by the idea of conceiving it as an empirically oriented and falsifiable philosophy of history with an emancipatory purpose. He then defined it in more methodological terms as a project combining causal explanation and hermeneutic understanding – a model based on his reading of Freudian psychoanalysis as involving, in essence, the removal of causal obstacles to self-understanding and thus resulting in the patient's liberation from avoidable constraints (Habermas, 1968b). Once we know the real reason, for example, why we are afraid of spiders which we know to be harmless, we are on the way to overcoming our fear. The same sort of model, Habermas argued, underlay the Marxist critique of ideology: once we understand why capitalism appears, misleadingly, as a just system based on agreement and contract, and is presented as such by bourgeois political economy, the way is open to a more accurate and empowering understanding of it as an avoidable system of social exploitation. In other words, Freudian and Marxian thought can be understood as paradigms of critical social science, oriented by and to an interest in emancipation.

Habermas (1973b) then came to feel that the trichotomy of empirical, hermeneutic, and critical sciences was too simplistic, especially in that reflection in the philosophical sense did not necessarily mean emancipation in practice. The truth, in other words, does not necessarily make us free, in the absence of other conditions. And some of the best historical sociology, for example, although it may aid reflection in the first sense, does not really fit Habermas's model of emancipatory science. In place of this model, he developed in the 1970s a more modest account of reconstructive science, exemplified, as noted earlier, by his emergent theory of communicative action and his theory of discourse ethics.

Just as some linguistic theories reconstruct in formal terms our competence as speakers, the theory of communicative action provides a theoretical reconstruction of a practice in which we regularly engage, whether or not we reflect explicitly and theoretically on it. As he put it in an interview (Habermas, 1991a, p. 111), he does not

> say that people *want* to act communicatively, but that *they have to*.... When parents bring up their children, when the living generations appropriate the transmitted wisdom of preceding generations, when individuals and groups cooperate, that is, get along with one another without the costly recourse to violence, they all have to act communicatively. There are elementary social functions that can only be satisfied by means of communicative action.

As we saw above, Habermas (1981) outlined this model in reference both to the traditions of social theory and to the history of Western modernity. He draws in particular on George Herbert Mead's analysis of self–other relations in interaction, and Durkheim's theorization of intersubjectivity and social solidarity in relation to the secularization of religion, what Habermas calls the "linguistification of the sacred," to illustrate some of the social theoretical roots of his own model of communicative action. Habermas goes on to show how Max Weber, who, in *The Protestant Ethic and the Spirit of Capitalism* and in his work as a whole, described the rationalization of the lifeworld in early modernity, also offered an account, complementary to that of Marx, of the reconfinement of human beings in an increasingly rigid and bureaucratized world. As Habermas shows, systematizing the central theme of Western Marxism expressed in Lukács's concept of reification, markets and bureaucratic power relations combine, in varying configurations, to reduce individuals' freedom to act both as individuals and collectively. This means, incidentally, that the postmodern critique of modernity is fundamentally misconceived, since it takes as essential to modernity features found in the capitalist form which it took, but logically separable from it. The task of critical theory, then, is to explore alternative historical and present-day possibilities (Habermas, 1981, volume 2, pp. 374–403).

Shortly after the publication of *The Theory of Communicative Action*, Habermas returned in his writing to the theme of morality which had concerned him in his theory of social evolution and to systematize the ethical principles which underlay that historical model. The American developmental psychologist Lawrence Kohlberg had traced the advance of children's moral reasoning to what Habermas called a post-conventional stage, at which the question of the validity of (often conflicting) moral principles is explicitly addressed. At this point, Habermas argues, ordinary moral reasoning overlaps with philosophical ethics, and this is the situation whch confronts us in the contemporary world, in which, as Max Weber put it, mutually opposed "gods and demons" compete for our allegiance. But where Weber leaves us impaled on the existential dilemmas with nothing to guide us except the imperative to choose in an authentic manner, Habermas insists that one can give compelling reasons in moral argumentation, just as one can in matters of fact.

Once again, it is an ideally informed consensus which would conclusively underwrite, and the more or less conscious pursuit of such a consensus which in practice underwrites, our judgments about justice and, to some extent, even our conceptions of the good. Post-conventional moral reasoning is inevitably a matter of dialogue or discourse, in which principles are justified if they can or could find, for the moment at least, the assent of all those who are or might be affected by them. More formally, according to the principle which Habermas labels U, a norm is morally right if "*All* affected can accept the consequences and the side effects its *general* observance can be anticipated to have for the satisfaction of *everyone's* interests (and these consequences are preferred to those of known alternatives)" (Habermas, 1983, p. 65).

There are strong echoes here, of course, of the Kantian notion of the universalizability of moral judgments, and of John Rawls's modified utilitarian theory of justice, in which inequalities are justified if they are to the benefit of the worst off, but in Habermas's model we also have to choose between alternative bases of moral judgment as well as between alternative applications of them. The same goes, Habermas argues, for the legal principles which abut onto moral ones. Precisely because there are substantial disagreements between alternative legal principles as well as over their interpretation, only the dialogue institutionalized in a functioning democratic state can legitimate the choice between these principles. Habermas's moral universalism is not, then, the arrogant gesture which it sometimes appears to be in the accounts of postmodern or antifoundationalist critics. It is, rather, intended as the only possible response to a situation of radical diversity of views and in which it is practically essential to be able to offer universalistic defenses of fundamental principles: "the concrete, particular moralities rooted in specific forms of life are only acceptable today if they have a universalistic kernel. For they must if it comes down to it (*im Ernstfall*) be able to prevent something like the Shoah happening again. Otherwise they are worth nothing and cannot be justified" (Dews, 1992, p. 226).

At the same time, however, it is not clear how *much* discussion a discourse ethics commits us to, nor how this might best be institutionalized. Communicative action, Habermas insists, is not the same as argumentation; the latter term denotes specific forms of communication – "islands in the sea of praxis" – but the expansion of communicative action at the expense of more authoritarian traditions forms a necessary basis for argumentative discourse to become more widespread. As he put it in another recent work, "What seems to me essential to the degree of liberality of a society is the extent to which its patterns of socialization and its institutions, its political culture, and in general its identity-guaranteeing traditions and everyday practices express a noncoercive form of ethical life in which autonomous morality can be embodied and can take on concrete shape" (Habermas, 1991b, p. 171). Habermas points to the variety of forums in modern societies, ranging from academic symposia to TV debates and parliamentary assemblies, in which specific moral and ethical issues are argued out.

Discourse ethics does not offer, then, a practical solution to concrete moral or ethical issues, so much as a set of recommended practices within which such solutions may be pursued (Habermas, 1983, p. 103). In this of course it resembles democratic theory, which it has also complemented and enriched – notably in its contribution to the conception of deliberative democracy. This to some extent resolves the issue raised in Germany by Albrecht Wellmer and in the USA by a number of critics as to whether discourse ethics should be understood more in relation to politics and the public sphere than in relation to morality in a strict sense. His discourse ethic is, Habermas concedes, necessarily somewhat formal. It is based on a procedure, that of practical discourse, rather than specific ethical prescriptions (Habermas, 1983, p. 103). It draws a sharp distinction between questions of justice and questions of the "good life"; the latter can only be addressed in the context of diverse cultures or forms of life or of individual life-projects (Habermas, 1983, p. 108). On the other hand, a universalistic morality can bridge the division between morality and law, in that both are based, in varying ways, on a relation to discourse. In Habermas's most recent major book, *Between Facts and Norms*, he develops the implications of this model for a theory of law and the democratic state.

Readers of Habermas at the end of the 1980s who were wondering what might be the political implications of his sometimes rather rarefied discussion of moral theory were given an answer in the slogan with which he ended his Tanner Lectures (Habermas, 1988b, p. 279): "A legal system is autonomous only to the extent that the procedures institutionalized for legislation and legal decision guarantee a non-partisan formation of opinion and will and thereby give moral procedural rationality access, as it were, to law and politics. No autonomous law without realized democracy." What Habermas offers in more detail in *Between Facts and Norms* is a full-blown political theory of law and the democratic state. Although law and morality are distinct, both moral and legal norms depend implicitly on what Habermas calls the discourse principle, that those affected by them could agree to them as participants in a rational discourse (Habermas, 1992b, p. 107). Modified to fit the three contexts of morality, law, and political democracy, the intuition embodied in the discourse principle, which aims "to explain the point of view from which norms of action can be *impartially justified*" (Habermas, 1992b, pp. 108–9), underpins the structural relations between them.

Law, especially constitutional law, is crucial for Habermas's argument because it bridges the gap between moral reasoning on the one hand, which can only exhort and rebuke those who ignore it, and political decision-making on the other, which is always at risk of arbitrariness, even when it is democratically legitimated:

> In less complex societies, socially integrating force inheres in the ethos of a form of life, inasmuch as this integral ethical life binds all the components of the lifeworld together, attuning concrete duties to institutions and linking them with motivations. Under conditions of high complexity, moral contents can spread throughout a society along the channels of legal regulation. (Habermas, 1992b, p. 118)

For Habermas, of course, democracy does not simply mean universal suffrage and majority rule. Although, for example, he accepts the legitimacy of majority voting in a system necessarily operating under time constraints, he insists that procedural rules of this kind must themselves be discursively justified. Habermas is at least as much concerned for the extent and quality of public discussion of political issues as for the details of institutional arrangements. In other words, he has returned to issues of the public sphere and public opinion which were the object of one of his first studies, but now armed with a much more substantial normative and empirical theory of the state:

> The rational quality of political legislation does not depend only on how elected majorities and protected minorities work within the parliaments. It depends also on the level of participation and education, on the degrees of information and the precison with which controversial issues are articulated – in short, on the discursive character of non-institutionalized opinon formation in the political public sphere. (Habermas, 1992b, p. 570; cf. Habermas, 1988a, p. 249)

Anyone advancing a theory of the state in the contemporary world has of course to confront issues of globalization and what Habermas (1998a) has termed the "postnational constellation." While Habermas's formal model of the democratic constitutional state (*Rechtsstaat*) was cast very much in traditional nation-state terms, his more informal reflections in interviews and occasional articles have focused on the challenges to state sovereignty posed not simply by the fact of globalization but also by the normative intuitions captured by the notion of a global public opinion or global civil society and political concepts of "cosmopolitan democracy" or "world domestic politics." As Habermas notes in one of his most recent contributions to this topic, a crucial question is "whether political communities can construct a *collective identity* beyond the limits of a nation and thereby satisfy the legitimacy conditions of a postnational democracy" (Habermas, 1998a, p. 136). His tentative answer is that a European federal state, developing a sense of solidarity on the basis of a common European history, albeit one of tension and divison, may serve as a testing ground and a basis for more ambitious experiments in cosmopolitan democracy, just as Europe earlier pioneered a nation-state structure and in large part imposed it on the rest of the world. "Europe's second chance" (Habermas, 1996) should not of course take the form of neocolonial arrogance, but nor should it be missed in a "postcolonial regression into eurocentrism" (Habermas, 1998a, p. 9).

The Person

Born in 1929, Habermas grew up in the small town of Gummersbach, near Cologne, Germany. He studied philosophy, history, psychology, and German literature at Göttingen, Zurich, and Bonn, where he obtained his doctorate in 1954 with a thesis on Schelling. After some journalistic work he became, in 1956, Adorno's research assistant at the Institute of Social Research in Frankfurt, newly re-established in Germany and the base of what had come to be called the "Frankfurt School." Here he participated in an empirical study on the political awareness of students (Habermas et al., 1961). From 1959 to 1961 he worked on his *Structural Transformation of the Public Sphere* (1962). After a period as Professor of Philosophy at Heidelberg, Habermas returned to Frankfurt in 1964 as Professor of Philosophy and Sociology, where he delivered the inaugural lecture on "Knowledge and Interest" (reprinted in Habermas, 1968b). Also at this time he published the essays entitled *Theory and Practice* (1963), a survey work, *The Logic of the Social Sciences* (1967), and some further essays grouped under the title *Technology and Science as Ideology* (1968).

In 1971 Habermas left Frankfurt for Starnberg, Bavaria, to take up, along with the physicist C. F. von Weizsäcker, the directorship of the newly created Max Planck Institute for the Study of the Conditions of Life in the Scientific-Technical World. Surrounded by some of the most brilliant younger sociologists in the country, many of whom have since become major theorists in their own right, he began to develop the theme of communicative action, which had been present but not particularly prominent in his earlier work, into the centerpiece of his theorizing. He published an enormous amount of material, including the well known *Legitimation Crisis* (1973) and culminating with the *Theory of Communicative Action* (1981). In 1982, he returned to a chair in Philosophy and Sociology at Frankfurt, where he taught until his retirement in 1994.

In the 1980s and 1990s, Habermas developed the implications of his theory of communicative action in three broadly distinct domains. First, he advanced what is generally called a "discourse ethics" or, more precisely, a "discourse theory of morality," in *Moral Consciousness and Communicative Action* (1983), *Justification and Application* (1991), and a number of essays. Second, in the critical history of philosophy, his critique of poststructuralism in *The Philosophical Discourse of Modernity*, based on a series of lectures, was published in 1985, *Postmetaphysical Thinking* in 1988, and *Texte und Kontexte* in 1992. Third, he has developed his moral theory into a theory of politics, law, and the democratic state, with a series of lectures on "Law and Morality" delivered in 1986, *Between Facts and Norms* (1992), and the essays published as *The Inclusion of the Other* (1996).

The above constitute what Habermas considers his "theoretical" works, but he has also published seven volumes of political writings and, most recently, a further volume of political essays, *Die postnationale Konstellation* (1998). Thus his work in social theory is complemented by a volume of writing on contemporary social and political issues which is itself the subject of at least one book-length study (Holub, 1991). Like Max Weber in Imperial Germany, and Karl Jaspers in the early years of the Federal Republic, he has come to be in some sense the intellectual conscience of the country. Like Weber, he is basically a thinker rather than a man of action, but one who intervenes in political issues when something, as he often puts it, "irritates" him. And although he rejects Weber's doctrine of the value-freedom of science, he insists, like Weber, on the distinction between scholarly and political discourse (Dews, 1986, p. 127).

Habermas has been concerned in particular with three sets of issues, past, present, and future. In the past, or more particularly in current uses of the past, he has repeatedly intervened over issues of the responsibility of Germany and of individual Germans for the Third Reich and the Holocaust. One of his earliest essays was concerned with the philosopher Martin Heidegger's refusal in the 1950s to confront his past as an active Nazi (Habermas, 1953). More recently, in the late 1980s, he initiated what came to be called the Historians'

Dispute (*Historikerstreit*) with an attack on what he saw as a concerted attempt by the West German Right to whitewash the past by historicizing it, relativizing the crimes of the Nazis as one episode among others in a world-historical past which was inevitably often tragic. This "damage settlement" (Habermas, 1987) – a term taken from the insurance industry – was all in order to create a new, confident national consciousness. Most recently, Habermas has intervened in support of the young North American historian Daniel Goldhagen against virulent attacks in Germany on his controversial attempt to demonstrate how widespread was German complicity in the Holocaust.

Of contemporary events which attracted Habermas's active involvement, undoubtedly the most important were the student protests of 1968. Habermas participated very fully in this movement, and although he came to criticize its extremism and had no sympathy for the desperate terrorism which followed its demise, he welcomed its long-term effect in modernizing the political culture of of the Federal Republic. More recently, as noted above, he defended ths liberal and enlightened strand of West German thought against attempts to return to a new (conservative) "obscurity" (Habermas, 1985b). Finally, the reunification of Germany has led Habermas into extended reflections both on Germany itself and on the future of the European nation-state in general. He has been a critical supporter of the European integration process, which he sees as opening up a possible future for a "postnational" world.

The Social Context

As will be clear from the previous section, Habermas spent the whole of his academic career, with the exception of guest professorships in the USA and elsewhere, in his native country, and he has been crucially concerned with the question which the philosopher Karl Jaspers (1966) made into a book title: where is the Federal Republic going? More concretely, as a member of what has been called the "Hitler Youth generation," drawn as a child into complicity with the most appalling regime of modern times, he was horrified both by the crimes of the Third Reich and by the unwillingness of most of his compatriots to face up to their responsibility for what had happened. For a long time the Nazi period was a taboo subject in schools; major universities conveniently passed over it in their official histories, and the naming of a new university after a leading opponent and victim of Nazism was seen as deeply controversial. Even in communist East Germany, where the history of the Third Reich was at least given the prominence it deserved, issues of personal or collective responsibility were not seriously raised.

The German past is, then, one crucial aspect of the social context of Habermas's life and work. Another was of course something which was common to all the major Western European states in what were called the "thirty glorious years" from the late 1940s to the early 1970s: democratic welfare states, rising prosperity, and full employment. Habermas's response, notably in *Legitimation Crisis* (1973), was to reformulate Marxist crisis theory in a suggestive model of the displacement of crisis tendencies from the economic base to the political and cultural sphere. He had earlier taken up and reformulated the critique of "technocracy," which had been fashionable in the fifties and sixties, concerned to construct a socialist response to the technological determinism deriving from the work of Heidegger, Arnold Gehlen, and Helmut Schelsky. In this context, Habermas also looked into the changing nature of political participation, the public sphere, and civil society – the last of course crucially invigorated in the years around 1968 by "citizen" initiatives and new social movements (Habermas, 1963, 1968b).

Soon after the publication of *Legitimation Crisis*, of course, the age of full employment came to seem lost forever in the aftermath of the first oil price shock of 1973; the political climate shifted to the right, with the rise to power of Ronald Reagan, Margaret Thatcher, and, in West Germany, Helmut Kohl. German neoliberalism was a muted affair compared to that in the USA and UK, but the political background was a good deal nastier, with political terrorism sparking off a peculiarly violent backlash in the "German Autumn" of 1977 and the following years, in which respectable intellectuals were often accused of sympathizing with terrorists. Habermas, and close associates such as Albrecht Wellmer (in Habermas, 1987), attempted to restore some sense of proportion to public debate on these issues.

The Federal Republic, which had muddled through the 1980s more or less effectively under Helmut Kohl's calm and complacent reign as Federal Chancellor, was surprised in the autumn of 1989 by the collapse of its poor sister-state, the German Democratic Republic, along with the other Marxist-Leninist dictatorships in Europe. The "national question" ceased to be the preserve of historians and (mostly right-wing) publicists and rapidly moved to the top of the political agenda. As usual with really important agenda items, it was dealt with perfunctorily, in a technical-fix reunification which left all the important issues unresolved. Habermas (1990) was one of many German intellectuals who argued that a crucial opportunity had been missed to rethink the constitution of the Federal Republic, rather than simply incorporating what were delicately referred to as the "five new states" or the "accession territory." These issues now remain to be confronted, as Habermas rightly insists, on a European and global stage.

The Intellectual Context

Habermas's thinking emerges from the flexible and interdisciplinary Marxist tradition of what came to be called the "Frankfurt School" of critical theory, based in the early 1930s and again from 1950 in the Institute for Social Research in Frankfurt. As Habermas showed in detail in his *Theory of Communicative Action*, this tradition draws on both Marx and Max Weber, on another non-Marxist, Weber's contemporary Georg Simmel, and on the father of "Western Marxism" (Anderson, 1976), György Lukács. In an autobiographical interview, Habermas recalls reading Lukács for the first time with great excitement but with a sense that his work was no longer directly relevant to postwar societies such as Western Germany. His thinking remained shaped, however, by a Western Marxist agenda emphasizing not just issues of capital and class but the interplay between capitalist exploitation and bureaucratic state rule, and their implications for individual identity and collective political autonomy.

Habermas's relationship to Frankfurt critical theory was somewhat indirect in the early stages of his career. He diverged from the two key members of the Frankfurt School who had returned to Germany, Theodor Adorno and Max Horkheimer, whose interests had become increasingly philosophical, in insisting that a revival of critical theory had once again to engage fully with the social and human sciences. He fully shared, however, Adorno and Horkheimer's concern with the way in which enlightenment, in the form of instrumental rationality, turns from a means of liberation into a new source of enslavement. "Already at that time" (the late 1950s), he has written, "my problem was a theory of modernity, a theory of the pathology of modernity, from the viewpoint of the realization – the deformed realization – of reason in history" (Dews, 1992, p. 187). This involved a working-through of the classics: Marx and Weber, but also Kant, Fichte, and Hegel – and of course ancient Greek thought.

This theoretical emphasis was, however, constantly combined, as in his early volume of essays, *Theory and Practice*, with a concern for the conditions of rational political discussion in modern technocratic democracies. Only the social sciences, broadly conceived, could provide the means to construct a genuinely contemporary critical theory of advanced capitalism, but their own positivistic deformation was itself part of the problem to be overcome. Habermas joined in the "positivism dispute" of the early 1960s in which these issues were battled out in Germany (Adorno, 1966), and devoted the following decade to a detailed historical critique of positivist social science and the elaboration of an alternative model of "reconstructive" science, of which his own theory of communicative action is an example. In *Knowledge and Human Interests* (1968b), Habermas brilliantly showed how positivism had limited our understanding of the natural and the social world and undermined the possibility of critique; this could, however, be reconstructed from the work of Kant, Fichte, Hegel, and Marx and shown to inspire, for example, Freudian pychoanalytic theory and practice. "Critical" sciences such as psychoanalysis or the Marxist critique of ideology, governed by an emancipatory interest in overcoming causal obstacles to self-understanding, bridged the gap between the natural or empirical sciences, oriented to the prediction and control of objectified processes, and the human sciences, oriented to an expansion of mutual understanding.

Earlier critical theory had distinguished itself from more orthodox variants of Marxism by its intense engagement with non-Marxist thought after Marx. Rather than writing off phenomenology, existentialism, or Heidegger's philosophy as a symptom of capitalist crisis, Adorno devoted major studies to Kierkegaard and Husserl, and a substantial part of *Negative Dialectics* (Adorno, 1966) to a discussion of Heidegger. Similarly, though in a more methodological vein, Habermas worked out his own models of critical and reconstructive science – the former in an engagement with Schutzian phenomenological sociology,

Peter Winch's development of Wittgensteinian philosophy into social theory, and Gadamer's Heideggerian philosophical hermeneutics. These, Habermas argued, could be brought into a complementary relation with one another and could then be further augmented by a more materialist reflection on the way in which our understanding of the social world (the common theme of these three currents of thought) is systematically distorted by relations of power and exploitation. In the 1970s, as noted earlier, he developed an idea of reconstructive science, seen as a systematic attempt to isolate the conditions and implications of practices such as linguistic communication and moral reasoning. Here it is linguistic theories of speech pragmatics which provide the paradigm, and social theory the detailed illustration.

Finally, Habermas's discourse ethics has been substantially developed in relation to English-language ethical and political theory. His polemical exchanges with Gadamer and the system theorist Niklas Luhmann have become major documents in their own right. Against Gadamer, he argued that understanding needed to be supplemented by a materialist critique of power and exploitation, which he justified with an appeal to a notion of social theory contrasted with Luhmann's technocratic conception. Habermas has developed his thinking in close contact with others, notably the philosopher Karl-Otto Apel, whose intellectual trajectory in many ways parallels his own. He has also been exceptionally willing to engage with critical discussions of his own work and more recent developments in critical theory in the work of Axel Honneth, Seyla Benhabib, and others – thus giving practical expression to the theoretical and political importance which he attaches to communication and dialogue.

Impact

Habermas came to be recognized relatively early in West Germany as a major social theorist. His standing as a political commentator was helped perhaps by his prominent role in 1968 and the attacks he suffered from both sides of the barricades. Outside the country, he was slower to attract a substantial following, in milieux largely ignorant of the Frankfurt School tradition and its characteristic concerns and modes of approach. Even with the turn to social theory and more politicized social science in the UK in the early 1970s, Habermas was perhaps not Marxist enough for the orthodox, who tended to favor structuralist variants of Marxism, and too Marxist or "theoretical" for others. His impact in the UK and France, for example, came largely as a result of growing interest in his work in the more diverse and pluralistic intellectual milieu of the USA.

In the 1980s and 1990s, however, and despite the somewhat forbidding character of many of his books, his reputation in the English-speaking world grew rapidly. As noted above, Habermas's work has been influential in a whole range of fields, and has become one of the principal reference points for much discussion in social theory and, for example, moral philosophy, legal theory, and theories of international relations. Historians and theorists of culture have also increasingly been influenced by his conception of the public sphere and other elements of his thought (see Calhoun, 1992). Critical theory in the broadest sense has been carried on by contemporaries such as Albrecht Wellmer and a third generation of thinkers including Axel Honneth, Hans Joas, Thomas McCarthy, and Seyla Benhabib – all of whom, in different ways, have responded to issues posed by post-structuralist, postmodernist, and feminist theory, and shown how Habermas's approach can be usefully developed and extended. Habermas's concern with historical sociology and theorizing states and social movements has been carried forward by, for example, Claus Offe and Klaus Eder. In a more speculative vein, Ulrich Beck's influential analysis of modernity in terms of risk again owes a great deal to Habermas. Finally, his discourse ethics and his more recent theorizing about law and the state have attracted enormous interest in areas of analytic moral and legal philosophy previously untouched by Habermasian concerns. This is currently one of the most active areas of research, and to some extent practical ethical and legal argument, which draw directly on Habermas's work, and Habermas has himself been working very substantially in this field.

His opposition to post-structuralism and postmodernism and his occasional polemics with the French philosopher Jean-François Lyotard and others have marked out one of the systematic lines of division in contemporary social theory, concretized to some extent in positions taken in relation to the Enlightenment. For Habermas, this should essentially be seen as a project, incomplete and ambiguous in many ways but no less worthwhile than when it was first articulated in the seventeenth and eighteenth centuries. Thus, while he accepts some of what has been said by postmodernists and others about a certain rigidity in Enlightenment and, more broadly, liberal thinking – as indicated in the title of one of his recent volumes, "The Incorporation of the Other" (Habermas, 1996) – he remains committed to these values and to a universalistic mode of thought and argumentation: again not despite, but precisely because of, the enormous diversity of values and cognitive orientations found in modern societies.

The rise of social theory since the beginning of the 1970s, and more particularly in the 1990s, as a relatively distinct domain of activity and a source of inspiration to the social sciences as a whole, has also been due in considerable part to Habermas's work. He has always been hard to place in disciplinary terms, working on the borders of social theory and philosophy, and always willing to venture into new fields, such as the analysis of language or law, as required by the development of his own work. In short, he has made it possible both to see the contemporary world differently, and to rethink the relations between theories in the social sciences, which are at least one of our main resources in understanding this world.

Assessment

Will people still be reading Habermas at the end of the twenty-first century? My feeling is that they should be, for several reasons. First, and irrespective of the direction to be taken by social theory in the century which is just dawning,

10

Anthony Giddens

Christopher G. A. Bryant and David Jary

The British sociologist Anthony Giddens has established himself as a theorist of global stature in each of the three main phases of his work: first, as a major interpreter of the classical tradition and its successors; second, as the author of structuration theory, a very influential treatment of agency and structure in which primacy is granted to neither; third, as a commentator on late modernity and globalization.

To an extent equalled, if at all, only by Jürgen Habermas, Giddens's work is distinguished by its comprehensive critical appropriation and imaginative reworking of the main concepts and perspectives of classical and modern theorists. Central to his early and middle work is an incisive critique of functionalism, evolutionism, and historical materialism. His structuration theory has found countless applications throughout the social sciences. The breadth and flair of his coverage of historical and global issues is no less striking. Significantly, he takes issue with currently fashionable conceptions of postmodernity, advancing instead an account of radicalized modernity in which changes characterized as postmodern by recent theorists (including postempiricist epistemology) are treated as already implicit in modernity. Latterly, Giddens has explored the implications of changing conceptions of self-identity, and new sources of risk, in a globalizing society. He has also started to define a new "utopian-realist" politics beyond left and right, a venture attractive to Britain's new Labour government. His cascading arrays of concepts have long caught the attention of social scientists; his reflections on self, society, and politics in a global order are beginning to inform wider publics.

INTRODUCTION: A GLOBAL SOCIAL THEORIST

Giddens is remarkable for the number of his publications, including some thirty-two authored and edited books between 1971 and 1997 (which have been translated into twenty-two languages), and nearly two hundred articles, essays, and reviews in academic journals, books and symposia, and magazines and newspapers. He is also unusual for the scale and scope of his work on three different dimensions. The first of these has to do with substance. Giddens has written on most developments in the social sciences except research design and methods. He has written commentaries on most leading figures, both living and dead, and most schools and traditions of social thought; he has worked on the ontology of the social and the self and has articulated the structuration theory with which his name is now everywhere associated; he has written on class, class societies, and the state; he has paid great attention to features of our own age of late, or "high," modernity and globalization and to their theorization; he has recently taken up issues of self and self-identity; and he currently is helping to specify a politics beyond left and right. In short, he is a world-renowned, a truly global, social theorist – but he is also a participant in debates in areas of special interest throughout the social sciences.

The second dimension is one of level. Giddens's writings range from discussions of fundamental, often somewhat abstruse, metatheoretical problems – as in *New Rules of Sociological Method* (1976a), *Central Problems in Social Theory* (1979) and *The Constitution of Society* (1984) – to very direct and effective books for students. The third dimension pertains to disciplinary range. Giddens is a sociologist who has been interested in anthropology and psychology since his undergraduate days, and who has engaged with developments, and prompted responses from critics, in philosophy, history, geography, linguistics, all the social sciences, management, social work, and psychotherapy.

To all of these can now be added an increasingly visible contribution to public debate in Britain in support of the center-left, including *New Statesman* articles and media appearances.[1]

Giddens would figure in most sociologists' lists of the top ten sociologists in the world today. His reputation extends, however, far beyond sociology. He has been described as Britain's best known social scientist since Keynes, and is well placed to become one of its most influential, having moved from King's College, Cambridge, to the directorship of the London School of Economics just four months before the Labour Party's triumph at the general election of May 1, 1997 after eighteen years in opposition. The new Labour government is dedicated to the "modernization" of Britain and seeks a politics of the "radical center." Quite what these might mean is still being debated and Tony Giddens is pleased to be one of the debaters outside government, but close to it, who is increasingly heard. Others close to the new government have joined the governors of the LSE. But though the *Sunday Times* (July 13, 1997) concluded "new Labour, new LSE," Giddens is anxious to stress that while he personally supports new Labour, the LSE as an institution does not, and must not, have any political alignment.

We will offer an overall comment on Giddens's *oeuvre* in due course but first it may be helpful to say something about his career to date.[2]

Giddens's Career

Anthony Giddens was born in 1938 in Edmonton, north London, the son of a clerk with London Transport. He was educated at a local grammar school, and then Hull University, where he read two nonschool subjects – sociology and psychology. At these he excelled, graduating with first-class honors in 1959. On graduation, he went to the London School of Economics, where he completed an MA thesis entitled "Sport and Society in Contemporary England." In 1961 he started as a lecturer in sociology at Leicester University. At Leicester he taught neither the second-year course in classical sociological theory (apart from three lectures on Simmel) – that was Ilya Neustadt's preserve – nor the third-year course on more recent developments in theory – this was given by Percy Cohen, whose *Modern Social Theory* (1968) is derived from it. Instead, he was primarily responsible for the third-year course in social psychology, in which he chose to link "social personality" to a number of other topics, including socialization, language, attitude formation, identity, institutions, and national character. In this and other courses, including lectures on Durkheim and suicide to a large first-year audience, he impressed not just with what he said but also with how he said it – with exceptional fluency and without notes. It was, it should also be emphasized, a significant time and place in which to make an impact. As T. H. Marshall (1982) and John Eldridge (1990) have each pointed out, Leicester in the late 1950s and the 1960s was one of the seedbeds of British sociology.

We do not wish to make too much of this early experience, but some features are worth noting. For a start, Giddens's version of sociology has always been open to developments in anthropology and psychology. Having been introduced to these in Hull, he found at Leicester a sociology department with an interest in developmental sociology and in-house teaching not only in anthropology but also in psychology. Indeed, it was through in-house psychology courses that Leicester sociology undergraduates first encountered Mead, Becker, and Goffman. Giddens also encountered a remarkable collection of teachers, including Norbert Elias – a key figure in the formation of the Leicester approach to sociology.[3]

Giddens mentioned to us in 1989 that he regarded all his work as one continuous project, which we have called "the making of structuration theory." In addition to their merits as commentary, Giddens's writings prior to *New Rules of Sociological Method* (1976a) have thus also to be seen as part of a larger venture, the critical appropriation of earlier traditions in order to secure a base upon which to build theoretical constructions of his own. Many of those with a special interest in, and respect for, the work of Elias argue that Giddens owes more to Elias in the conception and execution of this undertaking than he acknowledges (on Giddens and Elias, see Kilminster, 1991). Elias, after all, had developed a (con)figurational, or process, sociology which, like Giddens's later structuration theory, sought to overcome the dualism of agency and structure. In particular, Eric Dunning (1994), then and now a teacher at Leicester, has directly challenged our judgment (in Bryant and Jary, 1991) that we had no reason to question Giddens's claim that he never knew enough about Elias's (largely unpublished) work for it to have been a major intellectual influence. He did, however, attend Elias's first-year lecture course, which was organized around the theme of development, in 1961–2, the last time he gave it, and he did read volume 1 of the *The Civilizing Process* both in unpublished translation and later in German (Elias, 1939). Giddens, it should be noted, joined the University of Leicester in 1961 and left in 1969, but, such were their travels, in only four of those eight years were he and Elias in Leicester at the same time. Having said that, Giddens says how impressed he was by the personal example of Elias – the single-minded scholar willing to pursue a large-scale personal project, heedless of distractions, over very many years.

Dunning argues that ours is too individualistic an approach to influence. Elias was, he contends, the major contributant to a departmental culture which influenced Giddens more than he is able or willing to admit. As evidence for this claim, Dunning recalls the debates among the staff between the supporters of developmental sociology led by Elias and their opponents led by Cohen. The opponents supposed Elias to be "championing a regressive return to an old-fashioned and outmoded 'evolutionism' rather than arguing, as he was, for the synthesis of classical and modern themes, concepts and concern" (Dunning, 1994, p. 4). "To his credit," Dunning continues, Giddens "was one of those who grasped Elias's synthesizing aims." But, of itself, that does not indicate any particular debt to Elias. Indeed, Dunning effectively concedes as much with his next remark that, "while at Leicester, Giddens remained – by choice, I think – essentially an aloof outsider." Dunning thinks this helps to explain Giddens's inadequate grasp of Elias's work; we think it suggests that Giddens was his own man from the start.[4]

Giddens taught at Simon Fraser University, near Vancouver, in 1966–7. There he saw how difficult it was for a European Marxist head of department, Tom Bottomore, to cope with students whose radicalism far exceeded his own. In 1967–8 Giddens moved on to the University of California in Los Angeles. Southern California was, he says, a revelation. He tells how a trip to Venice Beach, where he encountered large numbers of strangely attired people engaged in unlikely pursuits, brought home to him how both European structural sociologies and the agenda of the European left had their limitations. Their preoccupations with class, authority, and political party offered little insight into the way of life of the hippies or the course of the anti-Vietnam War movement.

Southern California may have fired his imagination but Giddens would still seem to have felt obliged to take stock of European structural sociologies before moving on intellectually. His *Capitalism and Modern Social Theory* (1971a) and *The Class Structure of the Advanced Societies* (1973) precede the first book to address systematically questions of agency and the microfoundations of social order, *New Rules of Sociological Method* (1976a). Given the early North American experience, however, it is understandable not only that Giddens should, in due course, take up questions of agency, but also that he should eventually seek a politics *Beyond Left and Right* (1994a).

In 1969, Giddens left Leicester for a university lectureship at Cambridge and a fellowship at King's College. He belatedly acquired a doctorate in 1974 and eleven years later became the second holder of the chair of sociology. In 1986, he played a leading role in the establishment of the first new faculty at Cambridge for many decades, Social and Political Sciences, and was appointed its first dean. Giddens remained at Cambridge until 1996, but also made numerous visits to universities and other institutions all over the world. *The Consequences of Modernity* (1990a) originated in lectures given at Stanford University, California, in 1988, and he also greatly valued teaching at the University of California at Santa Barbara before and after the publication of the US edition of his textbook introduction to sociology (1989, 1991).

Between 1975 and 1978, Giddens was the editor for ten books published in the Hutchinson Sociology series, and between 1977 and 1989 he was the editor for over fifty books published in two series by Macmillan. Since 1978, he has been an editor of the journal *Theory and Society.* No doubt this experience stood him in good stead when in 1985 he joined with John Thompson and David Held to found Polity Press. Polity has since become one of the world's leading social science publishers, with well over three hundred titles currently in print, and Giddens has been directly involved with commissioning, editing, and promotion throughout, though, he admits, it is proving harder to keep this going while Director of the LSE.

Giddens's career developed interestingly in the 1990s. From 1989 he had three and a half years with a therapist. The experience deepened his interest in personal life and the emotions, and led to the discussions of the self, identity, love, and sexuality in *Modernity and Self-identity* (1991a) and *The Transformation of Intimacy* (1992b). He has told us how he came to make connections between his personal circumstances and developments in society and culture from the local to the global, and how he came to re-view the latter in light of the former.[5] Giddens's thinking on "dialogic democracy" (presented in *The Transformation of Intimacy* and *Beyond Left and Right*), for example, worked outwards from personal relations to global issues. He also says that therapy gave him the confidence to seek a public role for the first time. It was truly life-transforming; it persuaded him that he could make his future significantly different from his past.

This, then, is the context in which Giddens embarked on the new vein of writing on the human condition in an age of high modernity in the 1990s; increased his intervention in public debates via articles in the press, media appearances, and joint seminars with academics, journalists, politicians, etc.; and, in due course, sought a new job which would provide both a new challenge and an opportunity to promote the public value of social science, inform government, and influence opinion. He obtained the last with his appointment to the directorship of the London School of Economics. Ever the teacher, he has introduced at the LSE a weekly director's lecture (with attendances of up to a thousand students in its first year). It is too soon to say how successful Giddens's directorship will turn out to be, but he has already raised the media profile of the LSE as the place where the issues of the age are addressed and debated.

THREE PHASES IN THE MAKING OF STRUCTURATION THEORY

It is very generally accepted among sociologists and other social scientists that neither the holy trinity of Marx, Durkheim, and Weber, nor additions to the sainthood like Simmel, provided satisfactory ways of connecting micro- and macro-analysis or agency and structure. The same is generally said about subsequent developments, such as the structural-functionalism and the empirical, even empiricist, inquiry favored by the American mainstream from the 1930s onwards, and the variants of the interpretive tradition which were the principal alternative to the mainstream. The shortcomings of earlier ontologies of the social, and of the self, have thus invited correction, and from the 1970s onwards the numerous writers who have set out to supply it have generated a massive, protracted, and unconcluded debate (Bryant, 1995, chapter 3). It was in 1976, with the appearance of *New Rules of Sociological Method* (1976a) and "Functionalism: *après la lutte*" (1976b), that Giddens first offered his correction, "structuration theory." In terms of the breadth of the response he has generated in different disciplines and in different countries, Giddens is arguably the single most important figure in the whole debate.

Although structuration theory, as such, was only unveiled in 1976, it is possible to view Giddens's work prior to then as, in many ways, a preparation for it; and although its "summation" was published in 1984, in *The Constitution of Society*, it is possible to treat Giddens's work subsequent to then as, in many ways, a further development of it. Indeed, this is how Giddens himself presents it, notwithstanding the transformative consequences of therapy for his writings in the 1990s. It is thus feasible to identify three clear phases in Giddens's writing career. Each is a step in the making of structuration theory and in each works of a particular character predominate.

Exegesis and commentary

Before 1976, most of Giddens's writings offer critical commentary on a very wide range of writers, schools, and traditions. (The main exception is the work on suicide which extends beyond Durkheim and culminates in *The Sociology of Suicide* (1971b) and Giddens's revised theory of suicide (1977b).) The best known books in this phase are *Capitalism and Modern Social Theory: an Analysis of the Writings of Marx, Durkheim and Max Weber* (1971a) and *The Class Structure of the Advanced Societies* (1973). After publication of *New Rules of Sociological Method* (1976a), commentary is never Giddens's primary activity again – though commentaries continue to appear. He remains, it is generally agreed, a very knowledgeable, perceptive, and stimulating commentator.

In his engagement with the work of others, Giddens is, by his own admission, seeking to go beyond commentary to critical appropriation as a basis from which to develop a long-term project of his own – the making of structuration theory. In this he calls to mind the early Talcott Parsons (see Sica, 1991).

Structuration theory and the duality of structure

There is space here for only a brief account of some of the main features of the theory and an even briefer indication of some of the criticisms, developments and applications it has generated.

PRINCIPLES The second period, from 1976 to 1984, is dominated by intensive work on the elaboration of the principles of structuration theory. It opens with *New Rules* (1976a), includes *Central Problems in Social Theory* (1979), and reaches its climax in *The Constitution of Society* (1984). It involves a retreat from epistemology, on which Giddens had written penetratingly, and an engagement with ontology.

Giddens picked up the term "structuration" from (the French of) Piaget and Gurvitch, but his usage differs from theirs. With the objective of carrying social theory beyond classical conceptions, structuration theory makes critical appropriations from two main theoretical innovations in mid-twentieth-century sociology. On one front, Giddens engages with developments in action theory and social phenomenology. "The characteristic error of the philosophy of action," according to Giddens (1976a, p. 121), "is to treat the problem of 'production' only, thus not developing any concept of structural analysis at all," but he is able to take from action theories (especially from Schutz, Garfinkel, and the ethnomethodologists) conceptions of "methodical" or "practical" consciousness, which he then deploys against both Durkheim and Parsons. On another front, Giddens engages with the newer forms of structuralism, with their roots in linguistics, especially the work of Lévi-Strauss and Althusser. Although "the limitation of both structuralism and functionalism . . . is to regard 'reproduction' as a mechanical outcome, rather than as an active constituting process, accomplished by, and consisting in, the doings of active subjects" (ibid.), Giddens is able to derive from structuralism the notion of generative rules. Giddens's claims for the distinctiveness of structuration theory are illustrated in table 22.1.

Structuration theory attempts to supersede these deficiencies by showing how "social structures are both constituted by human agency, and yet at the same time are the very medium of this constitution" (ibid.), and by explaining how "structures are constituted through action, and reciprocally how action is constituted structurally (Giddens, 1976a, p. 161). This is what is meant by "duality of structure," the central concept in Giddens's structuration theory, and the means by which he seeks to avoid a dualism of agency and structure. It is also to conceive structures not "as simply placing constraints upon human agency, but as enabling" (ibid.), and to recognize, contrary to Foucault, the omnipresence of a dialectic of control whereby "the less powerful manage resources in such a way as to exert some control over the more powerful in established power relationships" (Giddens, 1984, p. 374).

Table 10.1 Modes of theorizing structure and agency

	Structuralist theories	*Voluntarist theories*	*Structuration theory*
Characterization of structure	Structures and cultures determine, shape, or heavily constrain.	Structures are the revisable products of free agents.	Structure is the medium and outcome of the conduct it recursively organizes.
Characterization of actors/agents	Actors' choices are illusory, marginal, and/or trivial. Actors are cultural dopes, the victims of circumstances or instruments of history.	Actors make real choices. Actors determine.	Actors are knowledgeable and competent agents who refexively monitor their action.

"To examine the structuration of a social system is to examine the modes whereby that system, through the application of generative rules and resources, is produced and reproduced in social interaction" (Giddens, 1976b, p. 353). Systems, for Giddens, refer to "the situated activities of human agents" (Giddens, 1984, p. 25) and "The patterning of social relations across time-space" (ibid., p. 377). They have an *actual* existence (or a real existence, in the economist's sense of real). Systems display structural properties but are not themselves structures. Structures, by contrast, refer to "systems of generative rules and resources" (Giddens, 1976a, p. 127), or, as Giddens later put it, to "rule-resource sets, implicated in the articulation of social systems" (Giddens, 1984, p. 377). They have only a *virtual* existence, "out of time and out of space" (Giddens, 1976a, p. 127). Structure only exists in the memory of knowledgeable agents and as instantiated in action.

Actors, for Giddens, are never cultural dopes, but knowledgeable and capable agents who reflexively monitor their action. In his stratification model of the actor or agent, Giddens distinguishes between the motivation of action which may be partly unconscious but is not necessarily so, the rationalization of action (agents' articulated reasons for action), and the reflexive monitoring of action (agents' knowledge of what they are doing). Rationalization always involves discursive consciousness, or verbalization; reflexive monitoring involves either or both of discursive consciousness and practical consciousness (unverbalized awareness). Giddens claims that many other theories have ignored practical consciousness, or what actors tacitly know but cannot put in words.

For Giddens, the structuring or "structuration" of social interaction, or social relations, across time and space always involves "three elements: the communication of meaning, the exercise of power, and the evaluative judgement of conduct" (Giddens, 1977c, p. 132) as represented in table 22.2. Taking the top line first, "Structure as signification involves semantic rules; as domination, unequally distributed resources; and as legitimation, moral or evaluative rules" (ibid., p. 133). Rules and resources are the properties of communities and collectivities; the modalities of the middle line have to do with the modes in which actors can draw upon rules and resources in the production of interaction.

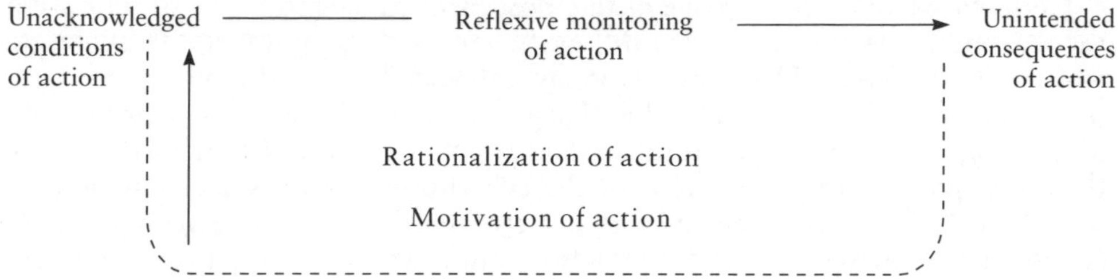

Figure 10.1 Stratification model of the agent and consciousness.
Source: Modification of combined figures from Giddens (1984, pp. 5 and 7), as in Bryant and Jary (1991, p. 9).

Table 10.2 Dimensions of the duality of structure

Structure	Signification	Domination	Legitimation
(Modality)	Interpretative scheme	Facility	Norm
Interaction	Communication	Power	Sanction

Source: Variation on Giddens (1976a, p. 122; 1979, p. 82; 1984, p. 29).

Table 10.3 Structures and institutional orders

S–D–L	Symbolic orders/modes of discourse
D(auth)–S–L	Political institutions
D(alloc)–S–L	Economic institutions
L–D–S	Legal institutions

S, signification; D, domination; L, legitimation.
Source: Giddens (1984, p. 32).

"'Interpretative schemes' are the modes of typification incorporated within actors' stocks of knowledge, applied reflexively in the sustaining of communication" (Giddens, 1984, p. 29). Facilities include command over people and resources, and norms include normative expectations of actors.

Rules, both semantic and moral, are the "techniques or generalizable procedures applied in the enactment/reproduction of social practices" (ibid., p. 21). Resources divide into allocative, or material, and authoritative, or nonmaterial; the former derive from dominion over things, the latter from dominion over people. Both are involved in the generation of power, the capacity to do; there is also, however, a dialectic of control, whereby the controlled, and not just the controllers, have an effect on the relation between them and the situation they share. "The most deeply embedded structural properties, implicated in the reproduction of societal totalities" (i.e groups, organizations, collectivities, societies), he calls "*structural principles*. Those practices which have the greatest time-space extension within such totalities can be referred to as *institutions*" (ibid., p. 17). Different institutional orders all involve signification, domination, and legitimation, but in different proportions, as table 22.3 shows.

Concern for time-space is one of the most distinctive features of structuration theory, and it has opened up fruitful exchanges with geographers. Drawing on sources as diverse as Heidegger, Lévi-Strauss and the *Annales* historians, Giddens demands that we avoid the sharp distinction between synchrony and diachrony favoured by structuralists and functionalists and that "we... grasp the time-space relations inherent in the constitution of all social interaction" (Giddens, 1979, p. 3). Time-space thus refers not to some framework, or set of coordinates, external to social interaction, but to the ways duration and extent enter into the constitution of social practices. Writing, for example, affords communication at a distance and over time, and clock timing affords the commodification of labor power.

CRITICISMS Layder (1994) has pointed out that what Giddens means by "structure" when he refers to the dualism of structure and agency which has bedeviled social science is the notion of pre-given objects or patterned realities. And what Giddens means by "structure" in the duality of structure which graces structuration theory are the rules and resources of the virtual order which are implicated in the reproduction of the actual order or social system. In other words, his resolution of the dualism of agency and structure works by discarding structure as conventionally understood by social scientists and substituting something quite different.

In 1982, Archer complained that structuration theory is unhelpful when trying to account for variations in degrees of voluntarism and determinism and degrees of freedom and constraint. In *The Constitution of Society*, Giddens responds by distinguishing different senses of "constraint" and by reminding us that there are no natural laws of society. He adds that

> The nature of constraint is historically variable, as are the enabling qualities generated by the contextualities of human action. It is variable in relation to the material and institutional circumstances of activity, but also in relation to the forms of knowledgeability that agents possess about those circumstances. (Giddens, 1984, p. 179)

This, however, does not deal with Archer's complaint. Are all these variations historically so contingent that structuration theory can say nothing further about them? Giddens gives a partial answer in terms of structural principles and structural sets. Structural sets, or structures (in the plural), refer to rules and resources which hang together to make a set. Take, for example, the following, very familiar, case of capitalism. The

> private property: money: capital: labor contract: profit

items in the set are internally related. One can also move from the set both to (a) the more abstract structural principle of capitalism, or class societies ("the disembedding, yet interconnecting, of state and economic institutions"; Giddens, 1984, p. 183), and (b) the less abstract structure, the rules and resources, which, via the dimensions or axes of structuration (signification, domination, and legitimation), are involved in the institutional articulation of capitalist societies. In assessing what options actors have, much depends on the strength of the internal connectives both within the structural set and between it and the rules and resources upon which actors draw. The options which actors perceive/conceive and enact can vary greatly in number and scope.

Thompson (1989), taking up similar issues, argues that there is more to structures than rules and resources, and the addition is not captured by the notion of structural principles. Instead, it has to do with the connections between, and distributions of, different rules and resources; alternatively, it is about why Giddens's rule-resource sets are setted as they are and what agents can do about them, or with them, other than just reproduce them. Thompson takes as an example Marx's analysis of the capitalist mode of production. It attends to the conditions which make possible capitalist production and exchange, from the circumstances which facilitate the formation of a "free" labor force to the principles and processes involved in the constitution of value and the generation of profit. These cannot, Thompson claims, satisfactorily be "forced into the conceptual mould of structure qua rules and resources" (Thompson, 1989, p. 69).

Both Archer's and Thompson's difficulties are connected to a complex of issues concerning the status of the virtual, voluntarism and determinism, and the nature of constraint. Archer (1982, 1988) has done more than anyone to tease them out. According to Giddens, structure refers to cognitive and moral rules and to allocative and authoritative resources, but it is virtual, not real, in that it exists only in instantiations in action and in memory traces. This amounts to saying structure is real only when it is activated. What Giddens calls rules Archer prefers to call the cultural system. She argues that "Since what is instantiated depends on the power of agency and not the nature of the property [of the rule or constituent of the cultural system], then properties themselves are not differentially mutable" (Archer, 1988, p. 88). In other words, Giddens's rules do not constrain because agents can conform to, modify, or reject them at will. She labels this the "ontological diminution of the cultural system." Giddens's response (1990b) is to say that of course structure, resources as well as rules, differentially enables and constrains, but it does so only as mediated by agents' reasons. Structural constraint cannot enforce like a causal force in nature. Even Marx's wage laborers, forced to sell their labor power, can, and on occasions do, reject one employer's labor contract for another, strike, go slow, and organize politically. Structure is virtual, it turns out, not just because it is out of time and out of space, but also because it does not alone determine. To this we would counter that structure, or better structures, are real (a) because, by Giddens's own admission, they differentially enable and constrain (it is, after all, a realist axiom that something is real if it has real effects), and (b) because, as Archer has pointed out, the differential potentials for enablement and constraint which structures offer have to do not just with agents' different activations of them but also with different properties which inhere in them.

DEVELOPMENTS AND APPLICATIONS Giddens's theory of structuration has been developed and applied by a very large number of scholars and researchers around the world in a very wide range of disciplines. We note just two of the developments immediately and will mention some applications later. Stones argues that what is missing from Giddens's theory of structuration is concern for the strategic context of action (Stones, 1991) or, as he now prefers, agent's context analysis (Stones, 1996). Like Cohen (1989), Stones notes how Giddens inclines either to bracket institutional analysis in his treatment of the strategic conduct of knowledgeable agents, or to bracket strategic conduct in his analysis of institutions as chronically reproduced rules and resources. By reworking Giddens's concept of knowledgeability in terms of strategic context, Stones directs attention to the agent's strategic terrain – "the social nexus of interdependencies, rights and obligations, asymmetries of power and the social conditions and consequences of action" (Stones, 1996, p. 98) which make up the perceived and perceivable possibilities of action and their limitations. In effect, Stones seeks a hermeneutically sensitive version of what Parsons (1937) called the conditions of action in his original voluntaristic theory of action. Strategic, or agent's, context analysis, so conceived, affords a critique of action, an examination of its conditions and limits; or, as Stones avers, it allows examination of counterfactual claims that agents could have acted other than they did by treating contexts as neither entirely fixed nor entirely fluid.

Stones indicates that there is potentially more to "knowledgeability" than Giddens himself makes explicit. In a similar vein, Bryant (1991) argues that there is potentially more to Giddens's "dialogical model" of social science application than he was originally able or willing to define. In particular, it overcomes many of the deficiencies of the engineering, enlightenment, and interaction models by aligning a post-empiricist philosophy of social science with the engagement of agents in a reconsideration of their reasons for action. What it does not provide is a rationale for a critical social science. For that one has to turn to the "utopian realism" of *The Consequencies of Modernity* and subsequent works.

Two limitations of Giddens's original theory of structuration remain. On the one hand, it has little to say about the formation and distribution of the unacknowledged and acknowledged conditions of action or about the differential knowledgeability of actors. On the other, it does not elaborate on individual and collective *transformative* projects, and the differential capabilities of actors to see projects through successfully, including the capacity to cope successfully with unintended consequences. Despite these limitations, however, it has proved highly attractive to empirical researchers. Critics such as Stinchcombe (1986) may deplore the self-indulgencies of Giddens's abstract social theory but, ironically, it is the work they consider most arid which researchers have found most useful. Literally dozens of researchers all over the world have applied elements of structuration theory in archaeology, education, geography, management theory, organizational analysis, political science, psychology, and religious studies. Giddens (1991b) has himself commended the use of structuration theory in Burman (1988) on unemployment in Canada, Connell (1987) on gender relations in Australia, and Dandeker (1989) on surveillance, bureaucratic power, and war.

To illustrate applications of Giddens, Bryant and Jary (1996) selected, from a very large number of possibilities: Shotter (1983) in psychology; Carlstein (1981) and Gregson (1986) in geography; Elchardus (1988) on time; Barrett (1988) and Graves (1989) in archaeology; Spybey (1984), Whittington (1992), and Yates and Orlikowski (1992) on management and organizations; Sydow and Windeler (1996) on inter-firm networks; Roberts and Scapens (1985), MacIntosh and Scapens (1990), and Boland (1993) in accountancy; Lee (1992) and Mellor (1993) on religion; and Shilling (1992) on education. Orlikowski (1992) on technology and Scapens and MacIntosh (1996) on accountancy are also worthy of note. DeSanctis and Poole (1994) have also elaborated how, drawing on Giddens, Bourdieu, and others, it is possible to construct "adaptive structuration theory." Most applications draw upon only a small part of Giddens's theory of structuration – principally the few elements outlined above – though no systematic review of the uses of Giddens across disciplines has yet been done.

Theorizing modernity: the personal and the global in a runaway world

Giddens has always been interested in modernity, as his early *The Class Structure of the Advanced Societies* (1973) confirms – indeed, he has always believed sociology's defining mission to be the analysis of the *modern* world – but it is only after his work on the principles of structuration theory reach their fullest elaboration in *The Constitution of Society* (1984) that he devotes most of his efforts to the analysis of late modernity.

THE CRITIQUE OF HISTORICAL MATERIALISM AND THE INSTITUTIONAL DIMENSIONS OF MODERNITY The two volumes of *A Contemporary Critique of Historical Materialism* (1981, 1985) provide a link between the second and third phases of Giddens's work. They address the core issues raised by evolutionism and its alternatives and provide new schemata for mapping the historical and contemporary relations between the state and economy in a "globalizing" world. Giddens concludes that:

1 There exists no necessary overall mechanism of social change, no universal motor of history such as class conflict.
2 There are no universal stages, or periodizations, of social development, these being ruled out by intersocietal systems and "time-space edges" (the ever-presence of exogenous variables), as well as by human agency and the inherent "historicity" of societies.
3 Societies do not have needs other than those of individuals, so notions such as adaptation cannot properly be applied to them.
4 Pre-capitalist societies are class-divided, but only with capitalism are there class societies in which there is endemic class conflict, the separation of the

political and economic spheres, property freely alienable as capital, and "free" labor and labor markets.

5 While class conflict is integral to capitalist society, there is no teleology that guarantees the emergence of the working class as the universal class, and no ontology that justifies denial of the multiple bases of modern society represented by capitalism, industrialism, surveillance, and the industrialization of warfare.

6 Sociology, as a subject concerned pre-eminently with modernity, addresses a reflexive reality.

The analysis of premodern, modern, and late modern societies along four partly independent, partly interdependent, dimensions – economic, political, military, and symbolic – none of which has primacy, is, at a minimum, distinctive (though compare Mann, 1986) and instructive. In particular, it attends to features of modernity which sociology has too often ignored: the growth of the administrative power of the state and the industrialization of warfare. It also explores the complex ways in which power figures in time-space distanciation (the stretching of social systems across time-space), including the ways not just nation-states and capitalism but also different types of "locale" – such as cities as "power containers" – exercise domination over both nature and persons. Giddens's critique of historical materialism is one most commentators, Marxist and non-Marxist, respect, even when they differ (see Wright, 1983; Callinicos, 1985; Dandeker, 1990).

A projected third volume which was to have dealt with state socialism and its alternatives never appeared. The defeats suffered by the left in Western Europe from 1979 onwards and the collapse of state socialism in Eastern Europe in 1989 revised Giddens's thinking about possible developments within late modernity and the value of any book focusing on traditional socialist agendas. Instead, *The Consequences of Modernity* (1990a), *Modernity and Self-Identity* (1991a), *The Transformation of Intimacy* (1992b), and *Beyond Left and Right* (1994a) offer striking and perceptive comment on the contemporary human condition, without providing a comprehensive and systematic examination of the economics and politics of late modernity. Reflexivity is the theme which links them all.

REFLEXIVE MODERNITY "The reflexivity of modern social life consists in the fact that social practices are constantly examined and reformed in the light of incoming information about those very practices, thus constitutively altering their character" (Giddens, 1990a, p. 38). But, contrary to Enlightenment expectations, knowledge has not led to certitude; instead, reason has lost its foundation, history its direction, and progress its allure. Even so, modernity has not given way to postmodernity but has assumed a new form, that of "radicalized modernity." For both Giddens and Beck (Beck, 1986; Beck et al., 1994) radicalized modernity refers to the new patterns of security and danger, trust and risk, which typify late modern societies; and trust and risk have to do with expectations of what both other people and abstract systems will do. Modernity is radicalized because the intensification of individual and institutional reflexivity in the absence of sure foundations for knowledge has a chronic propensity to "manufacture uncertainty" and generate reordering. It is also radicalized because processes of continuous rationalization are transforming the familiar contours of industrial society.

High modernity involves the disembedding, or lifting out, of social relations, practices, mechanisms, and competencies from their specific, usually local, circumstances of time and space ("locales"), and their extension, thanks to developments in communications, over much wider spans of time and space. The development of expert systems provides one example of the latter; "symbolic tokens" (media which circulate without regard to the characteristics of those who handle them – such as money) provide another. Both expert systems and symbolic tokens depend on trust, not in individuals, but in abstract capacities. "Trust is related to absence in time and space" (Giddens, 1990a, p. 33), and it "operates in environments of risk" (ibid., p. 54). This last is a reminder that living in late modernity is often unsettling and disorienting; it is disturbingly "like being aboard a careering juggernaut" (ibid., p. 53).

Table 10.4 sets out the differences between the conception of postmodernity which Giddens rejects and the conception of radicalized modernity which he endorses. One of the features of the contemporary world acknowledged by both postmodernists and Giddens is the plurality of intellectual formations and cultural spaces, but, *contrary to postmodern theories*, this need not preclude potential convergences, fusions of horizons, larger truths, or agreements on new beginnings. In the fourth row of the radicalized modernity column Giddens emphasizes the possibilities of universal truth claims and systematic knowledge, but he is reluctant to enter further epistemological debate and explain precisely how, given his general acceptance of anti-foundationalist and post-empiricist arguments, these are realizable (Bryant, 1992). There is often a lack of detail in Giddens's epistemological and political thinking. Sometimes this reduces its impact; on the other hand, it adds to the attraction for those who would build on it.

Disoriented or not, men and women in an age of high modernity are not subject to the fate and fortune of their premodern forebears; instead institutional and personal reflexivity, including the calculation of risk, inform social practice and continue to have a bearing on the course of events. Indeed, there is now, according to Giddens, a possibility that "life politics" (the politics of self-actualization) may become more salient than "emancipatory politics" (the politics of inequality); that new social movements may have more social impact than political parties (especially in conditions of "post-scarcity'); and that the reflexive project of the self and changes in gender and sexual relations may lead the way, via the "democratization of democracy," to a new era of "dialogic democracy" in which differences are settled, and practices ordered, through discourse rather than violence, the commands of duly constituted authority, or the separation of the parties.

Giddens's account of the opportunities presented by radicalized modernity is highly generalized. It lacks both justified identification of mediate political groupings – despite an obvious interest in feminism and new social movements

Table 10.4 A comparison of conceptions of postmodernity and "radicalized modernity"

Postmodernity	*"Radicalized modernity"*
1 Understands current transitions in epistemological terms or as dissolving epistemology altogether	1 Identifies the institutional developments which create a sense of fragmentation and dispersal
2 Focuses upon the centrifugal tendencies of current social transformations and their dislocating character	2 Sees high modernity as a set of circumstances in which dispersal is dialectically connected to profound tendencies toward global integration
3 Sees the self as dissolved or dismembered by the fragmenting of experience	3 Sees the self as more than just a site of intersecting forces; active processes of reflective self-identity are made possible by modernity
4 Argues for the contextuality of truth claims or sees them as "historical"	4 Argues that the universal features of truth claims force themselves upon us in an irresistible way given the primacy of problems of a global kind. Systematic knowledge about these developments is not precluded by the reflexivity of modernity
5 Theorizes powerlessness which individuals feel in the face of globalizing tendencies	5 Analyzes a dialectic of powerlessness and empowerment, in terms of both experience and action
6 Sees the "emptying" of day-to-day life as a result of the intrusion of abstract systems	6 Sees day-to-day life as an active complex of reactions to abstract systems, involving appropriation as well as loss
7 Regards coordinated political engagement as precluded by the primacy of contextuality and dispersal	7 Regards coordinated political engagement as both possible and necessary, on a global level as well as locally
8 Defines postmodernity as the end of epistemology, the individual, ethics	8 Defines postmodernity as possible transformations moving "beyond" the institutions of modernity

Source: Giddens (1990a, p. 150).

– and careful attention to the principles of structuration theory. Unfortunately, his most recent monograph, *Beyond Left and Right: the Future of Radical Politics* (1994a), does not repair these deficiencies. What it does do is explore the paradox of a political left, for long on the defensive, which had, in many respects, fewer radical inclinations than a market-oriented radical right intent on overthrowing tradition and custom at, it sometimes seemed, any cost. Dismissing without much argument any middle-way "market socialism," Giddens responds to the radicalism of the right by drawing on earlier forms of "philosophic conservatism," in combination with elements of socialist thought to construct a six-point framework for a reconstituted radical politics: (a) repair damaged solidarities; (b) recognize the centrality of life politics; (c) accept that active trust implies generative politics; (d) embrace dialogic democracy; (e) rethink the welfare state; and (f) confront violence.

A RUNAWAY WORLD This is hardly a framework, more an agenda – and arguably an agenda more principled than practical at that. Giddens's "brave new world" (1994b) may be worthy, but is it realistic? It may not all be the "argument-by-mantra" of which Judt (1994, p. 7) complains, but its connections with contemporary political agents and processes in both the state *and* civil society are, to say the least, underspecified. Could it be, however, that this will prove its strength, not its weakness? "There is no single agent, group or movement that, as Marx's proletariat was supposed to do, can carry the hopes of humanity," Giddens (1994a, p. 21) reminds us, "but there are many points of political engagement which offer good cause for optimism." Stop hankering after some new comprehensive, all-connecting, ideologically driven programme, Giddens seems to say, and, in this age of high modernity, do what you can where you can – for there is plenty that you can do in the home, workplace, community, and polity. Tony Blair, for one, is listening. Giddens was a guest at the Britsh Prime Minister's weekend residence, Chequers, on November 1, 1997.

Giddens continues to be fascinated by the notion "of a runaway world," and he chose it for the title of a conference in January 1997, which marked his assumption of the directorship of the LSE and the publication of four volumes of commentary on his work (Bryant and Jary, 1996). The conference asked, in effect, what could be done about, or in, a runaway world when there was great hope but less expectation that the imminent defeat of the Conservative government by new Labour at the ballot box would make a difference.

Giddens often links the image of a runaway world to that of riding a juggernaut (as in *The Consequences of Modernity*, chapter 5, and *Modernity and Self-identity*, chapter 1). We think the juggernaut metaphor has the wrong associations and should be abandoned. Juggernaut, in Hindu mythology, is the name of an idol carried in procession on a huge cart; in the past devotees are said to have thrown themselves in front of it. This ultimate in cultural dopism is plainly incompatible with Giddens's approach to human agency. "Runaway world" is more serviceable, but still presents problems. It suggests a world wholly out-of-control which had formerly been under control – both of which are exaggerations – but it also correctly implies that science, social science, and technology no longer offer the promise of any overall control. Indeed, some technologies – such as industrial processes which pollute, nuclear technology, and genetic engineering – are now as much constituents of a world out-of-control as means of controlling it; they are as much part of the problem, adding to manufactured uncertainty, as part of any solution.

The specter of a runaway world would seem to prompt three alternative responses. First, try to recover, or secure, control; fix the big picture. Second, resign oneself to loss, or absence, of control and retreat to the private and personal. In the circumstances of late modernity, this is more likely to focus on the self than on the soul. Third, go for limited and local control; accept that there is no one big picture, but fix bits of pictures as and when you can for the purposes in hand. In the last of these, positivism gives way to post-positivism, empiricism to post-empiricism, and ideological conviction to pragmatism; we are left as more or less chastened, or more or less emancipated, mourners at what Gray (1995), another contributor to the London conference, calls Enlightenment's wake.

Giddens is cheered, not chastened, by Enlightenment's wake. An age of endings, not just of the millennium but also of modernity and the politics of left and right, also suggests fresh beginnings. The burden of totalizing ambition has been lifted and a world of multiple possibilities beckons. It is interesting to compare his view of these possibilities with Edmund Leach's, because it is Leach's 1968 Reith Lectures for the BBC, *A Runaway World?*, which first planted the idea. Leach argued that developments such as the population explosion and the technological revolution had seemingly led to a runaway world, and "The runaway world is terrifying because we are gradually becoming aware that simple faith in the limitless powers of human rationality is an illusion" (Leach, 1968, p. 78–9). In its place, Leach advocated an evolutionary humanism. Some of its features we would question, but three of Leach's injunctions are worth noting three decades later. First, rethink science along, we would now say, post-empiricist lines. Second, engage with the world to make things happen; men and women can make a difference even if they cannot know all the differences they will make, and even if some of them turn out to be unwelcome. Third, do not be deterred by disorder; the times are always changing, and changing times are always out-of-joint; order is an illusion which affords a sense of security at odds with the inevitability of change. Those who participate in history, instead of looking on, can at least enjoy the present. That way, Leach continues, you can avoid becoming

> a lonely, impotent and terrified observer of a runaway world. A more positive attitude to change will not mean that you will always feel secure, it will just give you a sense of purpose. You should read your Homer. Gods who manipulate the course of destiny are no more likely to achieve their private ambitions than men who suffer the slings and arrows of outrageous fortune; but gods have much more fun. (Leach, 1968, p. 9)

There is a conceit, or perhaps a bravura, in Leach's claim that men and women are, or could be, god-like – except that Leach's gods do not determine the course of history, they just make things happen. What Giddens offers is more a version of men and women condemned to take risks but saved by their potential for dialogue. To put it in Weberian terms, gods might favor an ethic of ultimate conviction, but men and women are better served by an ethic of responsibility.

In Giddens's terms, this is the difference between utopianism and utopian realism, where the latter refers to the combination of realism and idealism in the envisaging of "alternative futures whose very propagation might help them be realised" (Giddens, 1990a, p. 154). Giddens's own utopian realism has at its heart his vision of the possibilities of the more socialized, demilitarized and planetary-caring global order variously articulated within the green, women's, and peace movements, and within the wider democratic movement. Our runaway world could even end up as an agreeable postmodernity (see figure 10.2).

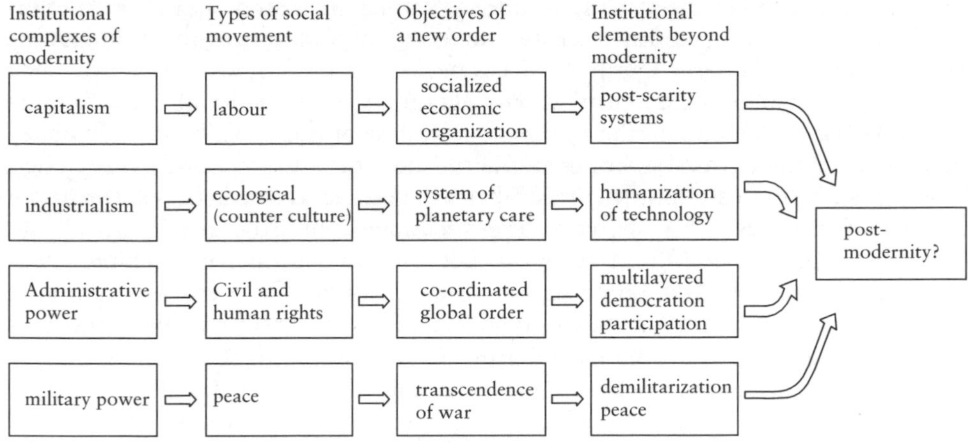

Figure 10.2 From modernity to postmodernity: Giddens's scheme.
Source: Held (1992, p. 34).

Like Habermas, Giddens presents the possibility of the dialogic, and ultimately democratic, resolution of differences.

EVALUATING GIDDENS'S OEUVRE

Giddens's commentary on leading figures, schools, and traditions is unsurpassed in volume, range, and consistent quality. It would be a commendable achievement even if he had done nothing else. But, of course, he has. It is arguable that of all the approaches to the agency–structure and macro–micro debates on offer, and they now run into double figures, Giddens's is the most persuasive – not least because of the long list of theorists and theoretical approaches he has critically appropriated.[6] The principles of structuration have also proved useful to an impressive number of researchers in a dauntingly wide range of disciplines. In addition, Giddens has done as much as anyone to make concern for time-space an essential of social theory and empirical research design.

Beginning with *The Consequences of Modernity* (1990a), Giddens has also played a leading role in establishing globalization and its concomitants as one of the biggest topics in contemporary social science. And, whatever the limitations of his more recent work, Giddens has coined, appropriated, and given currency to a host of concepts which can be expected to continue to figure in discourse about late or postmodernity for a long time yet: reflexive and radicalized modernity, institutional reflexivity, detraditionalization, manufactured uncertainty, and global risk environments, emancipatory politics and life politics or the politics of self-actualisation, narratives and projects of the self, the sequestration of experience and ontological security, the democratization of democracy and dialogic democracy, the pure relationship, the transformation of intimacy and confluent love, utopian realism, and many more.

To pay attention to the phases of Giddens's writing career and to aspects of his works is all very proper, but it misses the most important feature of his whole oeuvre – grand synthesis. Craib (1992), a perceptive but not always sympathetic critic, argues that Giddens's oeuvre, whatever its flaws, is probably the best there is at integrating (a) commentary, (b) theorization of the constitution of society and the self, and (c) analysis of premodern, modern, and late modern societies. Craib has his doubts about the feasibility of such grand synthetic ventures, but he also acknowledges that without them sociology could so easily fragment into a host of self-contained and self-absorbed specialities of ever-declining consequence for our understanding of the world at large. Giddens, perhaps more than any other single figure in sociology, is holding the whole discipline together and connecting it to other social sciences.

Having made what we believe to be a formidable case for Giddens, we now want to enter some criticisms of our own. There is, we believe, a pressing need for Giddens to develop further the principles of structuration theory in order to deal more convincingly with the objections raised by critics. The non-appearance of a major systematic treatment of economic and political relations in late modern societies, to fill the gap left by the abandonment of the projected third volume of the contemporary critique of historical materialism, is also a serious omission. The books of the 1990s offer brilliant sketches, countless *aperçus*, engaging prompts, and much else, but are still only a partial remedy. There are also unresolved tensions in Giddens's description of continuities and contingencies in modernity and his depiction of knowledgeable and capable agents in a runaway world.

Giddens has (potentially) provided some of the ingredients for a theory of *late* modernity, such as the focus on the dialogic resolution of issues and the acknowledgment of the continuing importance of traditions (see especially his contribution to Beck et al., 1994). He has also come close to reconsideration of "evolutionary" issues (see Jary, 1991; Craib, 1992), including the role of the aesthetic, the ludic, and perhaps also the religious dimensions of culture (see Tucker, 1993). It would, however, sometimes be more helpful to point up the similarities with Habermas than the differences. The similarities on the dialogic conception of knowledge and the justification of values, and on new social movements, are evident; despite his protestations, there is also the potential for an approach to evolution with some resemblance to Habermas's.

Much of Giddens's recent writing is innovative and speculative – too speculative for many critics. The early Giddens who eschewed judgments in *Capitalism and Modern Social Theory* (1971a) contrasts greatly with the pundit of the 1990s. The close referencing of the early and middle Giddens differs markedly from the light referencing of *The Consequences of Modernity* (1990a) and subsequent books. Rigorous scholarship and analysis have increasingly given way to invention and communication relatively unencumbered by literatures and *systematic* evidence. It would be a pity if Giddens should prove unable to find the time and the will to complete another major work which succeeds more fully in answering doubts about the principles of structuration theory, while at the same time connecting the core of the theory to an analysis of radicalized modernity in which more justified instances of utopian realism inform a thorough examination of its economics and politics – but even without it his achievement has been immense. For the moment, Giddens has other commitments. He wants to secure a brilliant future for the LSE in the difficult circumstances of the chronic underfunding of British universities, and a movement from elite to mass higher education in which greater institutional diversification is inevitable – no mean task. And he wants to contribute prominently and publicly to the fashioning of a politics beyond left and right in which the values of the center-left remain, but the strategies and the policies are rethought – no mean ambition.

Postscript 2002

Since this chapter was written, Giddens "the public intellectual" has won widespread public attention in Britain and access to politicians and their advisers in many countries all over the world. In the autumn of 1998 he published *The Third Way*, an attempt to define a politics beyond left and right for new Labour. Much of the force of Giddens's argument, and much of its appeal to Tony Blair and to politicians abroad, lay in the claim that socialism and the Old Left had died of exhaustion and maladjustment to a changed world, and their successors, neoliberalism and the New Right, unable to sustain the contradictions between market fundamentalism and conservatism, were now dying too. But what of the successor third way? According to Giddens (1998b, p. 64), "the overall aim of third way politics should be to help citizens pilot their way through the major revolutions of our time: *globalization, transformations in personal life* and our *relationship to nature*." In all three cases, Giddens argues (with echoes of Saint-Simon) that wise action on our part can make a difference to how these revolutions work themselves out.

Giddens's third way program has as its components the radical center, the new democratic state (the state without external enemies – a pre-September 11 formulation), an active civil society, the democratic family, the new mixed economy, equality as inclusion, positive (enabling) welfare, the social investment state, the cosmopolitan nation (which balances cultural pluralism and solidarity), and cosmopolitan (outward-looking) democracy. It is notable that Giddens's state still has a lot to do in making social investments, in regulating capitalism at home, and in reforming and devising the international institutions with which to combat market fundamentalism globally. Giddens has discussed the latter with George Soros and has edited a book on it with Will Hutton (Hutton and Giddens, 2000a).

Not all the concepts and ideas in Giddens's version of the "the third way" figure in Tony Blair's similarly titled Fabian society pamphlet, published shortly afterwards (Blair, 1998). In particular, Blair refers disparagingly to the "fundamentalist Left," but it is market fundamentalism and especially the minimal regulation of international capital markets that disturb Giddens more. Giddens's ecological concerns also do not make it into Blair's pamphlet, and nor does his critique of the self-exclusion of the privileged from the social mainstream. Blair's use of Giddens is selective, and his vision is less radical. Be this as it may, third way thinking (recast as the "new center" by Chancellor Schröder in Germany) has influenced governments in most of the European Union and beyond, and has secured plaudits from, *inter alia*, Romano Prodi, President of the European Commission, and Fernando Henrique Cardoso, President of Brazil. Such developments have enabled Giddens to edit a volume entitled *The Global Third Way Debate* (2001a: cf. Jary 2002).

Giddens also delivered the 1999 Reith Lectures on BBC radio. He took as his title *Runaway World* but omitted any reference to juggernauts. The lectures are prestigious and may have served to make some of his ideas more widely known, especially as three of the five were delivered outside Britain (in Delhi, Hong Kong, and Washington). Each lecture was followed by discussion, and among the questioners were Hilary Clinton and Tony Blair. Audio and video versions of the series were accessible on the World Wide Web, along with an interactive web site. Given that the lectures contained nothing new, the global multimedia were the message.

In May 2001, new Labour was re-elected in Britain with another huge majority but without the popular enthusiasm evident in 1997; the turn-out of only 59 percent was the lowest since 1918. Giddens had already responded to critics in *The Third Way and its Critics* (2000b); he now came up with *Where Now for New Labour?* (2002). His answers amount to more of the same; they are worthy, often complex, and far from populist. They represent as does so much of new Labour, and here there are again echoes of Saint-Simon, a politics without passion. In countries other than Britain variations of this failure to stir the voters have contributed to the recent electoral reverses of the center-left. Knowing this Giddens is prepared to speak again of ideology and the good society but what he has to say about balancing the state, civil society, and the market and differences between government, the state, and the public interest is still decidedly cerebral.

Giddens has taken part in a succession of private conferences with the leading politicians of the center-left on both sides of the Atlantic, including gatherings in the Clinton White House and at Chequers, the country house of the British prime minister. At the latest, in May 2002, he urged center-left leaders to be bolder in their programs for modernization. He has less of a following now than he had two or three years ago but this will not deter him. His is very much a long-term commitment to the renewal of social democracy. It should also be noted that his activism and his engagement with leading thinkers in many countries has served LSE well. Almost everyone associated with the school agrees that under Giddens's directorship it has become a much more exciting place to study and debate the issues of our globalizing age. The contemporary Giddens has proved a truly remarkable figure (see Bryant and Jary, 2001, esp. pt IV "The Public Intellectual," and ch. 12 "The Reflexive Giddens").

Notes

1 Three of these from 1995 have been republished as chapter 13, "Brave New World: the New Context of Politics," of Giddens (1996). We also hazard the suggestion that Giddens (1998a) may prove influential in the definition of a "third-way" political

project for Tony Blair's new Labour government. The best piece so far by a journalist on Giddens and his new political role is Boynton's in *The New Yorker* (1997).

2 We have, *inter alia*, drawn on our interviews with Giddens on April 26, 1989 in Cambridge and November 27, 1997 in London.

3 This is not to say that Elias's influence was necessarily evident to students at the time, as one of us, Chris Bryant, a Leicester graduate, can testify.

4 For another view of Elias at Leicester, see Brown (1987).

5 This is, of course, the opposite of C. Wright Mills's (1959) exercise of the sociological imagination, which moves from an examination of "the public issues of social structure" to an enlightening re-view of "the personal troubles of milieu."

6 But like others we sometimes wonder whether Giddens's synthesis sufficiently respects the nuances of the approaches it incorporates – a reservation only reinforced by his recent admission that he hardly ever reads books from cover to cover, he just uses lists of contents and indexes to fillet out the main bits (in the *Guardian*, Higher Education, January 14, 1997).

Bibliography

Writings of Anthony Giddens

Capitalism and Modern Social Theory. 1971a. Cambridge: Cambridge University Press.

The Sociology of Suicide (editor). 1971b. London: Frank Cass.

Emile Durkheim: Selected Writings (editor). 1972a. Cambridge: Cambridge University Press.

Politics and Sociology in the Thought of Max Weber. 1972b. London: Macmillan.

The Class Structure of the Advanced Societies. 1973. London: Hutchinson.

Positivism and Sociology (editor). 1974. London: Heinemann.

New Rules of Sociological Method. 1976a. London: Hutchinson (2nd edn, 1993).

Functionalism: *après la lutte.* 1976b. *Social Research*, 43, 325–66.

Studies in Social and Political Theory. 1977a. London: Hutchinson.

A Theory of Suicide. 1977b. In *Studies in Social and Political Theory*, chapter 9.

Notes on the Theory of Structuration. 1977c. In *Studies in Social and Political Theory*, appendix to chapter 2.

Durkheim. 1978. London: Fontana.

Central Problems in Social Theory: Action, Structure and Contradiction in Social Analysis. 1979. London: Macmillan.

A Contemporary Critique of Historical Materialism. Volume 1, Power, Property and the State, 1981. London: Macmillan (2nd edn, 1995).

Profiles and Critiques in Social Theory. 1982a. London: Macmillan.

Sociology: a Brief but Critical Introduction. 1982b. London: Macmillan (2nd edn, 1986).

Classes and the Division of Labour: Essays in Honour of Ilya Neustadt (editor with G. Mackenzie). 1982. Cambridge: Cambridge University Press.

The Constitution of Society: Outline of the Theory of Structuration. 1984. Cambridge: Polity.

A Contemporary Critique of Historical Materialism. Volume 2, The Nation-state and Violence. 1985. Cambridge: Polity Press.

Durkheim on Politics and the State (editor). 1986. Cambridge: Polity Press.

Social Theory and Modern Sociology. 1987. Cambridge: Polity Press.

Social Theory Today (editor with J. H. Turner). 1987. Cambridge: Polity Press.

Sociology. 1989. Cambridge: Polity Press (2nd edn, 1993; 3rd edn, 1997; US edn, *An Introduction to Sociology*. New York: Norton, 1991).

The Consequences of Modernity. 1990a. Cambridge: Polity Press.

Structuration Theory and Sociological Analysis. 1990b. In J. Clark, C. Modgil and S. Modgil (eds), *Anthony Giddens: Consensus and Controversy*. Lewis: Falmer Press, chapter 22.

Modernity and Self-identity: Self and Society in the Late Modern Age. 1991a. Cambridge: Polity Press.

Structuration Theory: Past, Present and Future. 1991b. In C. G. A. Bryant and D. W. Jary (eds) *Giddens' Theory of Structuration: a Critical Appreciation*. London: Routledge, chapter 8.

Human Societies: a Reader. 1992a. Cambridge: Polity Press (2nd edn, *Sociology: Introductory Readings*, 1997).

The Transformation of Intimacy: Sexuality, Love and Eroticism in Modern Societies. 1992b. Cambridge: Polity Press.

Beyond Left and Right: the Future of Radical Politics. 1994a. Cambridge: Polity Press.

Brave New World: the New Context of Politics. 1994b. In D. Miliband (ed.), *Reinventing the Left*. Cambridge: Polity Press, chapter 1.

Politics, Sociology and Social Theory: Encounters with Classical and Contemporary Social Thought. 1995. Cambridge: Polity Press.

In Defence of Sociology: Essays, Interpretations and Rejoinders. 1996. Cambridge: Polity Press.

Centre Left at Centre Stage. 1997. *New Statesman*, special edition, May, 37–9.

After the Left's Paralysis. 1998a. *New Statesman*, May 1, 18–21.

The Third Way: the Renewal of Social Democracy. 1998b. Cambridge: Polity Press.

Runaway World: How Globalisation is Reshaping Our Lives. 1999. London: Profile.

On the Edge: Living with Global Capitalism (editor, with Will Hutton). 2000a. London: Cape.

The Third Way and Its Critics. 2000b. Cambridge: Polity.

The Global Third Way Debate (editor). 2001a. Cambridge: Polity.

The Reflexive Giddens: Christopher G. A. Bryant and David Jary in Dialogue with Anthony Giddens. (2001b). In C. G. A. Bryant and D. W. Jary (eds) *The Contemporary Giddens: Social Theory in a Globalising Age*. Basingstoke and New York: Palgrave.

Where Now for New Labour? 2002. Cambridge: Polity.

Further reading

Archer, M. S. (1982) Morphogenesis versus Structuration: on Combining Structure and Action. *British Journal of Sociology*, 33, 455–88.

Archer, M. S. (1988) *Culture and Agency: the Place of Culture in Social Theory*. Cambridge: Cambridge University Press.

Barrett, J. C. (1988) Fields of Discourse: Reconstituting a Social Archaeology. *Critique of Anthropology*, 7(3), 5–16

Beck, U. (1986) *Risk Society: towards a New Modernity*. London: Sage.

Beck, U., Giddens, A., and Lash, S. (1994) *Reflexive Modernization: Politics, Tradition and Aesthetics in the Modern Order*. Cambridge: Polity Press.

Blair, T. (1998) *The Third Way: New Politics for the New Century*. London: The Fabian Society.

Boland, R. J. (1993) Accounting and the Interpretative Act. *Accounting, Organizations and Society*, 18, 125–40.

Boynton, R. S. (1997) The Two Tonys: Why Is the Prime Minister so Interested in What Anthony Giddens Thinks? *The New Yorker*, October 6, 2–7.

Brown, R. K. (1987) Norbert Elias in Leicester: Some Recollections. *Theory, Culture and Society*, 4, 533–9.

Bryant, C. G. A. (1991) The Dialogical Model of Applied Sociology. In C. G. A. Bryant and D. W. Jary (eds), *Giddens' Theory of Structuration: a Critical Appreciation,* London: Routledge, chapter 7.

Bryant, C. G. A. (1992) Sociology without Philosophy? The Case of Giddens' Structuration Theory. *Sociological Theory*, 10, 137–49.

Bryant, C. G. A. (1995) *Practical Sociology: Postempiricism and the Reconstruction of Theory and Application*. Cambridge: Polity Press.

Bryant, C. G. A. and Jary, D. W. (eds) (1991) *Giddens' Theory of Structuration: a Critical Appreciation*. London: Routledge.

Bryant, C. G. A. and Jary, D. W. (eds) (1996) *Anthony Giddens: Critical Assessments*, 4 volumes. London: Routledge.

Bryant, C. G. A. and Jary, D. W. (eds) (2001) *The Contemporary Giddens: Social Theory in a Globalising Age*. Basingstoke and New York: Palgrave.

Burman, P. (1988) *Killing Time, Losing Ground*. Toronto: Wall and Thompson.

Callinicos, A. (1985) Anthony Giddens – a Contemporary Critique. *Theory and Society*, 14, 133–66.

Carlstein, T. (1981) The Sociology of Structuration in Time and Space: a Timegeographic Assessment of Giddens' Theory. *Svensk Geografisk Arsbok*, 57, 41–57

Cohen, I. J. (1989) *Structuration Theory: Anthony Giddens and the Constitution of Social Life*. London: Macmillan.

Cohen, P. S. (1968) *Modern Social Theory*. London: Heinemann.

Connell, R. W. (1987) *Gender and Power*. Cambridge: Polity Press.

Craib, I. (1992) *Anthony Giddens*. London: Routledge.

Dandeker, C. (1989) *Surveillance, Power and Modernity*. Cambridge: Polity Press.

Dandeker, C. (1990) The Nation-state and the Modern World System. In J. Clark, C. Modgil, and F. Modgil (eds), *Anthony Giddens: Consensus and Controversy*. Lewis: Falmer Press.

DeSanctis, G. and Poole, M. S. (1994) Capturing the Complexity in Advanced Technology Use: Adaptive Structuration Theory. *Organization Science*, 5, 121–47.

Dunning, E. (1994) Towards a Configurational Critique of the Theory of Structuration. Paper presented at the 13th World Congress of Sociology, Bielefeld, Germany.

Elchardus, M. (1988) The Rediscovery of Chronos: the New Role of Time in Sociological Theory. *International Sociology*, 3(1), 35–59.

Eldridge, J. (1990) Sociology in Britain: a Going Concern. In C. G. A. Bryant and H. A. Becker (eds), *What Has Sociology Achieved?* London: Macmillan, chapter 9.

Elias, N. (1939) *The Civilizing Process. Volume I, The History of Manners*. Oxford: Blackwell (1978).

Graves, C. P. (1989) Social Space in the English Medieval Parish Church. *Economy and Society*, 18, 297–322.

Gray, J. (1995) *Enlightenment's Wake: Politics and Culture at the Close of the Modern Age*. London: Routledge.

Gregson, N. (1986) On Duality and Dualism: the Case of Structuration and Time Geography. *Progress in Human Geography*, 10, 184–205.

Held, D. (1992) Liberalism, Marxism and Democracy. In S. Hall, D. Held, D. McGrew, and T. McGrew (eds), *Modernity and its Futures*. Cambridge: Polity Press with Open University Press, chapter 1.

Jary, D. W. (1991) Society as Time Traveller: Giddens on Historical Change, Historical Materialism and the Nation-state in World Society. In C. G. A. Bryant and D. W. Jary (eds), *Giddens' Theory of Structuration: a Critical Appreciation,* London: Routledge, chapter 5.

Jary, D. W. (2002) The Global Third Way Debate. *Sociological Review*, 50, pp. 437–49.

Jary, D. W. and Jary, J. (1995) The Transformations of Anthony Giddens. *Theory, Culture and Society*, 12(2), 141–60.

Judt, T. (1994) How Much Is Really Left of the Left? *The Times Literary Supplement*, 4773(7), September 23.

Kilminster, R. (1991) Structuration Theory as a World-view. In C. G. A. Bryant and D. W. Jary (eds), *Giddens' Theory of Structuration: a Critical Appreciation,* London: Routledge, chapter 4.

Layder, D. (1994) *Understanding Social Theory*. London: Sage.

Leach, E. (1968) *A Runaway World?* London: BBC.

Lee, R. L. M. (1992) The Structuration of Disenchantment: Secular Agency and the Reproduction of Religion. *Journal for the Theory of Social Behaviour*, 22, 381–402.

MacIntosh, N. B. and Scapens, R. W. (1990) Structuration Theory in Management and Accounting. *Accounting, Organizations and Society*, 15, 455–77.

Mann, M. (1986) *The Sources of Social Power. Volume 1, A History of Power from the Beginning to AD 1760*. Cambridge: Cambridge University Press.

Marshall, T. H. (1982) Introduction to A. Giddens and G. Mackenzie (eds) *Social Class and the Division of Labour: Essays in Honour of Ilya Neustadt*. Cambridge: Cambridge University Press.

Mellor, P. A. (1993) Reflexive Traditions: Anthony Giddens, High Modernity, and the Contours of Contemporary Religiosity. *Religious Studies*, 29, 111–27.

Mills, C. Wright (1959) *The Sociological Imagination*. New York: Oxford University Press.

Orlikowski, W. J. (1992) The Duality of Technology; Rethinking the Concept of Technology in Organization. *Organization Science*, 3, 398–427.

Parsons, T. (1937) *The Structure of Social Action*. New York: McGraw-Hill.

Roberts, J. and Scapens, R. W. (1985) Accounting Systems and Systems of Accounting: Understanding Accounting Practices in Their Organisational Contexts. *Accounting, Organizations and Society*, 10, 443–56.

Scapens, R. W. and MacIntosh, N. B. (1996) Structure and Agency in Management Accounting Research: a Response to Boland's Interpretive Act. *Accounting, Organizations and Society*, 21, 675–90.

Shilling, C. (1992) Reconceptualising Structure and Agency in the Sociology of Education: Structuration Theory and Schooling. *British Journal of Sociology of Education*, 13, 69–87.

Shotter, J. (1983) "Duality of Structure" and "Intentionality" in an Ecological Psychology. *Journal for the Theory of Social Behaviour*, 13, 19–43.

Sica, A. (1991) The California–Massachusetts Strain in Structuration Theory. In C. G. A. Bryant and D. W. Jary (eds), *Giddens' Theory of Structuration: a Critical Appreciation,* London: Routledge, chapter 2.

Spybey, T. (1984) Traditional and Professional Frames of Meaning in Management. *Sociology*, 18, 550–62.

Stinchcombe, A. (1986) Milieu and Structure Updated: a Critique of the Theory of Structuration Theory. *Theory and Society*, 15, 901–14.

Stones, R. (1991) Strategic Context Analysis: a New Research Strategy for Structuration Theory. *Sociology*, 25, 673–95.

Stones, R. (1996) *Sociological Reasoning: towards a Past-modern Sociology*. London: Macmillan.

Sydow, J. and Windeler, A. (1996) Managing Inter-firm Networks: a Structurationist Perspective. In C. G. A. Bryant and D. W. Jary (eds), *Anthony Giddens: Critical Assessments, volume 4*. London: Routledge, chapter 93.

Thompson, J. B. (1989) The Theory of Structuration. In D. Held and J. B. Thompson (eds), *Social Theory of Modern Societies: Anthony Giddens and His Critics*. Cambridge: Cambridge University Press, chapter 3.

Tucker, K. H. (1993) Aesthetics, Play and Cultural Memory: Giddens and Habermas on the Postmodern Challenge. *Sociological Theory*, 11, 194–211.

Whittington, R. (1992) Putting Giddens into Action: Social Systems and Managerial Agency. *Journal of Management Studies*, 29, 693–712.

Wright, E. Olin (1983) Giddens' Critique of Marxism. *New Left Review*, 138, 11–35.

Yates, J. and Orlikowski, W. J. (1992) Genres of Organizational Communication: a Structurational Approach to Studying Communication and Media. *Academy of Management Review*, 17, 299–326.

11

Pierre Bourdieu

CRAIG CALHOUN

The most influential and original French sociologist since Durkheim, Pierre Bourdieu was at once a leading theorist and an empirical researcher of extraordinarily broad interests and distinctive style. He analyzed labor markets in Algeria, symbolism in the calendar and the house of Kabyle peasants, marriage patterns in his native Béarne region of France, photography as an art form and hobby, museum goers and patterns of taste, modern universities, the rise of literature as a distinct field of endeavor, and the sources of misery and poverty amid the wealth of modern societies. Bourdieu insisted that theory and research are inseparable parts of one sociological enterprise, and refused to separate them.

Bourdieu was born in 1930 in a small, rural village in the Pyrenees mountains. His very accent marked him as an outsider in elite Parisian academic life. But he rose from his humble origins to be at the top of his class at France's most elite educational institutions and eventually held the same chair at the Collège de France that Marcel and Mauss had occupied before him. Throughout his career, he insisted on the importance of advancing sociology as a science, combining empirical research with theory. At the same time, he was politically engaged, especially in the last years of his life. When he died, he was one of France's most prominent public figures, known especially for his criticisms of global neoliberalism and the imposition of an "American model" which favored taking funding away from state institutions and relying only on the private market, whether for education, culture, or pensions and welfare support (1998, 2002). A popular film was made about him and he was so famous that on the day of his death France's leading newspapers delayed publication to run the story on the front page.

TAKING GAMES SERIOUSLY

A former rugby player and a reader of the later Wittgenstein, Bourdieu was drawn to the metaphor of games to convey his sense of social life. But by "game" he did not mean mere diversions or entertainments. Rather, he meant a serious athlete's understanding of a game. He meant the experience of being passionately involved in play, engaged in a struggle with others and with our own limits, over stakes to which we are (at least for the moment) deeply committed. He meant intense competition. He meant for us to recall losing ourselves in the play of a game, caught in its flow in such a way that no matter how individualistically we struggle we are also constantly aware of being only part of something larger – not just a team, but the game itself. It is worth knowing that rugby (a game of running, passing, kicking, and tackling somewhat like American football, but played with more continuous motion, a bit like soccer) is one of the world's most physically intense games. When Bourdieu spoke of playing, he spoke of putting oneself on the line.

Social life is like this, Bourdieu suggested, except that the stakes are bigger. Not just is it always a struggle; it requires constant improvisation. The idea is directly related to Wittgenstein's (1967) account of language games. These are not diversions from some more basic reality but a central part of the activity by which forms of life are constituted and transformed. Learning a language is a constant training in how to improvise "play" in social interaction and cultural participation more generally. No game can be understood simply by grasping the rules that define it. It requires not just following rules, but having a "sense" of the game, a sense of how to play.[1] This is a social sense, for it requires a constant awareness of and responsiveness to the play of one's opponent (and in some cases one's teammates). A good rugby (or soccer or basketball) player is constantly aware of the field as a whole, and anticipates the actions of teammates, knowing when to pass, when to try to break free. A good basketball player is not simply one who can shoot, but one who knows when to shoot.

Games are strategic. There are different possible approaches to each contest, and to each moment in the contest. What makes for a good strategy is determined by the rules of the game, of course, but also by assessing one's opponent's strengths and weaknesses – and one's own. Originality or inspiration is only one factor among many in determining the outcome.

Whether a tennis player rushes the net is a complex result of numerous factors, not a simple, conscious decision. Indeed, if it is simply a conscious decision the player is probably already too late. The tennis player has a physical, bodily sense of how strong her own serve was, and an awareness (usually without words) of the shot her opponent is returning; thought and bodily action are not sharply separate. She also has an inclination to rush a lot or a little, to play risky or safe tennis, to be confident in her physical strength and speed, or to watch for angles or chip shots to throw a stronger opponent off balance. This is partly the result of years of experience, partly the result of coaching and disciplined practice. The coach may even use theory to help analyze the strengths and weaknesses of the player's game; for example, urging her to rush the net a little more, hang back at the baseline a little less. This can be long-term, general advice, or specifically targeted to the opponent the player faces today. Either way, however, the player's actual shots are actions that cannot be reduced to theoretical rules. They are improvisations. Sometimes they are inspired surprises, occasionally disastrous mistakes. But for a good player they are also embodiments of a highly consistent style. This is what Bourdieu termed a "habitus," the capacity each player of a game has to improvise the next move, the next play, the next shot.

We may be born with greater or lesser genetic potentials, but we are not born with a habitus. As the word suggests, this is something we acquire through repetition, like a habit, and something we know in our bodies, not just our minds. A professional basketball player has shot a million free throws before he steps to the line. Some of these have come in practice sessions, designed to allow the player to work on technical skills free from the pressure and chance of a game. But the player's practical experience – and learning – also came in real games, in front of crowds, with the hope of victory and the fear of letting down his teammates on his mind. Whether he has developed a relaxed confidence in his shot and an ability to blot out the noise and waving hands of the arena is also a matter of previous experience. It is part of the player's habitus. And the difference between a great athlete and a mediocre also-ran is often not just physical ability but a hard-to-pin-down mix of confidence, concentration, and ability to rise to the occasion.

The confidence that defines greatness is largely learned, Bourdieu suggested. It is learned in a thousand earlier games. On playgrounds, in high school, and in college, basketball players imagine themselves to be Michael Jordan – but they also learn that they are not. They do not jump as high or float as long; their desperate shots miss when his amazingly often went in. One of the most important points Bourdieu made is that this is precisely how our very experience of struggling to do well teaches us to accept inequality in our societies. We learn and incorporate into our habitus a sense of what we can "reasonably" expect. I, for example, would *like* to be a great tennis player, but have accepted that I am not. More basically, I have come to regard tennis as a mere recreation. I play it for fun, and sometimes play aggressively, but I do not play it for serious stakes. The games I play more seriously are ones I early learned I was better at, games involving words instead of balls, requiring more speed of thought and less of foot. I play these for greater stakes: my salary, my sense of career accomplishment, my belief that through my work I make a contribution to others. Then there are the games that matter so much to us that most of us play them whether we are good at them or not – love and marriage, raising children and trying to help them prosper, acquiring material possessions, or seeking religious salvation. It is our desire for the stakes of the game that ensures our commitment to it. But we do not invent the games by ourselves; they are the products of history, of social struggles and earlier improvisations, and of impositions by powerful actors with the capacity to say this, and not that, is the right way to make love, create a family, raise children.

To understand any social situation or interaction, Bourdieu suggested, ask what game (or games) the actors are playing. This is closely analogous to distinguishing the different institutional fields of modern life: education, law, family, and so forth. What is at stake in their play? The stakes determine what will count as winning or losing. The game may be literature, for example, and the players seek reputation and immortality (defined as inclusion in the canon of recognized great works). The game may be business, and the players seek wealth. It may be politics and they pursue power. The stakes of different games also shape the ways in which players will attempt to limit the field and preserve its autonomy. Precisely because they care about their literary reputations, therefore, authors of serious books are at pains to distinguish their field from "mere journalism."

Science too is a game, in this only partly metaphorical sense. It is strategic. It has winners and losers. It depends on specific sorts of resources and rules of play. And science has stakes, most notably truth. Scientists do not pursue truth out of simple altruism. It is an interest, not a *dis*interest. Commitment to truth – and to the specifically scientific way of pursuing truth (e.g. by empirical research rather than waiting for divine inspiration) – defines the field of science. But the participants in this field do not simply share peacefully in truth, they struggle over it. They seek to command it; for example, by controlling who gets hired in universities and research institutes, which projects get funded by national science foundations, which kinds of work are published in the most famous journals. They advance competing theories; they attempt to advance competing careers. Science works as a field devoted to truth because it provides players with organized incentives for pursuing their rewards – their victories in the game – by discovering and communicating genuine knowledge. It offers organized disincentives for lying, failure to use good research methods, or refusing to communicate one's discoveries.

The rules of each game are constraints on both the players and the ways in which players get things done. Players usually have to treat them as fixed and unchanging, but in fact they are historically produced. This means that they are subject to continual change, but even more that there is a great deal of investment in the existing organization of fields. When we improvise our actions, we respond to both the social and cultural structures in which we find ourselves and to our own previous experiences. We are able to act only because we have learned from those experiences, but much of what we have learned is how to fit ourselves effectively into existing cultural practices. We are constrained not just by external limits, in other words, but by our own internalization of limits on what we imagine we can do. We cannot simply shed these limits, not only because they are deep within us, but because they are part of our sense of how to play the game. In other words, they are part of the knowledge that enables us to play well, to improvise actions effectively, and maintain our commitment to the stakes of the game.

Person and Career

No culture prizes intellectuals more than France; in none are intellectuals celebrities of comparable magnitude. Pierre Bourdieu resented and contested (and profited from and used) this throughout his career. He challenged the legitimacy of "total intellectuals" with an opinion on every subject and an eye out for the TV cameras. He offered critical analysis of "the intellectual hit parade," mocking the presentation of scholarship as though it were popular music. He decried the power wielded by academic mandarins who control university appointments and research institutes. At the same time, Bourdieu became one of the most prominent French intellectuals of his generation and certainly the most influential and best known social scientist. He was on the cover of popular magazines, was the subject of television documentaries and news stories, saw his books on bestseller lists, and became a dominant force in parts (though only parts) of the academic world. He also become an intellectual mandarin himself. He not only held the most prestigious academic appointment in France, a chair at the Collège de France, he was also the head of a major research center and the editor of two journals. His work was supported by a small army of collaborators and assistants.

Amid all this, Bourdieu always thought of himself as an outsider, and though it is paradoxical, he had reasons. Paris exerts a power over French intellectual life that far exceeds that of New York, Boston, Chicago, and the San Francisco Bay area in America. The Parisian power structure is dominated by people who combine credentials from a handful of elite institutions with a smooth, urbane cultural style. They fluidly cross the lines of politics, journalism, and the university. Although a disproportionate number of the most creative figures are outsiders by family background, the power structure remains dominated by Parisians of elite class backgrounds. Many have known each other since childhood in a handful of highly selective schools, and quickly recognize and disdain outsiders. Into their midst in the 1950s, an adolescent Pierre Bourdieu came to study in the most elite of the Parisian *grandes écoles*, the École Normale Supérieure (ENS).

Bourdieu's father was the postmaster of Deguin, a small town in the Béarne region of Southwest France.[2] This is the rough French equivalent of coming from Appalachia or a remote part of Idaho. The regional dialect is strong and distinctive; the Béarnaise have resisted homogenizing efforts of the French state for generations. Both brilliant and hard-working, Bourdieu gained admission to a special, highly selective regional high school (the Lycée de Pau) and then to one of Paris's most famous secondary schools, the Lycée Louis-le-Grand. From there he entered the École Normale in 1951. Simply gaining admission to the ENS was a guarantee of membership in France's intellectual power-elite. Students were treated as members of the civil service from the moment they entered, taught to think of themselves as what Bourdieu (1989b) later termed "the state nobility." Some who started as outsiders simply assimilated, perhaps especially those whose talents were middle of the pack; Bourdieu excelled and also resisted. So did his ENS contemporaries Jacques Derrida (philosopher and literary scholar, founder of "deconstruction") and Michel Foucault (intellectual historian and cultural critic, possibly the most prominent of all the intellectuals of that generation, though now dead more than a decade). Derrida and Bourdieu graduated at the top of their class at the ENS and both became world-famous. But both remained in important ways outsiders to the Parisian intellectual elite. Neither was immediately chosen for major academic positions. Derrida for decades was barred from any of the major chairs of philosophy in France, teaching in a peripheral position even after he was one of the world's most famous and influential scholars. Bourdieu was able to make more of an institutional career only because of fortuitous circumstances.

On the one hand, he was fortunate to be supported early in his career by such powerful figures as Raymond Aron, a distinguished sociologist and journalist. On the other hand, and perhaps even more crucially, an institutional base for the social sciences had been created outside the traditional university structure. The École des Hautes Études en Sciences Sociales (EHESS) had been created (by transformation of an older institution). Bourdieu did not follow the approved path to a regular university appointment – for example, never writing a thesis for the *doctorat d'état*, the special higher degree that was the usual basis for professorships. More than that, he launched strong criticisms of a professorial elite that he thought focused heavily on defending an old intellectual order (and its own power) and minimally on advancing knowledge through research. Bourdieu allied himself with research, with new knowledge, rather than with those who sought instead simply to control the inheritance of old knowledge. This met with predictable disapproval from much of the university elite, but the existence of the EHESS gave Bourdieu an alternative base where he was able in the 1960s to establish a research center and publications program.

Though Bourdieu's writings on the problems of French higher education (especially Bourdieu and Passeron, 1964) influenced the student protests of the 1960s, he was not himself centrally involved in the activism. His approach to politics was more to intervene through producing new knowledge, with the hope that this would help to demystify the way institutions worked, revealing the limits to common justifications and the way in which power rather than simple merit shaped the distribution of opportunities. His views of the educational system reflected the disappointed idealism of one who had invested himself deeply in it, and owed much of his own rise from provincial obscurity to Parisian prominence to success in school. As he wrote in *Homo Academicus*, the famous book on higher education that he began amid the crises of 1968, he was like someone who believed in a religious vocation, then found the church to be corrupt. "The special place held in my work by a somewhat singular sociology of the university institution is no doubt explained by the peculiar force with which I felt the need to gain rational control over the disappointment felt by an 'oblate' [a religious devotee] faced with the annihilation of the truths and values to which he was destined and dedicated, rather than take refuge in feelings of self-destructive resentment" (Bourdieu, 1984, p. xxvi). The disappointment could not be undone, but it could be turned to understanding and potentially, through that understanding, to positive change.

Educational institutions were central to Bourdieu's concern, but both his sense of disappointment and his critical analyses were more wide-reaching. All the institutions of modernity, including the capitalist market and the state itself, share in a tendency to promise far more than they deliver. They present themselves as working for the common good, but in fact reproduce social inequalities. They present themselves as agents of freedom, but in fact are organizations of power. They inspire devotion from those who want richer, freer lives, and they disappoint them with the limits they impose and the violence they deploy. Simply to attack modernity, however, is to engage in the "self-destructive resentment" Bourdieu sought to avoid. Rather, the best way forward lies through the struggle to understand, to win deeper truths, and to remove legitimacy from the practices by which power mystifies itself. In this way, one can challenge the myths and deceptions of modernity, enlightenment, and civilization without becoming the enemy of the hopes they offered.

Bourdieu's perspective and approach were both shaped crucially by his fieldwork in Algeria. He studied Kabyle peasant life and participation in a new cash economy that threatened and changed it (Bourdieu and Sayad, 1963). He studied the difficult situation of those who chose to work in the modern economy and found themselves transformed into its "underclass," not even able to gain the full status of proletarians because of the ethno-national biases of the French colonialists (Bourdieu et al., 1963; Bourdieu, 1972). And during the time of his fieldwork, Bourdieu confronted the violent French repression of the Algerian struggle for independence. The bloody battle of Algiers was a formative experience for a generation of French intellectuals who saw their state betray what it had always claimed was a mission of liberation and civilization, revealing the sheer power that lay behind colonialism, despite its legitimation in terms of progress.

Bourdieu's formal education had been in philosophy, but in Algeria he remade himself as a self-taught ethnographer (Honneth et al., 1986, p. 39). It was in trying to understand Kabyle society that he shaped his distinctive perspective on the interplay of objective structures and subjective understanding and action. The experience of fieldwork itself was powerful, and helped to shape Bourdieu's orientation to knowledge. As an ethnographer, Bourdieu entered into another social and cultural world, learned to speak an unfamiliar language, and struggled to understand what was going on, while remaining necessarily in crucial ways an outsider to it. This helped him to see the importance of combining insider and outsider perspectives on social life. To be altogether an outsider to Kabylia was certainly to fail to understand it, but in order to grasp it accurately the ethnographer also had to break with the familiarity of both his own received categories and those of his informants. His job was neither to impose his own concepts nor simply to translate those of the people he studied. He must struggle, as the philosopher Bachelard (an important influence on Bourdieu) put it, to "win" the facts of his study.

One of the most basic difficulties in such research, Bourdieu came to realize, is the extent to which it puts a premium on natives' discursive explanations of their actions. Because the anthropologist is an outsider and starts out ignorant, natives must explain things to him. But it would be a mistake to accept such explanations as simple truths, not because they are lies but because they are precisely the limited form of knowledge that can be offered to one who has not mastered the practical skills of living fully inside the culture (Bourdieu, 1972, p. 2). Unless he is careful, the researcher is led to focus his attention not on the actual social life around him but on the statements about it which his informants offer. "The anthropologist's particular relation to the object of his study contains the makings of a theoretical distortion inasmuch as his situation as an observer, excluded from the real play of social activities by the fact that he has no place (except by choice or by way of a game) in the system observed and has no need to make a place for himself there, inclines him to a hermeneutic representation of practices, leading him to reduce all social relations to communicative relations and, more precisely, to decoding operations" (ibid., p. 1). Such an approach would treat social life as much more a matter of explicit cognitive rules than it is, and miss the ways in which practical activity is really generated beyond the determination of the explicit rules.

In this respect, Bourdieu took the case of anthropological fieldwork to be paradigmatic for social research more generally. The confrontation with a very different way of life revealed the need for both outsider and insider perspectives. Not long after he completed his work in Algeria, Bourdieu challenged himself by applying the method he was developing to research in his own native region of Béarne. The task, as he began to argue didactically and to exemplify in all his work, was to combine intimate knowledge of practical activity with more abstract knowledge of objective patterns, and, using the dialectical relation between the two, to break with the familiar ways in which people understand their own everyday actions. These everyday accounts always contain distortions and misrecognitions that do various sorts of ideological work. The classic example is gift-giving, which is understood as disinterested, voluntary, and not subject to precise accounting of equivalence, but which people actually do in ways that are more strategic than their self-understanding allows. Bourdieu's project was to grasp the practical strategies people employed, their relationship to the explanations they gave (to themselves as well as to others), and the ways in which people's pursuit of their own ends nonetheless tended to reproduce objective patterns which they did not choose and of which they might even be unaware.

This project was a profound intervention into Bourdieu's intellectual context. French intellectual life in the 1950s and 1960s produced two powerful but opposed perspectives in the human sciences: structuralism and existentialism. The former emphasized the formal patterns underlying all reality (extending ideas introduced to sociology by Durkheim and Mauss); the latter stressed that meaning inhered in the individual experience of being in the world, and especially in autonomous action. The two greatest and most influential figures in French intellectual life of the period were Claude Lévi-Strauss (the structuralist anthropologist) and Jean-Paul Sartre (the existentialist philosopher). Bourdieu's theoretical tastes were closer to Lévi-Strauss, but he saw both as one-sided. If existentialism greatly exaggerated the role of subjective choice, structuralism neglected agency. In a sense, Bourdieu developed an internal challenge to structuralism, incorporating much of its insight and intellectual approach but rejecting the tendency to describe social life in overly cognitive and overly static terms as a matter of following rules rather than engaging in strategic practice.

It is partly for similar reasons that Bourdieu chose not to write an abstract theoretical treatise summarizing his theory. He saw theory as best developed in the task of empirical analysis, and saw this as a practical challenge. Rather than applying a theory developed in advance and in the abstract, he brought his distinctive theoretical habitus to bear on a variety of analytic problems, and in the course of tackling each developed his theoretical resources further. The concepts developed in the course of such work could be transposed from one setting to another by means of analogy, and adapted to each. Theory, like the habitus in general, serves not as a fixed set of rules but as a characteristic mode of improvising (Brubaker, 1992). In an implicit critique of the dominance of philosophy over French social science, Bourdieu held that the real proof that a sociological project has value is to be demonstrated in its empirical findings, not in abstract system-building.

When Bourdieu left Algeria, he received a fellowship to the Institute for Advanced Study in Princeton and followed it with a stay at the University of Pennsylvania. While in the USA, he met the American sociologist Erving Goffman – another theoretically astute sociologist who refrained from abstract system-building in favor of embedding theory in empirical practice. Goffman had begun to develop a sociology that followed Durkheim's interest in the moral order, but focused on the ways this was reproduced in interpersonal relations by individuals with their own strategic investments in action. Rather than treating individuals as either autonomous or simply socially constructed, for example, Goffman (1959) introduced the element of strategy by writing of the "presentation of self in everyday life." His point was similar to that Bourdieu would stress: to show the element of improvisation and adaptation, rather than simple rule-following, and then to introduce agents as dynamic figures in the social order. Where Bourdieu's favorite metaphor was games, Goffman's was drama, but they shared the sense of social life as a performance that could be played better or worse, and which nearly always tended to the reproduction of social order even when individuals tried to make new and different things happen in their lives.

Goffman encouraged Bourdieu to take a position at the University of Pennsylvania, but Bourdieu felt that if he stayed in the USA he would be unable to develop the kind of critical sociology he wanted to create.[3] It was not simply that he wanted to criticize France rather than the USA, but that he wanted to benefit from inside knowledge while still achieving critical distance. This would present a challenge, but the challenge was itself a source of theoretical insight: "In choosing to study the social world in which we are *involved*, we are obliged to confront, in *dramatized* form as it were, a certain number of fundamental epistemological problems, all related to the question of the difference between practical knowledge and scholarly knowledge, and particularly to the special difficulties involved first in *breaking* with inside experience and then in reconstituting the knowledge which has been obtained by means of this break" (Bourdieu, 1988a, p. 1).

Bourdieu returned to France and took a position in the European Center for Historical Sociology, headed by Raymond Aron. Aron was an important early supporter of Bourdieu's, and made him a deputy in the administration of the Center. The two were never close collaborators, despite initial mutual respect, and they came into increasing conflict as Bourdieu became more critical of French higher education. Aron was a moderate conservative politically, and Bourdieu was aligned with the left. Perhaps more importantly, Aron was a defender of French academia and Bourdieu criticized its role in preserving class inequality (Bourdieu and Passeron, 1964). Things came to a head when student revolt broke out in 1968. Aron suggested that the problem lay primarily with the students and sought to limit – rather than expand – their involvement in the life of the university. Bourdieu was sympathetic to the students, though he thought them naively voluntaristic and inattentive to the deep structures that made for the reproduction of class inequality and the university as an institution (see Bourdieu and Passeron, 1967).[4] He made little public comment on the protests, but he did choose this moment to break with Aron and found his own Center for European Sociology. With him he took a remarkable group of collaborators whom he had attracted, including Luc Boltanski, Jean-Claude Passeron, and Monique de Saint Martin.

Together, this group (and new recruits) conducted a remarkable range of empirical studies. These put the perspective Bourdieu had developed to use in analyzing many different aspects of French social life. In 1975 Bourdieu and his collaborators also founded a new journal, *Actes de la Recherche en Sciences Sociales*. In its pages they not only took up different empirical themes but developed and tried out new ideas and theoretical innovations. *Actes* also translated and introduced work from researchers with cognate interests in other countries.

Almost simultaneously with the founding of his Center, Bourdieu published a kind of manual for doing sociology (Bourdieu et al., 1968). This differed from typical textbooks in presenting not a compilation of facts and a summary of theories, but an approach to sociology as an ongoing effort to "win social facts." Entitled *The Craft of Sociology*, it bypassed abstract codification of knowledge and endeavored to help students acquire the practical skill and intellectual habitus of sociologists. Bourdieu also put his craft to work in an extraordinary series of books and articles. His study (with Passeron) of *Reproduction: In Education, Society, and Culture* was initially the best known in English. It helped to establish a whole genre of studies of how education contributes to the reproduction of social inequality. In theoretical terms, however, Bourdieu's most important work of the period was *Outline of a Theory of Practice* (1972), probably his single most influential work. At almost the same time, he also published his most sustained study of French cultural patterns, *Distinction* (1979), and two books of essays. This remarkable corpus of work was the basis for his election to the chair of sociology in the Collège de France. He continued his remarkable productivity thereafter. Among the most important of his books are *Language and Symbolic Power* (1982), *Homo Academicus* (1984), *The State Nobility* (1989), *The Political Ontology of Martin Heidegger* (1988), *The Rules of Art* (1992), and *The Weight of the World* (1993). He also published several collections of articles, and the noteworthy collaboration with Loïc Wacquant, *An Invitation to Reflexive Sociology* (Bourdieu and Wacquant, 1992), which is among the best overall statements of Bourdieu's perspective on sociology.

In sum, Bourdieu's own educational experience at once gave him fantastic resources – a command of the history of philosophy, multiple languages, and skills in critique and debate – and alienated him from the very institutions that helped, as it were, to make him a star. The resources were not limited to intellectual abilities but included the credentials, connections and sense of the game that enabled him not just to become famous but to create new institutions. The alienation gave Bourdieu the motivation to pioneer a critical approach, rather than a simple affirmation of the status quo.

Bourdieu saw critical social science as politically significant, but he was careful to avoid "short-circuiting" the relationship between scholarly distinction and political voice. He resisted trading on his celebrity, and kept his interventions to topics where he was especially knowledgeable, such as education or the situation of Algerians in France. More recently, he wrote a bestselling polemic about television (1996) and several pointed essays on the ways in which market logic is being introduced into cultural life. His typical goal was to demystify the ways in which seemingly neutral institutions in fact make it harder for ordinary people to learn the truth about the state or public affairs. He called for an "internationale" of intellectuals (to replace the old Internationale of the working-class movement). In this spirit, he founded a review of books and intellectual debate, *Liber*, which appeared in half a dozen languages (though, curiously, not English). He also overcame a longstanding resistance to making public declarations of conscience by signing petitions, in order to work with other leading figures to suggest in the midst of the Yugoslavian wars that there were other options besides passivity and massive high-altitude bombing. The media and the state seemed to suggest, wrote Bourdieu and his colleagues, that there was a simple choice between the NATO military campaign and ignoring the horrors of ethnic cleansing that Milosevic and others had unleashed. Not so, they argued, for there were other possible approaches to stemming the evils, including working more closely with Yugoslavia's immediate neighbors. And it was worth noting that NATO's intervention had actually increased the pace of ethnic cleansing. As Bourdieu (1999) argued, the categories with which states "think" are powerful. They structure too much of the thinking of all of us in modern society; breaking with them is a struggle, but an important one.

More generally, Bourdieu's mode of intervention was to use the methods of good social scientific research to expose misrecognitions that support injustice. A prime example is the enormous collective study of "the suffering of the world" produced under his direction (Bourdieu, 1993). This aimed not simply to expose poverty or hardship, but to challenge the dominant points of view that made it difficult for those living in comfort, and especially those running the state, to understand the lives of those who had to struggle most simply to exist. The book thus included both direct attempts to state the truths that could be seen from social spaces of suffering, and examinations of how the views of state officials and other elites prevented them from seeing these truths for themselves. The misrecognition built into the very categories of official knowledge was thus one of its themes. Bourdieu and his colleagues entered the public discourse not simply as advocates, therefore, but specifically as social scientists.

In other cases as well, Bourdieu's interventions into public debate and politics took the form of trying to expose misrecognitions and false oppositions. Faced with the 1999 NATO war with Serbia, for example, he joined with other intellectuals in challenging the view that there were only two choices: accept Milosevic's ethnic cleansing or bomb Serbia. This view served the interests of certain elites, but obscured the real range of possibilities for action. Worried by the growing dominance of television over popular consciousness, Bourdieu (1998) wrote a short book analyzing its characteristic ways of collapsing the real range of possibilities into false choices and misrecognitions that support certain social interests at the expense of others. Indeed, throughout his work, one of Bourdieu's enduring concerns was with symbolic violence. By this he meant the ways in which people are harmed or held back not by force of arms but by the force of (mis)understanding. The very way in which knowledge is organized for the education of France's most elite students, for example, enshrines certain ways of thinking as right, or as simply "the way to think" (doxa) (see Bourdieu, 1989b, chapter 2). The most powerful forms of symbolic violence are not simply name calling, like saying the poor are lazy or immigrants greedy. Rather, they inhere in the very cognitive structure. Students (Bourdieu had in mind specifically students at France's *grandes écoles*) thus learn to categorize different ways of thinking, different kinds of cultural production, and different social values as higher or lower. It is easier for them later to rebel against a specific classification – say the view that jazz is lower than opera – than to resist the whole project of viewing the world hierarchically. Yet there is nothing intrinsic to the world that requires that all cultural objects be viewed on a scale from higher to lower; this is a specific, culturally reproduced way of thinking. And it is one that systematically encourages support for social hierarchies of other kinds and misrecognition of the actual nature of what people think, or do, or value.

When Bourdieu intervened in public debates, it was almost always in favor of free exchange. The work and social value of artists, writers, and intellectuals depends on such free exchange – an unhampered and open creativity and communication. It thus depends on maintaining the autonomy of the artistic, literary, and scientific or intellectual fields. Boundaries need to be maintained between serious intellectual pursuit of truth and discourses – however smart – that seek only to use knowledge instrumentally. In this, he stood clearly against those who would censor intellectual or cultural life in favor of their standards of morality or political expediency (see Bourdieu and Haacke, 1994).

FALSE DICHOTOMIES

Bourdieu (1988a) described one of the central motivations behind his intellectual work as a determination to challenge misleading dichotomies. The broad dualistic outlook of Western thought is expressed in the ubiquitous opposition of mind to body. It also takes the form of specific dichotomies basic to social science: structure/action, objective/subjective, theory/practice. Drawing on Gaston Bachelard and other philosophers critical of this dualistic outlook, Bourdieu set out to transcend it (see the critical discussion in Vandenberghe, 1999). It is crucial, he suggested, not just to see both sides but to see how they are inseparably related to each other. Seemingly fixed objective structures have to be created and reproduced; apparently voluntary subjective actions depend on and are shaped by objective conditions and constraints; knowledge and action constantly inform each other, rather than theory guiding practice by a set of fixed rules. Bourdieu sought to move sociology beyond the antinomy of social physics (seeing social life as completely external and objective) and social phenomenology (looking at social life through subjective experience) (Bourdieu and Wacquant, 1992, p. 7).

Take the opposition of theory to practice. This is ancient, a central theme as long ago as the philosophical writings of Aristotle. It contrasts knowing to doing, mental to physical activity. This conceptualization has several problems. First, it tends to neglect the kind of non-theoretical knowledge that is implicit in practical skills. Few of us can explain the physics of buoyancy in water, the mechanics of moving muscle and bone, or even the dynamics that make freestyle faster than breaststroke, yet we can swim. In a similar sense, craft workers are able to produce pottery and textiles (among other things) in ways that demonstrate huge amounts of learned knowledge, but which do not depend heavily on putting that knowledge into formal terms, or even into words. This neglect of practical knowledge both reflects and encourages a value judgment that mental work is "better" than physical labor. This was implicit in the class structure of ancient Greece, in which aristocratic men could afford the time for pondering philosophy, while slaves, commoners, and women took care of most material production.

Second, the theory/practice dichotomy encourages the view that practice is the application of theory, a form of rule-following. Behind this is an image of the mind (something distinct from the brain) moving the body like a puppet, giving directions to the muscles as the puppet master pulls strings. Bourdieu (along with a variety of philosophers including especially Wittgenstein) suggested this is misleading. When we perform practical tasks we are not necessarily following rules. Computer models of mental processing commonly suggest something like this because that is the typical nature of a computer program. But human activity involves a combination of discursive awareness and unconscious skill. A "simple" task like buttoning a shirt is not based on consciously following a set of rules (try to articulate what these would be!); rather, it is a practical ability that we learn through the discipline of repetition. We can only do it well when it becomes habitual. The same is true, Bourdieu suggested, not just for such physical tasks but for much more complex social tasks like choosing marriage partners or giving gifts. There *are* rules about such things, but on the basis of careful empirical observation and analysis in both Algeria and France Bourdieu suggested that the rules do not account adequately for what actually goes on. The rules are one part of the story, important to people when they discuss what is desirable, but their practical activity involves a constant adaptation to circumstances that call for going beyond rules. This does not mean that in coming to conclusions about such matters as who makes a good marriage partner people are not drawing on their knowledge. They are; and they are making judgments about potential for happiness, economic success, acceptance by their parents, etc. But these judgments are precisely not deductions from scientific theories in the way that, say, an engineer's conclusions that a bridge needs more structural supports may be. Similarly, Bourdieu described how Kabyle peasants resolve disputes, emphasizing that it is not by rigidly applying formal legal rules, but by making judgments – socially shared through conversation – about what is in accord with justice or honor.

Taking practice seriously implies, third, that we see society through the lens of what social actors are trying to do. Social science is typically built on a totalizing view. This is made possible by the fact that scientists are generally outsiders to the social situations they analyze, and by the fact that they can see how historical events have turned out. This gives the scientists some great advantages. They can know more than most actual social actors about the odds of their choices working out the way they want, and about the unintended consequences of their actions (Merton, 1936). But the scientists need to guard against forgetting the uncertainty under which all real people act. Recall the game analogy. The basketball player with the ball is not concerned with scientific analysis of the probabilities of making a shot from 25 feet. He is concerned with the particular options before him – who is open for a pass, how much time is left on the clock – as well as with his own desire to win and the risk that he will embarrass himself instead of being a hero. Players will respond differently. But all, Bourdieu suggested, respond by acting strategically, not by simply following rules. "To substitute *strategy* for *rule*," he writes, "is to reintroduce time, with its rhythm, its orientation, its irreversibility" (Bourdieu, 1977, p. 9). A good player will not always take the 25-foot shot under similar conditions, but sometimes fake and pass, and sometimes drive for the basket. The key to understanding strategy is not just that the actor wants to accomplish something, but that he or she is trying to do so under conditions of uncertainty. Not only is the future not yet settled, but the actor cannot see the whole of society, the player can only see the game from his or her particular position within it.

Fourth, the traditional idea of theory represents knowledge as passive understanding of the world. The implication is that there is a complete and potentially permanent logical order already existing behind society or culture, and that the task of the sociologist or anthropologist is only to decipher it. Not so, said Bourdieu, partly because every culture is incomplete and contains internal contradictions. It may be relatively structured, but not 100 percent so. As a result, social scientists should not try to represent culture simply as rules that people follow, but as the practical dispositions that enable people to improvise actions where no learned rule fits perfectly. These will not be uniform throughout a society, but will vary with the locations of people's different experiences within it. Those who have more resources (capital) may be better able to realize widely shared values. To take a mundane example, star athletes may be better able to get dates with the prettiest or most popular girls in a high school. It would be a mistake, however, to represent their behavior and luck as though it represented cultural rules from which everyone else deviated. And to grasp the workings of the high school culture, we would need to understand how other people experienced their different social locations, and how this influenced who they thought they could or should date, what they saw as attractive, and so forth. What we would see is a system not simply of rules, but of resources, practical dispositions, and strategies. Our knowledge would also become more critical – we would be aware of the inequalities in the high school in a way that a more conventional cultural theorist might not be, we would see ways in which conventional norms about social attractiveness are in fact a basis of discrimination.

Bourdieu's case was not for an action-centered sociology as opposed to one focused on structure. On the contrary, he sought to overcome this distinction, which he thought had limited sociology in the past. His effort was to develop a "genetic structuralism"; that is, a sociology that uses the intellectual resources of structural analysis, but approaches structures in terms of the ways in which they are produced and reproduced through action. Bourdieu had already analyzed dynamics of reproduction in several works of the 1960s, but the most influential statement of his developing theoretical approach came with the publication in 1972 of *Outline of a Theory of Practice*.

Bourdieu started with the assumption that most social scientists exaggerate "structure" rather than action, because emphasizing the orderly, recurrent, and enduring aspects of social life is what sets "objective" social science apart from everyday "subjective" viewpoints. Every introductory sociology student learns the difference between a personal point of view and a scientific one, between an individual experience or choice and a social pattern in experiences and choices. Students often learn Émile Durkheim's (1895) famous maxim that social facts should be treated as though they were "things" – in other words, hard, objective reality. The facts of social science, Durkheim argued, are external to individuals, endure longer than individual lifetimes, and have coercive power over individuals. The Durkheimian tradition, and these approaches to social facts, remained dominant in French social science when Bourdieu wrote *Outline*.

Bourdieu's first task in *Outline*, thus, was to show the "objective limits of objectivism." Real objectivity in social science starts by breaking with anecdotes and familiar understandings in order to grasp a deeper reality. This is not simply the sum total of the facts that happen to exist (as a purely empiricist view might suggest). Rather, it is the underlying conditions that make possible whatever facts exist. The idea is similar to that involved in grasping the difference between genetics and physical appearance. A man and a woman bring more or less fixed genetic possibilities to the creation of children. But which of these possibilities appear in any specific child is a matter of statistical probabilities. Simply generalizing from the empirical traits of an individual child or even several children may thus be misleading with regard to the underlying pattern of genetic determination. In the same sense, what is "objectively" the deepest "reality" in social life is not the surface phenomena that we see all around us, but the underlying structural features that make these surface phenomena possible. The "objectivist" task of sociology is to grasp these underlying structural features. For example, what are the underlying conditions for the production and distribution of wealth, as distinct from simply its presence or absence among our friends or others we know? But here we see also the limits to pure objectivism. By itself, objectivism cannot make sense of how the underlying conditions of possibility are translated into empirical actuality. This only comes about when they become the bases of human action, which is not altogether objective, but is based on practical subjective knowledge of the social world. Social theory needs, therefore, to study both objective structures and the ways in which human beings act. These are two sides of a dialectical relationship and not simply two distinct phenomena, because the ways in which human beings act are the result of practical dispositions that they develop through their experience of objective structures. This is why most action tends to reproduce structures, and change in social institutions is relatively gradual. If we did not grasp that social action is itself structured, it would be hard to explain why action did not simply dissolve all institutions into chaos.

Objectivist sociology tends to explain the structuring of action only as the result of external forces. We may be pushed in one direction, or constrained from going in another. Our action is governed by force, or by rules, or by obstacles. What this misses, said Bourdieu, is the extent to which social structure is inside each of us because we have learned from the experience of previous actions. We have a practical mastery of how to do things that takes into account social structures. Thus the way in which we produce our actions is already shaped to fit with and reproduce the social structures because this is what enables us to act effectively. But we internalize the social structures as we experience them – not as they exist in some abstract objectivist model. We develop our practical understanding of these structures through our learning of categories that are made available by our culture, but also through our own active development of understanding. On the basis of this combination of experience and cognition, each of us develops a practical disposition to act in certain ways.

> There is action, and history, and conservation or transformation of structures only because there are agents, but agents who are acting and efficacious only because they are not reduced to what is ordinarily put under the notion of individual and who, as socialized organisms, are endowed with an ensemble of dispositions which imply both the propensity and the ability to get into and to play the game. (Bourdieu, 1989b, p. 59)

Bourdieu's stress on the presence of social structure inside the actor was a challenge not only to objectivism, but to most forms of subjectivism. These are mirror images of each other. Subjectivists are prone to two basic errors. First, they are apt to ascribe too much voluntarism to social actors. Focusing on each occasion as though it is an opportunity for creativity and constructing a new reality, they neglect the extent to which people's very abilities to understand and choose and act have been shaped by processes of learning which are themselves objectively structured and socially produced. Second, subjectivist approaches commonly present social life as much less structured, much more contingent, than it really is. As Bourdieu (1989b, p. 47) wrote, "If it is good to recall, against certain mechanistic visions of action, that social agents construct social reality, individually and also collectively, we must be careful not to forget, as the interactionists and ethnomethodologists often do, that they have not constructured the categories they put to work in this work of construction." In other words, how we think about reality does shape what it is for us, but how we think about it is a result of what we have learned from our culture and experience, not simply a matter of free will.

Bourdieu drew on sociologists (like George Herbert Mead, Harold Garfinkel, and Erving Goffman) who paid attention to the ways in which social action shapes social structures, and stressed the ways in which *inter*action even shapes who the actors are and what strategies they pursue. At the same time, he remained sharply critical of philosophers (like Sartre) who wrote as though individual existence came before society. Bourdieu insisted on a dialectic of structure and action, but he also made it clear that he thought the crucial first step for social science came with the discovery of objective structure, and the break with everyday knowledge that this entails.

Winning the Social Fact

Social life requires our active engagement in its games. It is impossible to remain neutral, and it is impossible to live with the distanced, detached perspective of the outside observer. As a result, all participants in social life have a knowledge of it that is conditioned by their specific location and trajectory in it. That is, they see it from where they are, how they got there and where they are trying to go. Take something like the relations between parents and children. As participants, we see these from one side or the other. They look different at different stages of life and other different circumstances – as, for example, when one's parents become grandparents to one's children. Our engagement in these relationships is powerful, but it is deeply subjective, not objective. We know a lot, but what we know is built into the specific relationships we inhabit and into specific modes of cultural understanding. Much of it is practical mastery of how to be a parent or a child. This is a genuine form of knowledge, but it should not be confused with scientific knowledge.

Our everyday life involvements, Bourdieu suggested, invest us with a great deal of practical knowledge, but require us to misrecognize much of what we and other people do. Misrecognition is not simply error; indeed, in a practical mode of engagement every recognition is also a misrecognition. This is so precisely because we cannot be objective and outside our own relations, we cannot see them from all possible angles. Which aspects of them we understand and how reflects our own practical engagement in them and also the conditions for perpetuating the games in which we are participants. As Bourdieu (1980, p. 68) wrote,

> Practical faith is the condition of entry that every field tacitly imposes, not only by sanctioning and debarring those who would destroy the game, but by so arranging things, in practice, that the operations of selecting and shaping new entrants (rites of passage, examinations, etc.) are such as to obtain from them that undisputed, pre-reflexive, naive, native compliance with the fundamental presuppositions of the field which is the very definition of doxa.

"Doxa" is Bourdieu's term for the taken-for-granted, preconscious understandings of the world and our place in it that shape our more conscious awarenesses. Doxa is more basic than "orthodoxy," or beliefs that we maintain to be correct in the awareness that others may have different views. Orthodoxy is an enforced straightness of belief, like following the teachings of organized religion. Doxa is felt reality, what we take not as beyond challenge but before any possible challenge. But though doxa seems to us to be simply the way things are, it is in fact a socially produced understanding, and what is doxic varies from culture to culture and field to field. In order for us to live, and to recognize anything, we require the kind of orientation to action and awareness that doxa gives. But doxa thus also implies misrecognition, partial and distorted understanding. It was the doxic experience of Europeans for centuries that the world was flat. Thinking otherwise was evidence not of scientific cleverness but of madness.

The ideas of doxa and misrecognition allowed Bourdieu a subtle approach to issues commonly addressed through the concept of ideology. Marxist and other analysts have pointed to the ways in which people's beliefs may be shaped to conform with either power structures or the continued functioning of a social order. Ideology is commonly understood as a set of beliefs that is in some degree partial and distorted and serves some specific set of social interests. Thus it is ideological to suggest that individual effort is the basic determinant of where people stand in the class hierarchy. It is not only false, but it serves both to legitimate an unequal social order and to motivate participants. Common use of the notion of ideology, however, tends to imply that it is possible to be without ideology, to have an objectively correct or undistorted understanding of the social world. This Bourdieu rejected. One can shake the effects of specific ideologies, but one cannot live without doxa, and one cannot play the games of life without misrecognition. Misrecognition is built into the very practical mastery that makes our actions effective.

Nonetheless, symbolic power is exercised through the construction of doxa as well as orthodoxy. Every field of social participation demands of those who enter it a kind of preconscious adherence to its way of working. This requires seeing things in certain ways and not others, and this will work to the benefit of some participants more than others. Take the modern business corporation. It seldom occurs to people who work for corporations, or enter into contracts with them, or represent them in court, to question whether they exist. But what is a corporation? It is not precisely a material object, and not a person in any ordinary sense. As the Supreme Court Justice Marshall put it famously, the corporation has "no soul to damn, no body to kick." Yet corporations can own property, make contracts, and sue and be sued in courts of law. Corporations exist largely because they are recognized to exist by a wide range of people, including agents of the legal system and the government. In order to do almost any kind of business in a modern society, one must believe in corporations. Yet they are also in a sense fictions. Behind corporations stand owners and managers – and for the most part, they cannot be held liable for things the corporation "does." To believe in the corporation is to support a system that benefits certain interests much more than others, and yet to not believe in it makes it impossible to carry out effective practical action in the business world. This is how misrecognition works.

In addition to making misrecognition, and doxa, the objects of analysis, Bourdieu wished to remind us of their methodological significance. It is because ordinary social life requires us to be invested in preconscious understandings that are at least in part misrecognitions that it is a faulty guide to social research. A crucial first step for every sociologist is to break with familiar, received understandings of everyday life. To "win" social facts depends on finding techniques for seeing the world more objectively. This is always a struggle, and one that the researcher must keep in mind throughout every project. It will always be easy to slide back into ways of seeing things that are supported by everyday, doxic understandings – one's own, or those of one's informants. Some of the advantages of statistical techniques, for example, come in helping us to achieve distance on the social life we study. At the same time, however, we need to work to understand the processes by which misrecognition is produced, to grasp that it is not a simple mistake. It is not enough to see the "objective" facts alone. We need to see the game in which they are part of the stakes.

Habitus

Participation in social games is not merely a conscious choice. It is something we do prereflectively. We are, in a sense, always already involved. From childhood we are prepared for adult roles. We are asked what we want to be when we grow up and learn that it is right to have an occupation. We are told to sit up straight and speak when spoken to. We experience the reverence our parents show before the church – or before money or fame, depending on the parents. Out of what meets with approval or doesn't, what works or doesn't, we develop a characteristic way of generating new actions, of improvising the moves of the game of our lives. We learn confidence or timidity. But in either case much of the power of the socialization process is experienced in bodily terms, simply as part of who we are, how we exist in the world. This sense is the habitus.

Notoriously difficult to pin down, the term "habitus" means basically the embodied sensibility that makes possible structured improvisation.[5] Jazz musicians can play together without consciously following rules because they have developed physically embodied capacities to hear and respond appropriately to what is being produced by others, and to create themselves in ways which others can hear sensibly and to which others can respond. Or, in Bourdieu's metaphor, effective play of a game requires not just knowledge of rules but a practical sense for the game.[6] If this is a challenge to the static cognitivism of structuralism, it is equally a challenge to the existentialist understanding of subjectivity. Sartre created his famous account of the existential dilemma by positing "a sort of unprecedented confrontation between the subject and the world" (Bourdieu, 1972, p. 73). But this misrepresents how actual social life works, because it leaves completely out of the account the durable dispositions of the habitus. Before anyone is a subject, in other words, he or she is already inculcated with institutional knowledge – recognition and misrecognition.

The habitus appears in one sense as each individual's characteristic set of dispositions for action. There is a social process of matching such dispositions to positions in the social order (as, in another vocabulary, one learns to play the roles that fit with one's statuses). But the habitus is more than this. It is the meeting point between institutions and bodies. That is, it is the basic way in which each person as a biological being connects with the sociocultural order in such a way that the various games of life keep their meaning, keep being played.

> Produced by the work of inculcation and appropriation that is needed in order for objective structures, the products of collective history, to be reproduced in the form of the durable, adjusted dispositions that are the condition of their functioning, the *habitus*, which is constituted in the course through which agents partake of the history objectified in institutions, is what makes it possible to inhabit institutions, to appropriate them practically, and so to keep them in activity, continuously pulling them from the state of dead letters, reviving the sense deposited in them, but at the same time imposing the revisions and transformations that reactivation entails. (Bourdieu, 1990, p. 57)[7]

Think of an example – say the Christian church, a product of two millennia that still seems alive to members. They experience it as alive, but they also make it live by reinventing it in their rituals, their relations with each other, and their faith. Being brought up in the church helps to prepare members for belief (inculcation), but it is also something they must actively claim (appropriation). The connection between the institution and the person is the very way in which members produce their actions.

> Each agent, wittingly or unwittingly, willy nilly, is a producer and reproducer of objective meaning. Because his actions and works are the product of a *modus operandi* of which he is not the producer and has no conscious mastery, they contain an 'objective intention', as the Scholastics put it, which always outruns his conscious intentions. (Bourdieu, 1972, p. 79).

To return to an earlier example, each of us reproduces the idea of corporation every time we engage in a transaction with one – owning stock, renting an apartment, going to work – even though that may not be our conscious intention.

Bourdieu emphasized that habitus is not just a capacity of the individual, but an achievement of the collectivity. It is the result of a ubiquitous "collective enterprise of inculcation." The reason why "strategies" can work without individuals being consciously strategic is that individuals become who they are and social institutions exist only on the strength of this inculcation of orientations to action, evaluation, and understanding. The most fundamental social changes have to appear not only as changes in formal structures but as changes in habitual orientations to action. Bourdieu sought thus to overcome the separation of culture, social organization, and embodied individual being that is characteristic of most existing sociology.

Fields and Capital

As we saw above, one of the ways in which Bourdieu used the metaphor of "games" was to describe the different fields into which social activities are organized. Each field, like law or literature, has its own distinctive rules and stakes of play. Accomplishments in one are not immediately granted the same prestige or rewards in another. Thus novelists are usually not made judges, and legal writing is seldom taken as literature. But, although the fields involve different games, it is possible to make translations between them. To explain this, Bourdieu uses the concept of capital. His analysis of the differences in forms of capital and dynamics of conversion between them is one of the most original and important features of Bourdieu's theory. This describes both the specific kinds of resources accumulated by those who are winners in the struggles of various fields and the more general forms of capital – such as money and prestige – that make possible translations from one to the other. "A capital does not exist and function except in relation to a field" (Bourdieu and Wacquant, 1992, p. 101). Yet successful lawyers and successful authors both, for example, seek to convert their own successes into improved standards of living and chances for their children. To do so, they must convert the capital specific to their field of endeavor into other forms. In addition to material property (economic capital), families may accumulate networks of connections (social capital) and prestige (cultural capital) by the way in which they raise children and plan their marriages. In each case, the accumulation has to be reproduced in every generation or it is lost.

In short, there are two senses in which capital is converted from one form to another. One is as part of the intergenerational reproduction of capital. Rich people try to make sure that their children go to good colleges – which, in fact, are often expensive private colleges (at least in America). This is a way of converting money into cultural capital (educational credentials). In this form, it can be passed on and potentially reconverted into economic form. The second sense of conversion of capital is more immediate. The athlete with great successes and capital specific to his or her sporting field may convert this into money by signing agreements to endorse products, or by opening businesses like car dealerships or insurance agencies, in which celebrity status in the athletic field may help to attract customers.

Bourdieu's account of capital differed from most versions of Marxism. It was not backed by a theory of capitalism as a distinct social formation (Calhoun, 1993). Neither was it the basis for an economic determinism. Bourdieu saw "an economy of practices" at work insofar as people must always decide how to expend their effort and engage in strategies that aim at gaining scarce goods. But Bourdieu did not hold that specifically economic goods are always the main or underlying motivations of action or the basis of an overall system. By conceptualizing capital as taking many different forms, each tied to a different field of action, Bourdieu stressed: (a) that there are many different kinds of goods that people pursue and resources that they accumulate; (b) that these are inextricably social, because they derive their meaning from the social relationships that constitute different fields (rather than simply from some sort of material things being valuable in and of themselves); and (c) that the struggle to accumulate capital is hardly the whole story – the struggle to reproduce capital is equally basic and often depends on the ways in which it can be converted across fields.

In addition, Bourdieu showed that fields (such as art, literature, and science) that are constituted by a seeming disregard for or rejection of economic interests nonetheless operate according to a logic of capital accumulation and reproduction. It is common to think of religion, art, and science as basically the opposite of economic calculation and capital accumulation. Even fields like law are constituted not simply by reference to economic capital (however much lawyers may treasure their pay) but by reference to justice and technical expertise in its adjudication. This is crucial, among other reasons, as a basis for the claim of each field to a certain autonomy. This, as Bourdieu (1992, pp. 47ff) has argued, is the "critical phase" in the emergence of a field. Autonomy means that the field can be engaged in the play of its own distinctive game, can produce its own distinctive capital, and cannot be reduced to immediate dependency on any other field.

Bourdieu's most sustained analysis of the development of such a field focused on the genesis and structure of the literary field. He took up the late nineteenth-century point at which the writing of "realistic" novels separated itself simultaneously from the broader cultural field and the immediate rival of journalism. His book *The Rules of Art* (1992) focused equally on the specific empirical case of Gustave Flaubert and his career, and on the patterns intrinsic to the field as such. The emphasis on Flaubert was, among other things, a riposte to and (often implicit) critical engagement with Sartre's famous largely psychological analysis. *The Rules of Art* contests the view of artistic achievement as disinterested, and a matter simply of individual genius and creative impulses. It shows genius to lie in the ability to play the game that defines a field, as well as in aesthetic vision or originality.

Flaubert was the mid-nineteenth-century writer who, more than anyone else with the possible exception of Baudelaire, created the exemplary image of the author as an artistic creator working in an autonomous literary field. The author was not merely a writer acting on behalf of other interests: politics, say, or money. A journalist was such a paid writer, responsible to those who hired him. An author, by contrast, was an artist. This was the key point for Flaubert and for the literary field that developed around and after him. What the artistic field demanded was not just talent, or vision, but a commitment to "art for art's sake." This meant producing works specifically for the field of art.

Writers like Flaubert and Baudelaire made strong claims for the value of their distinctive points of view. This has encouraged the analysis of their products as simply embodiments of their psychological individuality. On the other hand, they wrote "realistic" novels, engaging the social issues of their day, from poverty to the Revolution of 1848. This has encouraged others to focus on the ways in which they reflected one or another side in those issues, interpreting them, for example, as social critics or as voices of the rising middle class. Bourdieu showed how this misses the decisive importance of the creation of a field of literature as art. This meant, first, that when Flaubert or Baudelaire wrote about the issues of their day, they claimed the distinctive authority of artists. Indeed, they helped to pioneer the idea that artists might offer a special contribution to social awareness that reflected precisely their "disinterestedness" – in other words, the fact they they were not *simply* political actors. Second, though, Bourdieu showed that this appearance of distinterestedness is misleading. It is produced to the extent that artists are motivated by interests specific to the artistic field and their place within it, and not merely serving as spokespeople for other social positions. In other words, artists are disinterested in the terms of some other fields precisely because of the extent to which they are interested in the field of art. The autonomy of this field is thus basic to the production of artists in this sense.

Painting as a modern artistic field is defined by the difference between producing "art" for the sake of religion, as in medieval decorations of churches, or for the sake of memory and money, as in some portraiture; and producing art for its own sake (Bourdieu, 1983). The latter approach does not mean that the painter stops wanting food, or fame, or salvation – though he may not consciously recognize how much he is driven by these desires. Rather, what it does is orient his creative work specifically to the field of art, and to the standards of judgment of others in that field. The artist in this sense doesn't just produce more of what the market wants, but endeavors to create works that embody his own distinctive vision and place in the field. He seeks recognition from other artists, and in his work reveals his debts to but also distinctions from them. It is because it becomes a field in this way, oriented to an internal communication and accumulation of specifically artistic capital, that the production of art becomes partially autonomous from popular and even elite tastes. Art may guide tastes (not just be guided by them), or it may operate outside the world of everyday tastes, but it may not be reduced to them. This liberates art from determination by its immediate social context, but it does not liberate artists from all interests in achieving distinction or accumulating capital. On the contrary, they are driven to innovate (rather than just reproducing the masterworks of a previous generation), and to innovate in ways that derive much of their form from the existing state of communication in the art field. The artistic habitus, thus, enables a regulated improvisation, working with the symbolic materials at hand to express at once the artist's original vision and the artist's individual claims on the field of art. Because the art field is relatively autonomous, its works can only be understood by those who master its internal forms of communication. This is why ordinary people find much modern art hard to understand, at least until they take classes or read the guiding statements offered by museum curators. From the mid-nineteenth century, art could become increasingly abstract partly because it was the production not simply of beauty, or of a mirror on the world, but of a communication among artists. This communication was driven simultaneously by the pursuit of distinction and of art for art's sake.

When we set out to understand the "creative project" or distinctive point of view of an artist like Flaubert, therefore, the first thing we need to grasp is his place in and trajectory through the field of art (or the more specific field of literature as art). This, Bourdieu recognized, must seem like heresy to those who believe in the individualistic ideal of artistic genius. It is one thing to say that sociology can help us understand art markets, but this is a claim that sociology is not just helpful for but crucial to understanding the individual work of art and the point of view of the artist who created it. Bourdieu took on this task in an analysis simultaneously of Flaubert's career, of his own implicit analysis of it in the novel *Sentimental Education*, and of the genesis and structure of the French literary field. In doing so, he accepted a challenge similar to that Durkheim (1897) took in seeking to explain suicide sociologically: to demonstrate the power of sociology in a domain normally understood in precisely antisociological terms.

The analysis is too complicated to summarize here. At its center lies the demonstration that Flaubert's point of view as an artist is shaped by his objective position in the artistic field and his more subjective position-takings in relation to the development of that field. For example, it is important that Flaubert came from a family that was able to provide him with financial support. This enabled him to participate fully in the ethic (or interest) of art for art's sake, while some of his colleagues (perhaps equally talented) were forced to support themselves by writing journalism for money. This is different from saying simply that Flaubert expressed a middle-class point of view. In fact, it suggests something of why middle- and upper-class people who enter into careers (like art) that are defined by cultural rather than economic capital often become social critics. Their family backgrounds help to buy them some autonomy from the immediate interests of the economy, while their pursuit of distinction in a cultural field gives them an interest in producing innovative or incisive views of the world. In other words, the objective features of an artist's background influence his work not so much directly as indirectly through the mediation of the artistic field.

Within that field, the artist occupies a specific position at any one point in time, and also a trajectory of positions through time. The position of an individual artist is shaped by the network of relationships that connect him to (or differentiate him from) other artists and by his position in the hierarchies of artistic producers defined by both the external market and the internal prestige system of the field. The actual position the artist occupies, however, is only one among a universe of possible positions. He could have made different friends and enemies, could have used his talent better or worse at earlier times, could have traveled abroad rather than staying in Paris. In this sense, the artist's biography (including both the objective resources he starts with and the uses he makes of them) describes a trajectory through the space of objective positions in the field (which itself may be developing and changing). This trajectory is produced partially by choices and by the way the artist played the game, as well as by material factors. At the same time, as we saw in considering the habitus, the way the artist plays the game is itself shaped by the objective circumstances he has experienced. As he sets out to produce any new work, the artist starts from an objective position in the field, and also engages in new "position-takings." That is, he chooses consciously or unconsciously from among the range of possible moves open to him.

In line with Bourdieu's overall approach, what we see here is the deep way in which subjective and objective dimensions of fields and practices are bound up with each other. "Paradoxically," he wrote, "we can only be sure of some chance of participating in the author's subjective intention (or, if you like, in what I have called elsewhere his 'creative project') provided we complete the long work of objectification necessary to reconstruct the universe of positions within which he was situated and where what he wanted to do was defined" (Bourdieu, 1992, p. 88). One important way in which the field as a whole shapes the work of a Flaubert, say, is by granting him the freedom to innovate, and to construct a vision of the world that is not immediately constrained by economic logic or political power. In other words, the artist gains his freedom in relation to his broader social context precisely by accepting the determinations that come with investment in the artistic field.

> The posts of "pure" writer and artist, like that of "intellectual," are institutions of freedom, which are constructed against the "bourgeoisie" (in the artist's terms) and, more concretely, against the market and state bureaucracies (academies, salons, etc.) through a series of ruptures, partially cumulative, which are often made possible only by a diversion of the resources of the market – hence of the "bourgeoisie" – and even of state bureaucracies.

That is, the pure writer needs resources from somewhere.

> These posts are the end point of all the *collective work* which has led to the constitution of the field of cultural production as a space independent of the economy and politics; but, in return, this work of emancipation cannot be carried out or extended unless the post finds an agent endowed with the required dispositions, such as an indifference to profit and a propensity to make risky investments, as well as the properties which, like income, constitute the (external) conditions of these dispositions. (Bourdieu, 1992, p. 257)

In this sense, the artist is not so much "disinterested" as "differently interested." The illusion of disinterest is produced by the way economic and cultural dimensions of modern societies are ideologically opposed to each other. The field of cultural production is defined as the economic world reversed (Bourdieu, 1993, chapter 1). It is one of the central contributions of Bourdieu's theory, however, to show that this is a misrecognition, and the opposition is really between different forms of capital. Directly economic capital operates in a money-based market that can be indefinitely extended. Cultural capital, by contrast, operates as a matter of status, which is often recognized only within specific fields.[8]

Bourdieu situated his logic of multiple fields and specific forms of capital in relation to a more general notion of "the field of power." The field of art thus has its own internal struggles for recognition, power, and capital, but it also has a specific relationship to the overall field of power. Even highly rewarded artists generally cannot convert their professional prestige into the power to govern other institutional domains. By contrast, business people and lawyers are more able to do this. The question is not just who is higher or lower in some overall system, but how different groups and fields relate to each other. Fields that are relatively high in cultural capital and low in economic capital occupy dominated positions within the dominant elite. In other words, university professors, authors, and artists are relatively high in the overall social hierarchy, but we would not get a very complete picture of how they relate to the system of distinctions if we stopped at this. We need to grasp what it means to be in possession of a very large amount of particular kinds of capital (mainly cultural) that trade at a disadvantage in relation to directly economic capital. This translates into a feeling of being dominated even for people who are objectively well off in relation to society as a whole. College professors, for example, don't compare themselves to postmen so much as to their former university classmates who may have gotten lower grades but made more money in business. Similarly, they experience the need to persuade those who control society's purse strings that higher education deserves their support (whereas the opposite is much less often the case; businessmen do not have the same need to enlist the support of college professors – though sometimes it can be a source of prestige to show connections to the intellectual world). This experience of being what Bourdieu called "the dominated fraction of the dominant class" can have many results. These range from a tendency to be in political opposition to specific tastes that do not put possessors of cultural capital in direct competition with possessors of economic capital. College professors, thus, may prefer old tweed jackets to new designer suits, or old Volvos to new Mercedes as part of their adaptation to the overall position of their field.[9]

Reflexivity

Analyses of the objective determinants of the tastes of college professors were not in Bourdieu's view simply an idle form of narcissistic self-interest. Rather, it is vital for intellectuals to be clear about their own positions and motivations in order to be adequately self-analytic and self-critical in developing their accounts of the social worlds at large. This is the necessary basis for both public interventions and the best social science itself. Just as an analysis can discern the combination of objective and subjective factors that come to produce the point of view of an author like Flaubert, so analysis can establish the grounds on which scientific production rests.

Bourdieu did not call for the study of the points of view of individual scientists, or a critical uncovering of their personal biases, so much as for the study of the production of the basic perspectives that operate within intellectual fields more broadly. These are collective products. Identifying them is a source of insight into the unconscious cultural structures that shape intellectual orientations. These may be general to a culture or specific to the intellectual field. We saw an example in considering the ways in which anthropologists may be prone to an intellectualist bias in describing action in terms of following cultural rules. This follows not only from the typical self-understanding of intellectuals, but from reliance on discourse with informants as a way of discovering how practices are organized. Grasping how this bias gets produced is a way to improve the epistemic quality of analyses.

Beyond uncovering such possible biases, reflexivity offers the opportunity to see how the organization of the intellectual or academic field as a whole influences the knowledge that is produced within it. A simple example is the way in which the differentiation of disciplines organizes knowledge. Each discipline is predisposed to emphasize those features that are distinctive to it, reinforce its autonomy, and give it special advantage in relation to others. Topics that lie in the interstices may be neglected or relatively distorted. Bourdieu attempted more systematically to analyze the social space of intellectual work, using a computational technique called correspondence analysis. This allowed him to identify similarities in the products, activities, and relationships of different intellectuals, and graphically represent them as locations in a two or more dimensional space. In his major book on the organization of universities and intellectuals, *Homo Academicus*, he used this technique to produce an overall picture of social space. This is useful for grasping the battle lines over specific intellectual orientations, and also the conflicts over using knowledge to support or challenge the social order. Law professors, for example, are more likely to be products of private schools and children of senior state officials, and not surprisingly also more likely to be supporters of the state and its elites. Social scientists, more likely to be the children of schoolteachers and professionals, and graduates of Parisian public lycées, tend toward a more critical engagement with the state. Obviously, these are relatively superficial attributes and Bourdieu offered much more detail. Paying attention to these sorts of differentiations among the different disciplines helps us to understand what is at stake when they struggle over intellectual issues – say, whether a new field of study should be recognized with departmental status – and also when their members engage in intellectual production.

Drawing on the example of the literary field, we can see something of what was at stake for Bourdieu here. His reflexivity was not aimed at negative criticism of science, but rather at improving it. He wished social science to be more scientific, but this depends not simply on imitating natural science but on grasping the social conditions for the production of better scientific knowledge.

Mere imitation of natural science (as in some economics) produces objectifications which make no sense of the real world of social practices because they treat social life as though it were solely material life with no room for culture or subjectivity. Bourdieu's analysis helps not only to show the limits of such an approach but to show why it can gain prestige and powerful allies, why it attracts recruits of certain backgrounds, and how it in turn supports the state and business elites. A better social science requires, as we saw earlier, breaking with the received familiarity of everyday social practices in order to grasp underlying truths. It requires reflexively studying the objective limits of objectivism. But it also requires maintaining the autonomy of social science, resisting the temptations to make social science directly serve goals of money or power. Just as literature depends on authors gaining the freedom to produce art for art's sake – with other members of the literary field as its arbiters – so science depends on producing truth for truth's sake, with other scientists as arbiters. This truth can become valuable for a variety of purposes. But just as there is a difference between basic physics and the use of the truths of physics in engineering projects, there is a difference between producing basic sociological knowledge and using this in business or politics. It is especially easy for social scientists to be drawn into an overly immediate relationship to money or power; it is crucial that their first commitment be to the scientific field, because their most valuable contributions to broader public discourse come when they can speak honestly in the name of science. At the same time, truths that social science discovers are likely to make many upholders of the social order uneasy, because they will force more accurate recognitions of the ways in which power operates and social inequality is reproduced.

These reflexive understandings of social science, and especially of the need for social scientists to uphold the autonomy of the scientific field, shaped Bourdieu's own interventions into public discourse. For most of his career, he shied away from open political involvement, and especially from the use of intellectual celebrity to further political ends. He was active on certain specific issues, for example concerning the rights of Algerians in France, where he had a direct knowledge of the issues at hand. And late in his life, he energetically combatted neoliberalism and the "tyranny of the market" that he feared would erase the differentiation of fields and a century of gains from social struggles.

Impact and Assessment

Bourdieu's work has had an exceptionally broad, but relatively uneven, impact in sociology.[10] His analyses of the educational structure have been basic to analysis of the role of education in the reproduction of social inequality. His influence over the sociology of education is strong, but in the English-speaking world at least, the impact of his analyses on the study of social stratification generally has been more limited. James Coleman assimilated Bourdieu's concept of cultural capital to Gary Becker's notion of human capital, and called, to Bourdieu's discomfort, for a social engineering effort to enhance both.

Research in social stratification has continued to be predominantly highly objectivist, concerned with descriptions of hierarchies and predictions of patterns of mobility, rather than taking up Bourdieu's challenge to understand the nature of reproduction. This would require a more temporally dynamic, historical approach. It would also require paying attention to cultural as well as material factors, and to the differentiation of fields and problems of the conversion of capital.

Bourdieu's influence on empirical research has been greatest in the sociology of culture. This stems in large part from the range and power of his own empirical studies of forms of artistic production and consumption, and especially of the pursuit of distinction. These have, indeed, played a basic role in creating the contemporary (and highly vibrant) subfield of sociology of culture and have also shaped the broader interdisciplinary field of cultural studies. *Distinction* is easily the best known of these works, and it is extremely widely studied and cited. Somewhat surprisingly, however, there has not been much systematic cross-national research attempting to replicate the study or establish differences in the organization of tastes in different settings. Observers (e.g. Fowler, 1997; Swartz, 1997) have remarked that France may have an unusually tightly integrated cultural hierarchy; it remains for Bourdieu's approach to shape a series of similar empirical studies of anything resembling comparable breadth. Bourdieu himself did comparative research on similar themes. *The Love of Art* (Bourdieu and Darbel, 1966), for example, focuses on attendance at museums. It is framed by the paradox that state support (and non-profit private organizations) make the great treasures of European art readily accessible to broad populations, most of whom ignore them. The achievement of democratic access is undercut by a widespread perception that the ability to appreciate art is something ineffable, an individual gift, intensely personal. This, Bourdieu and Darbel suggest, is simply a misrecognition underpinning the continued use of art to establish elite credentials in an ostensibly democratic but still highly unequal society. Their study (which looked at six European countries) was one of the earliest in a series of research projects that have established in considerable detail the empirical patterns in the appropriation of culture. Bourdieu did not limit himself to high culture, studying as well the "middlebrow" art form of photography, including that of amateurs (Bourdieu et al. 1965). In this and other research (including *Distinction*), he participated in a broad movement that was basic to the development of cultural studies. This was a challenge to the traditional dichotomy of high versus popular culture. Along with others, Bourdieu helped to debunk the notion that this represented simply an objective distinction inherent in the objects themselves, the nature of their production, or the capacities required to appreciate them. While Bourdieu and other researchers revealed differences in tastes, they showed these to be created by the system of cultural inequality, not reflections of objective differences.

Bourdieu is virtually unique among major theorists in the extent to which he focused on and became influential through empirical research. Nonetheless, it is probably his theoretical contributions that have had the largest and most general impact in English-language social science. This is an influence that reaches beyond sociology to anthropology, within which he was a comparably major theorist (with the influence of his work on Algeria and especially Kabylia predictably larger and that on France correspondingly reduced). Bourdieu's was probably the single most important theoretical approach to the sociology of culture. More than this, he helped to bring the study of culture into a central place in sociology. This means paying attention to culture – and struggles over culture – as a crucial part of all social life, not simply approaching cultural objects as a special realm or subfield.

An overall appreciation of Bourdieu's work, however, must resist reading it in fragments: the work on education distinct from that on art and literature, that on power and inequality distinct from that devoted to overcoming the structure/action antinomy. Bourdieu's key concepts, like habitus, symbolic violence, cultural capital, and field, are useful in themselves, but derive their greatest theoretical significance from their interrelationships. These are best seen not mechanistically, in the abstract, but at work in sociological analysis. The fragments of Bourdieu's work are already exerting an influence, but the whole will have had its proper impact only with a broader shift in the sociological habitus that lies behind the production of new empirical understandings.

Bourdieu's work has been criticized from various perspectives. The most general critical review is that by Jenkins (1992). His grumbling is widely distributed but (aside from complaints about language and French styles in theory) centers on three contentions. First, Bourdieu was somewhat less original than at first appears. This is not an unreasonable point, for Bourdieu's work was indebted to influences (like Goffman and Mauss) that are not always reflected in formal citations. Second, Bourdieu's conceptual framework remained enmeshed in some of the difficulties to which he drew attention and from which he sought to escape. His invocations of "subjectivism" and "objectivism," for example, were made in the service of encouraging a less binary and more relational approach. Nonetheless, they tend to reinstitute (if only heuristically) the very opposition they contest. Moreover, Jenkins (1992, p. 113) suggests, Bourdieu's approach entails reifying social structure while developing an abstract model of it; it becomes too cut and dried, too total a system. Third, for Jenkins Bourdieu remained ultimately, and despite disclaimers, a Marxist, and a deterministic one at that. His concept of misrecognition is an epistemologically suspect recourse to the tradition of analyzing ordinary understandings as "false consciousness." This raises the problems that: (a) if ordinary people's consciousness is deeply shaped by misrecognition, their testimony as research subjects becomes dubious evidence; and (b) the claim to have the ability to uncover misrecognition privileges the perspective of the analysts (and may even function to conceal empirical difficulties). Jenkins's reading of Bourdieu is filtered through English-language concerns, theoretical history, and stylistic tastes. Nonetheless, his points are serious and shared with other readers.

Most prominently, despite the "sheep's clothing" of his emphases on culture and action, Bourdieu is held by many critics to be a reductionist wolf underneath. That is, he is charged with adhering to or at least being excessively influenced by one or both of two schools of reductionistic social science:

Marxism and rational choice theory. It seems to me clear, for reasons given above (and also elaborated by Bourdieu), that he was not in any strict sense a follower of either of these approaches. He was certainly influenced by Marxism, but also by structuralism, Weber, Durkheim and Durkheimians from Mauss to Goffman, and a variety of other sources. Bourdieu's language of strategy and rational calculation is a different matter. It does not reveal adherence to rational choice theory; indeed, it does not stem from that source but from more general traditions in English philosophy and economics. Nonetheless, Bourdieu was concerned to show that a logic of interest shapes action, even when it is not conscious, and that economies operate in a general sense even in social fields that explicitly deny interest and calculation. "Economies" in this sense mean distributional effects – that social actors enter into interactions with different resources and receive different resources as results of those interactions. That actions cannot be altogether distanced from effects of this kind means, for Bourdieu, that they cannot be removed altogether from interest. This said, Bourdieu did not consistently find ways to express this most general sense of economism without seeming to many readers to espouse a narrower reduction to specifically economic concerns (Jenkins, 1992; Evens, 1999).[11]

The most biting critique of Bourdieu's alleged reductionism has been mounted by Alexander (1995). His attack is partly an attempt to underpin Alexander's own preferred approach to overcoming oppositions of structure and agency, one that would grant culture more autonomy and place a greater emphasis on the capacity of agents to achieve liberation through "authentic communication." Bourdieu, Alexander suggests, tried to make the sociology of knowledge substitute for the analysis of knowledge. That is, he tried to make accounts of how people take positions do the work of analyses of those positions and their normative and intellectual merits. In short, he was a determinist. Moreover, somewhat in common with Jenkins, Alexander sees Bourdieu as covertly accepting too much of the rationalism, structuralism, and Marxism he argued against:

> Since the early 1960s, Bourdieu has taken aim at two intellectual opponents: structuralist semiotics and rationalistic behaviorism. Against these perspectives, he has reached out to pragmatism and phenomenology and announced his intention to recover the actor and the meaningfulness of her world. That he can do neither . . . is the result of his continuing commitment not only to a cultural form of Marxist thought but to significant strains in the very traditions he is fighting against. The result is that Bourdieu strategizes action (reincorporating behaviorism), subjects it to overarching symbolic codes (reincorporating structuralism), and subjugates both code and action to an underlying material base (reincorporating orthodox Marxism). (Alexander, 1995, p. 130)

Alexander attempts to substantiate this critique by both theoretical argument and (curiously, because he seems to exemplify in more hostile form the very position he decries in Bourdieu) an account of Bourdieu's intellectual development and successive enmities. The latter side of the argument amounts to suggesting that Bourdieu was disingenuous about the sources of his work, but carries little theoretical weight in itself (Alexander's intellectual history is also tendentious). The former side raises a basic issue.

The strengths of Bourdieu's work lie in identifying the ways in which action is interested even when it appears not to be, the ways in which the reproduction of systems of unequal power and resources is accomplished even when it is contrary to explicit goals of actors, and the ways in which the structure of fields and (sometimes unconscious) strategies for accumulating capital shape the content and meaning of "culture" produced within them.[12] Bourdieu's theory is weaker as an account of creativity itself and of deep historical changes in the nature of social life or deep differences in cultural orientation. No theoretical orientation provides an equally satisfactory approach to all analytic problems, and certainly none can be judged to have solved them all.

Alexander makes a false start, however, in presenting Bourdieu as simply "fighting against" two specific traditions. His relation to each was more complex, as was his relationship to a range of other theoretical approaches. From the beginning, and throughout his work, Bourdieu sought precisely to transcend simple oppositions, and approached different intellectual traditions in a dialectical manner, both criticizing one-sided reliance on any single perspective and learning from many. It is neither surprise nor indictment, for example, that Bourdieu incorporated a great deal of structuralism; it is important to be precise in noting that he challenged the notion that semiotics (or cultural meanings) could adequately be understood autonomously from social forces and practices. Likewise, Bourdieu labored against the notion that the meanings of behavior are transparent and manifested in purely objective interests or actors' own labels for their behavior. But this does not mean that he ever sought to dispense with objective factors in social analysis.

It is appropriate to close on a note of contention, not just because Bourdieu had critics but because his theory is critical. It developed in a life of contentious, evolving, engagement with a wide range of other theoretical orientations, problems of empirical analysis, and issues in the social world. Bourdieu's theory is contentious partly because it unsettles received wisdom and partly because it challenges misrecognitions that are basic to the social order – like the ideas that education is meritocratic more than an institutional basis for the reproduction of inequality, or indeed that if the latter is true this is simply something done to individuals rather than something they (each of us) participate in in complex ways. As I have suggested – and, indeed, as Bourdieu himself indicated – it is also in a strong sense incomplete. It is not a Parsonian attempt to present a completely coherent system. It does have enduring motifs and recurrent analytic strategies as well as a largely stable but gradually growing conceptual framework. It does not have or ask for closure. Most basically, Bourdieu's theory asks for commitment to creating knowledge – and thus to a field shaped by that interest. This commitment launches the very serious game of social science, which in Bourdieu's eyes has had the chance to challenge even the state and its operational categories. In this sense, indeed, the theory that explains reproduction and the social closure of fields is a possible weapon in the struggle for more openness in social life.

Notes

1 See Taylor (1993) on Bourdieu's account of the limits of rule-following as an explication of action and its relationship to Wittgenstein.

2 Biographical sources on Bourdieu are limited. The best available general discussion of his life and work is Lane (2000); see also Swartz (1997), Robbins (1993), and Jenkins (1992). Various articles by Bourdieu's close collaborator Loïc Wacquant provide helpful interpretation; see especially his contributions to Bourdieu and Wacquant (1992). Fowler (1997) situates Bourdieu in relation to cultural theory. The essays in Shusterman (1999) and Calhoun et al. (1993) consider several different aspects of Bourdieu's work.

3 Back in France, Bourdieu was responsible for introducing Goffman's work and arranging the translation of several of his books.

4 In this regard, Bourdieu differed from Alain Touraine, the other most prominent French sociologist of his generation and also a member of Aron's Center. Touraine embraced the student revolt more wholeheartedly and his sociology presented a much more voluntaristic cast. He also broke with Aron and formed his own center (see Colquhoun, 1986).

5 The concept has classical roots, notably in Aristotle, was important to Thomism, and was revived for sociological use by Norbert Elias as well as Bourdieu; on Elias's version, see Chartier (1988).

6 The notion of "sense" carries, in French as in English, both cognitivist and bodily connotations: to "make sense" and to "sense something." When Bourdieu rewrote and slightly expanded *Outline* in the late 1970s – about the time it was first becoming known in English – he chose the French title *Le sens pratique*. This second version of *Outline* (which has never been comparably influential or as widely read as it deserves) has the English title *The Logic of Practice*, which sacrifices one side of the double meaning.

7 Writing sentences like this was part of Bourdieu's habitus, his connection to the academic game, not least because their very complexity forces us to make the effort to hold several ideas in mind at once, resisting the apparent simplicity of everyday formations. Nonetheless, they do not translate elegantly or read easily.

8 It is not always recognized – but should be – how much this aspect of Bourdieu's theory follows and extends Weber's (1922) analysis of class (economic position) and status.

9 Bourdieu's most sustained analysis of such issues occurs in *Distinction* (1979), a book that attempts "a social critique of the judgement of taste." It is a mixture of empirical analysis of the kinds of tastes characteristic of people at different positions in the French class hierarchy and theoretical argument against those who would legitimate a system of class-based classifications as reflecting a natural order. In other words, Bourdieu showed tastes not to reflect simply greater or lesser "cultivation" or ability to appreciate objective beauty or other virtues, but to be the result of a struggle over classification in which some members of society are systematically advantaged. Lower classes, he contended, make a virtue of necessity, while elites demonstrate their ability to transcend it. The results include working-class preferences for more "realistic" art and comfortable, solid furniture, and elite preferences for more "abstract" art and often uncomfortable or fragile antique furniture.

10 See Bourdieu's (1998) complaints about how he was understood in translation.

11 Evens's (1999) critique also carries the interesting challenge that Bourdieu did not demonstrate an ability to grasp the radically other, and thus the situated rather than universal and mutable rather than immutable character of the kind of action and social order he described.

12 Alexander (1995, p. 152) terms "unconscious strategy" an oxymoron. It is true that the notion invites misunderstanding and confusion, since it is hard to distinguish when it means that results fell into place "as if" there had been a strategy at work, and when it means that actors make a million small choices that add up to a strategy of which they are never consciously aware as such. In any case, Alexander fails himself to consider either of these possibilities clearly. The former is basic to modern economic analysis; the latter is at the heart of the idea of "sense of play," which Bourdieu argued should replace a mechanistic, rule-following approach to the production of action.

Bibliography

Writings of Pierre Bourdieu

Travail et travailleurs en Algerie (with A. Darbel, J.-P. Rivet and C. Seibel). 1963. Paris and the Hague: Mouton (translated as *Work and Workers in Algeria*, Stanford, CA: Stanford University Press, 1995).

Le Déracinement, la crise de l'agriculture en Algerie (with A. Sayed). 1963. Paris: Editions de Minuit.

The Inheritors: French Students and their Relation to Culture (with J.-C. Passeron). 1964. Chicago: University of Chicago Press (1979).

Photography: a Middlebrow Art (with L. Boltaski, R. Castel, J. C. Chamboredon, and D. Schnapper). 1965. Cambridge: Polity (1990).

The Love of Art (with Alain Darbel). 1966. Stanford, CA: Stanford University Press (1990).

Reproduction: In Education, Culture, and Society (with J.-C. Passeron). 1967. Beverly Hills, CA: Sage (1971).

The Craft of Sociology: Epistemological Preliminaries (with J.-C. Chamboredon and J.-C. Passeron). 1968. New York: Walter de Gruyter (revised edn 1999).

Outline of a Theory of Practice, translated by Richard Nice. 1972. Cambridge: Cambridge University Press (1977).

Distinction. 1979. London: Routledge and Kegan Paul (1984).

The Logic of Practice. 1980. Stanford, CA: Stanford University Press (1990).

Language and Symbolic Power. 1982. Cambridge, MA: Harvard University Press (1991).

The Field of Cultural Production, or: The Economic World Reversed. 1983. In *The Field of Cultural Production*. New York: Columbia University Press (1993), pp. 29–73.

Homo Academicus. 1984. Stanford, CA: Stanford University Press (1988).

The Forms of Capital. 1986. In John G. Richardson (ed.), *Handbook of Theory and Research in the Sociology of Education*. New York: Greenwood, pp. 241–58.

The Political Ontology of Martin Heidegger. 1988a. Stanford, CA: Stanford University Press (1991).

Vive la crise! For Heterodoxy in Social Science. 1988b. *Theory and Society*, 17(5), 773–88.

The Historical Genesis of a Pure Aesthetic. 1989a. In *The Field of Cultural Production*. New York: Columbia University Press (1993), pp. 254–66.

The State Nobility. 1989b. Stanford, CA: Stanford University Press (1996).

In Other Words: Essays towards a Reflexive Sociology. 1990. Stanford, CA: Stanford University Press.

Language and Symbolic Power. 1991. Cambridge, MA: Harvard University Press.

The Rules of Art: Genesis and Structure of the Literary Field. 1992. Stanford, CA: Stanford University Press (1996).

An Invitation to Reflexive Sociology (with Loïc Wacquant). 1992. Chicago: University of Chicago Press.

La Misère du Monde (editor). 1993. Paris: Seuil (translation as *The Weight of the World: Social Suffering in Contemporary Society*. Stanford: Stanford University Press, 1999).

Free Exchange (with Hans Haacke). 1994. Stanford, CA: Stanford University Press (1995).

On Television. 1996. New York: New Press (1999).

Practical Reason: On the Theory of Action. 1998. Stanford, CA: Stanford University Press.

Rethinking the State: Genesis and Structure of the Bureaucratic Field. 1999. In George Steinmetz (ed.), *State/Culture: State Formation after the Cultural Turn*. Ithaca, NY: Cornell University Press, pp. 53–75.

Acts of Resistance. 1998. New York: New Press.

Firing Back. 2002. New York: New Press.

Further reading

Alexander, Jeffrey C. (1995) The Reality of Reduction: The Failed Synthesis of Pierre Bourdieu. In *Fin de Siècle Social Theory*. London: Verso, pp. 128–216.

Brubaker, Rogers (1992) Social Theory as Habitus. In C. Calhoun, E. LiPuma, and M. Postone (eds), *Bourdieu: Critical Perspectives*. Chicago: University of Chicago Press, pp. 212–34.

Calhoun, Craig (1993) Habitus, Field, and Capital: The Question of Historical Specificity. In C. Calhoun, E. LiPuma, and M. Postone (eds), *Bourdieu: Critical Perspectives*. Chicago: University of Chicago Press, pp. 61–88.

Calhoun, Craig and Wacquant, Loïc (2002) Everything is Social. In Memoriam, Pierre Bourdieu (1930-2002). *Footnotes* (American Sociological Association), 30(2), 5, 10.

Calhoun, Craig, LiPuma, Edward, and Postone, Moishe (eds) (1992) *Bourdieu: Critical Perspectives*. Chicago: University of Chicago Press.

Chartier, Roger (1988) Social Figuration and Habitus. In *Cultural History*. Ithaca, NY: Cornell University Press, pp. 71–94.

Colquhoun, Robert (1986) *Raymond Aron: the Sociologist in Society, 1955–1983*. Beverly Hills, CA: Sage.

Dosse, François (1997) *Structuralism*. 2 volumes. Minneapolis: University of Minnesota Press.

Durkheim, Émile (1895) *The Rules of Sociological Method*. New York: Free Press (1988).

Durkheim, Émile (1897) *Suicide*. New York: Free Press (1988).

Evens, T. M. S. (1999) Bourdieu and the Logic of Practice: Is All Giving Indian-giving or Is "Generalized Materialism" Not Enough? *Sociological Theory*, 17(1), 3–31.

Fowler, Bridget (1997) *Pierre Bourdieu and Cultural Theory: Critical Investigations*. London: Sage.

Goffman, Erving (1959) *The Presentation of Self in Everyday Life*. New York: Anchor.

Harker, Richard, Mahar, Christian, and Wilkes, Chris (eds) (1990) *An Introduction to the Work of Pierre Bourdieu*. New York: St Martins.
Honneth, Axel, Kocyba, Hermann, and Schwibs, Bernd (1986) The Struggle for Symbolic Order: an Interview with Pierre Bourdieu. *Theory, Culture, and Society*, 3(3), 35–51.
Jenkins, Richard (1992) *Pierre Bourdieu*. London: Routledge.
Lane, Jeremy (2000) *Pierre Bourdieu: A Critical Introduction*. London: Pluto.
Merton, Robert (1936) The Unintended Consequences of Purposeful Social Action. In Robert Merton, *Sociological Ambivalence*. New York: Free Press (1982).
Robbins, Derrick (1993) *The Work of Pierre Bourdieu: Recognizing Society*. London: Macmillan.
Sayer, Andrew (1999) Bourdieu, Smith and Disinterested Judgment. *The Sociological Review*, 47(3), 403–31.
Shusterman, Richard (ed.) (1999) *The Bourdieu Reader*. Cambridge, MA: Blackwell.
Swartz, David (1997) *Culture and Power: the Sociology of Pierre Bourdieu*. Chicago: University of Chicago Press.
Taylor, Charles (1993) To Follow a Rule. In C. Calhoun, E. LiPuma, and M. Postone (eds), *Bourdieu: Critical Perspectives*. Chicago: University of Chicago Press, pp. 45–60.
Vandenberghe, Frederic (1999) "The Real Is Relational": An Epistemological Analysis of Pierre Bourdieu's Generative Structuralism. *Sociological Theory*, 17(1), 32–67.
Weber, Max (1922) *Economy and Society: an Outline of Interpretive Sociology*. New York: Bedminster Press.
Wittengensteir, Ludwig (1967) *Philosophical Investigations*. Oxford: Blackwell.

12

Jean Baudrillard

Douglas Kellner

French theorist Jean Baudrillard is one of the foremost critics of contemporary society and culture, and is often seen as the guru of French postmodern theory. A professor of sociology at the University of Nanterre from 1966 to 1987, Baudrillard took the postmodern turn in the mid-1970s, developing a new kind of social analysis that went beyond the confines of modern social theory. He is ultimately important as a critic of modern society and theory who claims that the era of modernity and the tradition of classical social theory is obsolete, and that we need a novel mode of social analysis adequate to the emerging era of postmodernity.

A prolific author who has written over twenty books, Baudrillard has commented on the most salient sociological phenomena of the contemporary era, including: the erasure of the distinctions of gender, race, and class that structured modern societies in a new postmodern consumer, media, and high tech society; the mutating roles of art and aesthetics; fundamental changes in politics and culture; and the impact of new media, information, and cybernetic technologies in the creation of a qualitatively different social order. For some years a cult figure of postmodern theory, Baudrillard moved beyond the problematic of postmodernism from the early 1980s to the present, and has developed a highly idiosyncratic mode of social and cultural analysis.

In this study, I discuss Baudrillard's thought in relation to the problematic of classical social theory.[1] Baudrillard's 1960s and early 1970s studies of the consumer society and its system of objects drew on classical sociological theory and provided critical perspectives on everyday life in the post-Second World War social order, organized around the production, consumption, display, and use of consumer goods. His work on the political economy of the sign merged semiological and neo-Marxian perspectives, to provide deep insights into the power of consumption and how it was playing a crucial role in organizing contemporary societies around objects, needs, and consumerism. His 1970s studies of the effects of the new communication, information, and media technologies blazed new paths in contemporary social theory and challenged regnant orthodoxies. Baudrillard's claim of a radical break with modern societies was quickly appropriated into the discourse of the postmodern, and he was received as the prophet of postmodernity in avant-garde theoretical circles throughout the world.

Baudrillard proclaimed the disappearance of the subject, political economy, meaning, truth, the social, and the real in contemporary postmodern social formations. This process of dramatic change and mutation, he argued, required entirely new theories and concepts to describe the rapidly evolving social processes and novelties of the present moment. Baudrillard undertook to explore this new and original situation and to spell out the consequences for contemporary theory and practice. For some years, Baudrillard was a cutting-edge, critical social theorist, one of the most stimulating and provocative contemporary thinkers. He became a cult figure and media celebrity of postmodernism during the 1980s, and while he continued to publish books at a rapid rate, a noticeable decline in the quality of his work was apparent. In retrospect, he can be seen as a theorist who has traced in original ways the life of signs and the impact of technology on social and everyday life.

EARLY WRITINGS: FROM THE SYSTEM OF OBJECTS TO THE CONSUMER SOCIETY

Jean Baudrillard was born in the cathedral town of Reims, France, in 1929. He told interviewers that his grandparents were peasants and his parents became civil servants (Gane, 1993, p. 19). He also claims that he was the first member of his family to pursue an advanced education and that this led to a rupture with his parents and cultural milieu. In 1956, he began working as a professor of secondary education in a French high school (*lyceé*) and in the early 1960s did editorial work for the French publisher Seuil. Baudrillard was initially a Germanist who published essays on literature in *Les temps modernes* in 1962–3 and translated works of Peter Weiss and Bertolt Brecht into French, as well as a book on messianic revolutionary movements by Wilhelm Mühlmann. During this period, he met Henri Lefebvre, whose critiques of everyday life impressed him, and Roland Barthes, whose semiological analyses of contemporary society had lasting influence on his work.

In 1966, Baudrillard entered the University of Paris, Nanterre, and became Lefebvre's assistant, while studying languages, philosophy, sociology, and other disciplines. He defended his "Thèse de Troisiême Cycle" in sociology at Nanterre in 1966 with a dissertation on "Le système des objects," and began teaching sociology in October of that year. Opposing French and US intervention in the Algerian and Vietnamese wars, Baudrillard associated himself with the French left in the 1960s. Nanterre was the center of radical politics and the "March 22 movement," associated with Daniel Cohn-Bendit and the *enrageés*, began in the Nanterre sociology department. Baudrillard said later that he was at the center of the events of May 1968, which resulted in massive student uprisings and a general strike that almost drove de Gaulle from power.

During the late 1960s, Baudrillard began publishing a series of books that would eventually make him world famous. Influenced by Lefebvre, Barthes, Georges Bataille, and the French situationists, Baudrillard undertook serious work in the field of social theory, semiology, and psychoanalysis in the 1960s, and published his first book, *The System of Objects*, in 1968, followed by *The Consumer Society* in 1970, and *For a Critique of the Political Economy of the Sign* in 1972. These early publications are attempts, within the framework of critical sociology, to combine the studies of everyday life initiated by Lefebvre (1971, 1991) and the situationists (Debord, 1970) with a social semiology that studies the life of signs in social life. This project, influenced by Barthes (1967, 1972, 1983), centers on the system of objects in the consumer society (the focus of his first two books), and the interface between political economy and semiotics (the nucleus of his third book). Baudrillard's early work was among the first to appropriate semiology to analyze how objects are encoded with a system of signs and meanings that constitute contemporary media and consumer societies. Combining semiological studies, Marxian political economy, and sociology of the consumer society, Baudrillard began his lifelong task of exploring the system of objects and signs which forms our everyday life.

The early Baudrillard described the meanings invested in the objects of everyday life (e.g. the power accrued through identification with one's automobile when driving) and the structural system through which objects were organized into a new modern society (e.g. the prestige or sign value of a new sports car). In his first three books, Baudrillard argued that the classical Marxian critique of political economy needed to be supplemented by semiological theories of the sign. He argued that the transition from the earlier stage of competitive market capitalism to the stage of monopoly capitalism required increased attention to demand management, to augmenting and steering consumption. At this historical stage, from around 1920 to the 1960s, the need to intensify demand supplemented concern with lowering production costs and with expanding production. In this era of capitalist development, economic concentration, new production techniques, and the development of new technologies, accelerated capacity for mass production and capitalist corporations focused increased attention on managing consumption and creating needs for new prestigious goods, thus producing the regime of what Baudrillard has called "sign value."

The result was the now familiar consumer society, which provided the main focus of Baudrillard's early work. In this society, advertising, packaging, display, fashion, "emancipated" sexuality, mass media and culture, and the proliferation of commodities multiplied the quantity of signs and spectacles, and produced a proliferation of "sign value." Henceforth, Baudrillard claims, commodities are not merely to be characterized by use value and exchange value, as in Marx's theory of the commodity; sign value – the expression and mark of style, prestige, luxury, power, and so on – becomes an increasingly important part of the commodity and consumption.

From this perspective, Baudrillard claims that commodities are bought and displayed as much for their sign value as their use value, and that the phenomenon of sign value has become an essential constituent of the commodity and consumption in the consumer society. This position was influenced by Veblen's notion of "conspicuous consumption" and display of commodities, analyzed in his *Theory of the Leisure Class*, which, Baudrillard argued, has become extended to everyone in the consumer society. For Baudrillard, the entire society is organized around consumption and display of commodities through which individuals gain prestige, identity, and standing. In this system, the more prestigious one's commodities (houses, cars, clothes, and so on), the higher one's standing in the realm of sign value. Thus, just as words take on meaning according to their position in a differential system of language, so sign values take on meaning according to their place in a differential system of prestige and status.

In developing his own theory, Baudrillard criticizes the mainstream view, which conceptualizes consumption in terms of a rational satisfaction of needs, with the aim of maximizing utility. Against this view, he contrasts a "sociocultural" approach which stresses the ways that society produces needs through socialization and conditioning, and thus manages consumer demand and consumption. For Baudrillard, the system of objects is correlated with a system of needs. Although he shares with American theorists such as Packard, Riesman, and Galbraith a critique of the assumption of a free, rational, autonomous ego which satisfies "natural" needs through consumption, he criticizes Galbraith's model of the production of artificial needs and management of consumer demand.

Baudrillard's argument is that critics of the "false," or artificial, needs produced by the consumer society generally presuppose something like true human needs, or a stabilizing principle within human nature that would maintain a harmonious balance and equilibrium were it not for the pernicious artificial needs produced by advertising and marketing. Yet there is no way, Baudrillard claims, to distinguish between true and false needs – at least from the standpoint of the pleasure or satisfaction received from varying goods or activities of consumption. In addition, he maintains that:

> What Galbraith does not see – and this forces him to present individuals as mere passive victims of the system – is the whole social logic of differentiation, the distinguishing processes of class or caste distinctions which are fundamental to the social structure and are given free rein in "democratic" society. In short, there is a whole sociological dimension of difference, status, etc., lacking here, in consequence of which all needs are reorganized around an *objective* social demand for signs and differences, a dimension no longer grounding consumption in a function of "harmonious" individual satisfaction. (Baudrillard, 1998, p. 74)

Baudrillard's focus is on the "logic of social differentiation" whereby individuals distinguish themselves and attain social prestige and standing through the purchase and use of consumer goods. He argues that the entire system of production produces a system of needs that is rationalized, homogenized, systematized, and hierarchized. Rather than an individual commodity (or advertisement) seducing a consumer into purchase (which Baudrillard equates with the primitive notion of mana), individuals are induced to buy into an entire system of objects and needs through which one differentiates oneself socially but is integrated into the consumer society. He suggests that this activity can best be conceptualized by seeing the objects of consumption as *signs* and the consumer society as *a system of signs*, in which a specific object, such as a washing machine or a car, serves as an appliance and acts as an element of prestige and social differentation. Hence, "need is never so much the need for a particular object as the 'need' for difference (the *desire for social meaning*)" (Baudrillard, 1998, pp. 77–8).

In *The Consumer Society*, Baudrillard concludes by valorizing "multiple forms of refusal" which can be fused in a "practice of radical change" (ibid., p. 183), and he alludes to the expectation of "violent eruptions and sudden disintegration which will come, just as unforeseeably and as certainly May 68, to wreck this white mass" of consumption (ibid., p. 196). On the other hand, Baudrillard also describes a situation where alienation is so total that it cannot be surpassed, because "it is the very structure of market society" (ibid., p. 190). His argument is that in a society where everything is a commodity that can be bought and sold, alienation is total. Indeed, the term "alienation" originally signified "for sale," and in a totally commodified society where everything is a commodity, alienation is ubiquitous. Moreover, Baudrillard posits "the end of transcendence" (a phrase borrowed from Marcuse), where individuals can perceive neither their own true needs nor another way of life (ibid., pp. 190ff).

Baudrillard and Neo-Marxism

By 1970, Baudrillard had distanced himself from the Marxist theory of revolution and instead postulated only the possibility of revolt against the consumer society in an "unforeseeable but certain" form. In the late 1960s, Baudrillard had associated himself with a group of intellectuals around the journal *Utopie*, which sought to overcome disciplinary boundaries and, in the spirit of the Situationist International, to combine reflections on alternative societies, architecture, and modes of everyday life. Bringing together individuals on the margins of architecture, city planning, cultural criticism, and social theory, Baudrillard and his associates distanced themselves from other political and theoretical groupings and developed idiosyncratic and marginal discourse beyond the boundaries of established disciplines and political tendencies. This affiliation with *Utopie* only lasted into the early 1970s, but it may have helped to produce in Baudrillard a desire to work on the margins, to stand aside from current trends and fads, and to develop his own theoretical positions – although, ironically, Baudrillard became something of a fad himself, especially in the English-speaking world.

Baudrillard thus had an ambivalent relation to classical Marxism by the early 1970s. On one hand, he carried forward the Marxian critique of commodity production which delineates and criticizes various forms of alienation, reification, domination, and exploitation produced by capitalism. At this stage, it appeared that his critique came from the standard neo-Marxian vantage point, which assumes that capitalism is blameworthy because it is homogenizing, controlling and dominating social life, while robbing individuals of their freedom, creativity, time, and human potentialities. On the other hand, he could not point to any revolutionary forces and in particular did not discuss the situation and potential of the working class as an agent of change in the consumer society. Indeed, Baudrillard has no theory of the subject as an active agent of social change whatsoever (thus perhaps following the structuralist and poststructuralist critique of the subject popular at the time). Nor does he have a theory of class or group revolt, or any theory of political organization, struggle, or strategy.

Baudrillard's problematic here is particularly close to the work of the Frankfurt School, especially that of Herbert Marcuse, who had already developed some of the first Marxist critiques of the consumer society (see Kellner, 1984, 1989a). Like Lukács (1971) and the Frankfurt School, Baudrillard employs a mode of thought whereby the commodity and commodification become a totalizing social process that permeates social life. Following the general line of critical Marxism, Baudrillard argues that the process of homogenization, alienation, and exploitation constitutes a process of *reification*, in which objects come to dominate subjects, thereby robbing people of their human qualities and capacities. For Lukács, the Frankfurt School, and Baudrillard, reification – the process whereby human beings become dominated by things and become more thinglike themselves – comes to dominate social life.

In a sense, Baudrillard's work can be read as an account of a higher stage of reification and social domination than that described by the Frankfurt School. Baudrillard goes beyond the Frankfurt School by applying the semiological theory of the sign to describe the world of commodities, media, and the consumer society, and in a sense he takes their theory of "one-dimensional society" to a higher level. Eventually, Baudrillard will take his analysis of domination by signs and the system of objects to even more pessimistic conclusions, where he concludes that the problematic of the "end of the individual" sketched by the Frankfurt School has reached its fruition in the total defeat of the subject by the object world (see below). Yet in his early writings, Baudrillard has a somewhat more active theory of consumption than that of the Frankfurt School's, which generally portrays consumption as a passive mode of social integration. By contrast, consumption in Baudrillard's early writings is itself a kind of labor, "an active manipulation of signs," a way of inserting oneself within the consumer society, and working to differentiate oneself from others. Yet this active manipulation of signs is not equivalent to postulating an active subject which could resist, redefine, or produce its own signs. Thus Baudrillard fails to develop a genuine theory of agency.

Baudrillard's first three works can thus be read in the framework of a neo-Marxian critique of capitalist societies. One could read Baudrillard's emphasis on consumption as a supplement to Marx's analysis of production, and his focus on culture and signs as an important supplement to classical Marxian political economy that adds a cultural and semiological dimension to the Marxian project. But in his 1973 provocation, *The Mirror of Production* (translated into English in 1975), Baudrillard carries out a systematic attack on classical Marxism, claiming that Marxism is but a mirror of bourgeois society, placing production at the center of life, and thus naturalizing the capitalist organization of society.

Although Baudrillard participated in the tumultuous events of May 1968, and was associated with the revolutionary left and Marxism, he broke with Marxism in the early 1970s, but remained politically radical, though unaffiliated, for the rest of the decade. Like many on the left, Baudrillard was disappointed that the French Communist Party did not support the radical 1960s movements, and he also distrusted the official Marxism of theorists like Louis Althusser, whom he found dogmatic and reductive. Consequently, Baudrillard began a radical critique of Marxism, one that would be repeated by many of his contemporaries, who would also take a postmodern turn (see Best and Kellner, 1991, 1997).

Baudrillard argues that Marxism, first, does not adequately illuminate premodern societies, which were organized around symbolic exchange and not production. He also argues that Marxism does not radically enough critique capitalist societies, and calls for a more extreme break. At this stage, Baudrillard turns to anthropological perspectives on premodern societies for hints of more emancipatory alternatives. It is important to note that this critique of Marxism was taken from the left, arguing that Marxism did not provide a radical enough critique of, or alternative to, contemporary productivist societies, capitalist and communist. Baudrillard concluded that the French communist failure to support the May 1968 movements was rooted in part in a conservatism that had roots in Marxism itself. Hence, Baudrillard and others of his generation began searching for more radical critical positions.

The Mirror of Production and his next book, *Symbolic Exchange and Death* (1976), a major text finally translated in 1993, are attempts to provide ultra-radical perspectives that overcome the limitations of an economistic Marxist tradition. This ultra-leftist phase of Baudrillard's itinerary would be short-lived, however, though in *Symbolic Exchange and Death* Baudrillard produces one of his most important and dramatic provocations. The text opens with a preface that condenses his attempt to provide a significantly different approach to society and culture. Building on Bataille's principle of excess and expenditure, Marcel Mauss's concept of the gift, and Alfred Jarry's pataphysical desire to exterminate meaning, Baudrillard champions "symbolic exchange" and attacks Marx, Freud, and academic semiology and sociology. Baudrillard argues that in Bataille's claim that expenditure and excess are connected with sovereignty, Mauss's descriptions of the social prestige of gift-giving in premodern society, Jarry's theater, and Saussure's anagrams, there is a break with the logic of capitalist exchange and production, or the production of meaning in linguistic exchange. These cases of "symbolic exchange," Baudrillard believes, break with the logic of production and describe excessive and subversive behavior that provides alternatives to the capitalist logic of production and exchange.

The term "symbolic exchange" was derived from Georges Bataille's notion of a "general economy," where expenditure, waste, sacrifice, and destruction were claimed to be more fundamental to human life than economies of production and utility (Bataille, 1988). Bataille's model was the sun which freely expended its energy without asking anything in return. He argued that if individuals wanted to be truly sovereign (i.e. free from the imperatives of capitalism), they should pursue a "general economy" of expenditure, giving, sacrifice, and destruction to escape determination by existing imperatives of utility.

For Bataille, human beings were beings of *excess*, with exorbitant energy, fantasies, drives, needs, and so on. From this point forward, Baudrillard presupposes the truth of Bataille's anthropology and general economy. In a 1976 review of a volume of Bataille's *Complete Works*, Baudrillard writes: "The central idea is that the economy which governs our societies results from a misappropriation of the fundamental human principle, which is a solar principle of expenditure" (Baudrillard, 1987, p. 57). In the early 1970s, Baudrillard took over Bataille's anthropological position and what he calls Bataille's "aristocratic critique" of capitalism, which he now claims is grounded in the crass notions of utility and savings, rather than the more sublime "aristocratic" notion of excess and expenditure. Bataille and Baudrillard presuppose here a contradiction between human nature and capitalism. They maintain that humans "by nature" gain pleasure from such things as expenditure, waste, festivities, sacrifices, and so on, in which they are sovereign and free to expend the excesses of their energy (and thus to follow their "real nature"). The capitalist imperatives of labor, utility, and savings by implication are "unnatural," and go against human nature.

Baudrillard argues that the Marxian critique of capitalism, by contrast, merely attacks exchange value, while exalting use value and thus utility, instrumental rationality, and so forth, thereby

> seeking a *good use* of the economy. Marxism is therefore only a limited petit bourgeois critique, one more step in the banalization of life toward the "good use" of the social! Bataille, to the contrary, sweeps away all this slave dialectic from an aristocratic point of view, that of the master struggling with his death. One can accuse this perspective of being pre- or post-Marxist. At any rate, Marxism is only the disenchanted horizon of capital – all that precedes or follows it is more radical than it is. (Baudrillard, 1987, p. 60)

This passage is highly revealing, and marks Baudrillard's switch to an "aristocratic critique" of political economy, deeply influenced by Bataille and Nietzsche. For Bataille and Baudrillard are presenting a version of Nietzsche's "aristocratic," "master morality," where value articulates an excess, overflow, and intensification of life energies. For some time, Baudrillard would continue to attack the bourgeoisie, capital, and political economy, but from a perspective which valorizes "aristocratic" expenditure and sumptuary, aesthetic and symbolic values. The dark side of his switch in theoretical and political allegiances is a valorization of sacrifice and death which informs *Symbolic Exchange and Death*.

On the whole, in his mid-1970s work, Baudrillard was extricating himself from the familiar Marxian universe of production and class struggle into a quite different neo-aristocratic and metaphysical world view. Baudrillard seems to assume at this point that precapitalist societies were governed by forms of symbolic exchange similar to Bataille's notion of a general economy. Influenced by Mauss's theory of the gift and countergift, Baudrillard claimed that pre-capitalist societies were governed by laws of symbolic exchange rather than production and utility. Developing these ideas, Baudrillard sketched a fundamental dividing line in history between symbolic societies – i.e. societies fundamentally organized around symbolic exchange – and productivist societies – i.e. societies organized around production. He thus rejects the Marxian philosophy of history, which posits the primacy of production in all societies, and rejects the Marxian concept of socialism, arguing that it does not break radically enough with capitalist productivism, offering itself merely as a more efficient and equitable organization of production rather than as a completely different sort of society, with a different logic, values, and life activities.

The Postmodern Break

Henceforth, Baudrillard would contrast – in one way or another – his ideal of symbolic exchange to the logic of production, utility, and instrumental rationality which governs capitalist (and socialist) societies. "Symbolic exchange" thus emerges as Baudrillard's "revolutionary" alternative to the values and practices of capitalist society, and stands for a variety of heterogeneous activities in his 1970s writings. For instance, he writes in the *Critique*: "The exchange of looks, the present which comes and goes, are like the air people breathe in and out. This is the metabolism of exchange, prodigality, festival – and also of destruction (which returns to non-value what production has erected, valorized). In this domain, value isn't even recognized" (Baudrillard, 1981, p. 207). He also describes his conception of symbolic exchange in *The Mirror of Production*, where he writes: "The symbolic social relation is the uninterrupted cycle of giving and receiving, which, in primitive exchange, includes the consumption of the 'surplus' and deliberate anti-production" (Baudrillard, 1975, p. 143). The term therefore refers to symbolic or cultural activities which do not contribute to capitalist production and accumulation and which therefore constitute the "radical negation" of productivist society.

At this stage of his thought, Baudrillard stood in a classical French tradition of extolling the "primitive" or premodern over the dissected rationalism of modern society. Baudrillard's defense of symbolic exchange over production and instrumental rationality thus stands in the tradition of Rousseau's defense of the "natural savage" over modern man, Durkheim's posing mechanical solidarities of premodern societies against the abstract individualism and anomie of modern ones, Bataille's valorization of expenditure and the "accursed portion" of pre-modern societies, or Mauss's or Lévi-Strauss's fascination with the richness of "primitive societies" or "the savage mind." But after deconstructing the modern master thinkers and his own theoretical fathers (Marx, Freud, Saussure, and his French contemporaries) for missing the richness of symbolic exchange,

Baudrillard will eventually question this apparent nostalgia for premodern culture and social forms.

In his mid-1970s work, however, Baudrillard posits another divide in history as radical as the rupture between premodern symbolic societies and modern capitalism. In the mode of classical social theory, he systematically develops distinctions between premodern societies organized around symbolic exchange, modern societies organized around production, and postmodern societies organized around simulation. Against the organizing principles of modern and postmodern society, Baudrillard valorizes the logic of symbolic exchange, as an alternative organizing principle of society. Against modern demands to produce value and meaning, Baudrillard calls for their extermination and annihilation, providing, as examples, Mauss's gift-exchange, Saussure's anagrams, and Freud's concept of the death drive. In all of these instances, there is a rupture with the logic of exchange (of goods, meanings, and libidinal energies) and thus an escape from the logic of production, capitalism, rationality, and meaning. Baudrillard's paradoxical logic of symbolic exchange can be explained as the expression of a desire to liberate himself from modern positions and to seek a revolutionary position outside of modern society. Against modern values, Baudrillard advocates their annihilation and extermination.

It should be noted that Baudrillard's distinction between the logic of production and utility that organized modern societies and the logic of simulation that he believes is the organizing principle of postmodern societies postulates a rupture between modern and postmodern societies as great as the divide between modern and premodern ones. In theorizing the epochal postmodern rupture with modernity, Baudrillard declares the "end of political economy" and of an era in which production was the organizing principle of society. Following Marx, Baudrillard argues that this modern epoch was the era of capitalism and the bourgeoisie, in which workers were exploited by capital and provided a revolutionary force of upheaval. Baudrillard, however, declared the end of political economy and thus the end of the Marxist problematic and of modernity itself:

> The end of labor. The end of production. The end of political economy. The end of the signifier/signified dialectic which facilitates the accumulation of knowledge and of meaning, the linear syntagma of cumulative discourse. And at the same time, the end simultaneously of the exchange value/use value dialectic which is the only thing that makes accumulation and social production possible. The end of the linear dimension of discourse. The end of the linear dimension of the commodity. The end of the classical era of the sign. The end of the era of production. (Baudrillard, 1993a, p. 8)

The discourse of "the end" signifies his announcing a postmodern break or rupture in history. We are now, Baudrillard claims, in a new era of simulation, in which social reproduction (information processing, communication, and knowledge industries, and so on) replaces production as the organizing principle of society. In this era, labor is no longer a force of production but is itself a "one *sign* amongst many" (Baudrillard, 1993a, p. 10). Labor is not primarily productive in this situation, but is a sign of one's social position, way of life, and mode of servitude. Wages too bear no rational relation to one's work and what one produces but to one's place within the system (ibid., pp. 19ff). But, crucially, political economy is no longer the foundation, the social determinant, or even a structural "reality" in which other phenomena can be interpreted and explained (ibid., pp. 31ff). Instead, we live in the "hyperreality" of simulations, in which images, spectacles, and the play of signs replace the logic of production and class conflict as key constituents of contemporary societies.

From now on, capital and political economy disappear from Baudrillard's story, or return in radically new forms. Henceforth, signs and codes proliferate and produce other signs and new sign machines in ever-expanding and spiralling cycles. Technology thus replaces capital in this story, and semiurgy, the proliferation of images, information, and signs, replaces production. His postmodern turn is thus connected to a form of technological determinism and a rejection of political economy as a useful explanatory principle – a move that many of his critics reject (see the studies in Kellner, 1994).

Symbolic Exchange and Death and the succeeding studies in *Simulation and Simulacra* (1994a) articulate the principle of a fundamental rupture between modern and postmodern societies and mark Baudrillard's departure from the problematic of modern social theory. For Baudrillard, modern societies are organized around the production and consumption of commodities, while postmodern societies are organized around simulation and the play of images and signs, denoting a situation in which codes, models, and signs are the organizing principles of a new social order where simulation rules. In the society of simulation, identities are constructed by the appropriation of images, and codes and models determine how individuals perceive themselves and relate to other people. Economics, politics, social life, and culture are all governed by the logic of simulation, whereby codes and models determine how goods are consumed and used, politics unfold, culture is produced and consumed, and everyday life is lived.

Baudrillard's postmodern world is also one of radical *implosion*, in which social classes, genders, political differences, and once autonomous realms of society and culture collapse into each other, erasing previously defined boundaries and differences. If modern societies, for classical social theory, were characterized by differentiation, for Baudrillard postmodern societies are characterized by dedifferentiation, or implosion. For Baudrillard, in the society of simulation, economics, politics, culture, sexuality, and the social all implode into each other, such that economics is fundamentally shaped by culture, politics, and other spheres, while art, once a sphere of potential difference and opposition, is absorbed into the economic and political, and sexuality is everywhere. In this situation, differences between individuals and groups implode in a rapidly mutating dissolution of the social and the previous boundaries and structures upon which social theory had once focused.

In addition, his postmodern universe is one of *hyperreality*, in which entertainment, information, and communication technologies provide experiences more intense and involving than the scenes of banal everyday life, as well as the codes and models that structure everyday life. The realm of the hyperreal (media simulations of reality, Disneyland and amusement parks, malls and consumer fantasylands, TV sports, and other excursions into ideal worlds) is more real than real, so that the models, images, and codes of the hyperreal come to control thought and behavior. Yet determination itself is aleatory in a nonlinear world where it is impossible to chart causal mechanisms and logic in a situation in which individuals are confronted with an overwhelming flux of images, codes, and models, any of which may shape an individual's thought or behavior.

In this postmodern world, individuals flee from the "desert of the real" for the ecstasies of hyperreality and the new realm of computer, media, and technological experience. In this universe, subjectivities are fragmented and lost, and a new terrain of experience appears, which for Baudrillard renders previous social theories and politics obsolete and irrelevant. Tracing the vicissitudes of the subject in contemporary society, Baudrillard claims that contemporary subjects are no longer afflicted with modern pathologies like hysteria or paranoia, but exist in "a state of terror which is characteristic of the schizophrenic, an over-proximity of all things, a foul promiscuity of all things which beleaguer and penetrate him, meeting with no resistance, and no halo, no aura, not even the aura of his own body protects him. In spite of himself the schizophrenic is open to everything and lives in the most extreme confusion" (Baudrillard, 1988, p. 27). For Baudrillard, the "ecstasy of communication" means that the subject is in close proximity to instantaneous images and information, in an overexposed and transparent world. In this situation, the subject "becomes a pure screen, a pure absorption and resorption surface of the influence networks" (ibid.).

Thus, Baudrillard's categories of simulation, implosion, and hyperreality combine to create a new postmodern condition that requires entirely new modes of social theory and politics to chart and respond to the novelties of the contemporary era. His style and writing strategies are also implosive, combining material from strikingly different fields, studded with examples from the mass media and popular culture in a new mode of postmodern theory that effaces all disciplinary boundaries. His writing attempts to simulate the new conditions, capturing its novelties through inventive use of language and theory. Such radical questioning of contemporary theory and the need for new theoretical strategies are thus legitimated for Baudrillard by the radicality of changes in the current era.

For instance, Baudrillard claims that modernity operates with a logic of representation in which ideas represent reality and truth, concepts which are key postulates of modern theory. A postmodern society explodes this epistemology by creating a situation in which subjects lose contact with the real and themselves fragment and dissolve. This situation portends the end of modern theory, which operated with a subject–object dialectic in which the subject was supposed to represent and control the object. In the story of modern philosophy, the philosophic subject attempts to discern the nature of reality, to secure grounded knowledge, and to apply this knowledge to control and dominate the object (nature, other people, ideas, and so on). Baudrillard follows here the poststructuralist critique that thought and discourse could no longer be securely anchored in *a priori* or privileged structures. Reacting against the logic of representation in modern theory, French thought, especially some deconstructionists (Rorty's "strong textualists"), moved into the play of textuality, of discourse, which allegedly referred only to other texts or discourses in which "the real" or an "outside" were banished to the realm of nostalgia.

In a similar fashion, Baudrillard, a "strong simulacrist," claims that in the media and consumer society, people are caught up in the play of images, spectacles, and simulacra, which have less and less relationship to an outside, to an external "reality," to such an extent that the very concepts of the social, political, or even "reality" no longer seem to have any meaning. And the narcoticized and mesmerized (some of Baudrillard's metaphors) media-saturated consciousness is in such a state of fascination with image and spectacle that the concept of meaning itself (which depends on stable boundaries, fixed structures, shared consensus) dissolves. In this alarming and novel postmodern situation, the referent, the behind and the outside, along with depth, essence, and reality, all disappear, and with their disappearance, the possibility of all potential opposition vanishes as well. As simulations proliferate, they come to refer only to themselves: a carnival of mirrors reflecting images projected from other mirrors onto the omnipresent television screen and the screen of consciousness, which in turn refers the image to its previous storehouse of images, also produced by simulatory mirrors. Caught up in the universe of simulations, the "masses" are bathed in a media massage without messages or meaning, a mass age where classes disappear, and politics is dead, as are the grand dreams of disalienation, liberation, and revolution.

Baudrillard claims that henceforth the masses seek spectacle and not meaning. They implode into a "silent majority," signifying "the end of the social" (Baudrillard, 1983b). Baudrillard implies that social theory loses its very object as meanings, classes, and difference implode into a "black hole" of non-differentiation. Fixed distinctions between social groupings and ideologies implode and concrete face-to-face social relations recede as individuals disappear in worlds of simulation – media, computers, virtual reality itself. Social theory itself thus loses its object, the social, while radical politics loses its subject and agency.

Nonetheless, he claims, at this point in his trajectory (i.e. the late 1970s and early 1980s), that refusal of meaning and participation by the masses is a form of resistance. Hovering between nostalgia and nihilism, Baudrillard at once exterminates modern ideas (the subject, meaning, truth, reality, society, socialism, and emancipation) and affirms a mode of symbolic exchange which appears to manifest a nostalgic desire to return to premodern cultural forms. This desperate search for a genuinely revolutionary alternative was abandoned, however, by the early 1980s. Henceforth, he develops yet more novel perspectives on the contemporary moment, vacillating between sketching out alternative modes of thought and behavior and renouncing the quest for political and social change.

In a sense, there is a parodic inversion of historical materialism in Baudrillard. In place of Marx's emphasis on political economy and the primacy of the economic, for Baudrillard it is the model, the superstructure, that generates the real in a situation he denominates the "end of political economy" (Baudrillard,

1993a). For Baudrillard, sign values predominate over use values and exchange values; the materiality of needs and commodity use values to serve them disappear in Baudrillard's semiological imaginary, in which signs take precedence over the real and reconstruct human life. Turning the Marxist categories against themselves, masses absorb classes, the subject of praxis is fractured, and objects come to rule human beings. Revolution is absorbed by the object of critique and technological implosion replaces the socialist revolution in producing a rupture in history. For Baudrillard, in contrast to Marx, the catastrophe of modernity and the eruption of postmodernity is produced by the unfolding of technological revolution. Consequently, Baudrillard replaces Marx's hard economic and social determinism, with its emphasis on the economic dimension, class struggle, and human praxis, with a form of semiological idealism and technological determinism where signs and objects come to dominate the subject.

Baudrillard thus concludes that the "catastrophe has happened," that the destruction of modernity and modern theory, which he noted in the mid-1970s, has been completed by the development of capitalist society itself, that modernity has disappeared and a new social situation has taken its place. Against traditional strategies of rebellion and revolution, Baudrillard begins to champion what he calls "fatal strategies" that push the logic of the system to the extreme in the hopes of collapse or reversal, and eventually adopts a style of highly ironic metaphysical discourse that renounces opposition and the discourse and hopes of progressive social transformation.

FROM PATAPHYSICS TO METAPHYSICS AND THE TRIUMPH OF THE OBJECT

Baudrillard's thought from the mid-1970s to the present revolves in its own theoretical orbit and provides a set of challenging provocations to modern social theory. During the 1980s, Baudrillard's major works of the 1970s were translated into many languages, and each new book of the 1980s was in turn translated into English and other major languages in short order. Consequently, he became world renowned as one of the master thinkers of postmodernity, one of the major avatars of the postmodern turn. Hence, he became something of an academic celebrity, traveling around the world promoting his work and winning a significant following, though more outside the field of academic social theory than within the discipline of sociology.

At the same time that his work was becoming extremely popular, Baudrillard's own writing became increasingly difficult and obscure. In 1979, Baudrillard published *Seduction* (1990), a curious text that represented a major shift in his thought. The book marks a turning away from the more sociological discourse of his earlier works to a more philosophical and literary discourse. Whereas in *Symbolic Exchange and Death* (1993a) he sketches out ultra-revolutionary perspectives as a radical alternative, taking symbolic exchange as his ideal, he now valorizes seduction as his alternative to production and communicative interaction. Seduction, however, does not undermine, subvert, or transform existing social relations or institutions, but is a soft alternative, a play with appearances, and a game with feminism, that provoked a sharp critical response (see Goshorn in Kellner, 1994).

Baudrillard's concept of seduction is idiosyncratic, and involves games with signs, which oppose seduction as an aristocratic "order of sign and ritual" to the bourgeois ideal of production, while valorizing artifice, appearance, play, and challenge against the deadly serious labor of production. Baudrillard interprets seduction primarily as a ritual and game with its own rules, charms, snares, and lures. His writing at this point becomes dedicated to stylized modes of thought and writing, which introduce a new set of categories – reversibility, the challenge, the duel – that move Baudrillard's thought toward a form of aristocratic aestheticism and metaphysics.

Baudrillard's new metaphysical speculations are evident in *Fatal Strategies* (1983, translated in 1990), another turning point in his itinerary. This text presented a bizarre metaphysical scenario concerning the triumph of objects over subjects within the "obscene" proliferation of an object world so completely out of control that it surpasses all attempts to understand, conceptualize, and control it. His scenario concerns the proliferation and growing supremacy of objects over subjects and the eventual triumph of the object. In a discussion of "ecstasy and inertia," Baudrillard discusses how objects and events in contemporary society are continually surpassing themselves, growing and expanding in power. The "ecstasy" of objects is their proliferation and expansion to the *N*th degree, to the superlative; ecstasy as going outside of or beyond oneself; the beautiful as more beautiful than beautiful in fashion, the real more real than the real in television, sex more sexual than sex in pornography. Ecstasy is thus the form of obscenity (fully explicit, nothing hidden) and of the hyperreality described by Baudrillard earlier taken to a higher level, redoubled and intensified. His vision of contemporary society exhibits a careening of growth and excrescence (*croissance et excroissance*), expanding and excreting ever more goods, services, information, messages, or demands – surpassing all rational ends and boundaries in a spiral of uncontrolled growth and replication.

Yet growth, acceleration, and proliferation have reached such extremes, Baudrillard suggests, that the ecstasy of excrescence is accompanied by inertia. For as the society is saturated to the limit, it implodes and winds down into entropy. This process presents a catastrophe for the subject, for not only does the acceleration and proliferation of the object world intensify the aleatory dimension of chance and non-determinacy, but the objects themselves take over in a "cool" catastrophe for the exhausted subject, whose fascination with the play of objects turns to apathy, stupefaction, and an entropic inertia.

In retrospect, the growing power of the world of objects over the subject has been Baudrillard's theme from the beginning, thus pointing to an underlying continuity in his project. In his early writings, he explored the ways that commodities were fascinating individuals in the consumer society and the ways that the world of goods was assuming new and more value through the agency of sign value and the code – which were part of the world of things, the system of objects. His polemics against Marxism were fueled by the belief that sign value and the code were more fundamental than such traditional elements of political economy as exchange value, use value, production, and so on in constituting contemporary society. Then, reflections on the media entered the forefront of his thought: the TV object was at the center of the home in Baudrillard's earlier thinking and the media, simulations, hyperreality, and implosion eventually came to obliterate distinctions between private and public, inside and outside, media and reality. Henceforth, everything was public, transparent, ecstatic and hyperreal in the object world, which was gaining in fascination and seductiveness as the years went by.

So ultimately the subject, the darling of modern philosophy, is defeated in Baudrillard's metaphysical scenario and the object triumphs, a stunning end to the dialectic of subject and object which had been the framework of modern philosophy. The object is thus the subject's fatality and Baudrillard's "fatal strategies" project an obscure call to submit to the strategies and ruses of objects. In "banal strategies," "the subject believes itself to always be more clever than the object, whereas in the other [fatal strategies] the object is always supposed to be more shrewd, more cynical, more brilliant than the subject" (Baudrillard, 1983, pp. 259–60). Previously, in banal strategies, the subject believed itself to be more masterful and sovereign than the object. A fatal strategy, by contrast, recognizes the supremacy of the object and therefore takes the side of the object and surrenders to its strategies, ruses, and rules.

In *The Fatal Strategies* and succeeding writings, Baudrillard seems to be taking social theory into the realm of metaphysics, but it is a specific type of metaphysics, deeply inspired by the pataphysics developed by Alfred Jarry. For Jarry:

> pataphysics is the science of the realm beyond metaphysics.... It will study the laws which govern exceptions and will explain the universe supplementary to this one; or, less ambitiously, it will describe a universe which one can see – must see perhaps – instead of the traditional one.
>
> Definition: pataphysics is the science of imaginary solutions, which symbolically attributes the properties of objects, described by their virtuality, to their lineaments. (Jarry, 1967, p. 131)

Like the universe in Jarry's *Ubu Roi*, *The Gestures and Opinions of Doctor Faustroll*, and other literary texts – as well as in Jarry's more theoretical explications of pataphysics – Baudrillard's is a totally absurd universe where objects rule in mysterious ways, and people and events are governed by absurd and ultimately unknowable interconnections and predestination (the French playwright Eugene Ionesco is another good source of entry to this universe). Like Jarry's pataphysics, Baudrillard's universe is ruled by surprise, reversal, hallucination, blasphemy, obscenity, and a desire to shock and outrage.

Thus, in view of the growing supremacy of the object, Baudrillard wants us to abandon the subject and to side with the object. Pataphysics aside, it seems that Baudrillard is trying to end the philosophy of subjectivity that has controlled French thought since Descartes by going over completely to the other side. Descartes's *malin genie*, his evil genius, was a ruse of the subject which tried to seduce him into accepting what was not clear and distinct, but over which he was ultimately able to prevail. Baudrillard's "evil genius" is the object itself which is much more malign than the merely epistemological deceptions of the subject faced by Descartes and which constitutes a fatal destiny that demands the end of the philosophy of subjectivity. Henceforth, for Baudrillard, we live in the era of the reign of the object.

Into the 1990s

In the 1980s, Baudrillard posited an "immanent reversal," a reversal of direction and meaning, in which things turn into their opposite. Thus, the society of production was passing over to simulation and seduction; the panoptic and repressive power theorized by Foucault was turning into a cynical and seductive power; the liberation championed in the 1960s was becoming a form of voluntary servitude; sovereignty had passed from the side of the subject to the object; and revolution and emancipation had turned into their opposites, snaring one more and more in the logic of the system, thus trapping individuals in an order of simulation and virtuality. His concept of "immanent reversal" thus provides a perverse form of Horkheimer and Adorno's (1972) dialectic of Enlightenment, where everything becomes its opposite – where Enlightenment becomes domination, where culture becomes culture industry, where democracy becomes a form of mass manipulation, and science and technology become part of an apparatus of domination.

Baudrillard follows this logic and a perverse and nihilistic metaphysics based on this vision into the 1990s, where his thought becomes ever more hermetic, metaphysical, and cynical. During the decade, Baudrillard continued playing the role of academic and media superstar, traveling around the world lecturing and performing in intellectual events. Some of his experiences are captured in the travelogue *America* (1988) and the collections of aphorisms *Cool Memories* (1990a) and *Cool Memories II* (1996a), which combine reflections on his travels and experiences with development of his ideas and perceptions. Retiring from the University of Nanterre in 1987, Baudrillard has subsequently functioned as an independent intellectual, dedicating himself to caustic reflections on our contemporary moment.

During the 1990s, Baudrillard published *The Transparency of Evil* (1993b), *The Gulf War Did Not Take Place* (1995), *The Illusion of the End* (1994b), and *The Perfect Crime* (1996), which continue his excursions into the metaphysics of the object and defeat of the subject. Bringing together reflections which develop his ideas and/or comment on contemporary events, the books continue to postulate a break within history in the space of a postmodern *coupure*, though Baudrillard himself usually distances himself from other versions of postmodern theory.[2]

The 1990s texts continue the fragmentary style and use of short essays, aphorisms, stories, and *aperçus* that Baudrillard began deploying in the 1980s, and often repeat some of the same ideas and stories. They contain few new ideas or perspectives, but are often entertaining, although they can be outrageous and scandalous. These writings can be read as a continual commentary on current social conditions, along with a running dialogue with Marxism and poststructuralist theory. Yet after his fierce polemics of the 1970s against competing models of thought, Baudrillard's dialogue with theory now consists mostly of occasional asides, and his mode of analysis consists of ruminating on contemporary events and trends.

Baudrillard develops in these works "theory fiction," or what he also calls "simulation theory" and "anticipatory theory," to simulate, grasp, and anticipate historical events which he believes outrun all contemporary theory. The current situation, he claims, is more fantastic than the most fanciful science fiction, or theoretical projections of a futurist society. Thus, theory can only attempt to grasp the present on the run and try to anticipate the future. However, Baudrillard has had a particularly poor record as a social and political analyst and forecaster. As a political analyst, he has often been superficial and off the mark. In the essay "Anorexic Ruins," published in 1989, he read the Berlin Wall as a sign of a frozen history, of an anorexic history, in which nothing more can happen, marked by a "lack of events" and the end of history, taking the Berlin Wall as a sign of a stasis between communism and capitalism. Shortly thereafter, rather significant events destroyed the wall that Baudrillard took as eternal and opened up a new historical era.

The Cold War stalemate was long taken by Baudrillard as establishing a frozen history in which no significant change could take place. In his mid-1970s reflections, he presented the Vietnam War as an "alibi" to incorporate China, Russia, and eventually Vietnam into a more rationalized and modernized world economic and political order (Baudrillard, 1983a, pp. 66ff), and in his book on the Gulf War he repeats this claim (Baudrillard, 1995, p. 85), thus failing to see the actual political stakes and reasons for the Vietnam War, as well as the significance of the struggles between capitalist and communist powers. On the whole, Baudrillard sees history as the unfolding of expanding technological rationality, turning into its opposite, as the system incorporates ever more elements, producing an improved technological order, which then becomes irrational through its excesses, its illusions, and its generation of unforeseen consequences. This mode of highly abstract analysis, however, occludes more specific historical determinants that would analyze how technological rationality is constructed and functions and how and why it misfires. It also covers over the disorder and turmoil created by such things as the crises and restructuring of global capitalism, the rise of fundamentalism and ethnic conflict unleashed in part as a response to rationalization and to the breakup of the bipolar world order, or to the passions of identity politics.

Baudrillard's reflections on the Gulf War take a similar position, seeing it as an attempt of the New World Order to further rationalize the world, arguing that the Gulf War really served to bring Islam into the New World Order (Baudrillard, 1995, p. 19). The first study, titled "The Gulf War Will Not Take Place," was initially published a few days before the actual outbreak of military hostilities, and repeats his earlier concept of "weak events" and frozen history. *Pace*

Baudrillard, the war took place, but this did not deter him from publishing studies claiming during the war that it was not "really taking place" and after the war asserting that it "did not take place." Although I have also argued that the "Gulf War" was a media spectacle and not a genuine war (see Kellner, 1992), Baudrillard does not help us to understand much about the event and does not even help us to grasp the role of the media in contemporary political spectacles. Reducing complex events like wars to categories like simulation or hyperreality illuminates the virtual and high-tech dimension to media events, but erases all their concrete determinants. Yet Baudrillardian postmodern categories help us to grasp some of the dynamics of the culture of living in media and computer worlds, where people seem to enjoy immersing themselves in simulated events (witness the fascination of the Gulf War in 1991, the O. J. Simpson trials during 1994–6, the Clinton sex scandals, and various other media spectacles throughout the 1990s, analyzed in Best and Kellner, forthcoming).

In *The Illusion of the End* (1994b), Baudrillard attacks head-on what he sees as current illusions of history, politics, and metaphysics, and gamely tries to explain away his own political misprognoses that we were in a frozen, glacial history stalemated between East and West, that the system of deterrence had frozen history making sure that nothing dramatic could henceforth happen, that the Gulf War couldn't take place, and that we were at the end of history. Baudrillard unleashes his full bag of rhetorical tricks and philosophical analysis to attempt to maintain these hypotheses in the face of the dramatic events of 1989–91, which he claims are in fact "weak events"; events are still on strike, history has indeed disappeared. He continues to argue that we have reached the end of modernity, with its political conflicts and upheavals, its innovations and revolutions, its autonomous and creative subject, and its myths of progress, democracy, Enlightenment, and the like. These myths, these strong ideas, are exhausted, he claims, and henceforth we have a postmodern era in which banal eclecticism, inertial implosion, and eternal recycling of the same become defining features.

In particular, with the collapse of communism, the era of strong ideas, of a conflicted world, of revolution and universal emancipation is over. Communism, in Baudrillard's reading, collapsed of its own inertia, it self-destructed from within, it imploded, rather than perishing in ideological battle or military warfare. With the absorption of its dissidents into power, there is no longer a clash of strong ideas, of opposition and resistance, of critical transcendence. With the embedding of the former communist regimes into the system of the capitalist world market and liberal democracy, the West no longer has an other to battle against, there is no longer any creative or ideological tension, no longer an other or alternative to the Western world.

In general, in Baudrillard's 1990s musings, the postmodern condition is one of absorbing otherness, of erasing difference, of assimilating and imploding all oppositional or negative forces into a viral positivity, in which the positive radiates throughout every interstice of society and culture, irradiating into nullity any negativity, opposition, or difference. It is also an era in which reality itself has disappeared, constituting the "perfect crime" which is the subject of a book of that title (Baudrillard, 1996b). Baudrillard presents himself here as a detective searching for the perpetrator of the "perfect crime," the murder of reality, "the most important event of modern history." His theme is the destruction and disappearance of the real in the realm of information and simulacra, and the subsequent reign of illusion and appearance. In a Nietzschean mode, he suggests that henceforth truth and reality are illusions, that illusions reign, and that therefore we should respect illusion and appearance and give up the illusory quest for truth and reality.

Concluding Reflections

Baudrillard has never been as influential in France as in the English-speaking world and elsewhere. He is an example of the "global popular," a thinker who has followers and readers throughout the world, though, so far, no Baudrillardian school has emerged. His influence has been largely at the margins of a diverse number of disciplines ranging from social theory to philosophy to art history, and thus it is difficult to gauge his impact on the mainstream of social theory, or any specific academic discipline. He is perhaps most important as part of the postmodern turn against modern society and its academic disciplines. Baudrillard's work cuts across the disciplines and promotes cross-disciplinary thought. He challenges standard wisdom and puts in question received dogma and methods. While his early work on the consumer society, the political economy of the sign, simulation and simulacra, and the implosion of phenomena previously separated can be deployed within critical social theory, much of his post-1980s work quite self-consciously goes beyond the classical tradition and in most interviews of the past decade Baudrillard distances himself from critical social theory, claiming that the energy of critique has dissipated.

Baudrillard thus emerges in retrospect as a transdisciplinary theorist of the fin-de-millennium who produces signposts to the new era of postmodernity and is an important, albeit hardly trustworthy, guide to the new era. In my view, Baudrillard exaggerates the break between the modern and the postmodern, takes future possibilities as existing realities, and provides a futuristic perspective on the present, much like the tradition of dystopic science fiction, ranging from Huxley to cyberpunk. Indeed, I prefer to read Baudrillard's post-1970s work as science fiction which anticipates the future by exaggerating present tendencies, and thus provides early warnings about what might happen if present trends continue. It is not an accident that Baudrillard is an aficionado of science fiction, who has himself influenced a large number of contemporary science fiction writers.

However, in view of his exaggeration of the alleged break with modernity, discerning whether Baudrillard's most recent work is best read as science fiction or social theory is difficult. Baudrillard obviously wants to have it both ways, with social theorists thinking that he provides salient perspectives on contemporary social realities, that Baudrillard reveals what is really happening, that he tells it like it is. Yet more cynical anti-sociologists are encouraged to enjoy

Baudrillard's fictions, his experimental discourse, his games, and play. Likewise, he sometimes encourages cultural metaphysicians to read his work as serious reflections on the realities of our time, while winking a pataphysical aside at those skeptical of such undertakings. Thus, it is undecidable whether Baudrillard is best read as science fiction and pataphysics, or as social theory and cultural metaphysics, and whether his post-1970s work should be read under the sign of truth or fiction.

In retrospect, Baudrillard's early critical explorations of the system of objects and consumer society contain some of his most important contributions to contemporary social theory. His mid-1970s analysis of a dramatic mutation occurring within contemporary societies and the rise of a new logic of simulation which sketched out the effects of media and information on society as a whole is also original and important. But at this stage of his work, Baudrillard falls prey to a technological determinism and semiological idealism, which posits an autonomous technology and play of signs, generating a society of simulation which creates a postmodern break and the proliferation of signs, spectacles, and simulacra. Baudrillard erases autonomous and differentiated spheres of the economy, polity, society, and culture posited by classical social theory, in favor of an implosive theory that also crosses disciplinary boundaries, thus dissolving social theory into a broader form of social critique.

In the final analysis, Baudrillard is perhaps more useful as a provocateur who challenges and puts in question the tradition of classical social theory than as someone who provides concepts and methods that can be applied in social or cultural analysis. He claims that the object of classical theory – modernity – has been surpassed by a new postmodernity and that therefore new theoretical strategies, modes of writing, and forms of theory are necessary. While his work on simulation and the postmodern break from the mid-1970s into the 1980s provides a paradigmatic postmodern theory and analysis of postmodernity that has been highly influential, and that despite its exaggerations continues to be of use in interpreting present social trends, his later work is arguably of more literary and philosophical than sociological interest. Baudrillard thus ultimately goes beyond social theory altogether, into a new sphere and mode of writing that provides occasional insights into contemporary social phenomena and provocative critiques of contemporary and classical social theory, but does not really provide an adequate theory of the present age.

Notes

1 For my earlier takes on Baudrillard, see Kellner (1989b, 1994, 1995, chapter 8) and Best and Kellner (1991, 1997, chapter 3). Other books on Baudrillard include Frankovits (1984), Gane (1991, 1993), Stearns and Chaloupka (1992), Rojek and Turner (1993), and Genosko (1994).

2 To those who would deny that Baudrillard is a postmodern theorist and has nothing to do with the discourse of the postmodern (e.g. Gane, 1991, 1993), one might note the positive uses of the concept of the postmodern in his most recent books (Baudrillard, 1994b, pp. 23, 27, 31, 34, 36, 107, passim; 1996a, pp. 36, 70, passim). *The*

Perfect Crime (Baudrillard, 1996b) does not use the discourse of the postmodern *per se*, but makes ample use of his classic categories of simulation, hyperreality, and implosion to elucidate a new virtual order opposed to the previous order of reality, the murder of which is "the perfect crime" (ibid., pp. 16, 83, 125, 128, passim).

Bibliography

Writings of Jean Baudrillard

The System of Objects. 1968. London: Verso (1996c).
The Consumer Society. 1970. Paris: Gallimard (1998).
The Mirror of Production. 1975. St Louis: Telos Press.
For a Critique of the Political Economy of the Sign. 1973 St. Louis: Telos Press (1981).
Simulations. 1983a. New York: Semiotext(e).
In the Shadow of the Silent Majorities. 1983b. New York: Semiotext(e).
The Ecstacy of Communication. 1983c. In Hal Foster (ed.), *The Anti-Aesthetic*. Washington, DC: Bay Press.
When Bataille Attacked the Metaphysical Principle of Economy. *Canadian Journal of Political and Social Theory*, 11(3), 57–62.
America. 1988. London: Verso.
Cool Memories. 1990a. London: Verso.
Fatal Strategies. 1990b. New York: Semiotext(e).
Symbolic Exchange and Death. 1993a. London: Sage.
The Transparency of Evil. 1993b. London: Verso.
Simulacra and Simulation. 1994a. Ann Arbor: University of Michigan Press.
The Illusion of the End. 1994b. Oxford: Polity Press.
The Gulf War Never Happened. 1995. Oxford: Polity Press.
Cool Memories II. 1996a. Oxford: Polity Press.
The Perfect Crime. 1996b. London and New York: Verso Books.

Further Reading

Barthes, Roland (1967) *Elements of Semiology*. London: Jonathan Cape.
Barthes, Roland (1972) *Mythologies*. New York: Hill and Wang.
Barthes, Roland (1983) *The Fashion System*. New York: Hill and Wang.
Bataille, Georges (1988) *The Accursed Share*. New York: Zone Books.
Best, Steven, and Kellner, Douglas (1991) *Postmodern Theory: Critical Interrogations*. London and New York: Macmillan Press and Guilford Press.
Best, Steven, and Kellner, Douglas (1997) *The Postmodern Turn*. New York: Guilford Press.
Best, Steven, and Kellner, Douglas (forthcoming) *The Postmodern Adventure*. New York: Guilford Press.
Debord, Guy (1970) *The Society of the Spectacle*. Detroit: Black and Red.
Frankovits, Alan (ed.) (1984) *Seduced and Abandoned: the Baudrillard Scene*. Glebe, New South Wales: Stonemoss.
Gane, Mike (1991) *Baudrillard. Critical and Fatal Theory*. London: Routledge.
Gane, Mike (ed.) (1993) *Baudrillard Live. Selected Interviews*. London: Routledge.
Genosko, Gary (1994) *Baudrillard and Signs*. London: Routledge.
Horkheimer, Max and Adorno, Theodor (1972) *Dialectic of Enlightenment*. New York: Herder and Herder.

Jarry, Alfred (1963) What Is Pataphysics? *Evergreen Review*, 13, 131–51.

Kellner, Douglas (1984) *Herbert Marcuse and the Crisis of Marxism*. Berkeley: University of California Press.

Kellner, Douglas (1989) *Jean Baudrillard: from Marxism to Postmodernism and Beyond*. Cambridge and Palo Alto, CA: Polity Press and Stanford University Press.

Kellner, Douglas (1992) *The Persian Gulf TV War*. Boulder, CO: Westview Press.

Kellner, Douglas (ed.) (1994) *Jean Baudrillard. A Critical Reader*. Oxford: Basil Blackwell.

Kellner, Douglas (1995) *Media Culture. Cultural Studies, Identity and Politics between the Modern and the Postmodern*. London: Routledge.

Lefebvre, Henri (1971) *Everyday Life in the Modern World*. New Brunswick, NJ: Transaction Books.

Lefebvre, Henri (1991) *Critique of Everyday Life*. London: Verso.

Lukács, Georg (1971) *History and Class Consciousness*. Cambridge, MA: MIT Press.

Pefanis, Julian (1991) *Hetrology and the Postmodern: Bataille, Baudrillard, and Lyotard*, Durham, NC: Duke University Press.

Rojek, Chris and Turner, Bryan (eds) (1993) *Forget Baudrillard*. London: Routledge.

Stearns, William and William Chaloupka (eds) (1992) *The Disappearence of Art and Politics*. New York and London: St Martins Press and Macmillan Press.

13

Judith Butler

Patricia T. Clough

Among feminist philosophers, Judith Butler is distinguished for her treatment of the body, her criticism of the social construction of gender, and her contribution to the development of "queer theory." While Butler's first book, *Subjects of Desire: Hegelian Reflections in Twentieth-century France* (1987), focuses on the criticism of Hegelian philosophy elaborated in the writings of Jacques Derrida, Michel Foucault, Jacques Lacan, and Gilles Deleuze, it was not until the publication of *Gender Trouble: Feminism and the Subversion of Identity* (1990) that Butler's work became central to the heated debates over poststructuralism which characterized intellectual and academic discourses in the last decades of the twentieth century. Butler's poststructural rereadings of feminist theory and psychoanalytic theory – aimed at exposing the presumption of heterosexuality in modern Western philosophy – made *Gender Trouble* an often referred to text. With the publication of *Bodies that Matter: on the Discursive Limits of "Sex"* (1993), Butler became one of the most recognized feminist philosophers of the late twentieth century.

The Work

Gender, bodies and the matrix of heterosexual desire

Butler's treatment of the sexed body begins as a criticism of the feminist theory of gender. As Butler sees it, the feminist treatment of gender as a social construction of sex leaves sex to the realm of unintelligible nature and, therefore, fails to question how the sexed body is constituted as such. So, Butler asks "what are the constraints by which bodies are materialized as 'sexed,' and how are we to understand the matter of sex and of bodies more generally..." (Butler, 1993,

p. xi). Social constructionism does not offer answers to these questions because social constructionism, Butler argues, typically has not focused on the "process of materialization that stabilizes over time to produce the effect of boundary fixity and surface we call matter" (ibid., p. xi). While Butler's reconsideration of social constructionism begins with a criticism of the feminist theory of gender, her treatment of bodily matter has larger implications for philosophy and social theory.

Butler's treatment of bodily matter is part of the deconstruction of the Subject. It is a rethinking of the way the Subject is figured in modern Western philosophy, especially its Hegelian tradition. In *Subjects of Desire* (1987), Butler rereads Hegelian philosophy through the writings of Derrida, Lacan, Foucault, and Deleuze. She argues that in Hegelian philosophy, the Subject is figured as the origin of thought as well as its end, so that the truth of thought can only be reached in the Subject's final realization of a full self-consciousness of itself. Because Hegelian philosophy makes the Subject a projective figure of coherency, a matter of a unified self-same identity, it also prescribes the Subject's bodily form and thereby excludes different bodily figures or different embodiments of thought. Only some bodies are allowed to matter. Only some bodies are culturally intelligible, and the cultural intelligibility of bodies depends on the exclusion of other bodies, making them unthinkable, abject, even unliveable.

Butler aims to make this exclusion visible and to give philosophical grounds for the possibility of other bodies. She begins by uncovering what she describes as "the regulatory norm of cultural intelligibility," which constitutes bodily matter. She argues that the regulatory norm of cultural intelligibility given in modern Western philosophy is the norm of sexual difference elaborated within a "matrix of heterosexual desire." This norm operates both in the engendering of subject identity and in making gendered subject identity a bodily matter in which there is coherency and continuity among sexual practice, gender, and desire. In other words, the norm of sexual difference within the matrix of heterosexual desire allows for subject identities with only this body with only this desire with only this sexual practice. What are not permitted to "exist," as Butler puts it, are subject identities "in which gender does not follow from sex and those in which the practices of desire do not 'follow' from either sex or gender" (Butler, 1990, p. 17).

In contrast to the treatment of gender as the social construction of sex, Butler argues that gender identities cannot presuppose sexed bodies; sexed bodies and gender identities are constructed at the same time. Genders and sexualities refer to the prior norm of sexual difference in the matrix of heterosexual desire. Butler even argues that the regulatory norm of cultural intelligibility is not only about genders and sexualities. In constituting the cultural intelligibility of bodies, the cultural norm of sexual difference also grounds what is conventionally understood as social reality, personhood, and self-identity.

To treat the historical specificity of the regulatory norm of sexual difference within the matrix of heterosexual desire, Butler makes use of Foucault's genealogical analysis of regimes of sexuality. She draws specifically on Foucault's treatment of the modern regime of sexuality, which, he argues, comes to characterize European society by the end of the eighteenth century, when the incest taboo is articulated in terms of the oedipal crisis, elaborated, most notably, by Sigmund Freud. In *The History of Sexuality* (1980), Foucault argues that Freud's elaboration of oedipality allows for the interpenetration of "the deployment of alliance" and "the deployment of sexuality."

The deployment of alliance, which orders sexual relations before the end of the eighteenth century, refers to the transmission or circulation of wealth in terms of a regulation of licit and illicit sexual partners. By the eighteenth century, the deployment of alliance begins to lose ground to the deployment of sexuality, without, however, the former ever being entirely supplanted by the latter. The deployment of sexuality shifts the regulation of sexual relations to the quality of sensations and pleasures, the control and disciplining of bodies, making the nuclear family central to the operation of the deployment of sexuality. According to Foucault, by the nineteenth century, the family has become the site at which alliance and sexuality are interfaced. The family is where the oedipalization of the incest taboo infuses alliance with sexuality; in the family, Foucault (1980, p. 109) argues, incest "is constantly being solicited and refused . . . an object of obsession and attraction, a dreadful secret and an indispensible pivot."

Drawing on Foucault allows Butler to argue that in the modern regime of sexuality, the oedipal law (of the father or the phallus or *le nom du père*) precedes the constitution of sexed bodies, offering a historically specific regulatory norm of cultural intelligibility. In other words, while the oedipal law is a juridical law, it also is generative as a regulatory ideal or norm. Oedipus generates the desires and the desiring bodies that as law it would seem to forbid. To put this in the deconstructive terms of Butler's criticism of modern Western philosophy, oedipus produces both culturally intelligible subject identities and unintelligible ones; furthermore, the latter are an exclusion constituting the intelligibility of the former. Bodies that are intelligible come to matter in the exclusion of ones which are made unintelligible, abject, and unliveable. As such, oedipus is an agency of power/knowledge which accrues power to itself as law even in the failure of lawfulness; that is, in the constitution of unintelligible bodies. As Butler puts it, echoing Foucault, "desire is manufactured and forbidden as a ritual symbolic gesture whereby the juridical model exercises and consolidates its own power" (Butler, 1990, p. 76).

Yet Butler wants to get closer than Foucault does to the process of engendering subject identity through which individuals also become sexed bodies. To do so, Butler returns to psychoanalysis through Lacan's rereading of Freud. What Lacan offers Butler is an understanding of the compulsion to repeat in unconscious fantasy; she will argue that it is through fantasy that the sexed body materializes along with the construction of a subject identity. It is in the notion of unconscious repetition that Butler also finds a possibility for resistance to the cultural norm of intelligibility – a possibility which Foucault does not offer. But, if Butler returns to psychoanalysis, it is not to forget Foucault. Although she argues that subject identity and the body are materializations or surfaces of unconscious desire in a "phantasmatic field," Butler also argues that it is the historically specific regime of modern sexuality which first makes "the phantasmatic field . . . the very terrain of cultural intelligibility" (Butler, 1993, p. 6).

In returning to psychoanalysis, Butler recognizes that Lacan's rereading of Freud also makes it apparent that the oedipal law of the phallus is not only juridical but also generative. For Lacan, this is because oedipus always fails. As Lacan explains it, with the imposition of the law of the phallus and the initiation of the oedipal crisis, the infant-child is subjected to the symbolic order. Specifically, the infant-child is commanded to give up pre-oedipal attachments and is commanded to do so by fully accepting either a feminine or masculine identity according to the norm of sexual difference and under the threat of castration. But Lacan also suggests that the imposition of the oedipal law of the phallus occurs when the infant-child already has initiated unconscious fantasizing, productive of an imaginary in which lost objects, such as the nourishing milk, have been displaced with fantasmatic objects, such as the mothers's breast or the mother herself, to which the infant's attachment has become passionate or erotic. Borrowing Wendy Brown's terms, Butler argues that it is these pre-oedipal "passionate attachments" which the infant-child elaborates in post-oedipal unconscious fantasy (Butler, 1997a, pp. 6–10).

That is to say, although pre-oedipal unconscious fantasy must be brought into line with the oedipal law of the phallus, post-oedipal unconscious fantasy seems rather to serve in producing a seeming conformity while allowing the refusal of complete adherence to oedipus. Indeed, Lacan suggests that the post-oedipal structure of the individual's unconscious resists oedipus in a fantasmatic elaboration of bisexuality: either there is an unconscious refusal to identify with only masculinity or femininity or there is an unconscious refusal of sexual difference altogether in fantasized hypermasculinity or hyperfemininity. Because oedipus carries with it the threat of castration, the post-oedipal fantasmatic elaboration of bisexuality is as well an elaboration of a denial of castration. So, the fantasmatic resistance to oedipus is a fantasmatic appropriation of phallicity or the phallic embodiment of a unified subject identity.

What makes Lacan's rereading of Freud so important is that it proposes that the subject's identity is only seemingly unified, only seemingly the same as, or one with, the subject's intentionality or conscious self. Even more importantly, the seeming unity of subject identity is itself a production of unconscious fantasy. It is because Lacan's rereading of Freud deeply troubles the notion of a unified subject identity that it has been so important to feminist theorists. In Lacan's rereading of Freud, feminist theorists have seen the possiblity of women's resistance to the feminine identity imposed with oedipus. As Jacqueline Rose (1986, pp. 90–1) has put it, "The unconscious constantly reveals the 'failure' of identity. Because there is no continuity of psychic life, so there is no stability of sexual identity, no position for women (or for men) which is ever simply achieved. . . . Instead . . . there is a resistance to identity at the very heart of psychic life."

Butler draws on various feminist treatments of Lacanian psychoanalysis, such as Rose's, in order to explore how the body is sexed – how the body is "at once a compensatory fantasy and a fetishistic mask" (Butler, 1993, p. 65). But Butler not only shows how the oedipal law of the phallus is a deployment of the norm of sexual difference. She also shows that it is a deployment of a compulsory heterosexuality. Beyond the feminist revision of Lacanian psychoanalysis, Butler shows that the norm of sexual difference is heterosexist.

Butler's argument is that the law of oedipus imposes sexual difference not only by prohibiting an incestuous heterosexual object choice – the mother for the boy and the father for the girl. But, along with this prohibition, let us say even prior to it, there also is a prohibition of the homosexual object choice – for the girl, the mother, and for the boy, the father. As Butler sees it, the loss of the homosexual incestuous object, unlike the loss of the heterosexual incestuous object, is denied completely; what Butler calls "the modality of desire," or what Freud refers to as "the sexual aim," also is denied. For example, in the case of the boy, not only is the father tabooed as an object choice, but the sexual aim or the act toward which the sexual aim tends also is tabooed. Given the norm of sexual difference, the tabooed aim is even figured as feminine; that is, treated as what a male should not desire to do because it is what a female desires to do. Because the losses of the homosexual object and aim are denied, they cannot be grieved and, therefore, cannot be internalized.

Rather than grieved, the loss, Butler argues, is "melancholically incorporated" and thereby kept alive in and as part of the one who cannot grieve. There is an "encrypting" of the loss in the body. It is as if "the body is inhabited or possessed by phantasms of various kinds" (Butler, 1990, p. 68). In the case of the boy, the father and the desire for the father are kept living in deadening the loss onto the infant-child's body, which is thereby made male. The infant-child's body becomes a male body by means of a melancholic incorporation. As Butler puts it, "incorporation literalizes the loss on or in the body and so appears as the facticity of the body, the means by which the body comes to bear 'sex' as its literal truth" (ibid., p. 71).

It is in terms of an oedipalized compulsory heterosexuality that Butler argues that the sexed body is the effect of a fantasmatic melancholic incorporation. The matter of the body is the effect of a literalizing fantasy: "the belief that it is parts of the body, the 'literal penis,' the 'literal vagina,' which cause pleasure and desire – is precisely the kind of literalizing fantasy characteristic of the syndrome of melancholic heterosexuality" (ibid.). The fantasmatic matter of the body even gives the "inside" (of the body) from which "true" or "real" sexuality is imagined to emanate. Butler suggests that through the fantasmatic constitution of the body the interiority of the subject is made from the outside. Or to put it in a more precise way, the fantasmatic constitution of the body makes it a surface of receptivity for all further projected images of socializing instruments and institutions, even though these images will seem to be internal to subjectivity or to come from "inside" the body. This is what Butler argues in *The Psychic Life of Power: Theories in Subjection*, when she proposes that the "melancholic turn" not only constitutes the sexed body. It also constitutes the ego, thereby initiating "a variable boundary between the psychic and the social, a boundary . . . that distributes and regulates the psychic sphere in relationship to prevailing norms of social regulations" (Butler, 1997a, p. 171).

In treating the interimplication of the psychic sphere and norms of social regulation, Butler not only employs Lacanian psychoanalysis; she also means to give a feminist turn to it by undoing the privilege afforded the phallus in Lacanian psychoanalysis. She rereads Lacan's account of the mirror stage into her treatment of the body as a fantasmatic construction or an "imaginary morphe." Because Lacan argues that the body's unity depends at first on an imaginary projection onto a reflective surface, Butler recognizes that Lacan's rereading of Freud "establishes the morphology of the body as a psychically invested projection" (Butler, 1993, p. 73). But Lacan also argues that the infant-child's subjection to the symbolic order is brought on with oedipus, when finally the pre-oedipal imaginary is subjected to the symbolic and the distinction between "having" the phallus (marked as masculine) and "being" the phallus for the other (marked as feminine) is enforced. Using Lacan's own argument against itself, Butler shows that as transcendental signifier, the phallus is itself an imaginary construct; it presupposes a psychic investment in the penis.

In one of her best known essays, Butler offers "the lesbian phallus" as a figural refusal of the distinction of being and having the phallus, thereby undermining the Lacanian notion of the phallus as the transcendental signifier of the oedipal law. Butler shows the phallus itself to be an imaginary projection or something more like an ideological construct constituted in a regulatory norm of cultural intelligibility. So, Butler treats the oedipal law of the phallus not as a universal law bearing a transcendental signifier of subject identity but as a historically and geopolitically specific ideological narrative of subject identity. Without simply denying oedipus, Butler unmasks its posture as bearer of the transcendental signifier of a universal law.

By reducing oedipus to a norm of cultural intelligibility, Butler undermines the dominance which oedipus obtains in its transcendental and universal posture. In doing so, Butler opens thought to other regulatory psychobiographic forms of the cultural norm of intelligibility – not only those that exist in different cultures at different times, but also those that might come to be in the future. Butler's work is especially aimed at a futurity where subject identity is not dependent on the abjection of others, such as is the case of the norm of sexual difference in the matrix of heterosexual desire.

In all this, Butler means to save the psyche not only from the heterosexism of psychoanalysis but also from the insensitivity to sexual difference in Foucault's genealogy of the regime of modern sexuality. Butler proposes that, while Foucault argues that bodies are materialized according to the regulatory norm of oedipus, he does not explore how oedipus specifies what Butler describes as "modalities of materialization" in terms of sexual difference; he therefore does not recognize that "principles of intelligibility... require and institute a domain of radical unintelligibility" (ibid., p. 35). Foucault does not recognize that bodies which are excluded and made unintelligible haunt the norm of cultural intelligibility and, therefore, all bodies.

Butler argues that it is this haunting which gives the psychic meaning of bodies and makes them a matter of politics. That is to say, because the psyche refers to the domain of radical unintelligibility brought into being with and for the constitution of cultural intelligibility, the psyche gives the possibility of changing the norm in the repetition of fantasy. As Butler puts it:

> If every performance repeats itself to institute the effect of identity, then every repetition requires an interval between the acts, as it were, in which risk and excess threaten to disrupt the identity being constituted. The unconscious is this excess that enables and contests every performance, and which never fully appears within the performance itself. The psyche is not in the body, but in the very signifying process through which that body comes to appear; it is the lapse in repetition as well as its compulsion, precisely what the performance seeks to deny, and that which compels it from the start. . . . the psyche is the permanent failure of expression, a failure that has its value, for it impels repetition and so reinstates the possibility of disruption. (Butler, 1991, p. 28)

For Butler, the threat of disruption which psychic repetition offers constitutes the possibility for a feminist and queer politics beyond both Lacan's and Foucault's treatments of oedipus. In Lacanian psychoanalysis, there is the possibility of psychic disruption, but it always returns to the law of oedipus; in Foucault, there is a realization that the law is a historically and geopolitically specific regulatory norm, but there is no articulation of the possibility of psychic disruption in relationship to changing the norm itself. For Butler, although the oedipal norm of cultural intelligibility is historically and geopolitically specific, it produces psychic repetition, which, however, is "a crucial resource in the struggle to rearticulate the very terms of symbolic legitimacy and intelligibility" (Butler, 1993, p. 3).

Performativity, *différance* and power

To specifically address the issues of a feminist and queer politics, Butler first elaborated the possibilities of psychic disruption in terms of the notion of gender performance, her example being "drag." Butler's argument is that because the body is a fantasmatic projection of a psychic repetition, the body renders the relationship of sex, gender, psyche, and subject identity as one of difference; that is, the body, sex, gender, psyche, and subject identity are interimplicated but not reducible one to the other. Each is constituted again and again or repeatedly materialized. The coherency of each is itself a performance; drag shows that the body, sex, and gender are all performed and that they are "falsely naturalized as a unity through the regulatory fiction of heterosexual coherence" (Butler, 1990, p. 137). Drag shows the potential for political change in repetition and the play of differences.

But Butler's critics often fix on the notion of drag, claiming that it presents a "ludic" or trivial response to political exigencies and the political, economic, or material conditions of everyday life (Ebert, 1993). These critics miss the larger philosophical project in which Butler is engaged; that is, the reformulation of bodily matter in terms of a deconstruction of the Subject. In *Bodies that Matter*, Butler argues that in no way is gender performance a matter of play in the trivial sense of choosing a gender at will; performativity is not, Butler argues, "the act by which a subject brings into being what she/he names, but, rather... the reiterative power of discourse to produce the phenomena that it regulates and constrains" (Butler, 1993, p. 2). For Butler, performativity, therefore, is to be thought along the lines suggested by Foucault in his reformulation of power.

For Foucault, power is neither a strength possessed by the individual, nor a structure or institution. Foucault argues instead that power is a process immanent to a field of forces that cannot be represented as such: "power... is the moving substrate of force relations which, by virtue of their inequality, constantly engender states of power but the latter are always local and unstable" (Foucault, 1980, p. 93). While power makes it possible to use its mechanisms as "a grid of intelligibility of the social order," Foucault nonetheless suggests that power is not reducible to the social order, which only retrospectively allows power to be given a name. Butler puts it this way: "power is the name that renders manageable what might be otherwise too unwieldly or complex, and what, in its complexity, might defy the limiting and substantializing ontology presuppposed by the name" (Butler, 1997b, p. 35). Naming is the constitution of an identity which disavows the differences at play in the multiplicity of force fields or the singular, subindividual, finite forces of chance and necessity.

In linking gender performance with Foucault's treatment of power, Butler is not giving a political practice as much as showing how politics arises out of the play of differences which gives the possibility of identity as well as the disidentification with names. In this sense, Butler's rendering of gender performance draws as much on Derrida's treatment of *différance* as it does on Foucault's treatment of power. For Derrida, *différance* refers to the indefinite deferral of identity in the play of differences. But *différance* also refers to the repression or unconscious disvowal of the endless play of differences, when an identity is constituted, including subject identity. To put it another way, *différance* is referred to in order to remember that identity and, therefore, disidentification and change arise out of the play of differences.

In *Excitable Speech: a Politics of the Performative* (1997b), Butler draws both on Foucault's treatment of power and Derrida's treatment of *différance* to discuss hate speech and those attempts made to legislate against speakers using it. To argue against censorship, Butler proposes that the agency of hate speech is not the speaker which the laws against hate speech usually imply. The force of speech to make a difference is in repetition and the possibility of change which repetition gives. For Butler, the subject who speaks hate speech is "clearly responsible" for the speech but not because the subject is the originator of that speech. Butler argues instead that "the speaker renews the linguistic tokens of a community, reissuing and reinvigorating such speech. Responsibility is thus linked with speech as repetition, not as origination" (ibid., p. 39). Butler even suggests that the person named in the speech and who suffers its traumatic effects can be understood in post-Althusserian terms. That is, although a person is hailed and subjected by the hate speech, the hate speech nonetheless allows the person to speak back; indeed, there seems to be a compulsion for the subject to speak the hate speech back and, therefore, to perform it differently.

Hate speech thereby puts the subject for whom it is intended into "linguistic life." As Butler sees it, hate speech is "a founding subordination, and yet the scene of agency" (ibid., p. 38). The subject so named will most likely respond by repeating the hate speech, but for other ends than those for which it was first articulated. In this repetition of hate speech, a counter to it is made possible, without requiring state censorship or returning to the idea of the sovereign freedom of the intentional subject. If censorship is undesirable, Butler argues, it is not only because it is depriving, thereby restricting subjects from certain expression. Censorship also is undesirable because it is formative, constituting subjects or "the domain of the sayable within which I begin to speak at all" (ibid., p. 133).

While Butler's treatment of hate speech relies heavily on Derrida's treatment of the reiterative force in speech, she also insists that speech is a bodily act; not only does speech deflect the body, it also conveys it. Butler, therefore, draws Derrida's treatment of *différance* back to the unconscious, just as she drew Foucault's treatment of power back to it. She argues that Derrida's treatment of reiteration needs to be supplemented. Butler offers to do so with a treatment of "community conventions" which are repeated and enlivened in speech and which are unconsciously embodied in the speaker, who is, therefore, "a repository or the site of an incorporated history" (ibid., p. 152).

Butler turns to Pierre Bourdieu, arguing that his treatment of "habitus" gives an account of how norms or community conventions are embodied in "non-intentional and non-deliberate ways." But Bourdieu's treatment of habitus only shows that social norms are unconsciously embodied, without, however, recognizing that the body is itself unconsciously or fantasmatically constructed in the first place. For Butler, Bourdieu's notion of habitus is therefore limited, but her discussion of it makes clearer what she finds problematic about Derrida's treatment of reiteration; that is, that he locates it at the structural level of the sign. Butler wonders if the compulsion to repeat and the possibility for change which repetition gives are not rather located in the speaker's embodied history or the psychic substrate of the speaker's body, which is a social matter; that is, a materialization of the unconscious repetition of a historically specific norm of cultural intelligibility. This shift in Butler's treatment of the body, drawing Derrida and Foucault back to psychoanalysis, is on behalf of a radical feminist rethinking of the sociality of matter.

The Person

Judith Butler was born in 1956 in Cleveland, Ohio. It was at synagogue that Butler first realized her interest in philosophy, especially Spinoza and existential philosophy. Because she had trouble behaving in class, Butler was made to take a tutorial with the rabbi. Being in trouble and thinking herself a trouble-maker seemed to enable Butler to "come out" during her high school years, where pre-Stonewall conditions still prevailed. Throughout it all, Butler's interest in philosophy remained.

After a year at Bennington College, she attended Yale, where, at the age of twenty-eight, she received a PhD in Philosophy in 1984. At Yale, her mentor was Maurice Natanson, whose interest in sociology and the social sciences left its mark on Butler's work. She was particularly drawn to the notion of "performative acts" and their sociality, and found Husserl's treatment of "constituting acts" especially suggestive. Along with her engagement with phenomenology, Butler read Hegel, Kant, and writers of the Frankfurt School. Her introduction to feminist theory came by way of a graduate seminar, where she met Nancy Cott. Cott encouraged Butler to go further with feminist theory. She did, and her first examinations of feminist texts dealt with those of Simone de Beauvoir and Monique Wittig.

Not long after completing her graduate study, Butler became one of a small group of scholars who were transforming the character of intellectual life inside and outside the academy. These scholars were publicized in a variety of new interdisciplinary journals which were founded in the late 1970s and early 1980s. Along with national and international conferences, these journals gave these scholars a broad popular appeal, making them intellectual stars. Butler quickly enjoyed and suffered wide public exposure.

Although she is at present the Chancellor's Professor at Berkeley and lives in California with her partner and their child, Butler has been a visiting lecturer at a number of academic institutions and has given innumerable conference papers. She has published five books in all and contributed to a number of edited works. She has been director and active on the board of the International Gay and Lesbian Human Rights Commission.

INTELLECTUAL CONTEXT

Feminist theory and psychoanalysis

If, in the early 1970s, feminist theorists had emphasized women's similarity to men in a demand for equality, by the late 1970s, feminist theorists emphasized women's difference from men, as well as women's similarity to each other, based on their shared experiences and identities, especially their experience of mothering and/or their identification with their mothers. Just less than a decade after feminist theorists had insisted on women's equality with men, feminist theorists, such as Nancy Chodorow and Adrienne Rich, turned to a reconsideration of the experiences and institution of motherhood, including the analysis of the deep, unconscious motivations which, as Chodorow proposed, led women to mother.

All through the 1980s, Chodorow's revision of Freudian psychoanalysis was especially influential in the feminist treatment of the family in Western, modern, industrial, capitalist societies and the revaluation of psychosexual reproduction of mother-centered parenting, fixed in the separation of the private and public spheres. But by the late 1980s, the revaluation of woman's experience, along with feminine sexuality, feminine subjectivity, and the feminine psyche, came under criticism for what was referred to as "essentialism." The presumption that all women share the same identity or experiences was profoundly questioned. It was argued instead that behind the essentialism of the feminist theory of gender of the 1970s and early 1980s, there is an unacknowledged standpoint located in the identities and experiences of white, middle-class women of Western Euro-American cultures.

But the feminist treatment of gender was criticized not only in terms of the differences of class, ethnicity, race and nation and their intersection in subject identities. Criticism also came from feminist theorists, who, in the tradition of British cultural studies, developed a post-Althusserian materialist feminism that made more extensive use of Lacan's rereading of Freud. While Chodorow's psychoanalytic approach draws on the object-relations school of ego psychology which revised Freudian psychoanalysis toward the interpersonal relationship of mother and infant/child, Lacan's reading of Freud turns psychoanalysis to the working of unconscious fantasy and the difference or division internal to the subject which unconscious fantasy maintains, and which makes the individual vulnerable to what Althusser referred to as "interpellation" or the individual's subjection to cultural norms.

Many feminist theorists who worked within the post-Althusserian, Lacanian tradition, while concerned with the infant/child/maternal experience, the family, and the private sphere, more often turned their attention to forms of cultural authority and legitmation – such as literature and narrative cinema, which were seen to mediate the private sphere, articulating the discourses of nation-state and civil society onto the individual by interpellating the individual as their subject. In their readings of cultural texts, feminist theorists, such as Jacqueline Rose, Annette Kuhn, Kaja Silverman, Mary Ann Doane, and Teresa de Lauretis, showed that what Althusser referred to as interpellation worked through the oedipalized norm of sexual difference, so that interpellation might better be understood as an engendering subjection of the individual to the symbolic order.

Although focusing on sexual difference in their engagement with Lacanian psychoanalysis, feminist theorists did not challenge, at least not at first, the psychoanalytic presumption of the link between oedipus and unconscious fantasy. Feminist theorists did not thematize the historical or geopolitical specificity of oedipus. How to treat the unconscious in terms of differences other than sexual difference, such as differences of race, class, ethnicity, and nation, was not addressed in early feminist deployments of Lacanian psychoanalysis. But there also was little attention given to "sexual orientation."

In this context, the 1990 publication of Butler's *Gender Trouble* provoked heated debate over "queerness." In reformulating the relationship of sex and gender, Butler not only drew on the various rereadings of Lacan provided by post-Althusserian feminist theorists. She also returned to the French feminists, especially to Luce Irigaray, who had critically engaged Lacan's rereading of Freud. For Butler, Irigaray leads the way in criticizing Lacanian psychoanalysis as part of a feminist deconstruction of Western philosophy.

In *Bodies that Matter* (1993), Butler especially draws on Irigaray's criticism of "phallomorphosis," which uncovers the way in which Western philosophy excludes the body from thought by figuring it as feminine. But even though the feminine is made to figure the body, Irigaray argues that it is a "specular" body; it is not the woman's body that the feminine figures in Western philosophy, but the exclusion of body from rational thought. In Western philosophy, the feminine, Irigaray argues, is of no essence other than that of matter, nature, the irrational. She further proposes that this exclusion of body in the figure of the feminine is a constitutive exclusion, productive of the internal coherence of rationality and the Subject of reason. In the exclusion of the body, not only is thought disembodied but different bodies cannot be imagined at all. In the end, although unmarked and displaced, there is only one body in Western philosophy – the masculine body. For Butler, Irigaray not only offers an understanding of the constitutive exclusion especially operative in the oedipalized norm of sexual difference; she also gives an imagination of different bodies, a future of difference.

Poststructural criticism and queer theory

At its publication, *Gender Trouble* was not only read as a criticism of the feminist theory of gender; it was also understood as a more general criticism of identity politics and the discourse of gay and lesbian liberation. Butler's work was central to the development of queer theory, a criticism of lesbian/gay theory, in which the accusation of essentialism leveled at early feminist theory is leveled at lesbian/gay theories of identity and experience as well. But even before queer theory was instituted, the taken-for-granted equation of lesbianism with a feminist identity or a woman-identified femininity had been challenged in the "sex debates" of the 1980s, when some lesbian feminists defended sexual practices that had been criticized as male-identified, such as S/M and butch/femme. By then, feminist theorists concerned with questions of race, class, ethnicity, and nation had also begun to refuse the notion of a unified lesbian identity or a uniform lesbian experience.

But queer theory is not just one part of a criticism of feminist theory or gay and lesbian theories of identity and experience. For a number of theorists, such as Diana Fuss, Lee Edelman, Michael Moon, Steven Seidman, Andrew Parker, Michael Warner, and Teresa de Lauretis, queer theory also represents the engagement of lesbian and gay theorists with the debates over poststructuralism. Poststructuralism provided the means for a deconstruction of homosexual identity in terms of the historical specificity of its deployment in relations of power/knowledge. For example, in the same year *Gender Trouble* was published, Eve Kosofsky Sedgwick published *Epistemology of the Closet*, in which she draws on Foucault, among others theorists, to offer a genealogy of the institution in the nineteenth century of the "homo/heterosexual definition." As Sedgwick describes it, the homo/heterosexual definition refers to a "world mapping by which every given person, just as he or she was necessarily assignable to a male or female gender, was now considered necessarily assignable as well to a homo- or a hetero-sexuality" (Sedgwick, 1990, pp. 1–2).

Sedgwick's treatment of the homo/heterosexual definition is not meant to give foundation to an identity politics by which the experiences of lesbians and gays are imagined to offer a standpoint of critical reflection in the production of knowledge. Instead, Sedgwick means to reject a radical distinction between homosexuality and heterosexuality; she offers a "universalizing view" of homosexuality rather than a "minoritizing view." If the latter proposes that the homo/heterosexual definition is important only for a "homosexual minority," the former suggests that it is of "determinant importance in the lives of people across the spectrum of sexuality" (ibid., p. 1). It is a universalizing view of homosexuality that Butler elaborates when she treats sexed bodies in terms of her argument that "there are structures of psychic homosexuality within heterosexual relations, and structures of psychic heterosexuality within gay and lesbian sexuality and relationships" (ibid., p. 121).

But, for Sedgwick, the homo/heterosexual definition is not only a matter of the unconscious fantasies of subject identity. It also is a matter of the fantasmatic configuration which is deployed in relationships of power/knowledge; that is, the homo/heterosexual opposition serves as metaphor for other oppositions, such as "innocence/initiation, natural/artificial, new/old, discipline/terrorism, canonic/noncanonic, wholeness/decadence, urbane/provincial, domestic/foreign, health/illness..." (ibid., p. 11). The homo/heterosexual definition, as Sedgwick sees it, especially contributes to the production and distribution of excusable ignorances and legitimated knowledges; that is, knowledges about which some can easily claim ignorance, but which others are all but forced to embody.

In treating the homo/heterosexual definition, Sedgwick offers a more general proposal that epistemology be displaced by an exploration of the practices of disciplinary knowledge – asking "how certain categorizations work, what enactments they are performing and what relations they are creating rather than what they essentially mean" (ibid., p. 27). For Butler, too, queering the norm of sexual difference within the oedipalized matrix of heterosexual desire demands a shift from epistemology to locating "the problematic (of knowledge) within practices of signification"; this shift, Butler argues, "permits an analysis that takes the epistemological mode itself as one possible and contingent signifying practice" (Butler, 1990, p. 144).

In making epistemology a contingent signifying practice and treating epistemological issues in the politicizing terms of rhetorics, narrative logics, or technical enframements, queer theory draws heavily on poststructural criticism of modern Western philosophy; it especially borrows from the deconstruction of the Subject given as the authorizing and synthesizing figure of rationality and objective knowledge. It is because of its deconstructive aspects that queer theorists joined feminist theorists who already had engaged poststructural criticism in order to uncover the unmarked aspects of the authorized subject of knowledge figured in modern Western philosophy and the discourses of the human sciences. Along with feminist theorists, queer theorists made legible the erased marks of gender, sexuality, ethnicity, class, race, and nation in the figure of authorized subject and, thereby, registered the exclusion of certain subjects from authorized forms of knowledge.

Still, queer theorists refuse essentialism and offer a different understanding of the subject and of knowledge than standpoint epistemologies do. Queer theorists refuse the claim that a more accurate knowledge or a stronger objectivity are possible from the perspective of dominated subjects who have been hitherto excluded from authorizing forms of knowledge. For this reason, queer theorists often support notions of hybridity, especially elaborated by postcolonial theorists in treating patchwork identities in the border crossing cultures of neocolonial diaspora.

All of this also means that queer theorists refuse to name the subject of political agency once and for all; they urge a different view of politics. If, as Butler's work at least suggests, agency must be referred to the play of differences, then politics cannot begin with a definite mapping by the individual subject of its oppression. Neither the individual subject nor the experience of oppression can be the simple origin of politics. Instead, what must be engaged at the start of politics is the reiterative force of difference by which the agency of subject identity and experience are dissimulated. For Butler, *différance* allows for "a democracy to come," as Derrida refers to it. Rather than an identity politics, Butler proposes a politics of "coalition" where it is possible to acknowledge the contradictions involved in coalitions and yet "take action with those contradictions intact" (ibid., p. 15).

Social Context

Butler's work is deeply connected with political, economic, and cultural changes that have occurred in the second half of the twentieth century, and that have seemed to some so profound as to warrant characterization of modern societies as postmodern and, therefore, to require rethinking of the assumptions of modern social theory. Butler is among those intellectuals who have contributed to the reformulation of social theory and who have done so in relationship to the "new" social movements, such as students' movements, women's movements, gay and lesbian liberation movements, race and ethnic pride movements. Linked to the transformations characteristic of postmodernity – decolonization, the transnationalization of capital in neocolonialism and the globalization of telecommunications – the new social movements have raised questions about representation, culture, and identity. In support of struggles against exclusion and contentions over resources for recognition and self-reflexivity, intellectuals connected to the new social movements instigated criticism concerned with the production, circulation, and legitmation of knowledge, and turned modern Western philosophy and the human sciences to reflect on their assumptions. They even raised questions about the assumptions of leftist discourse, often aiming criticism at Marxist theory for its reduction of culture, identity, and representation to the economic.

Throughout the 1970s and the 1980s, there was much writing accompanying the criticism of Western philosophy and the human sciences, which focused on the psychic losses and cultural deprivation due to oppressive relations of domination; a desire was aroused to recover subjugated knowledges hidden in obscure histories and traditions of women, gays, lesbians, persons of color, and of different ethnicities, classes, and nations. And there was a growing sensitivity to the intersection of race, class, gender, ethnicity, sexuality, and nationality that was elaborated in what is often labeled "identity politics." But this focus on culture, representation, and identity was not merely a rejection of political economic analysis. Identity politics seemed instead a register of changes in politics and capitalist economy that were destabilizing that configuration of family and national ideologies, the state and civil society, the public and private spheres long presumed in social theory, especially in the discourse on democracy.

By the late 1970s, it had become more apparent that, in Northern capitalist societies, post-Second World War political economics had been transformed, which profoundly affected Southern and neocolonial nations as well. Keynesian inspired state intervention in market economics through social welfare programs and fiscal and monetary policies was being challenged, while the spatial displacement of the crisis of capital accumulation had led to a transnationalization of capital and the transformation of the Fordist/Taylorist organization of capitalist production into the flexible accumulation or the flexible specialization of neo-Fordism.

Also more apparent were the effects of globalized telecommunications, which not only allowed for outsourcing and subcontracting that supported the just-in-time delivery systems and the small-batch production of a transnational neo-Fordist capitalist production. Telecommunications also promoted the centralization of financial services, permitting instantaneous movements of capital and, therefore, the growing autonomy of the financial system from production. All of this suggested that abstract knowledge or scientific information was displacing labor as central to the accumulation of capital and the creation of wealth. Under such conditions, a distinction between science and technology seemed no longer meaningful and, given the developments in telecommunications, especially the interfacing of teletechnology and computer technology, the distinction between technology and culture also seemed less meaningful, at least in many parts of the world.

All this led some social theorists to argue that representation, culture, and identity had become a matter of a worldwide extension of commodification and the increased alienation of individual subjects due to the pervasiveness of marketing and advertising images that saturate everyday life and obliterate the boundary between the real and the imaginary. Such a view has usually been held by those who would argue for a political economy of the sign to replace or enlarge a more traditional Marxist political economy. But the central place of knowledge or technoscience in transnational, neo-Fordist, capitalist production has also suggested a view of technoscience as the primary agency of power in postmodernity; as such, knowledges became the object of analysis in various cultural studies, offering some indication that the development of telecommunications is driven by something besides capitalism or commodification.

In fact, the globalization of telecommunications made it more apparent that there is a will to record and transmit everything everywhere to everyone all of the time which has been driving the technological developments of capitalist economies from the start. Such a will is visible not only in the development of teletechnology but also in possibilities such as the availability of banks of information about each of us – not only demographics of all sorts but also the more general treatment of individuals as ontologically specific databases of genetic information which can be exchanged among agents that may just as easily be computer programs as people. This will is "the will to truth" which poststructural criticism had treated in relationship to modern Western philosophy and the human sciences.

Perhaps poststructural criticism has been at the center of heated debate over the last decades of the twentieth century because its efforts to deconstruct the authority of modern Western philosophy and the human sciences could be read as both a register and an intervention in the transformation to transnational, neo-Fordist, capitalist production and globalized telecommunications. After all, inside and outside the academy, poststructural criticism caused an intellectual upheaval in arguing that the normative grounds for the truth claims of knowledge, which modern Western philosophy gives the human sciences, are culturally specific; it did this at a time when the "West" was becoming more closely engaged with "the rest" of the world and when simply presuming the universality of the normative grounds of the human sciences was becoming impossible. It was also a time of profound change in the relation of technology, culture, identity, and representation.

But even before poststructural criticism had become a full blown challenge to the presumptions of modern Western philosophy and the human sciences, feminist theory already had gone a long way in undermining the self-assurance of academic discourses. Throughout the 1970s, feminist theorists especially focused their criticism on the configuration of the private and public spheres, in terms of which the function of the woman is given over to the socialization of the infant-child for participation in the nation and the economy. In uncovering the sexual politics of the private sphere and in protesting the exclusion of women from the public sphere, the state, and the economy, feminist theorists initiated debate over culture, identity, and representation.

By the late 1980s, however, feminist theorists themselves were embroiled in a debate over the seeming indifference of early feminist theory to differences of race, class, ethnicity, and nationality. This trouble among feminist theorists resonated with a general debate over identity politics in terms of which different groups claimed that their specific experiences of exclusion and domination gave them a standpoint from which to more adequately understand structures of oppression and domination that shaped identities and experiences. Lesbian and gay theorists also engaged in identity politics; they presumed a standpoint epistemology based on shared experiences of oppression and domination. Nevertheless, by the 1990s, queer theory was receiving a great deal of attention inside and outside the academy, even though it refused identity politics and deployed poststructural criticism, as did postcolonial theory and critical race theory, in rethinking the liberal politics of protesting exclusion in the demand for full participation in the state, the public sphere, and the economy.

In its articulation of the possiblity of a queer politics and queer aesthetics, queer theory registered and fostered a change in the character of lesbian and gay communities. After Stonewall, lesbian and gay communities had gained visibility, as intellectuals, academics, writers, and artists produced works focused on gay and lesbian experiences. There also were lesbian and gay newspapers, journals, productions of mass media and popular literatures. By the 1980s these communities had spawned what Steven Seidman describes as "ethnic models of identity and single-interest group politics inspired by either a liberal assimilationist ideal or, in the case of lesbian-feminism a separatist ideological agenda" (Seidman, 1995, p. 121). When queer theory challenged the unity of homosexual identity or the notion of self-same identity, it challenged the grounds for an ethnic model of identity, single-interest politics, and the liberal assimilationist ideal, on one hand, and separatism, on the other.

The emphasis in queer theory on the performative allowed it to be linked instead with the militant politics of Act-Up and Queer Nation. While Act-Up has supported a confrontational politics of civil disobedience in an effort to obtain services and scientific research for HIV/AIDS, Queer Nation has focused on creating awareness and making visible links between queers situated in various social and institutional settings. Both strategies fit the situation of the post-welfare state; together they promoted negotiation from within government or social institutions, while agitating against them from without.

The militant performative aspects of queer politics especially challenged the notion of representation, because such politics are less about appeals for representation within the state and more about playing with the logics of exposure informing mass media. Queer politics has refused the legitimacy of the configuration of the private and public spheres. In the context of queer politics, not only is private life understood to be political, but public discourses, especially science, are understood to be deployments of power. Indeed, science is understood as a primary agency of power/knowledge and therefore is open to critical revision through direct political action.

For all this, queer theory became a target in the so-called "culture wars" waged by cultural conservatives attempting to reinstate the family as the foundation of democracy by reasserting "family values" against those perceived to have abandoned them, such as queers, feminists, and those engaged in identity politics around race, class, ethnicity, and nation. Queer theory was also implicated in the turn of the culture wars into the so-called "science wars," waged by rightist and leftist critics against intellectuals connected with identity politics, poststructural criticism, and cultural studies of science, who were criticized especially for the argument – no matter how differently elaborated – that science and power are inextricable and that, therefore, the reflexivity of the self-criticism of science must be rethought.

In 1996, when the Sokal affair brought the science wars to public attention, it may very well have marked both the culmination of the long period of critical rethinking of the assumptions of modern Western philosophy and the human sciences and a turn to the normalization of a number of these criticisms. Alan Sokal, a physicist at New York University, wrote an essay which pretended to be a legitimate work of science studies engaging poststructural criticism and feminist theory. It was published in *Social Text*, a journal of leftist cultural criticism. Shortly after the publication of the essay, Sokal announced in another journal that the essay was a hoax which had gone unrecognized as such by the editors of *Social Text* because of their certainty of the political correctness of the cultural studies of science. Sokal, a self-proclaimed leftist and feminist, argued for the necessity of recognizing the possibility of objective knowledge of reality without which leftist politics would be threatened. He thereby produced another version of the usual criticism of poststructuralism: that the insistence on the inextricability of science and power refuses all grounds for judging scientific representation.

Although the Sokal affair brought to a frenzy the anxiety of those leftists who for some time had been proclaiming the excesses of poststructural criticism, feminist theory, queer theory, postcolonial theory, criticial race theory, and the cultural studies of science, ironically it also showed the ongoing relevance of all of these for treating questions raised by the Sokal affair itself – questions about the production and circulation of knowledges, the political interests inherent in doing science and cultural criticism alike, and the relationship of science and the media.

Impact and Assessment

Although her work extends social constructionism to the constitution of matter and, therefore, proposes the possiblity of a social theory of materialization, Butler has nevertheless been criticized for ignoring the social and overemphasizing the discursive. Social and political theorists, including some who define themselves as materialist feminists and who draw on the Marxist tradition, have argued that Butler fails to historicize or to give the historical conditions of queer identities or queer theory itself (Benhabib et al., 1995; Hennessy, 1995; Seidman, 1995). More often than not, what is meant by historicizing derives from a contrast between Foucault's approach to the relationship of power/knowledge, upon which Butler draws, and a conjunctural analysis in which linkages between localized practices are thought to be conditioned by and, therefore, to reproduce a social formation such as late capitalism or postmodern capitalism. For the purpose of this comparison, Foucault's approach is described as referring to the linkages of discursive practices belonging only to local arrangements, while his notion of the discursive is reduced to cultural representations distinguishable from the historical, economic, or political relationships underlying cultural representations.

Although this description misrepresents and trivializes the more subtle treatment of discourse and power/knowledge which Foucault gives and which Butler elaborates in her work, it might be worthwhile to consider the centrality of technoscience or abstract theoretical knowledge in neo-Fordist transnational capitalist production as a historical conditioning of a focus on discourse, imaginaries, language, and representation in poststructural criticism generally, and Butler's work especially. Still, Foucault's treatment of discourse and power/knowledge is not merely a historical effect; it is also an intervention and, as such, it gives a new idea of history in the notion of genealogy. In using Foucault's notion of genealogy, Butler historicizes differently than a conjunctural analysis proposes to do. She historicizes the oedipal norm of cultural intelligibility, releasing the potential for change in its reiterative force. In doing so, Butler historicizes agency. She reveals the sociality of agency, which a conjunctural analysis cannot do, since such an analysis assumes an agency behind historical conditions, a revolutionary agency grounded in the intentionality of the human subject.

All this is important for feminist theory and social theory at the end of the twentieth century, when it must be recognized that oedipus and the configuration of national and family ideologies, the state and civil society, the private and public spheres presumed along with oedipus in modern Western philosphy and the human sciences may not be, everywhere or all of the time, the regulative normative ideal of a configuration of social spaces. It follows that the grounds of democratic and scientific representation can only be contingent. For example, in the case of neocolonialist states, it is difficult to ground democratic representation in the configuration of social spaces presumed in modern Western philosophical discourse; after all, women often are made to figure the patriarchal ideology of the nation against capitalist commodification, while they themselves may use their employment in the workforce of a multinational corporation as a site for resisting patriarchal family ideology. Butler offers another example of this complexification of the conditions out of which agency arises. She points to the difference between, on one hand, queers' "coming-out" and thereby naming and discursively constituting homosexuality, and, on the other hand, the military's naming and constituting homosexuality in its prohibiting opportunities for lesbians and gays to name themselves as such. Both examples suggest the need for subtlety in recognizing the impossibility of determining the social conditions of agency and, therefore, of democratic politics. The examples point to the need to attend to the timing of exposures, under- and over-exposure to social situations and media-eventness, where the configuration of the social spaces presumed in the discourse of Western philosophy and the human sciences may no longer exist, or where they may never have been relevant in the first place.

Butler's insistence on the contingency of foundations for normative or ethical judgments is crucial for rethinking democratic and scientific representation in postmodernity. Yet a criticism often leveled against Butler is that she does not even offer normative or ethical foundations for her own resistance to heteronormativity. But Butler's position is that normative and ethical judgments, while necessary to politics and science, are never free from communication or from the labor of cultural translation which those judgments are asked to ground. For this reason, Butler looks for foundations which can move – movable foundations, sensitive to timing as much as to spatial arrangements of the spheres of social life. Butler's work is not anti-foundational as has been argued; rather, it aims to rethink foundations. This is necessary philosophical work, when social theory must be allowed to be touched by the transformations of postmodernity.

Bibliography

Writings of Judith Butler

Subjects of Desire: Hegelian Reflections in Twentieth Century France. 1987. New York: Columbia University Press.

Gender Trouble: Feminism and the Subversion of Identity. 1990. New York: Routledge.

Imitation and Gender Insubordination. 1991. In Diana Fuss (ed.), *inside/out: Lesbian Theories, Gay Theories*. New York: Routledge.

Bodies that Matter: On the Discursive Limits of "Sex." 1993. New York: Routledge.

The Psychic Life of Power: Theories of Subjection. 1997a. Stanford, CA: Stanford University Press.

Excitable Speech: a Politics of the Performative. 1997b. New York: Routledge.

Further reading

Benhabib, Seyla, et al. (1995) *Feminist Contentions: a Philosophical Exchange*. New York: Routledge.

Clough, Patricia Ticineto (1994) *Feminist Thought: Desire, Power and Academic Discourse*. Oxford: Blackwell.

Ebert, Teresa (1992) Ludic Feminism, the Body, Performance, and Labor: Bringing Materialism Back into Feminist Cultural Studies. *Cultural Critique*, 23, 5–50.

Foucault, Michel (1980) *The History of Sexuality, Volume 1*, translated by Robert Hurley. New York: Vintage.

Hennessy, Rosemary (1995) Queer Visibility in Commodity Culture. In Linda Nicholson and Steven Seidman (eds), *Social Postmodernism, Beyond Identity Politics*. Cambridge: Cambridge University Press, pp. 142–83.

Rose, Jacqueline (1986) *Sexuality in the Field of Vision*. London: Verso.

Sedgwick, Eve Kosofsky (1990) *Epistemology of the Closet*. Berkeley: University of California Press.

Seidman, Steven (1995) Deconstructing Queer Theory. In Linda Nicholson and Steven Seidman (eds), *Social Postmodernism, Beyond Identity Politics*. Cambridge: Cambridge University Press, pp.116–41.

Index